Exposing the Elephants

Exposing the Elephants

Creating Exceptional Nonprofits

Pamela J. Wilcox

John Wiley & Sons, Inc.

Published by John Wiley & Sons, Inc., Hoboken, New Jersey.
Published simultaneously in Canada.

For general information on our other products and services, or technical support, please contact our Customer Care Department within the United States at 800-762-2974, outside the United States at 317-572-3993 or fax 317-572-4002.

Wiley also publishes its books in a variety of electronic formats. Some content that appears in print may not be available in electronic books.

For more information about Wiley products, visit our Web site at http://www.wiley.com.

Library of Congress Cataloging-in-Publication Data:

Wilcox, Pamela J.
Exposing the elephants : creating exceptional nonprofits / Pamela J. Wilcox.
p. cm.
Includes index.
ISBN-13: 978-1-118-95225-2 (paper)
ISBN-10: 1-118-95225-1 (paper)
1. Nonprofit organizations—Management. I. Title.
HD62.6.W55 2006
658'.048—dc22

2006008031

10 9 8 7 6 5 4 3 2 1

There's an elephant in the room.

It is large and squatting, so it is hard to get around it.

Yet we squeeze by with, "How are you?" and "I'm fine". . .

There's an elephant in the room.

We all know it is there.

We are thinking about the elephant as we talk together.

It is constantly on our minds.

For, you see, it is a very big elephant . . .

But we do not talk about the elephant in the room.

—Terry Kettering

About the Author

Pamela J. Wilcox is founder and president of SAVé—staff and volunteer excellence —an organization that explores new ideas and offers practical solutions for strengthening nonprofit leadership. She is committed to helping boards and CEOs build exceptional nonprofits from the inside—by removing the obstacles that impede nonprofit success.

An innovative executive with more than 20 years experience in nonprofit leadership, strategic planning, staff management, and day to day operations, Pamela works in the forefront of change, revitalizing nonprofit offices, devising new ways to optimize volunteer and staff talent, directing mergers, and developing new methods of strengthening board and staff leadership. Her experience as a nonprofit executive director, senior manager, and consultant combined with for-profit experience as CEO and senior executive, brings her a unique perspective that has consistently elevated the performance of individuals, teams, and organizations.

Pamela and her husband, Robert, live in Chicago. You can reach her at the SAVé Web site, www.saveadvisors.com or at pjwilcox@saveadvisors.com.

Contents

Preface

After completing a massive change effort for a large nonprofit, I resigned my position as executive director to chill out, enjoy my daughter's wedding, and quietly contemplate less strenuous career options.

As happens so often, inspiration came when it was least expected. Finding myself at a Christmas party with revelers from different nonprofits, I listened as total strangers recounted surprisingly similar tales of working woes. Though this was nothing new, hearing the same complaints yet again triggered an old intrigue. How can an industry that espouses such lofty ideals be so frequently devoid of them in practice? Why do nonprofits continually tout change, while basic problems remain the same? And most important, can those problems be resolved?

Then it struck me. Although we now live in a very different information-based world and nonprofits form a large, important sector of our economy, their inherent mindset about volunteers and staff has not changed in a century. And just as individuals must have the right mindset to succeed, so must organizations. In that moment, the idea for this book began to take shape.

Exposing the Elephants identifies and holds the old mindset and old dogmas up to the light of day. It is a guide to help nonprofits openly and honestly question cultural and ingrained standards and examine organizational parts and performance in a fresh new light.

Something I heard during a seminar led by *Leadership and the New Science* author Meg Wheatley stuck with me: "It takes just a small pocket of heretics to start a revolution." Let the revolution begin with *Exposing the Elephants*. The stakes for winning the battle are great indeed—success means nothing less than the forward acceleration of social and economic progress on all fronts of everyday life.

This book is dedicated to the heretics already in the midst of the fray—the special and wonderful group of volunteers and staff who have been my working partners throughout these many years. Despite flawed governance and management practices at many nonprofits, these talented people found ways of flying under the radar screen and working effectively.

Exposing the Elephants expresses their vision of what should be and forms a body of knowledge that supports their ongoing efforts. May it lend support and give courage to all forward-thinking boards and CEOs as they brave the small but powerful group of insiders who so frequently block real change.

Acknowledgments

In some ways writing a book is a solitary effort—in others it is a joyous group affair. Here, it is my greatest pleasure to acknowledge the group that made this book possible and to ask them to step into the spotlight and take a well-deserved bow.

My deepest and most heartfelt thanks go to my husband Robert and friend and former colleague Solveig De Sutter whose faith in this book and in my ability to write it never wavered—even when mine did. Robert held me together personally with emotional support, enthusiasm, and love, and contributed professionally with business wisdom and patient discussions. My dear friend Solveig devoted countless hours brainstorming ideas, editing drafts, and renewing my spirits through the dark writing days.

Many, many thanks go to my book review team comprising volunteer and professional nonprofit leaders. These people donated their precious time and provided wisdom for early book drafts—Sue Adlesic, Mary Ulich, and Gary Taylor. Other former colleagues and friends gave freely of their time to comment on drafts and provide good ideas—my fervent thanks to Rosemary Butler and Sabine Schwark. Others provided just the right idea at the right time—many thanks to friends and colleagues Valerie Holton, Jane Dahlen, Denise Reens, Cathy Koessl, Ron Hamburger, Judy Myers, and Deb Darr.

My thanks to Carolyne Washburne, who shaped the original book proposal, and my deepest thanks to Karla Heuer, whose insights and editing abilities contributed greatly to the final draft. I am deeply indebted to Susan McDermott, senior editor at John Wiley & Sons, Inc., for recognizing the potential of this book and being willing to take a chance on this new writer. Words can't express just how much her acceptance and enthusiasm for the project meant to me—my most heartfelt thanks to her, senior production editor Kerstin Nasdeo, and all the other fine people at Wiley who made this book possible.

Finally, it's difficult to do anything worthwhile without the support of your family and friends, the people that I've mentioned and other wonderful people that form my personal support system—a special thanks to my daughter Keri, her husband Steve, and the pups—you make my life a wonderful adventure.

Introduction

Exposing the Elephants is divided into three parts. Part I introduces the nonprofit industry and explores the public perception of nonprofits. Nonprofit dogma in general is defined, and the resulting "nonprofit trouble cycle" is explored.

Part II tackles the "what" and "why" of the five nonprofit "elephants," each elephant representing an uncomfortable truth that volunteer and staff leaders recognize but refuse to openly acknowledge. These "elephants in the room" dominate nonprofit meetings and undermine nonprofit actions.

Part III explores ideas and practices—elephant solutions—that can tame and transform unruly pachyderms into well-behaved friends. Successful tools and techniques for "bringing it home" are sprinkled throughout the chapters.

Live Lessons and *At the Salt Mines*

Really understanding how industry archetypes create problems in the internal workings of nonprofit life is essential. That's where *Live Lessons* and *At the Salt Mines* come in. *Live Lessons* are real situations derived from actual nonprofit organizations, or, as they say in television land, "situations torn from the headlines." Fictitious names protect the innocent and avoid embarrassment to all. Some situations derive from personal working experience and some from those recounted by colleagues or detailed in the media. All are representative of actual issues facing nonprofits each day.

At the Salt Mines are little docudramas depicting a *Live Lesson's* day-to-day effect on nonprofit operations. Too often, a concept is easily understood but difficult to apply to real life. Together, *Live Lessons* and *At the Salt Mines* help the reader understand not only the specific elephant, but also how it operates in the real world of volunteers and staff.

The concepts in *Exposing the Elephants* cross the boundaries of all types of nonprofit organizations. Nonprofits are a diverse bunch of organizations that do not always share the same purpose, function, or vernacular. This book makes no attempt to target discussion toward those differences; rather, its content applies to any nonprofit that is beyond the founding or start-up phase. Such an organization employs professional staff and engages in a variety of ongoing activities and programs that require daily management.

Terminology

Exposing the Elephants also uses certain conventions to describe nonprofits, volunteers, and professional staff, and it is useful to look at a few of the most commonly used terms.

Nonprofits

In this book the terms *nonprofits, nonprofit sector,* and *nonprofit industry* are synonymous and apply to nonprofits as a whole. *Philanthropic organization* refers to nonprofits that rely on donations, not dues; *membership organization* refers to groups that rely on dues rather than donation dollars. People who are part of these organizations are called *donors* and *members*, respectively. The use of terms such as *charities, foundations,* or *trades* is deliberate and refers only to that specific group or subgroup.

Volunteers

Volunteers refers to all persons who donate time to a nonprofit; volunteers may serve in an individual capacity or as part of an advisory group, committee, or board. *Volunteer committee* or *volunteer board* refers to the volunteers who serve as members of that committee or board.

Governing board or *board of trustees* are synonymous terms that refer specifically to a nonprofit's governing body or board. Corporations refer to the same body as a board of directors and, in fact, many nonprofits also use this term. The term *volunteer leader* refers to the governing board of directors and the chairs of other volunteer committees, boards, or board-appointed groups. *Volunteer leadership* refers to the governing board only. *Nonprofit leadership* refers to the board and CEO.

Professional Staff

The top staff officer of a nonprofit is referred to by different titles, depending on the custom of that nonprofit. Some of the more friendly terms are executive director, executive vice president, president, and in some international organizations, secretary general. Another title, *CEO*, although controversial, is starting to emerge at many nonprofits. Some feel that this is a corporate business term, and thus should not be used by nonprofits. This book espouses the view that the top staff officer at a nonprofit should be the chief executive officer, so this book uses the term *CEO*.

The term *professional staff* refers to the CEO plus all other paid staff members working at the nonprofit. The term *senior staff* refers to the CEO and all direct reports.

PART I

Promise versus Reality

CHAPTER 1

Nonprofits: A Closer Look

The luxury of doing good surpasses every other personal enjoyment.

—John Gay

Intense awareness of environmental issues; deep concern about poverty, hunger, homelessness; far-reaching cutbacks in government funding for social services, the arts, education; stringent requirements for professional licensing and continuing education; and a huge generation of baby boomers, having achieved the rewards of "doing well," now interested in "doing good"—the confluence of these and other factors has fueled explosive growth in a major sector of the U.S. economy.

Most Americans don't recognize nonprofits as a third economic sector, along with for-profits and government. Recognized or not, with over 100 million employees and unpaid volunteers, nonprofits represent one of the largest groups of employers in the United States. Nonprofit management is an acknowledged profession, with an increasing number of colleges and universities offering degrees in the discipline. Nonprofits also attract private-sector professionals who want to work for a higher cause. Clearly, nonprofits are big business in a big way. Yet this vast, diverse sector remains little understood by the public.

In This Chapter

To promote greater understanding of this puzzling mammoth, we examine the real size, scope, and impact of the nonprofit sector and demystify commonly held myths about it. With these myths set straight, nonprofits, volunteers, professional staff, and the public will be able to question the generalities surrounding nonprofits and refuse anything less than real results.

The Wide Reach of Nonprofits

Size of Nonprofit Sector

Nonprofits are almost 1.6 million in number and contribute 8 percent of the gross national product. That's over $1 trillion in revenues, according to the Internal Revenue Service (IRS).[1] Over the last 25 years, the 2.5 percent annual average growth rate for employment in the nonprofit sector outpaced that of for-profit business (1.8 percent) and government (1.6 percent). Nonprofit employees now constitute 9.5 percent of the total American workforce or 12.5 million employees.[2] In other words, 1 in every 12 Americans works for a nonprofit.

Another 83.9 million Americans or 44 percent of adults volunteer for these organizations and contribute 15.5 billion hours to charitable organizations alone.[3] Equally startling is the generosity of American households: 89 percent contribute to charitable organizations, with the average annual contribution being $1,620.[4] According to *Giving USA,* in 2004 that figure amounted to an historic high of $248,520,000,000.[5] Yes, you read that right—billions!

Clearly, the nonprofit sector is no cuddly cocker spaniel; it's a huge St. Bernard. It's important to note that the term "nonprofit sector" refers to nonprofits in the aggregate as all organizations granted tax-exempt status by the IRS. The nonprofit sector is widely diverse, and to fully understand its economic impact, it's helpful to review the major types of organizations and the terminology used within the sector.

Types of Nonprofits

Tax-exempt organizations are classified under Section 501(c) of the IRS tax code. Each type of organization is given a numerical subcategory number (e.g., 501(c)(1), 501(c)(2)). We'll focus on the three major types of nonprofits that make up the majority of what is commonly known as the nonprofit sector: (1) 501(c)(3), charitable and foundations; (2) 501(c)(4), welfare and advocacy; and (3) 501(c)(6), business leagues.

501(c)(3) Nonprofits The largest of the nonprofit subcategories are the 501(c)(3) religious, charitable, and similar organizations. This group totals almost 1,000,000 and consists mainly of charitable organizations (more than 800,000) and foundations (more than 100,000). This number could be even larger because certain organizations that would fall into this category, such as churches, are not required to apply for tax exemption.

Charitable organizations include those that provide care and services to the needy, such as the United Way, Salvation Army, and Catholic Charities, and also organizations such as hospitals, museums, orchestras, private schools, libraries, and public radio and television stations. Individuals, families, businesses, and communities can establish foundations (e.g., the Bill and Melinda Gates Foundation) as a way to support specific causes.

Charities and foundations also are the fastest growing segment of nonprofits. In fiscal year 2005 alone, the IRS received applications for 77,539 new 501(c)(3) organizations, representing almost 93 percent of all nonprofit applications received. The 15.5 billion hours of free labor cited earlier is what allows these organizations to serve a broad range of people at a far lower cost than private industry. Because many of these constituents would not be served by the profit-driven private market and would be supported only through government tax dollars, charitable organizations and foundations have a huge economic impact on individuals and the economy.

501(c)(4) Nonprofits The second largest subcategory is 501(c)(4), the social welfare or advocacy organizations. Included are 136,060 organizations such as the National Association for the Advancement of Colored Persons (NAACP), the National Organization for Women (NOW), and the National Rifle Association (NRA). These nonprofits participate in legislative advocacy, lobbying, and political campaign activities. They serve as a link between individuals and the broader political process, providing the means to bring group concerns to the public attention and to push for change not only for the group but also on behalf of the general public. Again, the economic impact of such governmental influence is significant.

501(c)(6) Nonprofits The third largest subcategory is 501(c)(6), business leagues. These are the more than 85,000 professional and trade organizations such as the American Bar Association and the National Association of Realtors that promote the business or professional interests of a community, industry, or profession. The real and potential impact of this group on research, professional training, and influence through endorsements permeates our daily lives. Nine out of every 10 adults belong to an association, and one only needs to contemplate the increase in prestige and sales of a product endorsed by the American Medical Association to understand the potential economic impact of these organizations.

Not only do nonprofits affect our economy directly through the constituents served and the revenue generated, but they also exhibit tremendous purchasing power and are a revenue source for other businesses. Associations alone pay $6 billion in health premiums and spend $2.2 billion on technology, $56 billion on meetings, $66 billion on travel and hotels, and more than $12.3 billion in state, local, and federal sales and income taxes.[6]

Although these three categories are the largest and most influential, there are a total of 27 categories of 501(c) tax-exempt organizations, including credit unions, social and recreation clubs, fraternities, and veterans groups. The wide diversity in types of nonprofits is one key to understanding some of the public misperception regarding nonprofits. The image conjured by the word "nonprofit" is subjective depending on one's personal experience with a certain type of organization.

The situation is further complicated by a lack of consensus on terminology within the sector. Even insiders are befuddled by the use of terms like "philanthropic organizations," the "independent sector," the "social sector," and "charities." Typically, people using these terms are referring only to 501(c)(3) organizations, but others may think they are referring to all tax-exempt organizations.

Terms like "membership organizations," "professional organizations," or "trades" might be used to describe all 501(c)(6)s, but they more commonly refer to that specific category within the 501(c)(6) category. Even associations that act as advisers to nonprofits lend to the confusion by being fragmented and divided by nonprofit type (e.g., the American Society of Association Executives (ASAE) primarily represents 501(c)(6)s, and the Donor's Forum primarily represents 501(c)(3)s).

Anyone researching the subject understands how risky it is to assume anything with regards to the meaning of such terms that appear in public discourse. Questions to clarify the user's meaning are always in order. Nor do these divisions lend anything other than confusion when it comes to discussing global issues. After all, men and women are distinctly different, but they share many more commonalities by being human beings. In a similar fashion, although distinct differences exist among the various nonprofit categories, nonprofits share many more characteristics such as culture and management practices.

The Role of Nonprofits

Clearly, nonprofits have a huge impact on the American economy and in the fabric of our lives. This impact is assumed in the very reason that the government provides tax-exempt status to such organizations. Nonprofits relieve a burden that otherwise might need to be supplied by the government or not at all. In fact, the trend for federal and state governments to shift social services to outside providers has fueled the growth of philanthropies.

Setting aside the tax dollar question and the public's general low esteem for public officials, you might be wondering why this nation would want to shift things like social services outside of government. The answer to that question lies in the differing expectations of how nonprofits versus for-profits perform the service role.

A study from the Johns Hopkins Comparative Nonprofit Sector project is illuminating.[7] The study considers five areas where we might expect the nonprofit role to differ from for-profit business: (1) service, (2) innovation, (3) advocacy, (4) leadership development, and (5) democratization.

Service Role Nonprofits, like for-profit companies, must make a profit (known as net revenues or surplus in nonprofit language) to remain in business. The difference is that any profit must be returned to the mission of that nonprofit, whereas corporations and businesses can distribute that wealth to shareholders, business owners, CEOs, and staff.

Because of this nonprofit distribution character, nonprofits are expected to perform services that are public or collective in manner, serving constituents that the private market cannot because they are not paid for or require a special element of trust. This leads us to expect services to be of higher quality. Because nonprofits are not profit driven and have access to volunteers and philanthropic support, services should be delivered for lower cost. Also, nonprofits like charities and foundations with donor support should be more inclined to serve those in greatest need.

Innovation Role Given the lack of bottom-line focus, nonprofits should be more flexible and adaptable than other organizations and more likely to take risks. They should be a haven for new ideas and a laboratory for identifying and solving public problems. This suggests that nonprofits should be pioneers in particular fields and serve as a source of innovation.

Advocacy Role Not beholden to the market, nonprofits should be able to push for changes in government policy and public or professional conditions. They should provide a way to bring group concerns to public attention.

Leadership Development Role Nonprofits are potentially vehicles for individual and group expression. Such organizations promote citizen participation and protect the interests of specific groups.

Democratization Role At their best, nonprofits can make an important contribution to fostering sentiments of trust, social obligation, and belonging among their own members and between those members and others in society—democracy in action. Specifically, the underpinnings of liberal democracy rest with the exemption of religious nonprofits. Such institutions provide separation of church and state and limit government's ability to use tax policy as a tool to promote one religion over another or tax a church out of existence.

Any one nonprofit may not perform all of these roles well, but a good case can be built that the public should expect them all to do so. How well they are performing against the barriers and the drawbacks faced are a subject that we'll return to repeatedly. Right now, though, let's redirect our attention to the current public perception of nonprofits.

Myths That Surround Nonprofits

In general, the public has a favorable impression of nonprofits, one that encourages tolerance and promotes a feeling to look the other way when something goes wrong. *Independent Sector* surveys continue to show that Americans express comparatively high confidence in nearly all charitable organizations while ranking corporations, government, and Congress among institutions in which they had the lowest confidence.

Unfortunately, the public's favorable image rests on some pretty squishy ground. If one is of an uncharitable mind, you might say that some of the perceptions are so wildly off the mark as to fall into the category of myth. The most common myths are:

- Nonprofits are "soft": altruistic, gentle people working in a smaller, less competitive, nurturing environment for the greater welfare of society
- Nonprofits "do good," not "make money": profit is bad, nonprofits are good
- Nonprofits aren't a business: absent are measurements like per-share price, sales per year, total profit
- Nonprofits operate well as a whole

Why are these myths so widely held and yet so untrue? And what effect, if any, does this public misperception have on the nonprofit sector?

Nonprofits Are "Soft"

The nonprofit sector isn't what anyone should consider small, kind, and warm. The industry is large, in effect a third sector of our economy, and its impact is felt throughout the economy and society. Although nonprofits come in all flavors and sizes, so do for-profit businesses. And, like large corporations, large nonprofits are fewer in number but rival their for-profit counterparts in influence both outside and within their respective industries.

One reason for the public's misperception is that the word "nonprofit" conjures up different images if you volunteer for a small struggling charity operating out of a room full of scarred metal furniture than if you work for the American Bar Association with floors of comfortable offices in downtown Chicago.

Nor, on average, are nonprofit professional staff leaders paid extremely low wages. Although a small charity dependent solely on community donations may pay a CEO only $30,000 per year, the 2002 median salary of CEOs at large nonprofits was $285,000 and the median total compensation for CEOs in all size associations was $142,800.[8] That may not rival the multimillion-dollar deals of Fortune 500 CEOs, but it might be argued that it's more in line with what corporate CEOs really should make.

The real whopper is the public perception of a warm and soft working environment. As anyone who has worked at nonprofits can attest, often the environment is far from nurturing and noncompetitive. Nonprofit culture tends to be marked more by hierarchy and turf protection than collaboration. For reasons that will become clear in Chapter 3, some volunteers view professional staff as unnecessary, paid overhead, and some professional staff view volunteers as a hindrance rather than a help.

In fact, Giovinella Gonthier, co-author of *Rude Awakenings: Overcoming the Civility Crisis in the Workplace,* cites nonprofits as the most uncivil workplace of all. Gonthier states: "They lose sight of their mission . . . a lot of these people think that the labor and employment laws that apply to for-profit corporations don't apply to them."[9]

Contributing to the public misperception, newspapers and magazine articles fail to mention that the rate of nonprofit staff turnover exceeds the turnover rate of for-profits. Articles tend to focus on "stress" and "low pay" as the main reasons for high nonprofit turnover rather than on the reality of the workplace. A huge reason for the high turnover of nonprofit staff is a work culture that is at best discouraging to creative, talented professionals and at worst actually toxic to worker productivity.

This same culture often extends to volunteers. Nonproductive committees, unclear volunteer roles, and weak volunteer boards stimulate the same kind of turnover of bright, talented volunteers. All in all, the nonprofit work culture often serves as a catalyst for the exodus of the best and brightest from the ranks of the organization.

Nonprofits "Do Good" Rather Than "Make Money"

Contrary to widely held belief, nonprofits must make a profit to stay in business long term, just like for-profit concerns. The difference between corporations and associations lies mainly in what happens to the profit.

A corporation can distribute profits to owners, shareholders, executives, and employees. The owner of a private business can put his or her profits right into a personal bank account. Nonprofits are prohibited from these practices and cannot distribute profits into any form of private or individual hands. Nonprofits do not exist to earn money for owners and employees; profits must be reinvested in the mission.

Anyone who has worked in both for-profit and nonprofit concerns can attest to the strong profit-making orientation of nonprofits. Specifically, nonprofit governing boards spend an inordinate amount of board time micromanaging the finance area. This means that the roles of the nonprofit and for-profit CFOs are both challenging—but in very different ways!

So, corporations and associations share a driving need to make a profit; they just do so for different reasons. Corporations must maximize "shareholder return" or "return on dollars invested"; nonprofits must maximize "member/donor return" or the return of mission results for dollars invested.

Nonprofits Are Not a Business, so Success Cannot Be Measured Quantitatively

Although great resistance and misunderstanding surrounds the term "nonprofit business," a business component exists in nonprofits and includes all management aspects of services, products, programs, and organization. Nonprofit business success equates to how innovatively or efficiently mission is fulfilled, and this success can be quantitatively measured.

The findings of Joseph Galaskiewicz and Wolfgang Bielefeld as they studied a sample of public charities in the Minneapolis–St. Paul area over a 15-year period are illuminating.[10] The results of that study clearly showed that nonprofits that became more business-like did not suffer as a result and, in fact, experienced significant growth in donations, commercial income, volunteers, and professional staff. The fact that these findings are in a sector where conditions are most resistant to business practices hints at similar and even more favorable findings for the membership sectors.

One of the current rages in the nonprofit sector that has been widely discussed in trade magazines and books is nonprofit measurement. Although flying under disguised headings like "how to convert good intentions into measurable outcomes," the intended result is quantitative measurement, but there is widespread disagreement on what to measure and how to measure it across the different subcategories of nonprofits.

It's a big challenge to find consensus in an immense, diverse sector, where the "but, we're different" excuse is a handy tool often employed by CEOs or boards to discount benchmark studies. A ready example is the operating ratios published by the American Society of Association Executives (ASAE). The potential for board misuse of these benchmark studies is so strong that often CEOs use that excuse to relegate the study to the bottom of their desk drawers.

Nonprofits Operate Well as a Whole

Most nonprofits operate well if the measurement is, "Does the job get done—are we helping people?" But the well-publicized problems since September 11 make it difficult to argue that all things are operating well. A look at the headlines from a cross-section of different types of nonprofits within a six-month period confirms that. The article "Grasso Quits NYSE Amid Pay Furor" refers to the forced resignation of New York Stock Exchange Chairman Dick Grasso amid a public outcry over a $139.5 million retirement pay package.[11] Articles detailing similar problems include "More AmeriCorps Follies," an editorial regarding the covering up of a program "rife with mismanagement and lack of financial controls";[12] "Nonprofit Ex-Worker Charged with Theft," detailing the former office manager of Tobacco Free Michigan's embezzlement of $50,000, the latest of several residents charged with embezzling money from area agencies;[13] "NASA's Culture Faulted in Crash," where the investigating board cited failures of NASA management in the *Columbia* shuttle disaster and concluded the space agency has "a broken safety culture."[14]

Not only headlines call into question just how well (or not) nonprofits are doing their jobs. Another meaningful indicator is the downward trend of membership and volunteers. Looking beyond the typical nonprofit explanations of a bad economy or a time-strapped public, donations and membership follow a basic economic principle: prices reflect reality and people's preferences. What the loss of members or donors really means is that these people feel that the nonprofit no longer has value compared to something else. More simply put, donors or members believe that their dollars receive a higher return elsewhere.

Higher Expectations Equal Better Nonprofits

Americans continue to express comparatively high confidence in the nonprofit sector. So far, the public cynicism regarding corporations has tainted, but not greatly permeated, their view of nonprofits. Yet, as discussed, some of this nonprofit optimism is based on public misperceptions about the sector. Either nonprofits begin to operate in the manner that warrants the current optimism, or they risk the wrath of a public that feels deceived as negative information surfaces about an increasingly visible sector.

Already there are ominous signs that portend such a public backlash. Since the September 11 tragedy, controversies such as the disbursement of the September 11 funds and the continuing travails of the Red Cross in handling such disasters have eroded public confidence. Media pundits like Bill O'Reilly, host of the cable news show *The Factor,* are increasingly taking aim at large nonprofit public targets like The United Way and The American Red Cross.

For-profit companies are becoming more vocal about the unfair advantage of nonprofits when both compete for the same market. They do have a point because the distinctions between nonprofits and for-profits have blurred tremendously since the enactment of the Model Nonstock Corporation Statute that was revised in 1987. This statute freed nonprofits to engage in business activities as long as these activities ultimately served charitable objectives. Although nonprofits are still prohibited from distributing profits to individuals, in practice it's becoming increasingly difficult to define standards by which this can be measured or enforced.

Lobbyist activities and the proliferation of associations and private foundations for less than charitable reasons are also being noticed. The IRS outlined plans for 2004 that increase its focus on the political activities of exempt organizations as well as the application process for tax-exempt status. As this book goes to press, the Senate Finance Committee headed by Senator Charles Grassley (R-IA) continues to consider legislation to curb abuses of the laws governing nonprofits. All of this even leads some people to make the dire prediction that the excesses of the nonprofit sector mean the elimination of tax exemption in the future.

This discussion makes the case for substituting a much higher expectation for nonprofit performance than the existing attitude of "Oh, what do you expect? It's just a nonprofit." After all, while companies make no bones about profits being their purpose, nonprofits derive tax exemption from the mission of contributing to the greater good of cause or profession. Even though vision, mission, and moral commitment are not in any sense exclusive to the nonprofit enterprise, the public trust in nonprofits is based on these concepts. Thus nonprofits have a greater calling, and a higher bar over which they must jump. Failure to do so betrays the public's trust.

Barriers to Meeting Public Expectations

The public should be able to trust nonprofits to perform their roles efficiently—roles of service, innovation, advocacy, leadership, and democratization. The Johns Hopkins Study also identified nonprofit limitations or barriers to achieving success.[15] Among the most important are "excessive amateurism or professionalism," "resources insufficiency," and an "accountability gap." Let's look closer at each of these barriers.

Excessive Amateurism or Professionalism Reliance on volunteer input or private charitable support can lead to ineffective operations and an inability to effectively deliver programs and services. However, excessive professional staff control can limit the involvement of members.

Resource Insufficiency The voluntary sector may not be able to generate revenues on the scale needed to cope with the range of human problems presented. Or, attention is directed to expense reduction rather than revenue growth, thus limiting resources.

Accountability Gap For-profit businesses are held accountable by the consumers of their products and secondarily by their board of directors. By contrast, accountability in nonprofits rests with the trustworthiness of the professional managers and the oversight of the board. The assumption that nonprofit managers are trustworthy because they cannot generate profits for themselves may no longer be valid. This, coupled with the likelihood that a nonprofit board provides less vigorous oversight, means accountability mechanisms are lacking.

These drawbacks are very real problems for almost every nonprofit. The ability to decrease or eliminate these barriers may well determine if nonprofit boards are going to shape and lead their organizations in a direction that supports the current public confidence or continue down the path of their less-respected corporate counterparts.

Nonprofits can't eliminate these barriers and transform into high-performance organizations while clinging to their current dogmas—staunchly held principles and practices that worked in a bygone era. Today's nonprofit dogmas generate a negative working culture that inhibits long-term success. Cultural problems cannot be processed away, nor can they be changed by ignoring the reality that they exist. Nonprofits must uncover and learn to recognize sector archetypes and adopt an updated consciousness regarding the basic equations of volunteers, staff, and organizational performance.

The light at the end of the tunnel is clear: reaching full potential is the brightly shining goal. Full potential means making great achievements in research and education, improving conditions for the disadvantaged, and attracting the best and brightest into a different kind of work, unlike the image of business today. The challenge is to create a new collaborative type of performance organization that employs the best of the for-profit world while avoiding its excesses, a place where work means something to the worker and to society.

Seeing the light at the end of the tunnel is not the same as building the tunnel that gets us there. Right now, nonprofit heads are trying to build that tunnel with new processes, while their minds are hopelessly mired in outdated beliefs. Only a different mindset can build that tunnel.

Notes

1. IRS SOI Tax Stats—IRS Data Books: 2001–2003, www.irs.gov/pub/irs-soi/02eo01as.xls (for tax-exempt organizations and other entities, total for 2003; accessed January 30, 2006); IRS SOI Tax Stats, www.irs.gov/pub/irs-soi/02eo03ty.xls (for total number of returns 501(c)(3) [1] and 501(c)(3) [4] to 501(c)(3) [9] for tax year 2002; accessed January 30, 2006).
2. *The Independent Sector,* s.v. "Nonprofit Almanac Facts and Findings, Employment in the Nonprofit Sector," www.independentsector.org/PDFs/npemployment.pdf (accessed July 18, 2003).
3. *The Independent Sector,* s.v. "Value of Volunteer Time," www.independentsector.org/programs/research/volunteer_time.html (accessed July 18, 2003).
4. *The Independent Sector,* s.v. "Giving and Volunteering in the United States 2001," www.independentsector.org/programs/research/gv01main.html (accessed July 18, 2003).
5. "Charitable Giving Rises 5 Percent to Nearly $250 Billion In 2004," *Giving USA Foundation,* www.aafrc.org/gusa/ (accessed July 14, 2005).
6. "Associations in a Nutshell," *American Society of Association Executives,* www.asaenet.org/ GeneralDetail.cfm?ItemNumber=8247 (accessed January 29, 2005).
7. Lester M. Salamon, Leslie C. Hems, and Kathryn Chinnock, "The Nonprofit Sector: For What and for Whom?" Working Papers of the Johns Hopkins Comparative Nonprofit Sector Project, no. 37 (Baltimore: *Johns Hopkins Center for Civil Society Studies,* 2000).
8. Elizabeth Schwinn and Ian Wilhelm, "Nonprofit CEO's See Salaries Rise," *The Chronicle of Philanthropy* (October 2003), www.philanthropy.com/free/articles/v15/i24/24002701. htm. *ASAE,* "Total Compensation Increased Modestly for 20 of 34 Positions within Associations in 2002," *ASAE* (June 2003), www.asaenet.org/newsroom/1,1989,showarticle=yes^articleId=54137,00.
9. Noah Isackson, "Giovinella Gonthier: A Civility Engineer," *The Chicago Tribune Magazine* (December 29, 2002): 8.
10. Joseph Galaskiewicz and Wolfgang Bielefeld, "Fact and Finding: Nonprofits in an Age of Uncertainty: A Study in Organizational Change," *The Independent Sector,* 2(1), 1999, www.independentsector.org/programs/research/factfind2.pdf (accessed February 15, 2004).

11. Kate Kelly, Susanne Craig, and Ianthe Jeanne Dugan, "Grasso Quits NYSE Amid Pay Furor," *Wall Street Journal,* sec. A1, September 18, 2003.
12. "More AmeriCorps Follies," *Wall Street Journal,* ed., August 7, 2003.
13. "Nonprofit Ex-Worker Charged with Theft," *Chicago Tribune,* news 21, May 7, 2003.
14. Jeremy Manier, "NASA's Culture Faulted in Crash," *Chicago Tribune,* news 1, August 27, 2003.
15. See note 7.

CHAPTER 2

The Nonprofit Dilemma

There is an ominous cloud in the distance though at present it be no bigger than a man's hand.

—Arthur Eddington

Each day more than 11 million nonprofit professionals and 100 million volunteers wake up and set off for their organizations full of energy and ideas. And each day a significant number return home frustrated and demoralized. What happens during the working day to cause such a transformation? How does it impact nonprofit performance? More important, what changes must occur to preserve rather than destroy such positive energy?

The lure of "doing good" rather than just contributing to corporate profits attracts an ever-increasing number of talented and caring people to nonprofits. Professional staff and volunteers are willing to forgo top salary dollars and/or donate precious time in return for the satisfaction of "making the world a better place."

Yet, nonprofits squander a great deal of this capital on issues of internal power and politics rather than issues of mission. The result is a sector that underperforms to expectations. A large gap exists between what nonprofits are today versus what they should be. The key to understanding this performance gap is opportunity lost. Nonprofits fail to convert new ideas and thinking into effective, lasting mission-based programs and services.

Rating Nonprofit Performance

By the yardstick of "does the job get done?" nonprofits receive a passing grade. Trade and professional organizations provide information, advocacy, and education; charities and foundations deliver needed services and grants to a wide variety of worthy causes.

Nonprofits fare much worse when the measurement is "fulfilling promise and potential." Too often, organizations settle for average performance and maintenance of existing programs, rather than innovation and the risk of new ventures. The continual use of hyperbole to announce the latest and greatest program masks the reality that few of these ballyhooed activities are delivered efficiently or have staying power. Rather, the sector mentality for new programs is "launch 'em and leave 'em." Initial grand announcements reflect programs that rarely continue in operation for more than a few years.

At the same time, members, donors, and the public are pressing nonprofits to stay true to mission, and with limited resources, to deliver more programs faster in a cost-effective, high-impact manner. This means that nonprofits must optimize resources and capitalize on opportunities such as the latest technology. The speed and success at which nonprofits do so in a volatile, changing environment will determine if donors and members remain with the organization.

Despite the turmoil these demands have caused in recent years, little has changed over the past century because most nonprofits are simply ill prepared and in the wrong position to seize opportunity. It's not that the sector doesn't embrace change; in fact, the call for change and the necessity to change comes from every conceivable medium and advisor. It's impossible to attend a nonprofit seminar or read an article without being hit over the head with the message that "old methodologies don't work."

The sector is awash in new processes, and presidents or CEOs are instantly hailed as innovative and forward-thinking leaders by implementing the fad of the moment. It's easier and more impressive to measure organizational performance in a new way than to tackle thorny root problems where rewards for solutions may accrue to the next president or CEO. The situation is much like that of dieters who embrace each new fad diet without changing their basic eating and exercise mindset. The fad diet works in the short term, but the pounds quickly return because the underlying reason for gaining weight is not addressed.

On and on it goes, and the more nonprofits undergo change, the more they remain the same. This is the exact opposite of what we might expect from a sector that is unhampered by shareholders and the demand for large profits. Nonprofits should be more flexible, adaptive, and innovative; they should be incubators for new ideas and a vehicle for transforming those ideas into lasting programs and services.

Expectations aside, the diet isn't working because the underlying reason for the nonprofit malaise—the sector's inherent mindset regarding volunteers and staff—has not changed. Current thinking worked and produced desirable outcomes when nonprofits were small and of necessity run by volunteers; however, this same thinking is not effective and is producing undesirable outcomes as the sector has matured and competitive conditions have changed.

A Flawed Nonprofit Mindset

In reality, nonprofits are trying to adapt to the 21st-century environment with early-20th-century thinking! This mindset is a collection of attitudes or archetypes—ideas and modes of thought derived from past experience that still exist in the unconscious thought of sector participants. Although it is not discussed openly, this core belief system is inherited by each new nonprofit generation.

Think of a nonprofit as a person who lacks the correct mindset for success. Such a person cannot succeed over the long term; no matter how many short-term successes are achieved, the underlying personality undoes the positive. The same concept applies to nonprofits; over the long term, flawed, nonprofit beliefs undermine and undo any positive short-term successes.

"If It Ain't Broke, Don't Fix It."

Although most nonprofit volunteers may not think so, nonprofits are broken, and they do need to be fixed. They are broken as the word refers to flowers (i.e., "having an irregular, streaked, or blotched pattern especially from a virus infection") and as it refers to landmasses (i.e., "being irregular, interrupted, or full of obstacles").[1]

No, nonprofits are not flowering landmasses, but given the previous discussion, these definitions of *broken* are useful. In general, nonprofits do not completely or fully fulfill their intended promise and potential. Irregular, interrupted, and full of obstacles certainly describes the "launch 'em and leave 'em" method of program development employed at so many nonprofits. Candid insiders might well describe the politics and infighting dominating the nonprofit working culture as a virus infecting the entire organization.

The Nonprofit Trouble Cycle

A familiar, cyclical pattern of calm and crisis plagues the nonprofit sector. The cycle is so common that we'll give it a name—the *Nonprofit Trouble Cycle*. Consisting of five distinct phases, the cycle has one overriding characteristic. The core problems remain unresolved at the end of the Trouble Cycle, and the "solutions" simply serve as catalysts for the next cycle.

The five phases of the Trouble Cycle are readily recognizable. In fact, you will be able to spot them easily. Here are the five phases of the Trouble Cycle, along with a short example to illustrate the concept:

1. *Stealth Phase.* Organizational problems are present but visible only inside the nonprofit; volunteers and/or staff raise the alarm but are ignored by the CEO and/or board. The climate becomes ripe for abuse.

   After the merger of two membership organizations, the new unified organization realizes a 20 percent increase in education revenue. But, there's also a 30 percent drop in expected dues revenue because some members who previously belonged to both organizations were counted twice.

   Despite warnings from education staff and volunteers that the education increases were a short-term event (a new regulation mandated certain courses), the finance committee raises budgeted education attendances in order to cover the dues shortfall. The board approves a budget that contains an additional 20 percent increase in joint education revenues.

2. *Infection Phase.* Problems intensify and become visible to more members and outside constituents. The CEO and/or board discuss the problems, but any action taken is cosmetic or hindered by committee politics, organizational process, or vested volunteers (volunteers driven by self-interest rather than mission).

   Over a three-year period, attendance at education courses and seminars fails to meet the projected budget. Department staff and knowledgeable volunteers continually explain that this is not a real shortfall; in fact, attendance for the new organization is really greater than that of the two previous organizations prior to the merger. Simply put, the falloff is just a return to the normal level of attendance prior to the regulatory-induced increase.

   The board asks the education committee and CEO to look into pricing, location, and so on—anything that improves the education figures.

3. *Crisis Phase.* The problems manifest as an abuse in the system, which precipitates an organizational crisis that is impossible to ignore. The board and/or CEO fixate on abuse symptoms and take corrective action.

   There's an accumulated $3.5 million education deficit by the end of year three. On top of already decreased dues revenue, the economy takes a downturn, and membership really declines. Leaders start to panic as they realize that, at that rate, reserves will be depleted in the near future.

   The board, CEO, and finance committee decide to immediately cut education staff and stop funding the development of new courses and seminars.

4. *Relief Phase.* Corrective action relieves symptoms, and the immediate crisis passes. Praise and credit for resolving the crisis are heaped upon the board and/or the CEO.

   These changes halt the deficits. Meanwhile, the economy starts to improve, and dues and education revenues improve. The organization is back in the black by year five. The board and CEO are credited with making the hard decisions that led to this success.

5. *Denial Phase.* Core problems remain unresolved and, in fact, are often exacerbated by the actions taken in the Relief Phase. The board and/or CEO dismiss the festering issues as just part of working out the kinks. The organization enters the Stealth Phase of a new Trouble Cycle.

   The real problem wasn't a decline in education or an overabundance of education staff. It was unrealistic expectations for education revenues by volunteer leaders who were inexperienced in education operations and did not listen to the knowledgeable input of education staff and volunteers. The situation was made worse by a CEO who knew the realities of the situation but kept quiet to please the board.

   The measures taken (i.e., firing staff, limiting course development, changing the kinds of seminars and locations) helped the short-term problem but limited the organization's ability to provide and efficiently manage the courses and seminars—precisely the things members prized. An improved economy masked the declining education attendance for awhile, but the complaints are heard, at first by staff and then by members, about the lack of development and offerings. Education revenues again start to decline.

Duration of the Nonprofit Trouble Cycle The length of each phase and the speed at which one Trouble Cycle turns into another are largely determined by two things: (1) the tenure of the Relief Phase's governing board and/or CEO and (2) the severity and outreach of the actual crisis. Long tenure and a severe crisis point to a lengthy and emotion-torn Denial Phase. Stressed out and battle weary, volunteer leadership doesn't want to revisit the same emotion-ridden issues. Also, their reputation rests with the corrective action taken, and that makes it difficult to publicly admit that a problem still remains.

Further complicating the situation is the fact that long-tenured boards or CEOs in organizations of high volunteer/staff turnover are the institution's memory. If no one recalls a decision or its maker, the tenured group can rewrite history to be whatever it wants. Without accurate knowledge of what did and didn't work, organizations are condemned to the lowest rung of the learning curve and vulnerable to repeating their mistakes.

Long tenure also equates to lengthy Stealth and Infection Phases, again because the tenured group turns a deaf ear when the same problems are brought forward. Staff members, in particular, are unlikely to bring such issues to an impartial board in the first place. The Infection Phase ends only with the arrival of an inquisitive new board and/or CEO or when an illegal act or something equally dire occurs.

Outside influences also affect the duration of each Trouble Cycle phase. A change in the competitive environment or a severe downturn in the economy often moves an organization directly from the Stealth Phase to the Crisis Phase. For example, a health care nonprofit relied on its annual conference for almost $1 million net revenue per year. Its trade show was the only game in town and, although many pointed out the danger of such a lopsided reliance on one product (Stealth Phase), the board/CEO never moved beyond the talking stage in diversifying revenue. Other competitors entered the market, and a dramatic decline in attendance, along with the resulting drastic decrease in revenue, immediately forced the organization into the Crisis Phase.

The Core Problem Remains The important thing to remember about the Nonprofit Trouble Cycle is that it ends the crisis by resolving the immediate symptoms or problems. But the core problems are not identified and just go temporarily underground, waiting to reappear in another guise or place within the nonprofit. The next iteration of the cycle is sure to germinate and often flowers when a new crop of volunteers or staff emerges.

A nonprofit's behavior in the Trouble Cycle is analogous to a homeowner who notices that the wallpaper in his bathroom is peeling. He sees the problem and thinks, "Aha! It's that cheap paper installed by the guy who sold me this place." So the homeowner buys expensive, beautiful, new wallpaper and hires a tradesperson to hang it. The bathroom looks great. But one day the paper starts to peel in a small corner. If the same homeowner is in the house, he at first ignores the tiny problem, but as it becomes more noticeable, he starts to blame the tradesperson.

Or the homeowner moves before the paper peels or patches the corner prior to selling his home. The next homeowner, given no knowledge of the previous owner's actions, jumps to the same conclusion and makes the same mistake. In both cases, the paper will continue peeling because the root problem is a periodic leak in a pipe behind the wall. But the length of this Trouble Cycle's phases depend on the tenure of the homeowner, his past experience with such problems, his honesty in admitting the patch job, and whether he has the curiosity to look beyond the immediate problem. However, if the intensity of the leak increases, water dripping down the wall will precipitate a quick move into Crisis Phase!

Clearly, the tendency for nonprofits to get stuck in the Trouble Cycle is a little like the pop definition of *insanity*—doing the same thing over and over again and expecting a different result. And that raises some logical questions: Why do nonprofits get caught in this perpetual Trouble Cycle? Can't they catch on after the first iteration? What are the core issues, and why do they go unnoticed and unresolved?

Short Volunteer Tenure Drives the Cycle The example of the homeowner with the peeling wallpaper illustrates one reason that nonprofits fail to recognize the Trouble Cycle: a short volunteer tenure—and sometimes that of a CEO—correlates with a lack of institutional memory. One governing board and/or CEO addresses a problem, and eventually they are supplanted by the next board or CEO. The old problem appears new to the incoming group unless some formalized method for institutional learning is established.

Also complicating the problem and hindering a volunteer president or board director from the ability to "see the world through fresh new glasses" is the *legacy syndrome*. Presidents and board directors have short terms of office and want to deal with big issues that promise quick resolutions. Unfortunately, the core issues that fuel the Nonprofit Trouble Cycle are not evident on the surface, and so are not easy to find or quick to resolve.

Great is the pain and little is the glory of touching core problems that everyone would rather pretend don't exist at all. And that brings us to the core issues.

NOTE

1. *Webster's Ninth New Collegiate Dictionary* (Springfield, MA: Merriam-Webster Inc., 1988), 181.

PART II

The Problem Elephants: Bad Behavior, Bad Results

There's an elephant in the room . . . But we do not talk about the elephant in the room.

—Terry Kettering

Uninvited Guests: The Elephants of the Nonprofit Sector

Ignoring the elephants—yes, nonprofits have more than one in the room—keeps nonprofits mired in a deep-rooted dogma, and this antiquated mindset drives the Nonprofit Trouble Cycle. The elephants overshadow all nonprofit activities and make every action more difficult. It's not that nonprofits are unaware that problems exist. Insiders are always discussing issues like the loss of mission focus, mismatch of board/CEO organization mindset, confusion of governance and management roles, absence of volunteer/staff teamwork, and lack of lasting results.

Yet, although widespread discussion centers on these problematic areas and new processes are continually thrown in their direction, volunteer and staff leadership rarely have what could be even loosely construed as meaningful dialogue about the root of these problems; they have totally different viewpoints about roles, responsibility, performance, and results.

So the topic that dominates all-staff or all-volunteer meetings is never broached in mixed company. Such conversations are politically incorrect, but because the problems are real and not resolved, they simmer just below the surface of every nonprofit meeting. This is truly dangerous territory, which nonprofits find safer and much easier to skirt around than to tackle head on.

The problems that nonprofits recognize in some form or other but choose to ignore are the elephants in the nonprofit room. All together, five major elephants stand in the way of achieving great nonprofit performance. Let's meet them briefly and then examine them extensively in Part II. They are:

- ***Mission Impossible* Elephant.** Nonprofit leaders think mission; they actually do politics and volunteer activities.
- ***Earth to Board* Elephant.** Boards and CEOs think they hear constituents; they actually hear volunteers and staff.
- ***Board Fiddles, Rome Burns* Elephant.** Boards think policy is synonymous with governance; in reality, they rubberstamp management policy while ignoring macro-governance policy.
- ***Smile, Not Skill* Elephant.** Volunteer leaders judge professional staff on likeability; professional performance is not valued or rewarded.
- ***Read My Lips* Elephant.** Talking substitutes for doing; rhetoric takes the place of achievement.

For now, it's enough to understand that these elephants are the underlying reason why nonprofits fail to recognize the Trouble Cycle. Like the leaking pipe in our wall-paper example, the nonprofit elephants lurk in the shadows waiting to sabotage the long-term success of any project.

Remember our comparison of nonprofit archetypes to an individual's paralytic mind-set. Such a person rarely achieves long-term success. Acquaintances and friends may see this person's drawbacks, but only a rare friend cares enough to actually help the person. Most people don't want the hassle, so they do nothing, but silently they register that flaw, and although that thought is relegated to the background and invisible on the surface, it colors interactions with that person. The same situation occurs with nonprofit elephants.

Most people are rarely willing to challenge the status quo at any time. Challenging nonprofit elephants is especially fraught with danger. First, ingrained beliefs are tough to change; certainly they aren't the kind of problem that boards like to address. Second, a board or CEO who challenges entrenched nonprofit beliefs is in a particularly vulnerable position. Boards face strong opposition from *vested volunteers,* people whose ego, power, and status hinge on maintaining the status quo. Board members do not want to make powerful enemies who might prevent their reelection or who hold grudges that hurt the members' careers when they reenter nonprofit ranks.

Also, boards can face opposition from their CEOs. CEOs understand how to work around elephants and may prefer the known devil to an unknown one. Or CEOs may resent or be incapable of handling new responsibilities. For example, a board wants to look at a new governance structure that holds the CEO more accountable; the CEO, however, wants greater responsibility but not accountability. The CEO enjoys stating "the board approved it" as a means of deflecting blame for unpopular decisions.

Conversely, CEOs are really in poor positions to challenge many of these elephants, because they risk riling powerful board directors or volunteers. Remember, boards determine CEO performance reviews, and powerful volunteers make powerful enemies. Also, as discussed in Chapter 4, agreeing publicly with the board while continuing to move in their own direction is one of the tactics CEOs use to keep boards happy. Certainly, experienced staff members other than the CEO also avoid the elephants like the plague. The fierce opposition to and the swift annihilation of professional staff who attempt to bring such issues to light is lesson enough to deter people.

No, the task of exposing the elephants in the nonprofit room and confronting hard truths is not an easy one, but these elephants are the core problems that drain the energy of top volunteer and staff leaders. In turn, they are the reason that so many nonprofits struggle just to remain average rather than pursuing the challenge to be truly great.

CHAPTER 3

The *Mission Impossible* Elephant

Everything should be made as simple as possible, but not simpler.

—Albert Einstein

Where's Mission?

Ask any nonprofit board member the question, "What's your mission?" and you will typically hear something noble like "providing humanitarian aid to the downtrodden" or "advancing the cause of dentistry." Sounds wonderful, but is this mission as stated really the mission in practice?

A close look at how nonprofit resources are deployed and organizational dollars spent can paint a different picture. Volunteer and professional staff leaders' energies are often consumed by infighting and politics. The mission results of volunteer activities frequently fail to outweigh the resources used. Worse yet, volunteers and staff seem aware of the situation but feel powerless to change it.

In This Chapter

In Chapter 3 we examine the granddaddy of all nonprofit archetypes, the *I'm the Expert* belief. This belief governs the *Mission Impossible* elephant and is a contributing factor to the behavior of many of the other elephants. Sometimes unconscious but always present, *I'm the Expert* detours organizational energy away from mission and toward politics and power struggles.

This chapter analyzes the subtle and not-so-subtle effects of *I'm the Expert* in daily nonprofit life. Specifically, we'll view the unhealthy dual operating structure that develops and view its destructive force first hand. The vehicles that transport us are *Live Lessons,* descriptions of actual nonprofits and situations (names have been changed to protect the guilty) and *At the Salt Mines,* little docudramas depicting day-to-day operations in the nonprofit workplace.

Chapter 3 concludes by estimating the organizational cost of the *Mission Impossible* elephant. In the process, we'll compare the resources dedicated to mission against those consumed by the volunteer/staff structure. Then you decide: What is the real mission of this nonprofit?

The *I'm the Expert* Archetype

I'm the Expert is the conscious or unconscious belief that member, donor, or constituent expertise in occupation or cause (the benefit or mission of the organization) translates to expertise in nonprofit management (the business of the organization). The thinking goes like this: The American Bar Association (ABA) is about the law profession, so being a lawyer provides the necessary experience for managing an organization whose mission is law; the American Heart Association is about heart health, so being a volunteer who cares and is knowledgeable about heart-healthy activities provides the necessary expertise for managing an organization whose mission is heart health.

This attitude, though subtle and a little hard to grasp at first, is omnipresent and dramatically shapes member, donor, or constituent assumptions and behavior. Let's test the validity of that statement a little. Think about your own nonprofit. Then see if you can identify with John's assumptions in the following example.

The Case of John

John is CEO of The Golden Years, a chain of retirement homes. He's a member of the Association for Retirement Home Management (ARHM), a large, multinational nonprofit. John owns a significant number of shares of Coca-Cola stock and is well versed in Coke's management issues. His neighbor heads a Coke division, and the two talk frequently. Coke and ARHM ask John to join their boards, and he accepts both positions.

John makes the following assumptions regarding his Coke directorship:

- He knows that being a Coke shareholder does not prepare him to run a large, complex business like Coke.
- He expects Coke's CEO to direct and be responsible for Coke's business policies, strategies, and operations.
- As a board member, John looks forward to representing the senior market and focusing on top-level issues regarding Coke's vision and competitive environment.

John makes the following assumptions regarding his ARHM board position:

- John is a successful retirement home manager and understands how his nonprofit should run as well as anyone. After all, ARHM is his profession.

- A longtime member, John knows that the board is ARHM's governing body, responsible for the vision, mission, policies, strategies, and overall functioning of the organization.
- John expects ARHM's CEO to manage the staff and national office, execute the board's direction, and provide necessary support for board and board committees. As a board member, he expects the board to make the major decisions and approve all policies, strategies, marketing, and products.

Why are John's assumptions different for Coke and ARHM? *I'm the Expert* drives his thinking. John believes that he knows all about ARHM because it's an extension of his own profession. However, he views Coke as a business needing a set of professional skills different than his own. He expects Coke's CEO to run the business, while he views ARHM's CEO as support to the board.

John is in good company. His attitude is widely shared by his peers, and a case might even be made that *I'm the Expert* was helpful in the past when the sector was small, volunteers plentiful, paid staff rare, and the pace of change slow. Women, especially, did not work outside of the home, and many were devoted full time to volunteer activities. But as discussed in Chapter 1, these conditions are rapidly changing. John's assumptions no longer hold true in today's nonprofit environment for two major reasons:

1. *The Nonprofit Sector Has Grown*. ARHM is a complex business, one that is very different than The Golden Years retirement home. As we'll discuss shortly, nonprofits have two distinct components: benefit and business. Although John's knowledge set transfers to ARHM's benefit component, he needs different skills to manage the ARHM's business component.
2. *Most People Can Only Devote a Limited Amount of Time to Volunteer Activities.* The volunteer role has constraints that run counter to the requirements of dynamic business management. These constraints handicap John's ability, as a volunteer, to manage ARHM.

A third aspect of *I'm the Expert* is that many members, donors, and constituents believe that those who are not expert in the benefit component, professional staff, cannot possibly care about the organization as much as those who are experts, members, donors, and constituents. Furthermore, the underlying assumption is that unpaid workers (volunteers) are there because they care, but paid workers (professional staff) are there for the money.

Taking this step further, members, particularly volunteers, judge staff competence by an "insider" standard that has nothing to do with professional skills. The thinking goes like this: Staff members do not know our field/benefit and cannot talk the language, so the staff is not competent. Volunteers do the work out of love, not money; they are trustworthy and paid staff is not.

This kind of *I'm the Expert* thinking leads to the natural conclusion that a nonprofit is best protected by volunteers, not staff driving all real decisions.

The Two Nonprofit Components

As nonprofits move beyond their early formative years, they add reoccurring programs, services, and products that require daily management. Professional staff is hired, and two distinct parts of the organization emerge. One is the cause or mission part, which we'll call the *benefit component,* and the other is the management or business side, which we'll call the *business component.*

The Benefit Component

The nonprofit benefit component is the volunteer, member, donor, or constituent knowledge domain. It is their passion, expertise, and experience in that organization's mission field. Going back to our previous example, a lawyer understands the field of law, is familiar with the daily life and needs of lawyers, and has content expertise in different areas of law. At its best, the benefit component gives nonprofits a very special ability to "stay close to the market" and to develop and promote programs cost effectively.

The Business Component

The nonprofit business component is the professional staff knowledge domain. It consists of their experience and skill in marketing, operations, education, or management of the nonprofit entity. Once a nonprofit has reoccurring programs and services, they must be effectively managed daily for optimum results. At its best, the business component provides a continual stream of well-managed programs, services, and products. This simple example using ARHM should help make the distinction between these two components clearer:

- ARHM produces a monthly magazine of cutting-edge strategies and techniques for retirement home management.
- Professional staff directs the magazine business component (i.e., the management of resources such as topic, authors, manuscripts, printing, marketing, distribution, and finance).
- Volunteers or members contribute magazine articles or content.
- Professional staff and volunteers share their respective talents and informed wisdom on market need and issues such as theme and topics.

This seems to make perfect sense. Two different components of an organization: each makes a unique contribution, while each shares the other's informed wisdom. Together, they contribute much more to the nonprofit than either could individually. Yet the failure of nonprofits to recognize and fully capitalize on this fact is the norm, not the exception. This failure is the lifeblood of the *Mission Impossible* elephant.

In addition, some subtleties other than *I'm the Expert* make members, donors, and staff reluctant to fully acknowledge the business component. Some of these ingrained thoughts and habits are:

- **Business Is Evil.** Many nonprofit members or donors strongly object to thinking of their nonprofit as a business at all. That word is too closely linked with the evils of a profit-driven corporate world, where many must work for pay. They volunteer, in part, to escape that world and to work for a nobler cause. Philanthropy and foundation staff in particular share these feelings. They chose to work for the greater good rather than for a profit-oriented business.
- **Professional Management Is Not Needed.** As a nonprofit expands, it's difficult for longtime members to understand that the organization is moving into a different phase that requires more professional management. In some ways, it's like the plight of business entrepreneurs who fail to recognize that their foundling skills must give way to the new expertise needed for growth. They fear losing control of something dear and giving up a powerful role with nothing to replace it.
- **It's Customary to Pay Lip Service to Business Management.** Because sector advisers and the media push the idea of nonprofits thinking more like a business, there is a tendency for boards to talk this language, but this is often just lip service. For example, a board recruits "a new caliber of CEO," one with a strong business focus and corporate experience yet in practice insists on approving the new CEO's every action.

That brings us to the second major issue that makes John's assumptions regarding ARHM incorrect. The volunteer role has constraints that run counter to the requirements of managing a dynamic business.

Constraints to the Volunteer Role

Volunteer Strengths: Benefit Component

A "volunteer" is one who enters into or offers himself for a service of his own free will; somebody who performs an act without being legally bound to do so and without expecting to be paid.

For most people today, volunteerism means giving a limited amount of time to a worthy cause or to an organization related to a profession or belief. Volunteers' passion, expertise, and experience are a plus to the benefit component. It keeps nonprofits in touch with constituents and ensures a continual supply of fresh ideas and content expertise for programs and services.

The fact that volunteers can give only limited time on a temporary basis does not limit their contribution to the benefit component. To the contrary, volunteers are more actively engaged in the organization, so the more the turnover and the more new constituents in that role, the better. New board members often offer fresh insights to the board charge of defining, maintaining, and protecting mission. Few would argue that in the areas like content development, expert volunteers provide services for free that, when charged at market rate, would cost millions. However, what is good for the benefit component is not so good for the business side.

Volunteer Limits: Business Component

The needs of the business component are quite different. Business is a serious activity requiring time and effort and the avoidance of distractions. Business activities occur every hour, day in and day out. Making informed decisions depends on people's ability to understand and react to what is happening at any given point in time. People expect bosses to understand the business, provide clear goals, reward good performance, and be available for coaching and mentoring as needed.

Geographically remote volunteers who serve limited terms are ill-equipped to manage a daily business. That's why nonprofits hire professional staff. Being a business manager means making a full-time commitment for pay that, rightly or wrongly in today's world, is not subordinate to the events of family and life. The strength of professional staff is the day-in, day-out application of specific experience and skills to effectively optimize mission goals.

The constraints on the volunteer role conflict with the requirements for managing the business component. Consider a comparison of the two in Exhibit 3.1.

EXHIBIT 3.1 VOLUNTEER CONSTRAINTS VERSUS BUSINESS CONSTRAINTS

Volunteer Constraints	Business Requirements
Limited meeting time: one to three in-person meetings per year	Day-in, day-out attention to business operations
Limited terms in office: typically one to three years	Full-time commitment for indefinite time frame
Limited training time and business area experience	Extensive experience in designated area: on-the-job training/succession planning
Limited accountability: few penalties for poor performance; volunteer time subordinate to job or life events	Accountability for job performance
Limited exposure to operations or professional staff: geographically remote and limited availability	Daily proximity to people and action

Volunteer and Professional Staff: Complementary Strengths and Weaknesses

Volunteers are not the only ones with constraints. Professional staff also has weaknesses and constraints:

- Isolation from the day-to-day world of the member, donor, or constituent
- Lack of in-depth benefit knowledge
- Lack of contact with a broad spectrum of members, donors, or constituents

Just as benefit and business components are different but complementary, so volunteer and staff roles are different but complementary. Eureka! We strike gold at last.

The constraints of volunteers are the strengths of professional staff; conversely, the constraints of professional staff are the strengths of volunteers. And that takes us back to a central point in our earlier discussion of the two nonprofit components. Benefit and business components complement one another—so do volunteers and professional staff. Each entity can and should make a unique contribution to its respective component.

Given this fact, it would make sense that professional staff manages the business component and volunteers the benefit component. Otherwise, if it were the other way around, companies like Coke would certainly fire their paid managers and hire volunteer ones. *I'm the Expert* encourages nonprofits to go in a different direction. Volunteers try to run the nonprofit business, and too often, staff attempts to manage both. In the process, neither brings their best talents forward nor appreciates the other's potentially unique contribution.

How all this happens is an interesting story, but before watching *I'm the Expert* in action, it's important to understand the roles and relationships of members/constituents and volunteers.

Roles and Relationships Defined

Members, Volunteers, and Vested Volunteers

Although they are often used interchangeably, the terms *member* (donor, constituent) and *volunteer* are not identical. Members include everyone who pays dues or donates to a nonprofit, while volunteers are a much smaller subset of members who personally donate time and energy to the organization. In other words, usually all volunteers are members, but not all members are volunteers.

The importance of this distinction cannot be overemphasized, because the motivation and behavior of the two groups can be quite different. Typically, nonvolunteer members are not actively involved in the governance, politics, and operations of a nonprofit. They care little about organizational structure or who controls decisions. What they do care about is outcomes. Members primarily judge a nonprofit on "bang for the buck" (i.e., the return of their dollar investment in the form of societal benefit, political clout, programs, service, and other mission-related activities).

Volunteers, however, work and are actively involved in nonprofit operations. They care about structure and process, sometimes even more than outcome. As discussed in more detail in the next section, one can think of volunteers as a large, unpaid workforce that, together with paid professional staff, is the personnel of a nonprofit. Volunteer and professional staff are the two workhorses that perform nonprofit work.

Being more a part of nonprofit action than members, volunteers are also more likely to take an active interest in governance and management. That's good, because volunteers are an extremely important, positive force for nonprofits. Most volunteers are well-intentioned people who care deeply about their nonprofit's mission. They channel that caring into tireless, selfless, and incalculable contributions for the nonprofit. Being in the know makes them especially valuable for experience, institutional memory, and oversight of governance and management.

There is, however, another side of the volunteer coin. As in general when positive traits carried to the extreme turn negative, so, too, does volunteer commitment taken to the extreme turn into obsession. That brings us to a very small subset of the total volunteers we'll call "vested volunteers." Exhibit 3.2 illustrates the relationships among members, volunteers, and vested volunteers.

EXHIBIT 3.2 MEMBERS, VOLUNTEERS, AND VESTED VOLUNTEERS

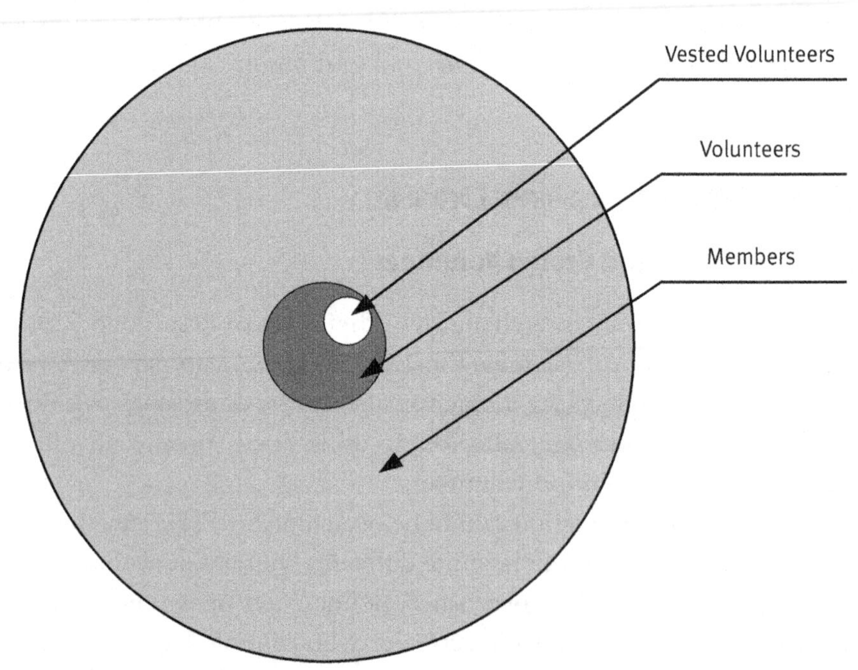

Vested volunteers are more concerned about their own vision and individual role within the nonprofit than with the nonprofit's needs as a whole. Their desire for personal power, prestige, or gain supersedes and clouds their vision of mission. They care deeply about the leadership and power structure of the nonprofit and are morbidly concerned about loss of power, especially if that power is perceived as moving to professional staff. Although small in numbers, vested volunteers wield an influence over a nonprofit that far exceeds their numbers.

Anatomy of a Vested Volunteer It's helpful to understand why people volunteer in the first place before tackling the issue of vested volunteers. The three most generally accepted reasons are:

- **Achievement:** personal gratification, giving back or contributing to the greater good
- **Affiliation:** belonging, networking, friends, and fun
- **Power:** personal power and fame

Most great volunteers are mission driven and motivated primarily by achievement and/or affiliation. Some want to help the less fortunate in society or do their part to make the world a better place. Others simply want to give back to an organization that helped them. Most like learning new skills and enjoying the camaraderie and contacts of peers along the way. The quality of volunteer talent follows the normal bell curve of any large group of people: a small number of outstanding, a large number of average, and a few not so good. But no matter what the talent level, a strong nonprofit encourages and accommodates all volunteers who are achievement or affiliation driven.

A problem arises when the question "How can I help my association?" becomes subordinate to "How can my association help me?" Unfortunately, this tends to occur over time with a few volunteers who may initially make strong contributions to mission. They begin their volunteer lives as talented individuals, gaining accolades and ever-increasing power as they travel along the path to committee or board leadership.

However, somewhere along this path, the vested volunteers become more committed to personal power than organizational mission. Slowly, as they spend huge quantities of time in critical volunteer roles, it becomes a "career." When they become committee chairs or board members, power becomes magnified.

Volunteer governance can be heady stuff. Board members may not hold a senior management position in their professional jobs, but as board members they can command a $25 million organization and a whole office of professional staff. They have all of the power without any of the drawbacks of a professional job. Livelihood does not depend on the position, there is no performance accountability, and everyone understands that volunteering is an unpaid role that may need to be subordinate to personal or life events at any time.

When a volunteer's ego and sense of role enjoyment grow out of control in this management-without-accountability-or-penalty world, a vested volunteer is born. A desire to maintain their role is paramount, so vested volunteers resist any change viewed as diminishing their power—and that includes almost anything that happens without their involvement. At the top of the list is a strong, independent professional staff that might alter that from which they derive such satisfaction.

Vested volunteers maintain the status quo through a surefire *I'm the Expert* tactic—a "this is or isn't what the members want" defense. In reality, the vested volunteer's position benefits only a small oligarchy of volunteers rather than the larger membership. However, because this fact often escapes board notice, vested volunteers wield great clout and play a large part in nonprofit problems.

Keeping these differences in mind, let's examine volunteer and staff roles in a high-performing nonprofit. How do members, volunteers, volunteer leaders, the CEO, and professional staff relate to each other? What are the logical roles and responsibilities for each of these entities?

High-Performing Roles and Relationships Diagrammed

The easiest way to understand nonprofit roles is to see them visually on an organizational chart. But a few caveats are in order before starting the diagram engine. The pros and cons of various governance structures can easily fill a book (and do). Such discussions are not the purpose of this book, but it is important to understand how things should work in a high-performing nonprofit. Otherwise, it is difficult to fully appreciate the *Mission Impossible* elephant's harmful behavior.

The governance structure that is most likely to support high mission achievement in a mature nonprofit is a "mission-fueled" or "market-fueled" model. Neither staff-driven nor volunteer-driven, in this model both entities work together under the mission umbrella, yet each makes a unique contribution toward mission goals. Beyond the following brief overview, we'll see in detail how mission-driven governance tames the *Mission Impossible* elephant in Chapter 8.

The Basic Parts Corporations are owned by their shareholders and private businesses by their founders and partners. However, the definition of nonprofit "owners" is not so distinct, which makes discussing who "owns" nonprofits painful and fruitless. Let's just assume that nonprofits are "owned" by their constituents: the members of a trade, professional or membership association, or donors/grantors/community constituents of a foundation or charitable nonprofit. For example, members or owners of the American Bar Association (ABA) are the lawyers, students, and vendors who pay dues. Donors or owners of the American Heart Association (AHA) are the people who contribute money/goods to the AHA.

EXHIBIT 3.3 MEMBER BOARD

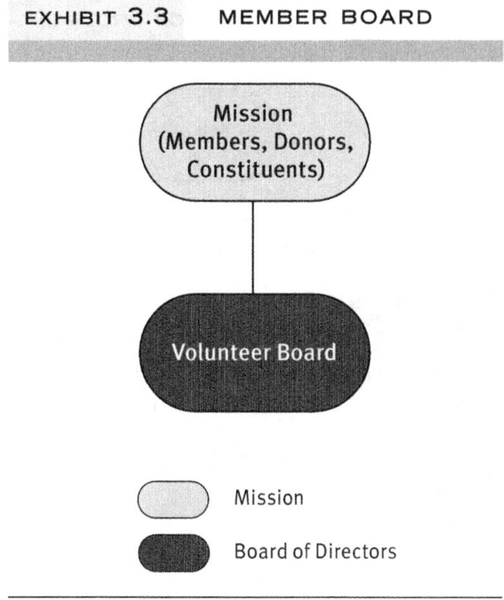

The ABA has more than 400,000 members. It would be impossible for such a large group to make decisions and act collectively in a timely fashion, so they are represented by appointed or elected volunteer boards. The role and relationship of members/donors to volunteer boards is shown in Exhibit 3.3.

Taking a little liberty with technical definitions, volunteer boards operate at the will and consent of members/donors, much like corporate boards are responsible to their shareholders. Boards must legally represent and protect the interests of these parties. A nonprofit board's legally defined responsibility is the discharge of duties in good faith, with the care and diligence of a prudent person, and in a manner believed to be in the best interests of the organization. In more practical terms, the board represents the interests and concerns of members and must transform their desires into mission. The board fulfills this responsibility and maintains oversight of the CEO and organizational activities through a collective process called "governance."

If a volunteer board is very large, it may delegate some of its responsibilities to an executive committee. This smaller group is empowered "under the will of the board" to act for the board and thus for the membership between meetings.

Board Work; Governance Process The board has three main resources to accomplish its work: the CEO (professional staff), volunteer staff, and outside parties (e.g., consultants, vendors). The board charges the CEO with managing the nonprofit business, and the board directs volunteers or outside resources as necessary to execute the governance process. A simple example is as follows: the board appoints a volunteer nominating committee for the governance process of board elections or hires an outside audit firm for the governance process of financial oversight.

EXHIBIT 3.4 BOARD/GOVERNANCE GROUPS

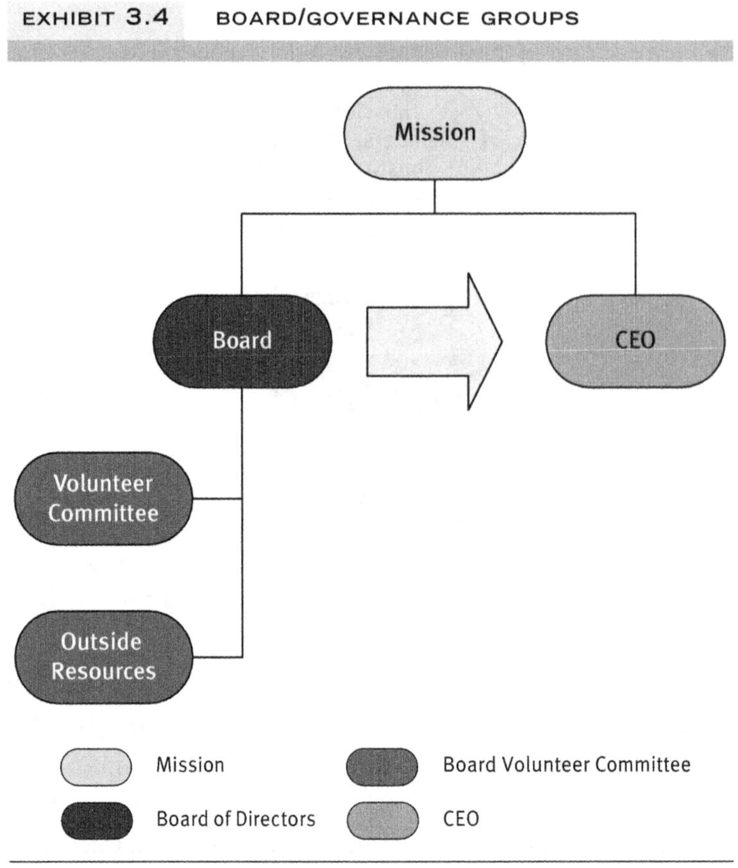

Let's add the board's governance resources to our diagram in Exhibit 3.4.

CEO Work; Business Process A high-performing board charges the CEO with directing the nonprofit business enterprise. Like the board, the CEO has three main resources available to accomplish the business process: professional staff, volunteer staff, and outside resources such as consultants or other vendors.

Let's add this final business process level to our diagram in Exhibit 3.5.

I'M THE EXPERT TAKES OVER

Common sense and management practice usually dictate that the head of a function directs the resources needed to perform that function. So we would expect the board to direct governance resources and the CEO to direct business resources—in other words, volunteers engaged in business process report to the CEO and volunteers engaged in governance process report to the board.

Remember *I'm the Expert*? How it encourages most boards and volunteers to avoid the term "business" or narrowly limits it to administrative support. And how volunteers

EXHIBIT 3.5 BOARD/CEO/BUSINESS GROUPS

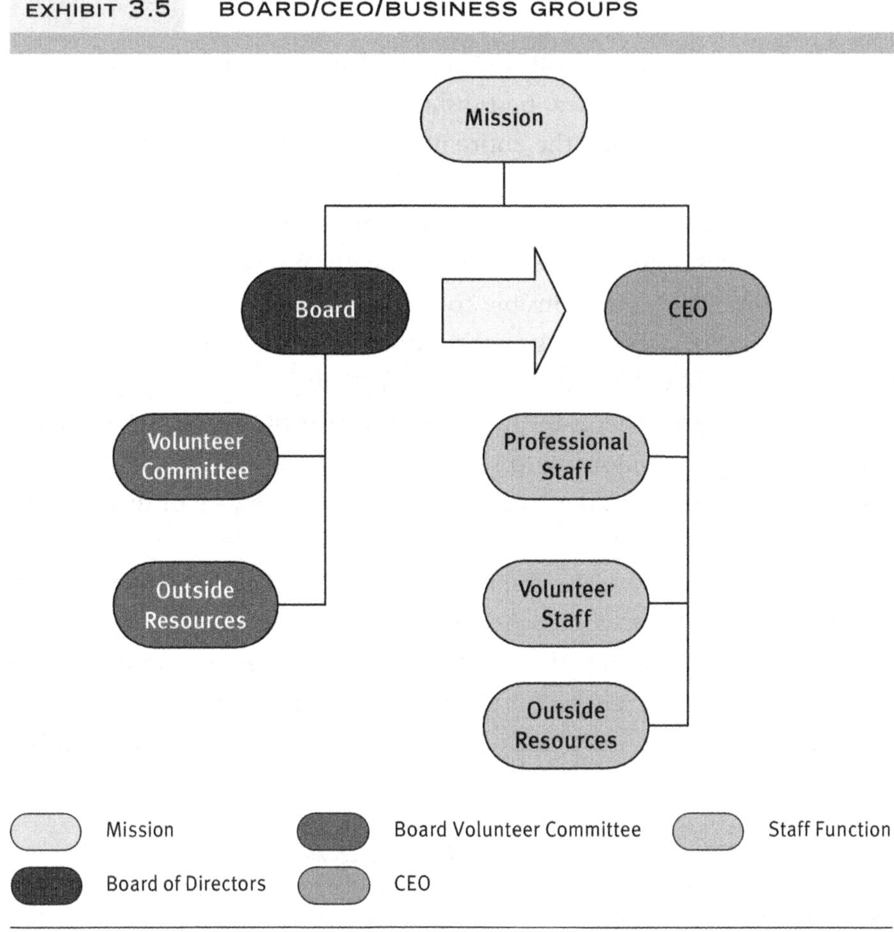

believe that they, not staff, must run the organization, albeit with staff support? Rarely do the people in charge report to the people they direct. Neither do volunteers report to staff.

Here's where the *Mission Impossible* elephant starts to trumpet its horn, and that sound heralds the birth of the dual operating structure. Volunteers report through a volunteer organization structure directly to the board, and professional staff reports through a staff organization structure directly to the CEO. In theory and on paper, volunteers and professional staff live in parallel universes that connect only at the board/CEO level.

Often a nonprofit's Web site and publications show only the volunteer structure; volunteer and staff structures are almost always listed separately. The subliminal implication is that volunteers are in charge and volunteer committees perform all the work of the organization. If staff is mentioned, it is usually as a source to contact for help.

The dual structure is the lifeblood of the *Mission Impossible* elephant. It creates confusion in roles, duplication of efforts, lack of accountability, and tortured communications —just the kind of environment that breeds power struggles, infighting, and minutiae!

The Dual Structure in Action

"Dirty little deeds, done dirt cheap" is a jingle that applies to the dual system. It precipitates pretend games that are at best dishonest and at worst demoralizing and disrespectful to all participants. And the entire nonprofit participates in these games, in one way or another.

Problems start with the practice of the board or its delegate appointing and overseeing all volunteer committees. The board is directly responsible only for governance process while the CEO is responsible for business process. Because most volunteer committees are engaged in business, not governance process, their work should be, and in reality is, overseen by the CEO and her or his staff.

So what board appointments mean to CEOs is that they must use a workforce formally appointed by and reporting to someone else. Even when a committee's work is managed by staff in practice, the committee may not be aware of that fact and thinks it reports to the board.

Wow! Doesn't it make your head spin to imagine the contortions necessary to thrive in this environment? In practice, working in the dual structure is sort of like rolling a ball uphill with your hands tied behind your back. One moves up the hill with confusion, duplication, and infighting nibbling at your heels. But there's nothing like experiencing havoc first hand, so let's make our initial foray into the real workplace.

A *Live Lesson*: "Two Does Not Equal One"

Introducing the Principals

Our subject nonprofit is CCE (Committees Committees Everywhere), a large professional association ($18 million operating budget with 100 employees). Exhibit 3.6 shows the organizational chart for CCE's top volunteer leadership levels. Other volunteer task forces and subcommittee groups not shown on the chart report to these groups—60 volunteer committees in all.

Exhibit 3.7 shows the organizational chart for CCE's top staff leadership levels. Again, other levels not shown on the chart report to these levels.

Although CCE follows the sector norm of showing separate volunteer and staff organization structures, CCE's bylaws state that the CEO reports to the executive committee. So, given this fact, Exhibit 3.8 shows how a combined CCE volunteer and staff chart might look.

The *Live Lesson* and four *Salt Mines* exercises that follow are based on real situations that occurred at CCE. Only the names—organization and people—have been changed. The star of this *Live Lesson* is education, always a "hot spot" because of its importance to mission and revenue. The action centers on CCE's seminar subcommittee.

Yes, it's true—in nonprofit land even committees have committees!

EXHIBIT 3.6 CCE VOLUNTEER ORGANIZATIONAL CHART

Audit Committee
Board
Nominating Committee
Executive Committee
Education Committee
Strategic Planning Committee
Publications Committee
Finance Committee
Public Relations Committee
Membership Committee
Leadership Committee
Seminar
Seminar Development
Conference Planning
Faculty
Editorial Board
Publications Review Board
Publications Review Board
Technology
Government Relations
Marketing
Membership
Chapters
Leadership Training
Board of Directors
Board Volunteer Committee
Staff Volunteer Committee

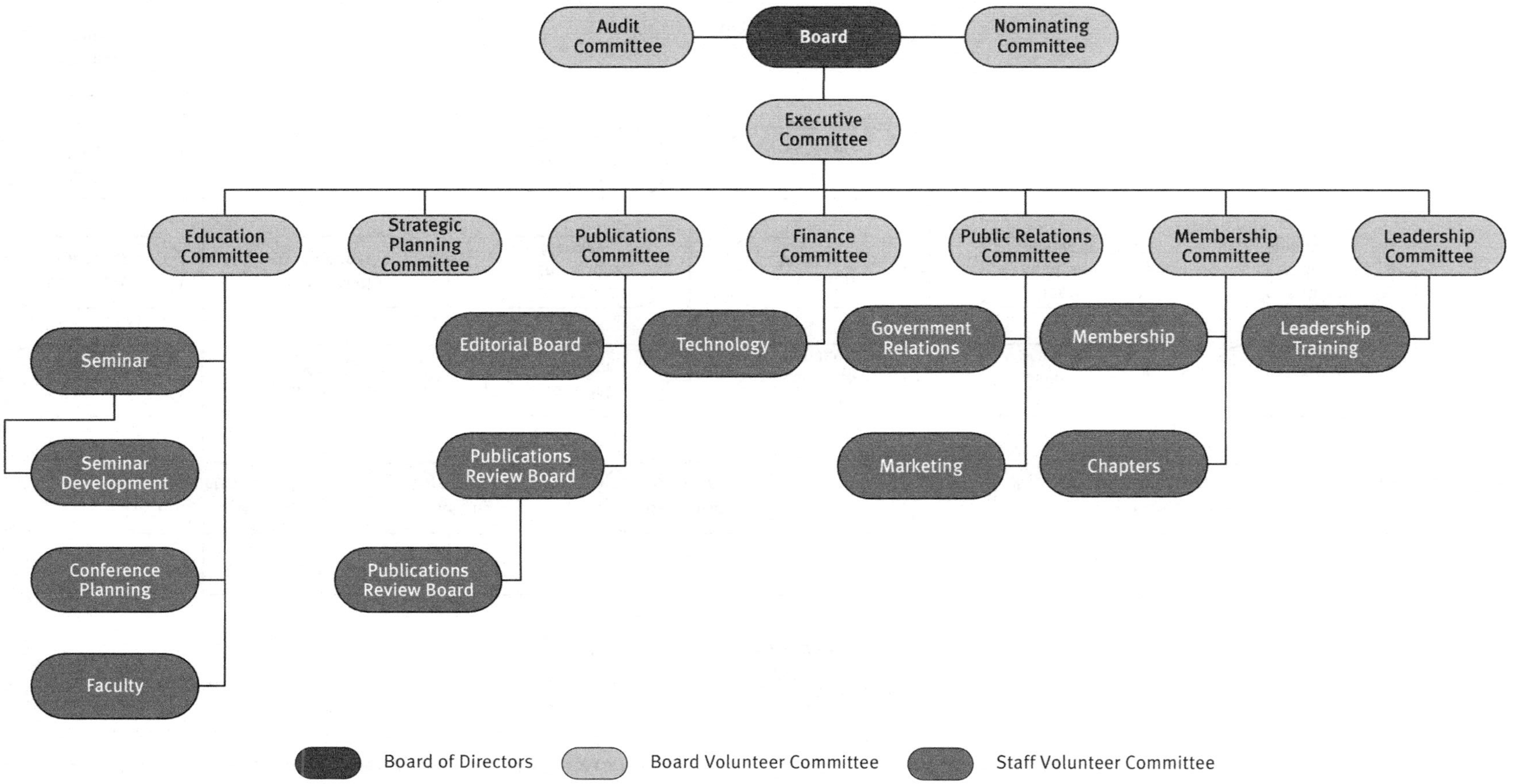

EXHIBIT 3.7 CCE STAFF ORGANIZATIONAL CHART

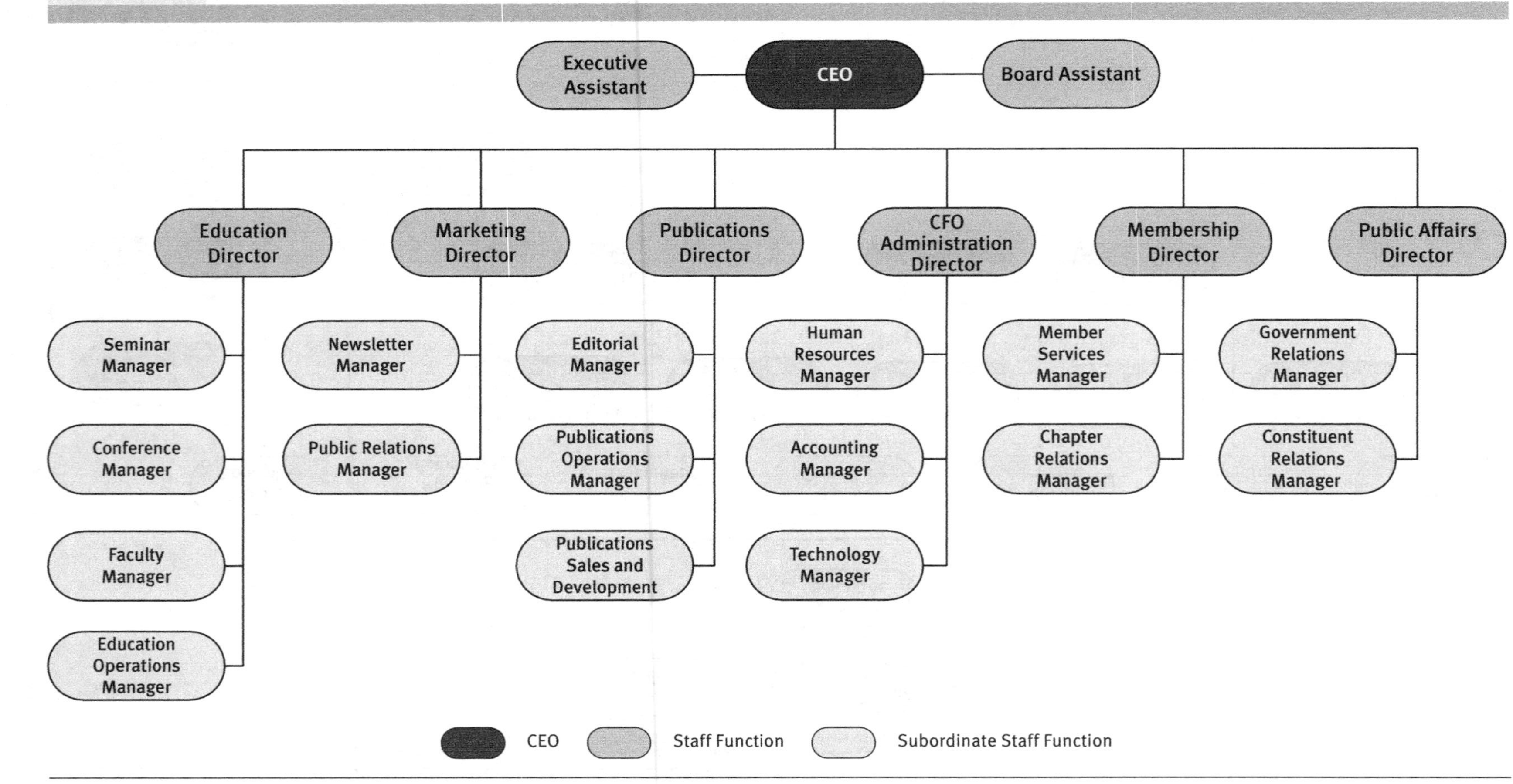
Executive Assistant
CEO
Board Assistant
Education Director
Marketing Director
Publications Director
CFO Administration Director
Membership Director
Public Affairs Director
Seminar Manager
Conference Manager
Faculty Manager
Education Operations Manager
Newsletter Manager
Public Relations Manager
Editorial Manager
Publications Operations Manager
Publications Sales and Development
Human Resources Manager
Accounting Manager
Technology Manager
Member Services Manager
Chapter Relations Manager
Government Relations Manager
Constituent Relations Manager
CEO
Staff Function
Subordinate Staff Function

EXHIBIT 3.8 CCE COMBINED VOLUNTEER AND STAFF ORGANIZATION CHART

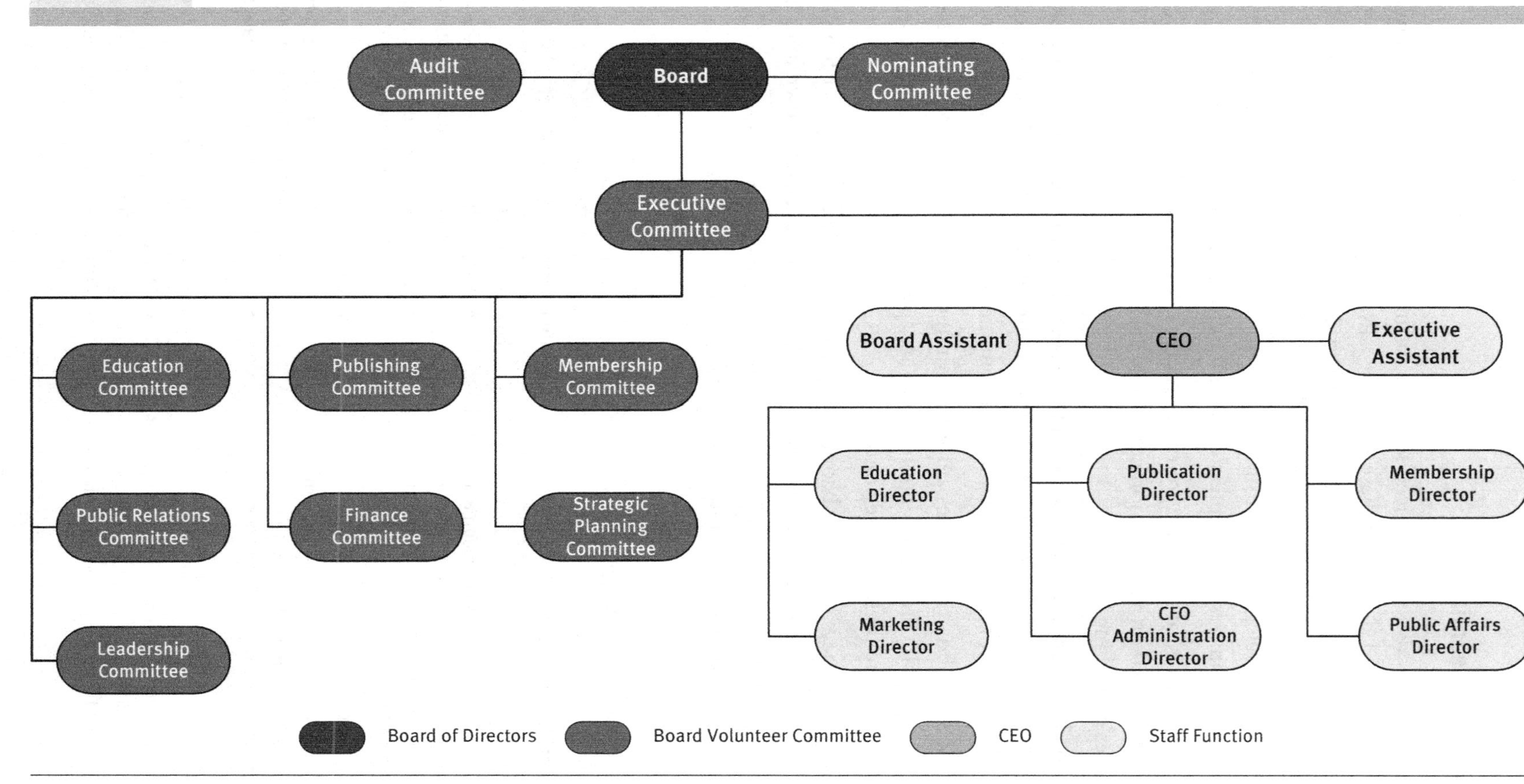

Live Lesson Essentials

- CCE offers reasonably priced seminars for member and nonmember professionals. Creating and delivering these seminars falls within the business component. The executive committee expects the CEO to deliver quality, mission-related seminars on a break-even basis (revenue equals expenses).
- The CEO delegates responsibility for seminars to the staff education director. She, in turn, manages both professional staff and volunteer staff resources.
- The board is largely unaware of education operations. Many board directors have never served on an education committee and believe that the education committee does everything.
- The board appoints seminar development subcommittee volunteers. Exhibit 3.6 illustrates the committee's reporting structure: seminar development subcommittee → seminar committee → education committee → executive committee → board.
- The CCE board delegates authority for appointing committee members to the president. The president's appointments are approved by the board, but this is simply a nod to the president's selections.
- Staff sends new seminar subcommittee appointees a welcome letter from the president. Included is a copy of the volunteer organizational chart (shown in Exhibit 3.6).
- Exhibit 3.9 shows the key responsibilities of the education/seminar committees and professional education/seminar staff.

EXHIBIT 3.9 KEY RESPONSIBILITIES

Volunteer Education Committees	**Professional Education Staff**
Education Committee • Exercises general supervision and control over content of education programs • Oversees the administration of all education programs	Education Director • Responsible for strategic oversight and development of education programs • Recommends new programs and terminates unprofitable ones
Seminar Committee • Recommends seminar policy to the education committee • Oversees the development of seminar content and materials	Seminar Manager • Recommends new seminar policy and ensures adherence to current policies • Manages seminar development and delivery
Seminar Development Subcommittee • Plans, develops, maintains, and updates seminars • Ensures the quality of seminar materials	Education Operations Manager • Manages the editorial and production process for education products • Ensures adherence to production and editorial cost budgets

- The cast of CCE is:

  Board President: Bob

  CEO: Charles

  Education Chair: Susan

  Seminar Subcommittee Chair: Tony

  Education Director: Robin

You have the *Live Lesson* basics—now on to the *Salt Mines*. Fasten your seat belts; it's going to be a bumpy ride!

Salt Mines #1 (Situation)

The elected president, Bob, appoints a capable volunteer, Fred . . .

- Fred reads his welcome letter and looks at the committee chart and job descriptions. Before his appointment, he talked with Bob, who stressed the committee's great work and CCE's fine seminars.
- Fred also receives a letter from department staff containing the staff organizational chart and job descriptions. Bob told him that staff is a great help.
- At the first seminar subcommittee meeting, Fred is puzzled by the active participation of the staff director, Robin. He assumed that staff was there just to help the committee.
- Fred raises one of his pet peeves under new business, the high price ($50 each) of seminars. Robin explains why seminars must be priced at break-even or above.
- Even after the subcommittee chair, Tony, confirms Robin's explanation, Fred is upset. And so is another new committee member. They believe that pricing is the committee's purview.
- After two hours of heated discussion, Fred makes a motion to change the price to $35. The motion is defeated.
- Fred is angry at Robin, Tony, and the other "do-nothing" subcommittee members. He calls Bob to complain as soon as he returns from the meetings.

Salt Mines #1 (Aftermath)

A crash of role confusion and power struggles . . .

- Fred is really angry at Robin. He thinks: "Who does she think she is anyway? She's not even a member, yet she's telling the committee what to do. Nor does she understand our needs; $35 is more than enough." He is convinced Robin just wants the revenue so she can keep her job.

- Fred tells Bob and everyone who will listen that staff is creating real problems by being too involved in member affairs. Robin has too much control, and Tony won't do anything about it. Bob calls Charles, the CEO, and Charles talks to Robin about the issue.
- Meanwhile, Fred lobbies other board and committee members; each talks with several friends about the situation. Pretty soon, Tony, Charles, and Robin are all receiving calls and e-mails. They have agreed to "keep each other in the loop" regarding the situation.

Salt Mines #2 (Situation)

A vested volunteer, Joe, is appointed . . .

- The seminar committee recently turned down Joe's new seminar proposal, for which he would be paid a development fee and an honorarium to teach the seminar. The topic was already under development, and Robin knows that Joe's work on previous projects was incomplete and late.
- Joe has friends on the executive committee. He corners two of its members at break, and they think his idea is great. They don't remember that the executive committee approved a seminar with the same topic at a previous meeting.
- The two executive committee members talk to one of their friends, a new seminar committee member from their city.
- Because this committee member is new and knows little about the already approved seminar, she agrees to resubmit Joe's proposal to the subcommittee.
- Although the developer has already been selected and the initial phase is underway on the approved seminar, two new subcommittee members also want to revisit the situation and consider Joe's proposal. Tony states that the matter is closed, and the meeting moves on.

Salt Mines #2 (Aftermath)

A crash of approvals and decision-making authority . . .

- Meanwhile, Joe decides to talk with the education chair. Why should he accept a "no" from a lower committee? He's really counting on the income from development and teaching.
- Joe knows that the executive and education committee won't challenge him on the details of the project. Heck, they love his seminar, and they always bend over backward to be fair to a fellow member, especially when he tells them that Robin just doesn't like him.

- The new subcommittee members are on Joe's side. Tony isn't listening to them, but they are complaining to Bob and others.
- Bob is getting uneasy. Both Fred and Joe are complaining about Robin, and he's hearing the same from others. He must talk to Charles (CEO) again; there may be a problem here.

Salt Mines #3 (Situation)

The board appoints an unsuited volunteer, Jane . . .

- Jane helped President Bob get elected. She wants a committee appointment and thinks the seminar development subcommittee is interesting. Although Jane has no background in seminars, she's really interested in learning. Bob appoints her.
- At the first subcommittee meeting, Jane asks basic questions about everything. The normally two-hour meeting spills into three hours, and many agenda items do not get addressed.
- Jane volunteers for two review groups and one development group. She's not well versed in the topics under development, but she's willing to learn. Plus, she likes editing and wants to volunteer her skills to edit book and seminar materials.

Salt Mines #3 (Aftermath)

A crash of learning versus contribution . . .

- Experienced subcommittee members are grumbling about Jane. She received Robin's premeeting materials just like the rest of them, so why didn't she read them?
- As the professional education director, Robin's excited about using her talents and experience to work on some new ideas that surfaced during the committee meeting, but she's swamped. President Bob and Subcommittee Chair Tony want to talk with her. So does her staff, and there are all those after-meeting administrative details, and she must set up calls, and so on, so that the subcommittee can complete its work.
- Jane's really irritated. Why can't Robin help her more? There was no time to read all that material she sent. Why couldn't she get together before the meeting and brief her? And, Tony! He shut her down each time she asked a question.
- Robin's in a bind. Jane has no background as an editor and, even if she did, Robin has a staff editor trained in manuscript structure and editing. And, Robin has a degree in education structural design, so there's little need for editorial help. Robin asks the chair to find something for Jane to do.
- After the meetings, Jane sees Bob at a work function. She tells him how much she likes the committee members, but is frustrated with Tony and Robin. They are

ignoring her offers to help, and serving on this committee is just not as much fun as she expected.

Salt Mines #4 (Situation)

Board and executive committee relations . . .

- Seminar A was expected to yield large attendance and earn plenty of money. Instead it tanked—and tanked in a spectacular way that affected education's overall bottom line.
- A board member can't understand how this happened. Why was so much riding on this one seminar? He doesn't accept Bob's explanation that a recap of the executive committee's discussion of the seminar was in his last board report. He feels, and so do many of his colleagues, that the executive committee failed to highlight this item and fully explain the risks.
- After all, the board approved the seminar based on the recommendation of the executive committee. But, as the board members begin to talk among themselves, they agree that the executive committee probably just approved the seminar based on the endorsement of the education committee.

Salt Mines #4 (Aftermath)

A crash of mistrust and a need for a scapegoat . . .

- A board member is talking with her colleagues. "Darn," she says, "this happens all the time. We only meet face to face twice a year, but the executive committee talks all the time. Of course, they're better informed, and they continually withhold essential information."
- One of her colleagues responds, "Yes, I'm sick and tired of it too and don't trust them. They are making decisions without consulting the board. But, when you think about it, they're just volunteers like us. It's really Charles (the CEO) who should have known better."
- More board members join the group, and the discussion continues. "The executive committee can't really be responsible for knowing all the details of the seminar. Isn't that the education committee's job?"
- Several members mention their discussions with Fred and Joe. Maybe the problem is with Robin. Or perhaps Charles didn't give the executive committee enough information to make an informed decision. Isn't that what we pay staff to do—prevent these kinds of losses?

Life in the *Salt Mines* Yikes, yikes, and double yikes, yikes! If you've never worked in a nonprofit, it may seem like these *Salt Mine* situations cannot be real. But if you are a current or former nonprofit worker, these instances may be mild compared to your own experiences.

Plus, this slice of nonprofit life is just a glimpse at one CCE area. Multiply these situations times the total number of CCE's functions and committees, and you begin to see the total impact on nonprofit productivity and achievement. Before leaving the fun of the *Salt Mines,* let's take a moment to summarize the major lessons that can be gleaned from our *Live Lesson.*

A Primer of Lessons from "Two Does Not Equal One"

Lesson One: People Will Find Their Own Path if Left Out in a Fog. It Just Might Not Be the Right Path.

Where duplication exists for no good reason, involved parties must and will struggle to find their own path through the fog. Each defines roles and boundaries differently along the path, and inevitably clashes of opinion lead to dissension.

Duplication is rampant in CCE's organizational charts and job descriptions. Often, the same responsibilities are assigned to two different entities—committee and staff.

The strengths and weaknesses of groups of people (committees) differ greatly from those of individuals (staff). Committees are good vehicles for vetting a variety of ideas or gaining input from diverse constituents, while individuals are better vehicles for "doing" or quick response. Yet common committee job duties include "doing" words like: "oversee development," "oversee the administration," and "exercise general supervision over content."

How can a group of volunteers that meets once or twice a year "oversee and supervise" a process where action occurs daily? Exactly how does one committee coordinate another committee's work anyway? And even if the committee could perform these tasks well, the same tasks appear in other committee and staff descriptions. If more than one entity performs essentially the same task, why are both needed, and who is accountable for the outcome?

A look at CCE's committee responsibilities is illuminating:

- **Seminar development subcommittee:** develops seminars
- **Seminar committee:** oversees seminar development; approves seminars
- **Education committee:** has general supervision over content of education; approves seminars
- **Executive committee:** approves or declines seminars
- **Board:** approves seminars via passing executive committee "board report" and motions

Does each of these entities contribute something unique to the mission goal of great seminars? And if they don't, why do they exist? What do the executive committee and board lend to this process? And because the committees meet only once or twice a year, as a practical matter, how do they reject a seminar? If the topic is not approved, it may be six months until the committees meet again, and by that time the topic may be obsolete. Where's staff in this equation? Education Director Robin shares many of the same responsibilities as those assigned to the committees, so who is accountable for what?

The fog of duplication rises to the very top of the volunteer and staff levels. Consider the responsibilities of CCE's 40-plus-member board, the 9-member executive committee, the board president, and the CEO, as shown in Exhibit 3.10.

A universally accepted definition of "general powers" doesn't exist on planet Earth, and even if it did, associations and corporations would interpret it differently. In fact, poll 10 executives on general powers and duties of management, and you get at least 12 different answers. The possibilities for new definitions are endless in a structure where the president, executive committee, and board change frequently.

Our worst fears are confirmed by *Salt Mines* participants. Robin, with advanced degrees in curriculum design and more than ten years of education management experience, sees her job as "directing and administering" education programs. Fred sees that charge as a committee responsibility. Jane sees her committee role as primarily fun and learning, while Robin and the subcommittee chair see it as performing a mission-crucial task. President Bob sees committee appointments as one way of rewarding volunteers and friends, while CEO Charles sees them as filling specific functions for a needed volunteer workforce.

The fog of roles and responsibilities inherent in the dual structure at CCE encourages a continuous battle among participants to establish boundaries and turf. By the time those definitions are hammered out, a new appointment cycle of volunteers or turnover of professional staff starts the battle anew.

EXHIBIT 3.10 RESPONSIBILITIES OF BOARD, EXECUTIVE COMMITTEE, PRESIDENT, AND CEO

Board	Executive Committee	President	CEO
Governing body of CCE	Conducts the business affairs of CCE	Supervises, directs, and controls the affairs of CCE with the general powers and and duties of management usually vested in the president of an association or corporation	Has the general powers and duties of management usually vested in the position of executive vice president of an association

Talented volunteers and staff will struggle out of this fog once, twice, maybe even three times if they truly love what they do. But think of the talent and energy wasted in this struggle. It's truly tragic, because at some point the struggle becomes too much, and another talented volunteer or staff person fades away in the fog—lost to the nonprofit forever.

Lesson Two: You Can't Blame the Horse for Dying When You Hold His Nostrils Closed!

Accountability without responsibility is unfair, but accountability without authority and control of resources is a recipe for disaster.

Although "responsibility" and "accountability" are often used interchangeably, *Exposing the Elephants* draws a subtle but profound distinction between the terms. "Responsibility" refers to the specific area and set of activities that an entity is responsible for (e.g., a finance director is responsible for the finance department and all its processes and activities).

"Accountability" refers to the totality of those responsibilities, to the global outcome of all this activity (e.g., the finance director is accountable for the accurate records of all financial activities). Accountability is accepting the responsibility for outcomes, including problems created and solutions to fix those problems; if a record is incorrect, no matter the cause, the finance director is accountable for rectifying the situation.

Any experienced person in the workplace understands that it must be very clear who's assigned to a project and who's in control. That person must be given true authority and held accountable for project outcomes. If outside people perceive that the authority is false, the project will most likely fail. Unfortunately, nonprofits often ignore this basic business concept.

Practically speaking, when a board or a board president appoints volunteer staff for business processes, the board is keeping the authority but assigning responsibility to the CEO. This fact does not escape volunteers, who see the board, not the CEO, as overseeing the committee's work.

This strikes right at the heart of why no one in a nonprofit is accountable when there is a problem. Responsibility is spread throughout the dual structure from the start, so that everyone is responsible, which, of course, means that no one is accountable. Multiple layers of committees and boards touch a task, as do multiple staff members. Ultimately, the board retains control and authority over all, but that doesn't mean that it accepts accountability in the event of a major problem. How many times does the board fire itself instead of the CEO?

Accountability is only one of the problems with board appointments of volunteer staff. Using our CCE *Salt Mine* example, the seminar committees are part of the resources (volunteer staff) that Education Director Robin needs to develop seminars. If she's lucky, the president may seek her counsel on committee requirements; more likely he'll make his appointment based on his criteria alone.

Robin understands education process, knows the volunteer and staff skills needed, and is accountable for outcomes, in this case, great seminars. Yet President Bob, who does not have that knowledge, selects her volunteer workforce. This affects the committee process and can create problems for Robin and Subcommittee Chair Tony. Some of the problems are:

- **Deadwood:** There are committee members who are relatively harmless (Jane) but take the seat of a working member; the remaining subcommittee members and staff pick up the slack. In addition, they must devote extra energy to educate Jane, whose term will end before she can use her new skills.
- **Troublemakers:** There are committee members who place self-interest above subcommittee goals (Joe). They tie the committee process in knots and lower the group's overall productivity. It only takes one bad apple to grind committee progress to a halt.
- **Infighting:** Committee and staff authority is continually up for debate and challenge. With no initial counseling about staff's role, Fred's *I'm the Expert* thinking immediately challenges Robin's position. Other volunteers may go directly to the president and board with their opinions and desires, which gives a volunteer and/or staff person a black mark and puts everyone on the defensive.
- **Committee Proliferation:** There is a tendency for the number of committees to grow. The president or board have no idea how seminars get done and so are susceptible to a member's appeal of "getting more members involved"—in other words, the more committees, the more seminars.
- **Time Drain:** The president, executive committee, board, and staff spend an inordinate amount of time on committee appointments and maintenance. The first task a new CCE president and board faces is filling what are often hundreds of committee appointments. The CEO's office must track appointments, create letters, publish directories, and send mailings. Each committee receives initial education materials and ongoing communications from their staff counterpart.

It isn't rocket science to realize that a whole lot of organizational energy goes into the care and feeding of committees. That could make sense if—and it's a big if—the committee produces enough results to warrant this cost.

Lesson Three: Ignorance of the Law Is No Excuse for Breaking the Law.

The nonprofit board that rubber-stamps committee work is like a naïve parent who never says no.

Every child knows that the quickest route to getting one parent's permission is to pretend that the other one already said okay. Woe to the naïve parent who falls for this ploy more than once!

Ideally, approval, formal sanction of endorsement, comes after a thorough consideration of all facts and an understanding of related factors and outcomes. The assumption is that approving entities possess the necessary experience and skill to take action.

A look at CCE's volunteer chart provides a strong clue that you can't make that assumption. The executive committee directly approves the work of seven committees plus the CEO and indirectly the work of 60 committees. The board approves the executive committee's work and everyone else's indirectly. Executive committee members who are part-time volunteers meeting once or twice per year rarely have time to consider the facts thoroughly for all of the lower committees' work, and they may not have the background to understand the details and ramifications of that work.

The only way this system works is by rubber-stamping, the nod that says, "We approve it, too." This takes different forms; sometimes the approval means "we trust that committee, so this is just a formality" or, more often, it's simply that the board as the highest authority officially signs off on everything.

Sometimes rubber-stamping creates resentment from a board that feels forced into approving things while being left out of the information loop, but mostly rubber-stamping makes the organization feel good. It gives the illusion of productivity by keeping everyone busy, and it reassures people that the organization is being protected by volunteers—the pesky *I'm the Expert* rearing its ugly head again.

These good feelings quickly evaporate when something major goes wrong, because responsibility is diffused throughout the system. So when there's a problem like CCE's tanked seminar, everyone points the finger at someone else. Lower committees are off the hook because the education committee approved it; that committee is off the hook because the executive committee approved it; the staff director is off the hook because it's a committee decision; and the executive committee is off the hook because the board approved it.

The board is left holding the bag, and that makes boards angry. So it's rare that nonprofits in this situation identify the real problem. Is the board really going to say, "We're part of the problem, and we'll fix it by giving up some perceived control"? Instead, the board commonly points its fingers at the usual suspects: not enough information or lack of proper controls.

Not enough information means that someone in the chain did not provide the information needed for the board to make an informed decision. Now, that's a Catch-22, because a common board complaint is that it can't digest all the information it currently receives from the staff and committee. It doesn't seem logical that even more information would avoid the problem.

If the problem is identified as a lower committee issue, or, as happens more frequently, as the CEO or staff going amuck, the convenient solution is adding controls. If it's a lower committee, just create another committee to check that committee's work. If it's the CEO or staff, decrease the span of control and add more approval levels.

This brings us to a curious dichotomy in volunteer leadership thinking as a whole. Although firmly entrenched in the *I'm the Expert* archetype most of the time, volunteers tend to discard this thinking in times of crisis. Then they revert to citing the limits of the volunteer role. Volunteer leaders make the important decisions, but, after all, they are just unpaid volunteers who can't devote all their time to the nonprofit. So it's unreasonable to hold volunteers accountable when things go wrong.

If the problem is bad enough, volunteers often seek a review of their governance and management structure. Task forces and special planning committees get together with thousands of dollars worth of consultants, and a new governance structure is birthed and announced with great fanfare. But this new governance structure is too often the same book with a new cover. The real solution, as we'll find in Part III, lies in taming the nonprofit elephants.

Lesson Four: How Do We Waste Thee? Let Me Count the Ways.

The sum of Lessons One through Three is an accumulation of waste that spells PIT.

It's no mistake that the first letters of Productivity, Integrity, and Talent spell "pit." That's exactly the gaping hole that nonprofits dig when they ignore the presence of the *Mission Impossible* elephant.

Waste of Productivity What greater good is achieved by the ongoing struggle to interpret roles and boundaries? The wasted energy as volunteers and staff kick off a new cycle of the "What's My Job?" game is simply mind-boggling! It flies in the face of the need for a committee to hit the ground running or risk accomplishing nothing innovative during its short term.

Unfortunately, it's rare that a committee innovates. Most settle for maintaining (i.e., spending time productively in monitoring and updating existing programs or spending time nonproductively in reviewing and approving the work of other committees and staff).

Unless a particular committee's output contributes to mission, the effort spent to appoint, train, and maintain that committee is a net productivity drain. Considering how much time the new president or board spends in the first six months making committee appointments, the staff effort to administer committee appointments, the ongoing need to communicate with and train new committee members and mediate struggles as parties carve out their niches, committees begin life with a productivity deficit. They must accomplish something just to break even! It's easy to do the math: Assume a modest nine people on each CCE committee and roughly 60 committees with nine members per committee. That's 540 volunteer members to appoint, track, train, and maintain. That's wasted productivity unless every one of the committees is the best entity for the job and contributes significantly to mission.

It's impossible to overstress the negative effect of this productivity drain on talented volunteers and staff. The very people who are most capable of executing action are instead tied up training those who either lack the necessary skills and experience or will not be able to apply their learned skills given a short term in office.

Productivity waste proliferates in communication. Twice the effort is needed to keep volunteers and staff aware of each other's activities in the dual structure, and the timing of information must be in sync. Misunderstandings and conflict ensue when inadvertent errors cause someone or some layer not to receive the same information as the other. Some may feel that the omission is deliberate, while others act on outdated information. In the age of e-mails, it's unbelievable how quickly these little misunderstandings take on a life of their own: In no time, there are 10 or 20 e-mails that take many man-hours to resolve.

Again, the result is a net productivity loss without any corresponding mission result. It is simply impossible for a nonprofit to reach its full potential when volunteer and staff resources spend a significant portion of their day in such nonproductive activity.

Waste of Integrity Pretense is a way of life in nonprofits. Volunteers and staff pretend that committees report to the board even while being directed by staff. Committees prove their worth to the board by claiming total credit for a successful seminar that was a joint staff and committee effort. A CEO publicly praises the wonderful volunteers while talking negatively about those same efforts to staff. The executive committee makes a show of presenting a project to the board for approval while knowing it is already a *fait accompli*.

Where do all these pretend games lead? Integrity takes a hit when words and actions don't match reality. Staff and volunteers see through these games and lose respect for the principal players. A working environment of disrespect and mistrust develops. Whom do you trust when interpretation changes with each new board and committee? When do you accept praise when false praise is the norm?

In truth, capable, contributing volunteers cringe at taking credit falsely, and creative staff professionals resent having their contributions undervalued. Especially harmful to a culture of respect is the well-meaning nonprofit practice of tacking on the "special thanks to staff" at the end of each event. Without a supporting reality, such comments smack of a patronizing nod rather than a true acknowledgment of professional efforts.

This kind of working environment negatively impacts a nonprofit in two major areas: teamwork and innovation. An effective team is one that melds individual efforts into a collective accomplishment beyond what can be achieved by any one member. This process only happens with open communication. Open communication exists only in a trusting environment, and a trusting environment relies on the integrity of participants. Integrity, trust, and mutual respect are the foundation for good volunteer committees and volunteer/staff teams.

Innovation likewise thrives best in a trusting culture that is open to risk. Lack of trust produces bureaucratic, risk-adverse people. The continual struggle among volunteers and between volunteers and staff produces a bureaucratic work environment where covering your trail with paper and not venturing anything new is the way to survive. In fact, an old nonprofit axiom is "accomplishment is punished, doing nothing is rewarded."

This "protect-your-backside" work environment encourages lots of activity and movement but little real mission accomplishment. In such an environment, process is king, not results. But talented and productive volunteers and staff live for results, not process, and that brings us to the last and ultimately most lethal category.

Waste of Talent The most damaging effect of *I'm the Expert* and the dual structure falls upon the most talented, potentially innovative and achieving volunteers and staff. The commonality shared by such people is a love for doing, an open mind for change, and a need to achieve—precisely the traits that can transform an average nonprofit into a high-performing one. But the bureaucratic environment found in most nonprofits cultivates the opposite. A bureaucratic "gotcha" mentality develops where there's a tremendous downside for taking visible risks but little downside for doing nothing.

Professional staff talents are also wasted by low volunteer performance expectations. Talented, innovative staff leaders join a nonprofit to put their professional skills to work in achieving meaningful results. Yet directly or indirectly, the board and volunteers make the administrative care and feeding of volunteer committees a top priority.

This practice makes both staff and committees unhappy. Staff people, who are bogged down with administrative work, try desperately to find time to achieve results. At the same time, committees lament the fact that the staff fails to get to "the big issues" and often cite a "failure of staff support" as the reason why they are not achieving more. The internal dissonance burns out innovative managers. High performers eventually give up and move on. Over a period of time, performance levels fall. The volunteers and staff left are sufficient to maintain the organization, but not to innovate or meet new challenges.

Talented volunteers burn out for a different reason. Well-intentioned boards believe that every willing volunteer is a good volunteer and should get an appointment. A particularly egregious practice is the "shut-up appointment." A member is bothersome or creating trouble for the president or a board member, so he or she is "kept quiet" with a committee appointment. The chance of some of these appointments going awry is pretty strong. When that happens, the last thing that a board or president wants to do is confront the problem volunteer. It's much easier to look the other way than to risk losing a member, colleague, or large donor.

When talented volunteers are on committees with problem volunteers or on committees where staff does all the work, they get tangled in the inevitable power struggles.

One day they realize that they are spending more time frustrated and angry than in contributing to mission results. They give up their volunteer role and move on.

Boards need to realize that not every volunteer is a productive volunteer. Volunteering for a certain committee is not a right of membership. The fear of losing a member and/or donor should pale in the face of losing the most talented volunteers. Taking the time to deal with bad appointments is like pruning a tree: trimming the limbs encourages new growth; eliminating the pruning encourages slow death. Retaining poorly placed volunteers or vested volunteers pushes talented volunteers out the door and acts as a deterrent to members who are potentially new, productive volunteers.

Many problems can be avoided if a good appointment is made in the first place. The best chance of that happening improves if the person responsible for the final outcome (in the case of business process, that's staff) selects the volunteer resources. If Robin and her chair choose the seminar subcommittee members, they will pick the best resources and accept the responsibility to counsel and coach those resources if a problem occurs.

The last sentence may cause a great weeping and gnashing of teeth—staff select volunteers—heresy! Chapter 8 will show that with the proper safeguards in place, this is one way to make the entire nonprofit stronger.

The Pit It's time to measure the size of this pit and estimate the costs of maintaining the machinery. To do that, we'll need to make some assumptions that admittedly are open to challenge and debate. Yet the reality of the work experience of the brave nonprofit women and men across the country bears witness to the probability that these assumptions are accurate.

Where's the Mission?

We've watched the *Mission Impossible* elephant operate. A fog of confused roles and responsibilities envelops CCE. Let's evaluate the cost of that fog by living with Robin at the office during the week that follows CCE's convention.

Education Director, This Is Your Life!

The following is the information and assumptions needed to understand Robin's week:

- CCE's official workweek is 37.5 hours. Office hours are 8:30 A.M. to 5:00 P.M., and employees have an unpaid lunch hour.
- Robin's base salary is $75,000 per year. Benefits are an additional 35 percent of base.
- The previous *Salt Mines* situations occur during CCE's annual convention. The convention concluded on Saturday morning.

- Robin, the CEO, and most of the board and committee chairs go home on Sunday and are back in their respective offices on Monday.
- Robin normally arrives at the office by 8:00 A.M. She returns from convention with a two-foot-high stack of paper that comprises the motions and activities from all the education committees.

Exhibit 3.11 is an hour-by-hour diary of Robin's week. The summary of time spent is shown in parentheses and categorized as follows:

- **Mission:** work directly related to mission programs and services
- **Committee Administration:** work directly related to committee politics or support
- **Unpaid—Mission:** mission work done outside official CCE working hours
- **Unpaid—Nonmission:** nonmission administration work done outside official CCE working hours

Add the Numbers—Is It Mission or Is It Volunteers? Yes, this really is how senior professional staff, volunteer chairs, and board presidents spend a great deal of time. Let's total Robin's time in Exhibit 3.12.

Robin spent 77 percent of her time on nonmission committee activities. Converting that to salary dollars, CCE pays Robin \$1,499 per week (\$75,000 × 35% benefits ÷ 52 weeks × 77%) to do administrative work with committees and \$448 per week to do mission work. Viewing this from a different perspective, volunteers receive \$1,499 worth of Robin per week; the entire membership receives \$448 per week.

Many things are troubling about this equation, but two things especially stand out. First, because Robin is mainly occupied with administrative work, CCE could save a lot of money by hiring an administrative assistant for \$35,000. Ah, but you may notice that on her own time, Robin does a considerable amount of mission work for which an administrative assistant is not qualified. Aren't members lucky to have someone of Robin's caliber donating her time to the nonprofit? Well, that's one way of looking at it—right up until the time that Robin walks out the door.

Second, members finance the nonprofit through dues, donations, program consumption, or sponsorships. Yet the bulk of the membership receives only 23 cents of each dollar, while a very small group of volunteers receives 77 cents. If you're a volunteer, be honest! Looking back over those meeting minutes with a critical eye, did your committee really produce more than 77 percent worth of results? If not, the nonvolunteer members are receiving an extremely low yield for their investment dollars.

So far, we've just looked at Robin. What about Charles? And what about the volunteers with whom Robin interacted? For the sake of argument, let's assume the same ratio of committee/mission work applies to volunteers. Using an Independent Sector study that estimates the total annual value of volunteer time at \$239.2 billion, this means that \$184 billion of volunteer time is also wasted on nonmission-related activities.[1]

EXHIBIT 3.11 ROBIN'S WORKWEEK

Monday

8:00 A.M.–8:30 A.M.	Robin arrives at the office. She scans the 100-plus e-mails that accumulated during her absence, answering the most immediate. Her seminar director, Tom, walks in. (Mission unpaid: 30 minutes.)
8:30 A.M.–10:00 A.M.	Tom asks what happened at the meetings. He wants the "inside scoop" on how Bob handled Fred. Robin reviews the seminar items with Tom and then tells him about the executive committee's request to "reconsider Joe's application." They discuss what to tell the current developer. She asks Tom to send Jane the additional information that she requested. (Committee administration: 90 minutes.)
10:00 A.M.–10:30 A.M.	Robin's phone rings constantly throughout the morning. Plus, her other four directors want to speak to her about convention actions. Charles schedules a senior staff meeting at 9:00 A.M. on Tuesday to go over executive committee actions, so Robin schedules a 2:00 P.M. meeting that afternoon with her staff. (Committee administration: 30 minutes.)
10:30 A.M.–noon	The CEO stops by to discuss his conversation with Bob after the executive committee meeting. Bob wants Fred's pricing issues considered by the seminar subcommittee so that Fred "feels better" and "this doesn't create issues" with other members. The CEO reassures Robin that he knows that pricing is up to her, but would like her to "go through the motions." The executive committee also asked that the subcommittee review Joe's proposal again. Robin explains that another developer is already working under contract when Charles cuts her off by saying "just give it another look." Also, he'd like a rework of the budget for an executive call on Friday. (Committee administration: 90 minutes.)
noon–12:30 P.M.	Robin takes a walk around the block to cool off and grabs a sandwich to eat at her desk. (Nonmission unpaid: 30 minutes.)
12:30 P.M.–2:00 P.M.	Robin receives phone calls from different committee members who are just "catching up" on what happened on pet projects. Robin tries to organize her notes and minutes for the meetings on Tuesday. (Nonmission unpaid [unused lunch]: 30 minutes; committee administration: 60 minutes.)
2:00 P.M.–5:00 P.M.	Robin patches together all her previous notes and numbers on the tanked seminar. She does several more education budget scenarios and meets with various managers to adjust these forecasts. (Committee administration: 180 minutes.) **Robin previously submitted two budgets, one "best case" and the other "worst case" for what she explained was a risky seminar. Now, because of the board/executive committee controversy, she must redo the same figures, even though the seminar came in slightly better than her worst-case scenario.
5:00 P.M.–6:30 P.M.	Robin responds to e-mails and calls regarding programs underway, plus starts drafting the formal communications and minutes that must go out to all committees after the meetings. (Mission unpaid: 60 minutes; nonmission unpaid: 30 minutes.)

Tuesday

7:30 A.M.–8:30 A.M.	Robin meets with a developer who is teaching a new course offering. She needs to fax him documents when she returns to the office. (Mission unpaid: 60 minutes.)

(continues)

EXHIBIT 3.11 ROBIN'S WORKWEEK (CONTINUED)

8:30 A.M.–noon	Robin just makes it into the office in time for the senior staff meeting. The meeting runs overtime due to new, unbudgeted projects approved by the executive committee. Most sound good but may not be viable due to a number of questions raised by the senior staff. Charles wants them to review the situation and see what can be done before his Friday executive committee call. (Mission: 60 minutes; committee administration: 150 minutes.) ** The new projects are not in the mission plan.
noon–2:00 P.M.	Robin skips lunch and tries to catch up on voice mail and e-mails. She prepares her notes for her 2:00 P.M. meeting. (Nonmission unpaid: 60 minutes; committee administration: 30 minutes; mission: 30 minutes.)
2:00 P.M.–5:00 P.M.	Robin reviews committee, executive, and board actions with her staff at their meeting. She listens as her directors echo the same complaints that she made in the morning senior staff meeting. All reluctantly agree to do yet another budget forecast and discuss the new projects with their committees. Another 2:00 P.M. staff meeting is set for Thursday. (Mission: 60 minutes; committee administration: 120 minutes.)
5:00 P.M.–7:00 P.M.	Robin takes care of pending projects related to member education newsletters and ongoing programs. She suddenly remembers the fax promised to the developer and sends it. She goes home. (Mission unpaid: 120 minutes.)
Wednesday	
8:00 A.M.–10:00 A.M.	Robin tries to respond to the "nonemergency" voice mail and e-mails that accumulated since Monday. Two calls are from her Tuesday developer meeting: one, asking about the fax as he's taken off work to prepare for the course; the second, voicing his anger over receiving it so late. (Nonmission unpaid: 30 minutes; mission: 30 minutes; committee administration: 60 minutes.)
10:00 A.M.–noon	Joe calls Robin and asks if the subcommittee reviewed his proposal yet. Robin calls Tony to discuss the situation. He blows a gasket as he hears that the executive committee wants a relook at Joe's proposal. He wants the education committee chair, Susan, involved and says that "he'll take care of this with Bob." Robin is to talk with Susan and continue work with the previously selected developer. Robin tells Tom to continue with the existing developer. (Committee administration: 120 minutes.)
noon–2:00 P.M.	Robin works through lunch. She calls Joe. She tells him that the chair is reviewing the file and will call him. Tom calls her later to say that the developer is unhappy. It seems that someone from the development subcommittee called him about Joe right after the meeting. He's decided to stop working until Robin or Tom "has the courtesy to call and tell him what was going on." Robin soothes Tom and the developer's feelings. (Nonmission unpaid: 60 minutes; committee administration: 60 minutes.)
2:00 P.M.–4:00 P.M.	Robin works on her budget reforecast for the CEO. Susan calls. The developer left her a voice mail hopping mad because he's being left out of the loop. Robin explained the situation and that both she and Tom called the developer as soon as they knew about the executive committee's action. Susan was sympathetic and said she'd call and soothe the developer's feelings also. Robin asks her to do what

EXHIBIT 3.11 ROBIN'S WORKWEEK (CONTINUED)

	she can to get the project back on time. (Committee administration: 120 minutes.)
4:00 P.M.–7:00 P.M.	The online education director comes in with an emergency related to a current program. He wants to "brainstorm" solutions, but Robin can only spare 30 minutes for him as she has a regularly scheduled conference call with faculty at 4:30; they agree on a course of action. The conference call goes way over as members want to discuss all the convention happenings. Robin is too tired to look at her e-mails and goes home. (Mission: 60 minutes; nonmission unpaid: 90 minutes; mission unpaid: 30 minutes.)
Thursday	
8:00 A.M.–noon	Robin goes over each area's reforecast figures and reworks them until the forecast is acceptable. She goes over every detail regarding the tanked seminar, but the numbers are the same as previously submitted; however, she does some different scenarios of cutting various programs and services. (Nonmission unpaid: 30 minutes; committee administration: 210 minutes)
noon–5:00 P.M.	Robin works through lunch. She finishes drafting the meeting minutes and goes over details with her administrative assistant, who will produce the final version. Then she meets with various staff members who have questions related to their areas. She reviews and approves the final minutes. Robin finishes her newsletter regarding the meetings and e-mails to the committees. (Nonmission unpaid: 60 minutes; mission: 120 minutes; committee administration: 120 minutes.)
5:00 P.M.–7:00 P.M.	Robin responds to accumulated voice mails, e-mails, and office mail. (Mission unpaid: 60 minutes; nonmission unpaid: 60 minutes.)
Friday	
8:00 A.M.–noon	Robin takes the first half hour to prepare for the 9:00 A.M. senior staff meeting; the meeting goes poorly. The senior staff does not have confidence in the new figures. Fred has convinced several board members that the tanked seminar is due to the high cost of seminars. Although pricing was not an issue, and the board approved the project, the executive committee is now discussing a member task force to look into why the seminar failed. Bob is going to call the education chair and ask him for task force names, and he'd like Jane's input and help with this task force. (Nonmission unpaid: 30 minutes; committee administration: 210 minutes.)
noon–5:00 P.M.	Robin again skips lunch. She attempts to call the education chair to warn him. She knows that unexpectedly hearing from Bob in this way will upset him. She wants to work together and figure out a strategy for how to handle the mushrooming problem. She spends the remainder of the afternoon fielding calls regarding this matter from different education committee members. (Nonmission unpaid: 60 minutes; committee administration: 240 minutes.)
5:00 P.M.–8:00 P.M.	Robin cleans up all the voice mail, e-mail, and office items that accumulated during the week, and then goes home. (Mission unpaid: 60 minutes; nonmission unpaid: 120 minutes.)

EXHIBIT 3.12 ROBIN'S TIME CHART

Days of Week	Mission	Committee Administration	Unpaid: Mission	Unpaid: Nonmission
Monday	0 minutes	450 minutes	90 minutes	90 minutes
Tuesday	150	300	180	60
Wednesday	90	360	30	180
Thursday	120	330	60	150
Friday	0	450	60	210
Total	360	1,890	420	690

% of time spent on mission = 23%
% of time spent on committee administration and nonmission = 77%

Summing It Up

Measured in terms of resource and dollars, what is CCE's mission in practice? Nonprofit boards won't say "our mission is volunteers," yet if the talent of a majority of volunteer and staff leaders is spent on nonmission committee work rather than mission-related endeavors, the mission in practice *is* volunteers. Said another way, rather than being a resource that helps achieve mission, volunteers are the mission!

We'll heed the lessons learned in this chapter and find ways to tame the *Mission Impossible* elephant in Part III.

NOTE

1. *Giving and Volunteering in the United States 2001,* Independent Sector, November 2001. ISSN: 1040-4082.

CHAPTER 4

The *Earth to Board* Elephant

Men (and women) occasionally stumble over the truth, but most of them pick themselves up and hurry off as if nothing ever happened.

—Winston Churchill

A Reality Check

Boards have a tendency to become immersed in a self-made, comforting cocoon of unreality that fails to reflect the actual state of the organization or the will of its members. Often overly optimistic, sometimes overly pessimistic, the board's distorted view of "what's happening out there" can be a major obstacle in the path of effective governance.

The board is not entirely to blame for its actions; the CEO and volunteers are the lens through which the board perceives the nonprofit world. If that lens is distorted, so also is the board's perception. Given time and dollar constraints, it's understandable that boards interact most frequently with the people who drive nonprofit activities. However, in the absence of focused efforts to offset this view, the tendency to rely on such a small subset of nonprofit people isolates the board from the opinion of its broader membership or constituency.

Put most simply, the board should represent and act on behalf of members and mission. It cannot govern effectively without placing its finger accurately on the pulse of its constituents-at-large and the organizational environment. The prevalence of the *Earth to Board* elephant in nonprofits is a sure sign that many boards need more work in this area.

In This Chapter

Using the duties of governance as a prism, we'll discuss the board's two main relationships—volunteers and CEO—and see how these relationships shape the board's world.

Then, we'll see the ways that boards inflict self-pain and how all of these factors combine to influence board decision making.

A *Live Lesson,* "Intentional Grounding Is Not a Foul" will illustrate Chapter 4 concepts, and *Salt Mine* exercises will clearly show the day-to-day consequences of feeding the *Earth to Board* elephant.

The Siren Call of "Members"

The duties of a board are discussed further in the next chapter. For now let's informally summarize them as *CAPS*:

- Connect with members
- Articulate member needs
- Protect member assets
- Supervise CEO and organization

Intuitively, it's difficult to imagine how a board can effectively discharge these duties without inhabiting the same space as members, constituents, and the CEO. However, the board encounters some very real roadblocks and challenges in its path to connecting with these entities.

Connect and Articulate

Board expert and author of *Boards That Make a Difference,* Dr. John Carver believes that a governing board is the on-site voice of "owners" (e.g., members in a membership organization, people of similar conviction in an advocacy nonprofit, and the community in a community-based group). Boards represent the owners and must connect with them in order to determine and articulate owners' needs and opinions.

A nonprofit board's relationship with owners can be loosely compared to that of the business sector with shareholders; corporate boards must speak for shareholders and be available to investors. On the surface, a nonprofit board's ability to stay in close contact with its constituents might appear a simpler task than a corporate board's charge to stay in touch with shareholders. After all, a nonprofit member is usually "one of them," a member or constituent, and mixes with other members or constituents at meetings and other nonprofit events. So, it seems logical to expect that a board member would be in sync with the constituency-at-large.

Board Member or Member

The feeling that one's viewpoint is similar to that of others is a common belief. However, this belief is quickly tested and disproved. Board members cannot assume that their viewpoints or even that of the board as a whole represents the members' mindset unless circumstances, facts, or objective surveys support that assumption.

Nor does mixing with the attendees at nonprofit meetings assure that the board is hearing the voice of the general constituency. Volunteers and volunteer committees form the large core of meeting attendees at many nonprofit meetings. Along with the CEO, these are the people with whom the board spends most of its time. In other words, the board likely receives the bulk of "member" information through volunteers.

Volunteer or Member

A sizable group of informed, engaged volunteers is generally a huge positive for a nonprofit. Volunteers are a caring contingent of the organization and an important barometer of membership attitudes. The danger arises when the board places all of its eggs in the volunteer basket.

Volunteers are a small subset of the membership population as a whole, usually less than 5 percent of the membership. Blurring the lines between volunteers and members fails to distinguish their often different points of view and makes a board vulnerable to two things: (1) Informed volunteers can provide a *mirror effect;* they positively reflect the board mindset. Or, (2) the even smaller subset of volunteers, vested volunteers, can lend a *vr-room effect;* they amplify negative feedback.

The Mirror Effect

A good analogy to describe the *mirror effect* is thinking of the main character in the movie, *Dorian Gray*. Gray was the gentleman who saw an eternally youthful and beautiful image in the mirror while his portrait reflected his true aging self. An informed, engaged board and volunteer team see the same reflection in the mirror while the broader membership gazes at a very different portrait.

Part of the reason for this phenomenon is that volunteers are more likely to talk directly with the board. They are privy to the many discussions and information preceding board action, and volunteer leaders especially understand the obstacles and inevitable compromises inherent in group consensus. Largely unaware of these backroom activities, most constituents are likely to judge board actions at face value and on merit rather than as the best selection given the circumstances.

A small headline in a Chicago newspaper, "AARP Backs out of Retirement Forums," seems to illustrate the point well.[1] The American Association of Retired Persons (AARP), the nation's largest advocacy group for older Americans, endorsed the Republican Medicare legislation in 2003. Given its members' desire for prescription drug benefits, the AARP undoubtedly felt that a flawed bill that provided some drug coverage was better than no bill at all.

The backlash from its 35 million members indicated a very different opinion. While members destroyed their cards outside of Washington headquarters, AARP staff handled an average of 1,500 protest calls per day. Only 18 percent of AARP members wanted Congress to pass the Medicare package, according to a survey commissioned by the American Federation of Labor and Congress of Industrial Organizations (AFL-CIO).[2]

The negative feedback garnered embarrassing national attention and eventually forced AARP to cancel a series of planned forums with the Social Security Administration.

The Vr-Room Effect

The *vr-room effect* is the magnified clout that vested volunteers give to certain issues if a board fails to distinguish input based on self-interest rather than mission. What really stirs up vested volunteers is the potential for any change that is not specifically championed by this group. Vested volunteers flock like bees to honey at the slightest mention of governance or management change. Although the root motive in resisting such change is fear of losing personal power or control, they publicly employ the most potent weapon in their arsenal: "Members (or constituents) want/don't want . . ."

Members want is an extremely effective mantra. Using it implies a selfless motive of championing something for the public good. The mantra is magic in a nonprofit. *Members want* assumes many shapes, but the following are some of its most common forms. All are calculated to, and succeed in, raising doubt and fear in the collective board's heart.

- **We're a Member Organization.** This is the *I'm the Expert* archetype at work. The board hears . . . *members must be in control.* The reality is that vested volunteers want to retain their control.
- **We Tried It Once, and It Didn't Work.** The board hears . . . *members don't want to try this again.* The reality is that vested volunteers want the issue shelved.
- **No One Else Is Doing It.** The board hears . . . *this must be risky if other nonprofits aren't doing it, and our members don't want us to take risks.* The reality is that vested volunteers are justifying inaction.
- **Other Nonprofits Are in Worse Shape.** The board hears . . . *we're doing better than most so members don't want us to change.* The reality is vested volunteers are preventing change by pointing out that others are in a worse situation.

The vested volunteers' mantra works well because most board members are well-intentioned, capable people who try hard to act in the best interest of members or constituents. They tend to judge others by their own standards, so they are not inclined to question motives or identify self-interest in another member or constituent.

Nonconfrontational by nature, most board members seek to please and appease the membership that elected them. Vested volunteers are often respected members, sometimes with long and distinguished volunteer pasts. They may even be the mentors and sponsors of current board members. So, *members want* has a multiplier effect when vested volunteers pronounce it.

The Vr-Room Effect and the Change Process

Vested volunteers can stop potentially beneficial governance or organizational change in its tracks. The exaggerated *vr-room effect* of vested input is not the only reason for their success.

Boards are challenged to understand and accept the realities of the change process. Sector pundits lead boards to believe that the end product of collaboration and transparency of information is a frictionless acceptance of change by members and constituents. If boards apply enough effort to communicate and illustrate change benefits, everyone will agree and the change will be embraced.

The reality is that even in the best of circumstances, not everyone will be happy during or at the end of a change process. Consider a bell curve of average opinion. Under most conditions, one-third will passionately care, one-third will passionately disagree, and another one-third will be indifferent.

In reality, all of the collaboration and communication in the world will not make hardcore vested volunteers accept changes to their domain. This is not to say that collaboration, transparency, and communication are not important tools of successful change initiatives. Adept use of these tools usually gains the buy-in of rational people, but this must be tempered with an understanding that some people are not rational, and a small vested group may never accept the change.

Board leadership is essential to navigate change's troubled waters. First, if boards want to shape a new consensus, they must be willing to risk alienating those who have a vested interest in maintaining the status quo. They must understand that important changes will anger a particular constituency and be prepared to distinguish self-interested "member's want" input from true "members want" input.

Most of all, boards must be aware that tough decisions always earn enemies, and it's not their job or the CEO's job to make everyone happy or have everyone like them. Dissent and anger don't necessarily signal a bad job of communicating. Boards must lead the organization in the right direction.

Because the *vr-room effect* is so common in nonprofits and leading change is such an essential board role, both play a central part in the *Live Lesson* in the next section. The *Lesson* also showcases our next subject, a tactic sometimes employed by CEOs and others called the *Everything Is Wonderful* game.

Protect and Supervise

Boards have a fiduciary duty to protect nonprofit assets. To do so, they must identify and monitor critical indicators of financial risk and exposure. Financial oversight by the board is an important topic, but one that is fully explored in the next chapter. For now, let's limit our discussion to the board's oversight of the CEO and organizational activities.

The word "oversight" implies that the overseers understand what they are overseeing. For example, a panel of judges selecting artwork for a juried art show should understand what constitutes fine art. Likewise, the board should understand what constitutes good CEO management in order to effectively oversee the CEO. Just as art judges evaluate entrants against an objective set of requirements, so should boards evaluate and monitor CEO performance against an objective set of measurements.

However, not only do most boards set CEO expectations too low, far too few boards set objective, measurable CEO outcomes at all. They may shrug and say, "of course, we set CEO goals," but such goals are seldom tied to measurable mission outcomes (e.g., implementation of a member-accessed database with a user approval rating of 5). More often, CEO goals are process oriented and subjective (e.g., manages the staff or supports the board).

The lack of measurable CEO outcomes coupled with a board's less than complete understanding of ideal CEO performance is fertile ground for CEO gamesmanship. In essence, the "tail wags the dog" because the CEO, not the board, is the overseer of CEO and organizational performance. One tool that greatly assists the CEO in this endeavor is skill at playing the *Everything Is Wonderful* game.

The CEO *Everything Is Wonderful* Game

Boards, made up of short-term, busy volunteers, want good news from the front. They want happy volunteers whose ideas are immediately executed, lots of highly visible organizational activities, and a positive, can-do attitude from CEO and staff.

Ideally, what does every CEO want? A happy board that is satiated with good news! Fortunately for the CEO, such news is relatively easy to convey. Given the common lack of nonprofit institutional memory, some CEOs maintain long tenure and are held in great regard by telling members exactly what they want to hear: everything is wonderful. The three cardinal rules of the *Everything Is Wonderful* game are:

1. Say "yes" to all board requests.
2. Be upbeat and put a positive spin on organizational activities.
3. Withhold negative information for as long as possible.

Let's look specifically at how these rules and the *Everything Is Wonderful* game are played in two important areas: (1) board and organizational activities and (2) board and staff.

Nothing but Blue Sky In many nonprofits, the CEO ensures that all information from staff to board is funneled through the CEO. In such a nonprofit, the board is unlikely to personally understand the business of the organization and is unlikely to ask the probing questions that shed light on CEO performance.

This situation gives CEOs the opportunity to convey information in whatever manner is most advantageous to them. Ironically, the board is especially vulnerable to this situation when it tries hard to live by what is a very good governance principle in concept. The principle is this: boards should govern, not manage staff. The CEO, not the staff, is the board's direct report, and the board should not involve itself in staff affairs. In making a well-intentioned attempt to avoid meddling with staff, boards veer off to the opposite extreme of limiting board contact to the CEO only.

This is akin to CEOs speaking only with their managers because all the other employees do not report to them. It is a very good way to become entirely isolated from what is really happening in the organization. All boards struggle to some degree with this principle of governance. The key to solving their dilemma lies with understanding the difference between simple information flows back and forth with staff and directives for action given to staff. Put succinctly, it's fine to talk, but it's wrong to direct.

It's wise for board members to discuss organizational events with both the CEO and staff. The board simply cannot let itself be intimidated into not asking questions of staff and accepting everything through the CEO's filter. In fact, one sign of a trusting, collaborative culture is when information runs rampant throughout all levels of the organization. That kind of information flow builds the knowledge base that is so needed for good organizational decision making.

The art of staying in touch yet not usurping another's authority is a skill set essential to the CEO and board. Done right, such informal discussions are a handy technique for informally monitoring organizational activities and contributing to board wisdom. Without board discussion and training on the topic, board members are quite likely to do it wrong. Conversation quickly translates into managing, which is why CEOs draw the line so narrowly regarding information flow.

So, which comes first, the chicken or the egg? Does the CEO limit information because of a dysfunctional board, or is the board dysfunctional because information is limited? The answer is probably a little bit of both, but the result is the same. The board is isolated from the real state of organizational activities, and this hinders its ability to accurately monitor activities or the CEO. Meanwhile, CEOs construct "reality" on their terms, and thus determine how the board evaluates organizational performance and the CEO.

An unfortunate by-product of this process is that boards can lose respect in the eyes of professional staff. Most nonprofit professionals can recount instances where they were unwilling witnesses as the CEO either deliberately misled the board or put a too-positive spin on an activity that everyone but the board knew had little chance of success. Either way, staff secretly hopes that boards will ask the right questions and uncover the truth. The fact that they fail to do so undermines the staff's opinion of board competence —and indicates tacit approval of the CEO's conduct.

If boards passively permit CEOs to filter most information, they cannot accurately monitor organizational activities or the CEO. Neither can boards discharge their duty by enforcing a positive environment that forces a can-do attitude down everyone's throat.

The Can-Do Staff A top-notch, hardworking staff that is achieving measurable mission-related outcomes is a reflection of a high-performing CEO. But too often, staff may be hardworking, but their output is activity, process, and volunteer administration, not results. Because a hardworking staff that focuses on volunteers garners great volunteer accolades, boards often fail to distinguish between the two kinds of hardworking.

CEOs enjoy high performance marks from the board in either case. They know that boards view high staff and high CEO performance synonymously. However, CEOs are truly performing well only if staff achieves mission-related results. One might argue where the ultimate problem lies, board or CEO, but the reality is that an activity-focused staff is a reflection of an activity-driven CEO. What's really happening is that the CEO is setting a low standard of performance that is being reflected throughout the nonprofit.

More activities will produce even more good news! The CEO curries favor with the board by agreeing to whatever activity the board proposes. This can-do attitude fits nicely with the volunteer archetype that sees the CEO as an administrative manager who is only there to execute board orders. So the board feels good, and the CEO looks good. But, assuming there are no resources available or a real mission-driven need for the board request, what happens to that "yes" once the CEO leaves the boardroom?

There are two time-honored CEO methods of executing that "yes activity." One is the "dump-it," and the other is the "mush the peas around the plate" tactic. The "dump-it" is when CEOs just drop the project on senior staff regardless of their current workload. If a manager voices displeasure, CEOs shift the blame to unreasonable board demands. CEOs use the "mush the peas around the plate" tactic when they do as little as possible to move the matter forward. Committee discussions go around in circles with no staff attempt at summation, which gives CEOs the ability to answer status questions with "it's waiting for a committee decision."

Publicly, the activity will be announced with great fanfare, but it never gets off the ground or dies a slow death at some stage of development. By the time this becomes obvious, a well-liked CEO rarely shoulders the responsibility. Remember, in the dual nonprofit organizational structure, accountability is diffuse. There are an infinite number of places to off-load responsibility for a project that has gone wrong. Most likely, the project simply drops off the radar screen as the next board comes into office.

The CEO's positive, can-do attitude garners favorable board ratings, so it makes sense that the CEO also expects staff to be positive and answer in the affirmative to whatever volunteers ask. In fact, veteran staff people often operate by an unwritten rule—never say anything negative to a volunteer. Negative news is not happy news. It tends to have two major consequences. First, people get blamed when something goes wrong.

Second, volunteers tend to rush in and fix a problem, and staff learns quickly that despite the best intentions of volunteers, their actions often make matters worse.

An extreme example of this is a situation that happened to a peer. An associate executive director for a health care nonprofit, she was having significant philosophical differences with the CEO and his dishonesty to the board. She was hopeful that things would improve because she had talked candidly about the CEO with a sympathetic board member. That board member promptly confronted the CEO regarding the issues. Roughly a month after this conversation, the executive director fired her, citing "loss of faith in her management abilities."

Is it surprising that experienced staff answers "great" to a board member's perfunctory "how's it going?" This creates a forced positive working environment and fosters what Jonathan Ross describes as the "pneumatic effect": "when positive affect is enforced on people, negative feelings are pushed down in one place, but they are likely to pop up again somewhere else, often in a least expected place."[3] This may explain why small situations kick off what appear to be inappropriate or extreme reactions in volunteers and staff.

A focus only on the positive restrains authentic dialogue, the kind of genuine conversation that the board needs to have to stay in touch with the CEO and organization. The *Earth to Board* elephant thrives on the fact that volunteer and staff leaders sit in the same room together but withhold the really important things they would like to say.

The Board's Worst Enemy

A well-known nonprofit axiom is that it takes just one dysfunctional volunteer to hold the entire system hostage, and there's at least one on every board and committee. Let's look at the characteristics of high-performing and not-so-high-performing boards. High-performing boards do the following:

- Have open, informed, fact-based discussions that lead to intelligent, consensus decisions
- Take transparent actions that are publicly supported by all board members
- Make actions based on organizational interest, not self-interest
- Accept responsibility for board performance

Contrast that with the not-so-high-performing behavior espoused in this newsgroup posting by an exasperated CEO:

> WELCOME TO THE BOARD
>
> This information has been compiled to help you assimilate into the board:
>
> - Make certain that you complain about something at each meeting. Even if the subject is minor, make it into something major.
> - Speak in a loud, concerned tone like you know everything; this impresses everyone with your knowledge of the organization.

- Give unsupported advice freely. It isn't necessary to provide actual assistance . . . the advice is enough.
- Always complain about not receiving information from the office, implying that you were overlooked because of a conspiracy or inefficiency on the part of staff. It's a bonus if you imply both.
- Attend board meetings infrequently, but don't worry about wasting your time reading past minutes . . . staff will catch you up.
- Always revisit past board decisions and continue discussion until the rest of the board makes the decision that you wanted in the first place.
- Don't help assimilate the growing number of new, clueless board members; board orientation is a staff responsibility.
- Whatever increases your personal stature is good for the organization.

Although tongue-in-check, this is a too-realistic view of dysfunctional board members. These members feel that the act of volunteering time is enough; staff gets paid to do the work. Worse yet, they believe that meeting and talking is the actual board work.

This is an affront to the majority of board members, who are hardworking, exhibit good board behavior, and are committed to high board performance. It's equally true that these members are often hesitant to confront dysfunctional members and tend to appease them rather than require that they correct their bad behavior. Yet, just one dysfunctional vested volunteer on the board can wreak havoc with consensus decisions and create a crisis of confidence for the entire board.

The dysfunctional board member may also conflict with the CEO. In that case, the inclination of the CEO is to provide an even tighter filter on information, so the entire board suffers. There's no end to the problems such dysfunctional individuals cause, and anyone participating in a committee or group activity can recite them by heart. One major problem that does bear further discussion is how dysfunctional individuals influence board decision making and, in turn, the change process.

Consensus Decisions Are Not Always Intelligent Decisions

A consensus decision is not an intelligent decision when the decision is not reality-based. This occurs in two situations: (1) when achieving consensus is more important than the decision itself, and (2) when the wrong input, facts, and assumptions guide the decision. In both cases, a dysfunctional board member plays at least a part.

The first situation in which consensus trumps decision occurs when powerful volunteer factions want different things. The board wants to give each faction a little of this and a little of that, thus making everyone happy. When consensus is finally reached, the board is just relieved to have something with which everyone can live. It doesn't step back and ask, "Does the decision itself make sense? Does it resolve the issue?"

The following example illustrates the problem: In an attempt to correct past election abuses, the board of a membership nonprofit decided to change how board members were nominated. The board created a regionally elected nominating committee under the assumption that regions would select seasoned people for the committee. Instead, they selected people with little or no board experience. As a result, the very problem the board wanted to resolve, weak board nominees, continued.

Although some of the board members suspected that the real problem was with the structure and process of the committee, they didn't want to tackle the problem head-on. Another board member was one of the architects of the elected nominating committee idea. She was strongly vested in keeping the committee concept, and, in addition, the board as a whole was fearful of taking something away from the regions.

Board discussions were long and angst-ridden. The board became focused on finding a solution that was acceptable to all. The consensus decision was to create a convoluted formula of board appointments and regional elections. The board felt good because, at last, everyone could agree. But the decision added another confusing layer and didn't answer the real issue, which is that an elected nomination committee is unlikely to yield the kind of candidates needed for a high-performing board.

This example is also a good one to illustrate the second situation: how the wrong input leads to a less than intelligent consensus decision. Jim Collins says it well in his book, *Good to Great:* "you need to get the right people on the bus"[4] and then, you need to ask the right questions.

A group of vested volunteers controlling board elections was the root problem that the elected nominating committee really intended to solve, but one of the current board members was also part of this vested group. The board wanted buy-in, so it placed some of the vested group on the task force that was to propose election changes to the board.

Although well-intentioned, the board's actions were like asking the fox how to best protect the henhouse. A strong, current board member chaired the group and spent her time trying to head off the worst of the group's proposals, which left little time to discuss the best ideas. The group insisted on a member survey that consisted of loaded questions answered by a select group of volunteers.

In effect, the board put the wrong people on the task force bus and asked biased questions that slanted input in a certain direction. Vested parties guaranteeing vested input combined with a strong board desire for harmony is a recipe for unintelligent board decisions. And the vested input was presented as "members want."

A *Live Lesson*: "Intentional Grounding Is Not a Foul"

Introducing the Principals

Our subject nonprofit is BCDA (Better Consensus Decisions Association). BCDA is a $6 million social organization with 150 chapters at college campuses (14,000 dues-paying college members) and 300 alumni chapters (100,000 alumni members; 8,000 dues-paying alumni members). BCDA board terms are two years. Our *Live Lesson* focuses on BCDA's strategic planning process and its effort to create and implement a five-year strategic plan.

Live Lesson Essentials

- A large-scale membership survey indicates that:
    1. BCDA should become more relevant by providing lifetime, not just college, programs and services.
    2. BCDA needs a greater national presence.
    3. BCDA volunteers have increasingly limited time.
- Based on survey results, Board A creates BCDA's first five-year strategic plan. Three key plan objectives are:
    1. Create relevant programs; increase paying alumni members. (Addresses survey need for lifetime programs)
    2. Broaden focus from regional to national; create a national marketing presence. (Addresses survey need for greater national presence)
    3. Move from volunteer to staff managed; implement a new board governance/ staff management board model. (Addresses survey need of limited volunteer time)
- The plan takes two years to pass and five years to successfully implement. Exhibit 4.1 illustrates the timeline, major events, and players in this *Live Lesson.*

Now that you understand the players and events of "Intentional Grounding is Not a Foul," let's move into the *Salt Mines* and the primer of lessons that follow.

Salt Mines #1: (Situation)

The board listens to the CEO . . .

- Sean (CEO 3) and Board B are struggling with plan implementation in Year 4. Sean is trying to hire and train a management staff; among his new hires are Finance Director Peggy and Membership Director Tom.
- Board A, tired from the battle to get the strategic plan approved, left office without meeting with Board B or providing guidance on plan implementation.
- Board B, with no blueprint from Board A, is swamped with appointing people to working committees and filling volunteer positions in the new volunteer structure. It is also orienting Sean.
- Sean, whose past experience is with a stable nonprofit, is busy executing board demands. Although Sean feels that the board is going in all directions at once, he tries to accommodate every request.

EXHIBIT 4.1 TIMELINE AND EVENTS

Year 1	Year 2	Year 3	Year 4	Year 5	Year 6	Year 7	Year 8	Year 9
Survey Board A →			Board B →		Board C →		Board D →	
CEO 1 →	CEO 2	Plan Approved						
		CEO 3 (Sean) →			CEO 4 (June) →		CEO 5 (John) →	

Calendar of Events

Year 1

- The membership survey is completed. Board A proposes a five-year strategic plan. The plan is controversial and meets with volunteer resistance.

Years 2–3

- In year 2, Board A is reelected in a contentious battle with plan opponents during the annual conference. CEO 1 gets forced out for what Board A views as partisan conduct because she supported opposing board nominees.
- Board A hires CEO 2, then fires CEO 2 within the year.
- Board A hires CEO 3 (Sean).
- The five-year strategic plan is approved during the annual meeting held at the end of Year 3.

Years 4–5

- Board B takes office shortly after Sean is hired. Only two Board A members continue on Board B.
- Sean and Board B must fill in the specifics of the plan and implement it. BCDA is losing money and discontent is becoming evident.
- Board B forces Sean's resignation at the end of Year 5.

Years 6–7

- Board C takes office. The majority of Board B is reelected, but the two Board A members leave.
- Board C hires CEO 4 (June).
- June is faced with a much larger deficit than Board C anticipated. June and Board C bring BCDA back in the black by the end of Year 7.
- June and Board C accomplish the three key plan objectives.
- Board C is operating under its new board model. Delegates must pass related constitutional changes at the annual conference (end of Year 7).
- The changes fail at Year 7's annual meeting.
- June resigns just as Board D takes office. Over half of Board C leaves also.

Years 7–8

- Board D hires CEO 5 (John).

- Board B is concerned about finances because monthly reporting has been sketchy since the new structure, regions, and committees were put into place. Sean and Peggy tell the board not to worry. Things are fine and, anyway, accounting is a staff function under the new board governance/staff management model.
- Board B is getting negative volunteer feedback about Membership Director Tom. It passes the information along to Sean, who sees this as interference in staff affairs.
- Sean feels that Tom is getting a bum rap and that his performance is really okay. Sean takes no action.

Salt Mines #1: (Aftermath)

The board is the CEO . . .

- Sean knows that his new senior staff is spread thin with conference calls every night and meetings on the weekend, but he keeps meting out new board requests at each staff meeting. One senior staff member complains, "This is not an effective way to solicit dues and is very time consuming. And, I don't have the staff to make these changes." Sean's response is: "I'm frustrated with the board too, but just do your job. If it doesn't work well, it's the board's responsibility."
- Finance Director Peggy seems to have finances under control. She provides Sean with handwritten sheets of the budget to date. Sean's relieved that one person on his staff is taking charge, especially because no one else is trained on how the accounting system works. However, the board is approving things like free education and small expenses continually without considering the costs in the aggregate. Peggy does likewise.
- Sean's glad that the board trusts Peggy too and is satisfied with the financial summaries that she provides. As Peggy told Sean, "If I give the board too much finance information, it will just ask more questions. The more information, the greater the board's micro-management."
- Sean's relationship with Board B is deteriorating as he fails to respond to complaints about Membership Director Tom. Sean isolates himself as staff members are bombarded directly with board requests and work. Employees start leaving BCDA.
- Board B is fed up with Sean's support of Tom. It resolves the problem by creating a new staff organization structure without Tom's position. Organizational chart in hand, the board goes into action.
- Tom is "retired." Sean and some of his staff resign. Board B appoints a former board member as interim CEO until June (CEO 4) is hired at the end of Year 5.
- By now, only one director is left on senior staff, and other key employees are gone. Major plan objectives remain unimplemented.

- June's first charge is to hire new senior staff. She discovers a large budget shortfall for Year 5 and a projected shortfall for Year 6 that is far in excess of Sean's and Board B's forecast.

Lesson Primer *Salt Mines* #1: It's Easier to Do Someone Else's Job but Much Better for the Organization if You Do Your Own

Ideas, plans, and implementation are linked. Every hour not spent in upfront planning is likely to equate to four hours of problem fixing on the back end.

As the popular saying goes, "ideas are cheap, but implementation is hard." Board A created a grand vision that changed virtually every piece of BCDA. Moreover, the plan held a massive cultural shift from volunteer to staff-managed and a desire to elevate BCDA as a player in the national scene. This grand plan engaged and fired the imaginations of members—and promised volunteers great things to come.

As they say, ideas without plans are just dreams. Board A focused on the big picture and outlined grandiose ideas in well-penned documents. It drastically changed and increased the governance, volunteer, and staff management structures without any organizational resources in place and with no projections on what resources were needed or total costs. They dumped everything into Board B's lap under the assumption that "the board governs and staff implements." Board A exited the scene, leaving a newly hired CEO in its wake.

Although it would have been difficult, Board B might have had a chance to succeed if it and Sean were experienced in a board governs and staff manages model, or if Board B and Sean were not new. But Board B was new, and BCDA did not have an institutionalized, orderly process for handing down knowledge from one board to the next. Board B took ownership of Board A's plan with little real knowledge transfer and without an implementation plan.

Sean also was new, and like the board not experienced in managing large-scale change. Worse yet, the needed senior staff and volunteer resources didn't exist, yet Sean gave the board the false reality that a limited and inexperienced staff could support the continually increasing number of committees and board requests. He placed staff at odds with the board by blaming the board for the heavy workload.

All in all, it took BCDA almost four years on the back end to fully implement the original plan. That time and a great deal of volunteer disappointment and organizational expense could have been avoided if Board A realized that its job was not just to create a grand plan, but to understand and provide for organizational resources and implementation oversight.

Actions Always Trump Words Board B hired Sean to implement a key plan objective—a staff-managed organization. In this model, the CEO, not the entire staff, reports directly to the board, and it's the board's responsibility to oversee Sean's performance and to deal directly with him when there are problems.

Board B members came from a culture of volunteer management. As volunteers, they did the work and fixed problems as they arose. So when Sean failed to act in the case of the membership director, Board B regressed to its comfort zone and took care of the problem. What Board B actually did was ignore its oversight job of managing the CEO in favor of acting as the CEO. In no uncertain terms, Board B's actions told the staff that BCDA's strategic plan of the board governs and staff manages was just words. The board, not the CEO, was still managing.

More Committees Does Not Equal Fewer Resources Board B was at the opposite ends of the spectrum when it accepted Finance Director Peggy's financial summaries in lieu of detailed monthly reports. Her excuse that new regions and a different accounting system made monthly reporting difficult was plausible, but if no reports existed, Peggy and Sean could not substantiate that finances were in good shape.

Both the board and Sean trusted Peggy, but trust without adequate oversight is a failure of both governance and management. Both the board and CEO must act as a prudent person would, and a prudent person would not assume that all is well in the absence of any supporting evidence. A prudent board cannot be intimidated with an "it's my job, not yours" answer in such an important area as finance.

Finally, a governance restructure is a dangerous time for the absence of financial reporting because spending can spin out of control quickly. Board B was enveloped in a fantasy world in which new regions, new task forces, and new committees operate without additional staff or financial resources.

Despite his responsibility to oversee Peggy, Sean was unaware of the expenses the board was approving and Peggy was paying. One of the CEO's prime responsibilities is ensuring and reporting an accurate financial position to the board.

Consumed with implementation activities, it's easy to see how things slip through the cracks, but that's a poor excuse for multiple cost centers escaping CEO and board notice. All of those cost centers added up to a nasty surprise—an unexpectedly large loss as an initiation for Board C and CEO June.

Salt Mines #2: (Situation)

Board C fully implements plan objectives . . .

- After almost seven years of false starts and great expense, things are cooking. Board C and June (CEO 4) partner under the new model and deliver key plan objectives (i.e., new initiatives to address alumni/programs, new image campaign, and board governance/staff management model).
- Volunteers alienated by past BCDA political problems begin to return. Board agendas become focused on major issues, and a strong staff team is hired and operating. Volunteers and members comment favorably on the changes, and a host of new initiatives are underway.

- Nominations for Board D occur six months prior to the annual meeting. Past Board A championed Perry (a former Board A member) for president, but Perry does not win nomination.
- Until the nominations, former Board A voiced approval of Board C's plan efforts. In fact, some expressed great joy that, at last, their plan was being implemented. However, Board A is sure that June influenced the nominating committee to reject Perry. Board A now begins to express severe misgivings about the powers of a CEO who "is not one of them" under the new model. It tells other key volunteers that members want the board in charge, not the CEO.
- Jack, a Board C member, is close to Board A and drafted some of Board A's original plan. Jack tells Board C, "If Board A objects to our changes, we'd better go back and reexamine our decisions. They're an important part of our membership, and we don't want the kind of dissension that marked Year 2's elections."
- Jack leads the charge to solicit "member" feedback that is, in reality, vested volunteer input. Board C holds conference calls with Board A. Board A cannot articulate which of the changes are wrong or how they deviate from the plan, just that Board C's governance model is "not what it envisioned." More and more information is supplied; the answer to each question leads to more questions and more requests for different information.
- Polly, also a former Board A member and a nonvoting member of Board C, approved the board model initially, and then failed to read the materials or attend discussion and training meetings. She's talked with Board A and is now convinced that the new model gives too much power to the CEO and staff; she secretly supports Board A.
- Jack and Polly voice their concerns to various Board C members. As with any major change, members are not entirely comfortable with their decision. Some begin to think, "Maybe this isn't what members want. Maybe we're jeopardizing everything BCDA values."

Salt Mines #2: (Aftermath)

A board divided will fail . . .

- Board C is spending its meeting time revisiting the decision to adopt a new board model and addressing Board A's concerns. Jack leads many of the discussions of whether the new model is really what members want.
- Jack cautions everyone to remain objective because it will be seen as partisan if they support their own model too strongly. Polly undermines the board's message with volunteers at every opportunity, and Board C is hit from all sides by newly alarmed volunteers.

- Board C is consumed with these endeavors in the months prior to the annual meeting. Meanwhile, Board A continues to lobby delegates to vote against the changes. It negatively spins the information provided by Board C and uses it as fuel in a calling campaign. The distortions are folded into an extensive, secret document with the clear message of "vote no or risk losing everything dear to BCDA."
- The majority of Board C finally wakes up and commences its own lobbying campaign shortly before the annual meeting. About half the board strongly supports the effort, adeptly discussing the issues and educating their regions. Jack plays both sides of the fence, telling each party what it wants to hear, and Polly now openly partners with Board A in opposition. The remainder of the board is conflicted and provides no effective support.
- Board A hands out their secret document to delegates at the annual conference a day before the vote. The delegate body narrowly votes down the constitutional changes. The regions lobbied by effective Board C members vote yes. June resigns at the end of the meeting.

Lesson Primer *Salt Mines* #2: If You Take Your Eyes Off the Ball, Someone Else Moves It Downfield

You must identify what "it" looks like in order to find "it."

A great misconception perpetuated on nonprofits is that change can occur without dissent if one just makes a big enough effort to include and communicate with everyone. That's just not true! Collaborate and communicate until you're blue in the face, but vested volunteers who benefit from the status quo will fight to their last breath against any change to that status quo.

That's why boards must be very clear that governance changes support the mission and plan purpose. They must be prepared for the dissonance that proposing such changes will create. Otherwise, it's difficult to hear volunteer concerns and continue to believe that a difficult decision is the right one.

Board C and June worked through some very tough times to interpret Board A's vision and implement the plan. Gradually, and with the backing of the board, June, staff, and volunteers began new initiatives that were favorably received by members. For the first time in BCDA history, Board C's governance policies clearly outlined board and CEO responsibilities and identified critical board oversight criteria. Things were finally beginning to jell.

That was precisely the problem; things were jelling without Board A at the helm. It liked a board-governed, staff-managed board model in concept, but not the actuality of a strong CEO. Perry failing to win nomination was a wake-up call. As Board A blamed CEO 1 in the past, it also felt that June played a part in Perry's failed presidential bid. With that kind of power and without one of their own heading the board, Board A feared that June might be stronger than the board. The fact that Board C's governance model safeguarded against such an event made no difference.

Board A knew that some volunteer leaders were unhappy because of the past problems with implementing the plan. They capitalized on this discontent by focusing lobbying efforts on this group. Although a relatively small number of volunteers, they carried great weight with the delegate vote in their regions—the *vr-room* effect in action!

Board A got away with this strategy because, in effect, it didn't define how plan concepts worked in practice, nor was it sullied by the mistakes made during implementation. In a clear example of distorted institutional memory, volunteers had no idea that Board A was partially accountable for the fits and starts and excessive cost of the plan implementation. By the time that Board C conquered the deficits and made the plan happen, some regional leaders had run out of patience. Board C's rhetoric sounded like all the other rhetoric; Board A was able to paint the fable of itself as the white knight that once again rides in to rescue BCDA from Board C's incompetence.

Board C as a whole was slow to discern the vested concerns of Board A, and it did not want to risk alienating powerful members. Yet, Board A's actions in the Year 2 elections, the timing of current concerns, and the methods employed to disseminate misinformation should have clearly signaled the possibility of vested concerns.

Board C got tangled in the genuine concerns voiced by volunteers, which brings us to another pitfall into which boards fall. Volunteers who genuinely believe that they are acting in the best interest of the nonprofit may not really be doing so. Board A members were sincerely convinced that BCDA would be harmed by the new governance structure, but that doesn't mean that their conclusion was correct. Separating the wheat from the chaff is the kind of uncomfortable but necessary judgment call that board leadership demands.

Don't Supply Ammunition for Your Opponent's Weapon Board C made the right move in reaching out to Board A initially, but Board A was a moving target. For example, not having articulated upfront how plan concepts worked made it easy to say "that's not what we had in mind." Upon receiving information addressing one concern, Board A simply raised three more issues. Board C should have cut its losses and focused on shoring up support and winning the vote of delegates.

Instead, Board A kept Board C busy trying to match its board model to "what Board A had in mind." In continuing to supply information, Board C kept feeding the elephant, consuming board time and energy, and supplying needless detail that Board A distorted successfully in its delegate handout.

Nor did Board C adequately address the misconduct of its own members, who actively used confidential board information to undermine the board's position. It permitted Jack to play both sides of the fence, continually discussing previous board decisions although providing no new facts—a clear violation of the board's governance policy.

For a time, he even convinced Board C that it should remain neutral and not actively support its own position.

Board C knew another dysfunctional member, Polly, was actively working against them. Yet they failed to censure Polly or revoke her privilege to sit at the board table even though she was an ad hoc, nonvoting board member. Keeping your enemy close is a dangerous strategy that requires purposeful action; otherwise, it's the equivalent of loading the bullets into your opponent's gun.

The lack of a unified board that actively supported its position created substantial doubt regarding the value of the governance model in volunteer minds, giving Board A even more ammunition. Board C took its eye off the primary goal: winning the delegate vote. Thus it failed to put the finishing touch on a model that was delivering the mission results articulated by the membership as a whole (Year 1 survey).

Play with Your Own Deck, and Cut Your Own Deal Although dissension and criticism are part of the change process, usually the rational majority of members are won by a clear, consistent message of real facts and benefits. Board C did not create such a message. The new governance structure was yielding mission and plan results, board policies made CEO/board roles clear, and board oversight was much stronger than in the past. Yet Board C failed to highlight the fruits of the new model's efforts, and thus failed to move the battle to its own backyard.

Board C yielded its advantage to Board A's "members want the board, not staff, in charge" turf. While Board C dithered, Board A was unified and used information, time, experience, and a strategic campaign to win the delegate vote.

Salt Mines #3: (Situation)

Board D focuses on reconciling all differences . . .

- Confirmed at the annual meeting, Board D dedicates its term (Year 8) to communications and making peace with all factions. Its goal is to be open and transparent on all things and to make Board A and all volunteers feel included and heard.
- Board D feels that an important criterion for hiring a new executive director is that the person be a member who will focus on volunteer relations and the retention and management of June's staff.
- John, CEO 5, is hired. June's senior staff team stays and successfully continues to work on the new endeavors set into place during Board C's term. Most of the programs are doing quite well, and finances continue to improve.
- Board D retains some of the innovations of the previous board model, such as advanced agenda planning and member outreach. Meetings go well.

Salt Mines #3: (Aftermath)

Maintenance is high, innovation is low . . .

- Board D feels relieved that the past two years went smoothly. The president reports that "they balanced the budget, mended fences, and hired staff." Board D, CEO 5, Board A, and volunteers are happier; things run with less conflict because everyone is on the same page.
- All of the senior staff attends board meetings with John. That way, Board D is kept current on the details of activities. John is focused on college chapter concerns that often consume a major part of board discussions.
- Although finances and programs are doing well, these endeavors are the continuation of changes and new initiatives begun by Board C and June. John and Board D undertake no new major projects.
- Board A feels better because they are back on various influential board groups and part of the task force to evaluate a new plan. They feel that their successful effort to defeat Board C's governance model is one of the main reasons the organization is doing so well.
- Some of Board A is on the nominating committee for the next board. Board E is elected at the end of Year 9 and includes close friends of Board A. Board C members who strongly supported the defeated governance model are mostly gone from Board E and no longer active in the national structure.

Lesson Primer *Salt Mines* #3: Happiness Is No Guarantee of Success

Volunteer needs are not member or constituent needs . . .

BCDA did a broad-based membership survey. Presumably, it asked the right people the right questions. If so, the survey input accurately represents the will of the members at large.

Board A's grand vision, based on survey input, interpreted that will. Again, assuming a correct interpretation, Board C took actions that fulfill the membership's three key objectives: (1) more paying alumni and new lifetime programs, (2) a national identity campaign, and (3) a strong board governance/staff management model.

In lieu of another large-scale survey effort indicating different membership direction, Board D's focus on communications, volunteer contentment, and college chapters reflects the will of a small group of volunteers rather than the membership. More significantly, though Board D and staff maintain many of Board C's new programs, innovation in the form of new major initiatives has stopped.

Controversy and Dissension Are the Handmaidens of Change A lack of controversy is not necessarily a positive sign. Innovation and change always require some dissonance. Passionate, strong people will clash when discussing differing ideas, but out of that process comes unique thought. Change occurs when someone is willing to push the envelope and risk dissent. An example that comes quickly to mind is online discount brokerages. Using the Internet to deliver brokerage services created great dissonance among full-service brokers, but some firms moved quickly beyond that dissonance to develop innovative hybrids. Others did not want brokers to be unhappy, so they did not pursue change. These firms suffered greatly as survival forced them into the same decisions down the road.

Too often, nonprofit boards and CEOs are rewarded for doing nothing and punished for taking action. Board C and June brought forward innovation and successful change; in the process, vested volunteers were unhappy about that change.

Board D brought the various factions back together, everyone was happier, but innovation ceased. Nonetheless, institutional memory recorded only the appeasement. In an ironic paradox, history discredits the change makers and credits the solution to the vested volunteers who created the problems. The smooth operations and success of Years 8 and 9 are recorded as successes for Boards A and D. In reality, much of that success is the flowering of Board C endeavors that are successfully maintained and carried forward by experienced senior staff and volunteers.

Maintaining is not enough, as the slow-to-react brokerages found out. BCDA's original membership survey identified environmental pressures that will probably intensify down the road. This implies that BCDA cannot simply maintain but must innovate to stay even. If environmental pressures intensify (e.g., there is a continual decrease of volunteers willing to donate major chunks of time), BCDA is vulnerable to committing the same mistakes as in the previous nine years, because it has failed to correctly identify the causative factors.

The Economic Cost of the *Earth to Board* Elephant

Many of the emotional and intellectual costs to BCDA of not tackling the real issues are the same as those discussed in the *Mission Impossible* Elephant (i.e., waste of people, talent, and resources on internal endeavors rather than mission output). Thus, here we focus on the economic loss to the organization when a board's reality doesn't match members' reality or the actual situation.

The previous *Salt Mine* exercises illustrate the difficulty that boards face in governing when members are not unified and committed to finding the voice of the whole. Mission is the guidepost that develops a strategic plan. Adherence and reference to that mission and plan are essential if boards are to effectively evaluate actions, seek input, conduct board business, make decisions, and monitor CEO performance.

As we have just seen, vested interests from volunteer and/or staff diverted BCDA's board from finalizing its new board model and creating the kind of culture that cultivates innovation and change. The best way to measure the economic cost of the *Earth to Board* elephant is to anticipate how the organization might go forward if the governance changes stayed in place—and then estimate the cost of the opportunity lost.

Opportunity Lost

The real cost of the *Earth to Board* elephant is this failure to seize new opportunities (e.g., creating a funding source that opens a new line of cancer research; developing an innovative program for tutoring disadvantaged children; or designing workshops that train professionals and improve the lives of millions). Internally, opportunities lost might be the failure to institutionalize learning, to share informed wisdom among volunteers and staff, or to risk a new procedure, program, product, or service.

The conundrum is how we measure what we cannot see. Concrete things such as the cost of personnel are easy to measure, but opportunity lost is difficult to measure and easy to ignore, which is a big reason why it's largely ignored by nonprofits. However, opportunity lost is real and can be measured by making reasonable assumptions. We just assume that the opportunity is seized, not lost.

Let's pretend that BCDA delegates approved the board's governance model. June and the new board seized an opportunity that presented itself in Year 8. The revenue and/or cost reductions that flow from this new opportunity over time is the cost of BCDA's lost opportunity.

Lost Opportunity Assumptions

Setting aside what really happened in our BCDA *Salt Mines,* let's assume the following:

- BCDA's delegate body approved the constitutional changes, and the new governance model became institutionalized.
- Board C created an excellent orientation of all previous board actions and delivered it to Board D. Board C also remained available for coaching Board D members as needed and helping reconcile volunteers to the change.
- June doesn't resign and Year 8 begins with an experienced CEO.
- Board D and June have clear, strong, and defined roles under the new model. June, who is confident in her role and with strong backing from the board, continues the sometimes contentious struggle of bringing new programs forward.

BCDA Seizes a New Opportunity in Year 7

- Collegiate members express their desire for employment help after graduation.
- A current BCDA college training program provides leadership training for chapter leaders that is similar to corporate management training. Participants practice learned skills in real life by leading their chapter and managing chapter operations.

- Knowing that BCDA's juniors and seniors want postgraduation employment, June and Board D seize the opportunity to partner with companies:
  - June approaches major corporations that correspond in identity and location with BCDA's largest university chapters. Companies partner with BCDA to develop joint BCDA/corporate management training criteria. The companies agree to recognize BCDA graduates who successfully complete the joint BCDA/company training.
  - Certification is included for the graduates. BCDA graduates have an edge for management training or job openings at partner companies. Or, they can use the program certification as a plus on their resumes when applying at a non-partner company.

Calculating the Cost of Lost Opportunity

Now, let's look at the economic costs of losing this opportunity to satisfy member needs.

The Partnership Over Ten Years BCDA implements the idea over three years. In the first year, BCDA has five corporate partners; after ten years, the number of companies in the program expands to 50 via regional partnerships.

Revenue Increases and Cost Reductions

1. More students are attracted to chapter positions, because the BCDA training program improves their postgraduation employment chances. This provides a better pool of chapter officers and, in turn, produces stronger chapters. It also attracts a higher number of prime students to BCDA chapters, and retains a greater number of active junior and seniors in the chapter.

   Assuming a modest 10 percent increase of students:
   - Current chapter member revenue = $1.2 million
   - 10 percent increase = **$120,000 per year** additional dues revenue
2. The new BCDA program garners national recognition because no other competing nonprofit offers such a program for its collegiate chapters. This gives BCDA a competitive advantage when universities are looking for new chapters.

   Assuming that BCDA opens chapters at three new locations during the ten years:
   - Although expenses outweigh revenue in the first several years after opening, after ten years the new chapters start to contribute revenue.
3. University administrators recognize the value of the training program, so problems with administrators are down. BCDA realizes lower expenses by not sending national staff and volunteers to the school and not hiring additional college chapter staff to serve the higher number of college chapter members.

Assuming five trips less per year for 100 chapters and .5 less employee:

- $800 per trip × 5 = **$4,000 per year**
- Expenses for .5 employee = **$15,000 per year**

4. BCDA creates a series of additional educational programs for college members who are part of the corporate partnership. Some of these programs are applicable to concerns of BCDA partner corporations, so corporations fund program development. Development cost is $50,000 per program.

   Assuming that BCDA is averaging one corporate-sponsored education development project per every two years:

   - Development revenue = **$50,000 per every two years**

5. Projects like this successful BCDA corporate partnership raise volunteer and staff pride in BCDA. Such activities make members and donors feel that they are receiving value for their dollars. Happy alumni members contribute more in donations to BCDA's foundation.

   Assuming that the foundation donation level is currently $300,000 in alumni donations:

   - Proud alumni donate 10 percent more, or a **$30,000 per-year** increase in alumni revenue.

6. Professional staff is attracted by the reputation of BCDA. BCDA can be increasingly selective about the people it hires. As the quality of BCDA staff continues to increase, better ideas and programs result.

Adding these hard dollar totals, the additional annual net revenue after the tenth year for this single program alone is almost **$200,000.** The actual figure would probably be much higher because some potential revenue is not estimated in our example, and successful programs tend to spin off other successful ones. So, the total cost of losing this one opportunity is $200,000 per year.

Summing It Up

Whenever there is a mismatch between reality and culture, a nonprofit will not realize its full potential. This is masked by the fact that the nonprofit still accomplishes things and volunteers may be content, but such a nonprofit will never inspire the minds of staff and volunteers to seize the opportunity to become great.

Notes

1. "AARP Backs Out of Retirement Forums," *Chicago Tribune,* sec. 1, December 16, 2003.
2. Laurie McGinley, "How AARP Chief Ended Up on Hot Seat," *Wall Street Journal,* sec. 1, November 20, 2003.
3. David Jewel, "Hesitations about Appreciative Inquire," *ODNC Beacon,* vol. 1, issue 2 (2003): 7.
4. Jim Collins, *Good to Great* (New York: HarperCollins, 2001), 41.

CHAPTER 5

The *Board Fiddles, Rome Burns* Elephant

Things which matter most must never be at the mercy of things that matter least.

—Goethe

WHOSE JOB IS IT?

One of the most frequently heard phrases in the nonprofit world is, "Boards create policies and strategies, staff implements them." The implication is that anything labeled "strategy" or "policy" is the domain of board and governance, not staff and management.

The misunderstandings that result from this belief occur just as frequently as the statement itself. Logically, nonprofits would quickly grind to a halt if this concept were a reality. How could a board comprising part-time volunteers who meet infrequently and who are removed from day-to-day operations possibly create all the policies and strategies necessary for the efficient functioning of a multilevel organization?

The question is why such an unworkable concept is so firmly rooted in the nonprofit mindset.

In This Chapter

The *Board Fiddles, Rome Burns* elephant exists because creating policy and strategy only at the board level simply doesn't work in the real world. This chapter examines the problems inherent in this way of thinking and offers a different mindset that works more effectively in today's dynamic, information-based workplace. Along the way, we'll sort out the macro-policies and strategies that really do belong at the board level.

A *Live Lesson,* "Behind CEO Mismanagement Lurks Board Failure," illustrates how the presence of the *Board Fiddles, Rome Burns* elephant negatively affects the nonprofit and what happens as a board neglects its critical oversight duties. Last, we estimate the cost that nonprofits pay for neglecting the store.

Policy and Strategy Uncensored

The Stereotypes of Policy and Strategy

Part of the reason for the current policy and strategy mindset lies with public stereotypes, and the rest can be traced to the *Mission Impossible* and *Earth to Board* elephants.

Popular thought connects policy and strategy with high-level thinking and planning —the domain of top managers. Everything else is implementation—the domain of middle managers and employees. A quick look at the literal definitions of and synonyms for strategy and policy breaks those stereotypes.

- **Policy.** A program of actions adopted by an individual, group, or government, or the set of principles on which they are based. Synonyms include *rule, strategy, guiding principle, guideline,* and *procedure.*
- **Strategy.** A carefully devised plan of action to achieve a goal, or the art of developing or carrying out a plan. Synonyms include *plan, policy, approach,* and *tactic.*

Clearly, strategy and policy have much broader meanings. A simple example proves the point: An administrative assistant to the president is given a draft memo and directed to correct, copy, and circulate the final to employees. The assistant must have a carefully devised plan (strategy) for completing and delivering such a memo and applies the rules for grammar and structure (policy) appropriate for revising the memo. This assistant is not a manager, but nonetheless is engaged in policy and strategy appropriate for the work level.

It's absurd to think the administrative assistant's policies and strategies should be approved by the board.

Enter *Mission Impossible* and *Earth to Board* Our two pachyderms, *Mission Impossible* and *Earth to Board,* reinforce the policy and strategy stereotypes of the nonprofit world. In addition, *I'm the Expert* says that volunteers must be in charge, which leads to the dual volunteer/staff organizational structure. Naturally, the top of that structure, the volunteer board, owns policy and strategy, and everyone else implements.

Neither volunteers nor sector advisors provide any dose of realism that might counteract the stereotypes. They simply provide the *mirror effect,* reflecting the board's own opinion that it owns policy and strategy.

A quick look at sector writings makes the point. An American Society of Association Executives (ASAE) publication states, "Strategy and direction setting are seen as the responsibility of the board. Accountability for the detail and implementation of strategy is assumed by member and staff workgroups."[1] A large association management company newsletter on volunteer and staff leadership states, "Leadership . . . has authority to set direction, make decisions and create policy. Management assures that staff and volunteers follow the direction set by the board and 'do things right.'"[2]

It's doubtful that the authors of these statements intend them to be taken literally. The entanglement of volunteer and staff leader responsibilities is common, and advisors are always looking for a quick, acceptable way to define those roles. Besides, they believe that everyone knows they are talking about overall, not management policy and strategy. But do they?

Good Words Taken Literally

Concepts unrefined by practical examples often get mangled as they are applied in the workplace. One person's global policy is another person's department policy. As Doug Macnamara, President of Banff Executive Leadership Inc., discusses in his article, *Creative Abrasion: Ensuring that Board-Executive Relationships Enhance Organizational Leadership:*

> Difficulties arise not only when one group steps into the other's domain but also when one group doesn't do their work sufficiently and the other does.[3]

Both of these situations exist as boards struggle with policy and strategy approvals. In one camp, boards drive themselves and CEOs crazy by faithfully trying to understand and approve every policy and strategy. Their agendas are full of discussions, with CEOs diligently supplying ever more paper and explanations. At some point, such a board is comfortable—or becomes comfortable with not being comfortable—and approves the action.

In the other camp, boards just rubber-stamp whatever the CEO or volunteer committee recommends, making board approval just a formality. In both cases, only a small portion of board time is spent with policy and strategy that relates directly to the board's governance or CAPS duties (**C**onnect, **A**rticulate, **P**rotect, **S**upervise). In the process, boards assume ownership for the outcomes of policies whose applications they can neither see nor monitor. That presents a world of problems.

Policy and Strategy in the Proper Place and Time

Policy and strategy do exist at more than just the board level. Going back to our earlier example, the president's administrative assistant uses policy and strategy to complete and distribute a memo. The assistant has policies from the president that determine distribution groupings, policies or rules of grammar that determine memo style and content, and strategies for how to distribute the memo and juggle the workload.

The administrative assistant's policy and strategy don't fit into the bucket of "governance" (e.g., they are not related to the global running of the nonprofit). Yet they are policy and strategy all the same. Perhaps policy and strategy shouldn't be defined by labels of governance/management at all, but by the nature and placement of policy and strategy within the organization.

Most people working within an organizational chart instinctively understand that their area has policies and strategies, but they may have difficulty articulating why this is so. In efficient organizations, the correct explanation is that each level of an organization is delegated a span of authority and accountability within a given time horizon, including the power to create policies and strategies appropriate for that span of control.

An interesting twist to this discussion is that the span of control and time horizon decrease exponentially with each successive level. In other words, the higher the organizational level, the broader the span of control and the longer the time horizon over which those activities occur. Rather than using the yardstick of "is it governance or management?" for determining the owner of a policy, the defining questions then become: (1) What is the span of control? and (2) How long is the time horizon?

The board has the greatest span of control and time horizon. Its responsibilities are global responsibilities—directing the benefit component and overseeing the business component. Most of the board's activities occur in the future, so its time horizon is very broad.

The board delegates a smaller span of control with a proportionately lesser time horizon to the CEO. The CEO still has a global span of control and a long time horizon, but this role is restricted to the business component of the nonprofit. Much of the CEO's time is spent in activities that occur within a one- to five-year time horizon.

CEOs delegate a still-smaller span of control and proportionately more limited time horizon to their direct reports. Those reports focus mainly on their specific department and current-year activities. In turn, department directors delegate a smaller span of control and more limited time horizon to their direct reports, and so it goes on down to the very bottom of the organizational chart.

One reason that boards are tempted to approve all policy and strategy is because much of nonprofit work has both a benefit and a business component. So boards may need a little help in determining where a policy should reside. The key lies with asking three simple "W" questions:

1. *Where does the activity under the policy reside?* Global (business and benefit), business, or department
2. *What is the span of control?* Global, business, or department
3. *When does the activity occur?* Current year, within five years, or into the future

Boards that regularly think through this exercise and ask the "W" questions are more likely to drive policy and strategy to the level where it belongs. Here are four familiar nonprofit activities:

1. Developing fiscal policy (e.g., goals for percentage of net revenue, percentage in reserve, percentage allocation to programs)

2. Creating and managing the current-year budget
3. Developing the budget for building expenses
4. Paying the office mortgage

Exhibit 5.1 shows how boards might answer the "W" questions.

The Importance of Delegating Strategy and Policy Authority

It is important to delegate policy- and strategy-making authority to the right level because we now operate in a knowledge society. In the words of seminal thinker Peter F. Drucker in his book, *Managing in the Next Society*:

> The next two or three decades are likely to see even greater technological change than has occurred in the decades since the emergence of the computer, and also even greater change in industry structures, in the economic landscape, and probably in the social landscape as well.
>
> We are rebuilding organizations around information. . . . Every relay doubles the noise and cuts the message in half. The same holds true for most management levels . . . they serve only as relays.[4]

Pushing policy and strategy decisions throughout the nonprofit is not just an altruistic attempt to satisfy people's need for autonomy. Autonomy to make policy and strategy decisions at the lowest levels are essential if nonprofits are to make timely decisions and react effectively to continually changing conditions.

It's obsolete thinking to believe that a board can wait until the next meeting to address a sudden change in environment or respond to local needs. Nonprofits and workplaces are now too complex to centralize all policy and strategy at the board or CEO level. Furthermore, like in other ages, opportunities never before dreamed of will emerge as the Information Age progresses. Those opportunities will present themselves throughout the nonprofit, and are ripe for the plucking by empowered knowledge workers.

EXHIBIT 5.1 DETERMINING POLICY LEVELS

Activity	Span of Control	Time Horizon	Policy Body
Fiscal policy (fiscal oversight)	Global benefit and global business	Current year to infinity	Board
Budget (executive)	Global business	Current year	CEO
Drafting budget for building expenses (finance)	Finance division	Current year	Financial director
Paying the mortgage (accounting)	Accounting department	Monthly	Financial manager

The Fear of CEO and Staff Policy Making

The concept is relatively simple: the level of the nonprofit that is responsible for a given activity and accountable for results is in the best position to create meaningful policy and strategy for that area. The conundrum for nonprofits stuck in the current mindset is that this kind of autonomy means giving up volunteer control. The *I'm the Expert* archetype makes many volunteer leaders fear that giving power away to the CEO and staff means going away from mission and constituents.

Yet that fear is totally unfounded for several reasons. If boards understand their role, create strong board policies, live by those policies, and engage fully in proper oversight, it is impossible for a strong CEO and staff to guide the nonprofit away from mission and constituents. Examples of nonprofit problems that made the headlines illustrate the point.

1. *The Statue of Liberty–Ellis Island Foundation:* "None of the directors who approved (the CEO's) compensation were aware of the amounts that the (CEO) earned from consulting, and several directors were never told that (the CEO) had separate consulting arrangements."[5]

   Board Oversight Failure: Risk management is a key board responsibility. Board approved CEO ethics and disclosure statements would have revealed the problem.

2. *Beard Foundation:* "According to the New York State attorney general's office, the organization has not filed tax returns in two years."[6]

   Board Oversight Failure: Board approved fiscal policy should state that the CEO is charged with the timely filing of all regulatory reports, including tax returns.

3. *New York Stock Exchange:* "By disregarding their Constituent's values, the board imperiled the exchange's reputation."[7]

   Board Mission Oversight Failure: In awarding their chairperson an exorbitant pay and retirement package, the board failed to scan the outside environment and understand that lavish pay for regulators was unseemly in the post-Enron era.

In such cases, the tendency is for boards to perceive the problem as too much CEO autonomy, which causes the board to delegate even less. But the actual problem is their focus on daily CEO work instead of doing board work—creating risk management policies that limit CEO power and protect the nonprofit.

Volunteers should not fear a loss of control, because delegating authority does not work in a vacuum. Each level's power is limited by the policies and strategies of the levels above. Thus CEOs may be responsible for creating the programs that fulfill mission, but they do so under the board's mission and CEO policies, and by seeking the informed wisdom of board, volunteers, and staff throughout the process. The board operates under its own governance policies but seeks the informed wisdom of the CEO, key volunteers, and constituents when creating and administering those policies.

Board-Level Policy and Strategy

Mission Policy and Strategy

Now with general concepts of policy and strategy firmly in mind, let's turn our attention to what boards should be doing. Constituents, members, and stakeholders delegate the responsibility of defining and implementing a nonprofit's global mission and vision to the volunteer board. Although few people would disagree that mission policy and strategy fit squarely into the governance bucket, there's no common thought regarding exactly what "mission and vision" policy is.

On reams and reams of paper, nonprofits continuingly define and redefine the words *mission* and *vision*. Vision is the future, mission is the goal; vision is where you want to be, mission is where you are—no, no, vision is a slogan, so discard it; instead, figure out the business that you're in. Or, there's always Jim Collins's BHAG or "Big Hairy Audacious Goal." Everyone gets dazzled and confused in the glitter and new print, and that means lots of activity and learning in order to create basically the same thing.

With so much advice on mission and vision, it's no wonder that boards go off in different directions as they sit in a room trying to answer the "what's our mission and vision?" question. So, it's also no surprise when boards give up on defining mission and default to the more tangible work of business processes like strategic plan tactics, marketing campaigns, and which program to offer—unfortunately, all things that fall under the CEO's job description.

Mission Statements At the other end of the spectrum, boards and staff get hung up for endless hours deciding on the right words, and then finally proudly announce a new mission statement. What comes out are lofty words framed in language that is not meant for the human tongue. A slogan-ridden workforce stifles a big yawn as it throws the paper into a drawer.

So what's a board to do? One extremely practical piece of advice is to sit back and forget all the terminology and hype. Consider what you're trying to accomplish. What is the intended outcome of the mission statement? Nonprofits, philanthropies, and memberships exist for mission. The mission is to make a difference in society or in the life of an individual. Too often, only charitable, foundation, and social service nonprofits are seen in this light, but professional, trade, and social groups also exist to make a difference for their particular group, in the individuals served, and ultimately in society.

Boards must capture this difference and capsulate it in a clear and concise statement that has the power to lift people's vision and make everyone feel that they make a difference. When that happens, mission statements are not words on paper or something that volunteers and staff must memorize; mission is what they feel.

A mission statement that really captures the fundamental reason for an organization's existence is unlikely to totally change very often, but it will need tweaking as the outside world evolves and conditions change. The board is the guardian that looks outward for changes in demographics, the economy, the profession, the community, and society, and new opportunities, and boards need to revise mission policy as necessary to keep mission vital and relevant.

The challenge in creating good mission statement policy is to avoid the temptation to tinker with words or style when no substantive inside or outside change drives a revision—however, the temptation to do so is almost overwhelming with each new board and strategic plan.

Mission Goals and Strategic Plans Beyond the mission statement, boards create other mission policies and strategies that are captured in a strategic plan. But, unlike what takes place in many nonprofits, the bulk of the strategic plan is not the domain of boards. That's because what nonprofits commonly call a strategic plan is really an operating plan, and most of the strategies in the plan relate to achieving business objectives.

Harrison Coerver, a well-respected longtime nonprofit management advisor, states bluntly:

> I've rarely encountered a board that could craft strategy. . . . I'm not even sure that group processes are the best way to develop strategy. What boards can do is come to some agreement on what the association's priorities should be. They struggle when it comes to how they should achieve those objectives.[8]

This may seem a little harsh, but it does define workplace reality. It breaks from the old nonprofit mindset that sends anything strategic to the board and substitutes the idea that the best strategy comes from the right person in the best position to develop that strategy. A volunteer board is the right body to define mission vision and goals. The CEO is the right person to create the objectives, strategies, and programs to reach those goals.

Let's look at a simple example of how these concepts fit together in practice.

Strategic Vision (Global [Benefit and Business]: Board's Responsibility)

- Mission: Protect democracy for U.S. citizens
- Mission Goals:
    1. Citizens will have accurate and safe voting methods.
    2. Polling places will be fully staffed.

Current Year Strategic Plan (Global [Business]: CEO Responsibility)

- Mission Goal 1: Citizens will have accurate and safe voting methods.

    Objective 1.1: Automated voting machines will be operative in 75 percent of precincts.

    Objective 1.2: Public awareness and training campaigns will run in all major cities.

- Mission Goal 2: Polling places will be fully staffed.
  - Objective 2.1: Provide two captains for each precinct.
  - Objective 2.2: Provide two security guards for selected high risk areas.

When the board and CEO work together in this manner, the output is not "a plan" that takes months and months of board and staff time to assemble. The board keeps mission policies relevant and current on an ongoing basis, not just at a given point in time. The CEO keeps a predictable schedule for ensuring an approved operating plan is in place at the beginning of and throughout the fiscal year. And both CEO and board work together to modify the plan as necessary throughout the year.

Boards are truly excited and energized when, instead of rubber-stamping work done by staff or talking about process issues, they can be independent and engaged in important, meaningful work that considers the constraints of their volunteer role. Think about it: being guardian of the benefit component both inside and outside the nonprofit; organizing and interacting with members, constituents, communities, and other stakeholders through methods like coffees, blogs, "cafes," or town hall meetings; or interacting with expert board guests on key trend information. That's the board that most of us would like to serve on and, hopefully, will be part of in a world where nonprofits define governance and business strategy clearly. But until then, many board agendas look pretty much like the one that follows.

Oversight Policy and Strategy

A board's oversight responsibilities fall broadly into four categories:

1. Oversight of mission
2. Oversight of CEO
3. Oversight of business component
4. Oversight of board effectiveness

We'll touch only briefly on board policy and strategy as it relates to the oversight of mission and of the CEO. Mission oversight, including the need to instill and monitor mission throughout the nonprofit and outside world, was discussed in the previous section, and the board's role in oversight of the CEO will be addressed comprehensively in Chapter 6.

Here, our discussion will center on board oversight of the business component, particularly the finance and governance process. The best way to see how this currently works in practice is to review some sample board minutes.

Board Minutes Tell the Tale One nonprofit's minutes posted online tells us quite a bit about how board agendas focus on nongovernance process and financial activities.

Board Actions:

1. Approved budget
2. Accepted recommendations of task force
3. Directed staff to develop relations with other nonprofits
4. Elected officers
5. Gave authority to the task force to negotiate with vendor
6. Selected convention dates
7. Made plans for midyear strategic planning session
8. Authorized $3,000 for planning facilitator

The problem with this list of actions is that almost all of the board's time is being directed toward internal processes. "Accepting the recommendations of a task force"—why and for what outcome? "Directing staff to develop relations with other nonprofits"—board CEO policies should delegate that responsibility to the CEO. "Give authority to a task force to negotiate with a vendor"—a group of people won't negotiate with a vendor, a staff person will.

This is not board work and certainly is not the kind of work that fires the soul of passionate board leaders. Now, let's focus on one of these board actions in the area of finance—"approved budget"—and ask our "W" questions:

1. *Where does the activity under the policy reside?* Business component
2. *What is the span of control?* Business
3. *When does the activity occur?* Current year

If the activity occurs in the business component, the span of control is business, and the activity is current year, why is the board doing this work? The budget is primarily a management tool for CEOs, a way of projecting, tracking, and managing daily income and expense items, yet most board agendas are filled with budget related discussion. Even if we ignore the duplicative efforts involved, part-time board members, no matter how astute in the ways of business and finance, know much less than CEOs who run the organization day to day. They are not in the position to either manage the budget better or detect when CEOs are manipulating figures. So the question remains: Why are boards so preoccupied with budget?

Boards Fear Finance One answer is culture—*I'm the Expert* thinking dictates volunteer control, and boards believe that the more time spent on finance, the better protected the nonprofit. The other answer is fear. Especially now, with highly visible corporate and audit firm problems, auditors are pressuring boards to take a more active stance in the finance area. That makes board members even more fearful that a failure to understand every intricacy of finance translates into a failure of fiduciary responsibility.

The Sarbanes-Oxley Act, which was meant to bring some sorely needed accountability to for-profit boards, is scaring already paranoid nonprofit boards into more financial micromanaging. It's ludicrous to think that a nonprofit's part-time, unpaid volunteers can or should be trained to know everything that the full-time CEO or finance director does. However, what can be expected is that board members possess the degree of financial literacy necessary to perform their financial oversight function and that they do this job. Otherwise, as we will see in the upcoming *Live Lesson,* a rampaging *Board Fiddles, Rome Burns* elephant has disastrous consequences.

Board Fiscal and Risk Management Policies A board does not fulfill its fiduciary duty by a hands-on approach to finance (e.g., approving the budget after endless meetings and explanations from staff, "managing" investments with an investment committee and an annual meeting with the investment firm, and monitoring every cost line). A board protects the assets of constituents and organization by assessing major risk, creating and monitoring risk management policies, and overseeing CEO and organization.

The point is driven home by a second look at our previous examples. The Statue of Liberty Foundation board probably spent a great deal of time on fiscal detail and activities, yet failed to create and monitor a risk management policy that included CEO ethics and conflict of interest. Likewise, the Beard Foundation had numerous meetings, yet failed to create and monitor a fiscal policy that covered timely filing of regulatory returns.

Fiscal and risk management policies provide guidelines to CEOs and clearly outline the limits to CEO power (e.g., board approval is required before using investment funds or entering into partnership agreements; board notification when operating funds fall below six months' reserve). Once in place, boards must monitor that such policies are followed. How boards do this and how they create effective fiscal and risk policies will be covered more in Chapter 10.

Right now, a special word is in order about two board committees commonly linked with financial oversight—the finance and audit committees.

About Finance Committees Unless a nonprofit is so large that fiscal responsibility must be allocated to a small group, as a practical matter finance committees are a waste of organizational and CEO resources. The reason is that such committees duplicate the work of the CEO and board. Finance committees are often charged with reviewing monthly statements, assessing the investment portfolio, and reporting on financial activities to the board. These activities rightly fall under the CEO, and fiduciary oversight of these activities rests with the board as a whole.

Another reason that finance committees don't work in practice is the composition of the committee itself. Finance committees often attract independent members who have little financial background but "a desire to know more about finance" or vested volunteers with an agenda. The CEO or staff finance director spends endless hours educating the committee and dealing with the vested member without any discernable independent committee output. This is a waste of organizational resources and a failure of the board to properly execute its fiduciary responsibility.

It's difficult to find an example where a nonprofit board creates and monitors strong fiscal and risk management policies and needs a finance committee to add more worth. However, the opposite situation where the finance committee makes things more difficult and actually takes value away from the finance process is much easier to find. Consider the following:

> The board of a large advocacy organization had an asset allocation policy in place, but portfolio trades had to be approved by the board. With the stock market rising rapidly, the investment company recommended stock purchases in place of a bond that was maturing. The CEO brought the recommendation to the board (time: four days), but one director, unhappy with the current investment firm, convinced the board that it was time to shop for a new one.
>
> The board asked the CEO to take the request to the finance committee; the finance committee met via phone and asked the CEO to look for new firms (time: one month). The CEO got bids from three firms (time: two months) and then went to the finance committee (time: one month) with the recommendation to retain the current firm. The committee agreed and recommended the same to the board. The board accepted its recommendation (time: one month).
>
> After almost six months, the board authorized the CEO to retain the investment firm and execute the trade. Of course, by then six months' market appreciation evaporated as funds sat as non-interest-earning cash, and the stock opportunity was also gone.

Any vendor, in this case the investment company, only performs well if it is managed on a day-to-day basis; the CEO should direct business processes including trades. The board does set investment policy (asset allocation), but abdicates the selection of a new investment firm to the finance committee—and that committee promptly transfers the responsibility to the CEO. The end result is that board and finance committee activity and approvals do not protect nonprofit assets; they simply drain the energy of the CEO. Instead, real protection would come if the board holds the CEO accountable for managing the business component, while doing its real job, fiscal policy and oversight.

About Audit Committees Audit committees are a different story. Used properly, such committees are an essential part of the board's fiscal monitoring process. Ideally, an audit committee should be independent of the CEO; the committee's board-delegated powers include hiring and managing outside auditors. Audit committee members must be free of any conflicts of interest and should possess a certain level of financial skills. Their charge is to meet with the auditors, review the annual audit, report highlights and issues of interest to the board, and recommend any necessary changes to fiscal policy or oversight.

The audit committee performs an essential function for the board that does not duplicate CEO efforts. The audit report is an important monitoring tool that tells boards how well CEOs perform their fiduciary duties, and control of the audit committee should always rest with the board. Ironically, the common practice in many nonprofits is just the opposite—CEOs, not boards, select and control the auditors.

Educating Constituents Before we leave this area, it should be noted that boards face a big challenge in convincing themselves, as well as volunteers and other constituents, that the CEO, not the finance committee, is the best manager of their assets. In no other single area are boards so squarely caught between the need to delegate to CEOs the autonomy to do their job well and the pushback from volunteers who fear staff control.

Too often, the result is that boards spend an incredible amount of time on finance details that contribute little toward protecting the organization's assets. Furthermore, the righteous feeling of spending so much time in financial areas creates the false sense of security that the board is attending to its fiduciary duties, while in reality the board is avoiding them.

Boards will need to educate themselves and their constituents that a CEO with strong board oversight will maximize and protect organizational assets, whereas finance committees will not. Strong CEOs who have clear direction and backing from the board will find additional revenue sources and move expenses to their lowest efficient level; finance committees and volunteers will not. It's not for the lack of desire or sincerity of intent on their parts; it's that volunteer constraints prevent the continuity of leadership and daily attention to detail needed to manage business activities.

Board Oversight in Other Organizational Activities

What happens when boards step outside their governance role and approve operating policies or strategies in areas other than finance? The example that follows is the best way of illustrating the quagmire that ensues:

- **The CEO presents the latest membership policies to the board for approval.** Even the CEO doesn't know all the nitty-gritty details because the policy was constructed by department directors in conjunction with their staff. But the CEO is comfortable that the policy fits the desired behavior and is within the span of control delegated to directors.
- **The CEO presents the recommendation to the board with as much detail as possible.** One of the board members served on the membership committee for years and delves into every detail. Finally, the member convinces the board to tweak the part of the policy that covers an activity that's been a nagging problem

for a long time. Neither the CEO nor other board directors understand or care about this detail, but the changes seem harmless, so the board approves them.

- **The CEO brings the policies back to the membership directors.** The tweaking affects several major details that could negatively impact revenue and expense projections. Plus these changes have been a bone of contention between the board director and membership chair for quite some time; the membership committee has continually declined to approve the changes.
- **The next step depends on the CEO.** A strong, capable CEO will bring the policy back to the board table. A lot of effort and resources are wasted as the approval process starts all over again. Or, a board-pleasing CEO will simply tell the staff directors that "the board approved it, so do it." Not only will the membership committee be upset, but resources will be wasted as the staff director and chair try to work around the new policy—or worse yet, actually follow the policy and lose members.

This kind of situation is repeated countless times when boards try to approve anything that is called policy or strategy. How much more time for doing would be freed if the CEO and department directors had autonomy and were accountable for appropriate policies? How much more time would the board have if it didn't have to approve such policies?

These are just a few of the questions on our mind as we embark on the next *Live Lesson,* "Behind CEO Mismanagement Lurks Board Failure." In this *Lesson,* exactly what the example volunteer board is doing at their normal board meetings is unclear; probably, like most nonprofit boards, full agendas precipitate hours of discussions. However, what is clear is, though this board gives every appearance of being in charge, in reality, when it comes to governance, they are sound asleep in their chairs.

A *Live Lesson*: "Behind CEO Mismanagement Lurks Board Failure"

Introducing the Principals

Our subject nonprofit is a respected, centuries-old museum that we'll call the Big USA Museum (BUM). BUM is funded by private donations, county property tax dollars, and museum fees. The county publicly owns the building and the exhibits, and the private nonprofit, BUM, manages the museum. Some county officials sit on the museum board, and the county makes annual contributions to the museum.

Thanks in part to a new theater, science wing, and some hugely popular exhibits, the BUM budget has grown from $10 million to $21 million in just three years. But despite record growth, the BUM president and CEO have just startled everyone by announcing a huge deficit, and we're about to discover why.

Live Lesson Essentials

- Museum fortunes seemed assured five years ago as BUM's much-respected CEO, Jack, resigned after a six-year tenure. Through his leadership and private fundraising, the museum added an IMAX theater, a new science center, and a large gift shop.
- As Jack took his leave, the museum was fresh off a successful fundraising campaign that was earmarked to help repay the more than $18 million in bonds that were needed to fund the expansion.
- Since Jack's departure, there's been instability at the executive level. In the four years hence, the CEO position was vacant for almost two years, and two CEOs have come and gone.

Salt Mines #1: (Situation)

The board hires a CEO—and hires a CEO . . .

- The board takes a year after Jack's departure to find his replacement. New CEO Bob was a controversial president of a state university and held administrative and faculty positions prior to that. Peter, the volunteer board president, praises Bob's skills saying, "The museum is a place of education." The board is awed by Bob's credentials—his extensive background in African studies, ability to speak native dialects fluently, and books and research projects in England, Vietnam, and Egypt.
- After one year Bob gets into a salary dispute with one of the county representatives on the museum board and resigns. When he leaves, the board feels that the budget is in balance, and things are running well. They let a senior staff that worked well together for a long time temporarily, as a group, assume Bob's duties.
- A year later, the board hires a new CEO, Carl. He's an Oxford scholar and archeologist who comes to BUM, according to the press release, "after leading a $25 million expansion for a well-known science institute.

  Carl is very excited: "This fulfills a big dream of mine. My proudest achievement at my last position was making the science institute a more visitor-friendly place, which resulted in a financial turnaround. My first priority here will be to learn about the community."
- Peter, the board president, introduces Carl to the rest of the board members at a reception in his honor. He's telling everyone how lucky they are to find another creative genius just like beloved former CEO, Jack. He tells another board member, "Well, for once the paper quoted me correctly; I do think that we finally found

someone creative and that he also has broad public appeal and entrepreneurial knowledge."

- Things seem to go great for the next six months. The museum wraps up the year with a wildly successful African exhibit that sets record attendance. And the county that owns the museum facility, land, and exhibits is close to approving a package that guarantees a 10-year annual cash contribution, capital improvements help, and backing of existing museum debt in a new lease/management agreement.
- Shortly before the deal is to be finalized in March, the chief financial officer (CFO) Ted answers a local reporter's question about the success of the African exhibit, and also mentions that the museum may have a \$150,000 deficit for the fiscal year, but "it's just a one-time thing caused by the fundraising and expense cycle—and a long-overdue capital fund drive."
- Ted resigns two months later. A reporter calls CEO Carl to ask about the departure of his long-tenured CFO. Carl tells the reporter that the deficit may be as high as \$3.6 million. Realizing what he just did, Carl picks up the phone to give the board president, Peter, the same bad news before it hits the papers.
- As headlines of the projected shortfall hit, Carl is quoted as saying, "Cash is tight and layoffs may be necessary," and Peter is saying, "I was surprised at the disclosures, but the board has confidence in Carl, who started in the middle of past year. Carl is the answer, not the problem."
- When reporters ask about Ted's departure shortly after the initial announcement, Carl has kind words for the departing CFO, talking about his crucial role in the county lease agreement. But by year-end, he's quoted as saying, "Financial savvy is not my strong suit. I handed things over to Ted. For the first year he was really CEO, and I was learning."
- As the growing financial scandal widens, CEO Carl suddenly resigns in June. In an act of serendipity, Carl's alma mater runs a two-page spread on his accomplishments in that month's alumni magazine. The article reported that under Carl's leadership the museum just finished its strongest financial year since 1900. Ted is quoted as saying, "The old museum model of living off endowments and tax levies just doesn't work—exhibits and private funding does."
- The board president, Peter, takes over Carl's job until the board can find a new CEO. In July, Peter resigns citing "family reasons." An existing board member, Larry, becomes the new president and also acts as interim CEO.
- In September, the board passes up three experienced museum executives, including a financial manager for a renowned institution, and selects an existing county executive, Terry, as the new CEO. President Larry announces the appointment by saying, "Terry's our choice. I was initially hesitant about his lack of museum experience, but he really convinced me. He has proven fundraising experience, proven leadership skills, and the ability to start quickly."

Salt Mines #1: (Aftermath)

And hires a CEO and hires a CEO . . .

- In the year that the senior staff runs the organization after CEO Bob leaves, they add six new vice-president positions and many new staff members. The board, in effect, treats CFO Ted as the interim CEO, relying on him for budget, finance, and operating information, but they give him no official authority to act as CEO.
- When CEO Carl comes aboard in August, the fundraising vice-president, Sarah, who the board respects for substantially increasing donations, resigns when she does not get the CEO position. Carl hires Sarah's replacement the following April, and funds the new fundraiser's commute from another state. This person quits three months later.
- A day after Carl's talk with reporters, board members wake up to smell the coffee and this newspaper headline: "Museum President Forecasts a $4M deficit." BUM president Peter and CEO Carl talk to reporters about the $4 million shortfall and another possible $3 million for the first three months, but they don't tell the board.
- Carl's resignation sets off a round of criticism by board leaders who still support him. In general, the board blames the CFO, Ted, for the problems, not Carl. The board president, Peter, publicly praises the departing Carl in the paper, saying, "He's not the cause of the museum's problems. His leaving makes it even harder to climb out of our financial problems."
- Later disclosures reveal that despite Carl's public statement that his number-one priority was getting to know the community, at museum expense he was commuting back and forth to the museum from his out-of-state home for the first seven months of his tenure—and working just four days a week.

Lesson Primer *Salt Mines* #1: The Benefit of Not Understanding a Problem Is the Opportunity to Face It Again

The chances of hiring the right CEO without understanding the real state of the nonprofit are a million to one.

Take the time to reflect and reassess—the museum needs an experienced manager . . .

Everyone loved CEO Jack—and with good reason. Under his direction the museum became a national, not just a regional, force. His creativity and a long-tenured, experienced staff set the museum on an expansion course that grew assets from $2 million to $35 million and visitors from 400,000 to almost 1 million.

But all this expansion—the new science center, theater, store, and exhibits—came at a price. Museum coffers were full after the big fundraising campaign, but a considerable debt load, more than $18 million, had developed. Some new programs like the store were already running a deficit. And, in the year following Jack's departure, the museum went from running annual surpluses of $2 million to $5 million to running a deficit of $600,000. Clearly, the seeds of the future disaster were planted if the board had looked closely.

Former CEO Jack was a strong manager, actively directing all aspects of the museum, doing both CEO and board oversight jobs well. Board members were lulled into a false sense of security, and board oversight drifted during Jack's time, remaining on cruise control right up to the time of the $4 million shortfall headline. In reality, Jack left the museum in a vulnerable position. All the creative pieces and that amazing growth needed equally spectacular management. But the board completely missed that a shift to management mode was needed; it just wanted a new CEO who was similar to Jack.

After leaving the organization adrift without a CEO for a year, the board replaced Jack with another academic—Bob. He tried to tackle a growing expense problem by laying off some staff. However, he laid off an immensely popular curator in the process, and a county official started questioning Bob's salary, so that was the end of Bob.

Don't follow one mistake with another—the museum needs an experienced leader...

Although CEO Bob had spoken about a cash crunch and laid off staff, the museum board still acted as though everything was fine. Again, it did not take the time to reflect on the real state of the museum, nor confront the political problem with county officials that always simmered just below the surface and adversely affected Bob's ability to manage.

Not understanding that senior staff had been two years without strong CEO leadership, the board put senior staff as a group in charge while they once again searched for a CEO like Jack. Unfortunately, the senior staff had neither the experience nor the authority to make CEO decisions. A needed capital campaign was put on hold while the fundraising VP jockeyed for the CEO role, and a CFO who might be able to manage a $10 million budget with adequate cash flow now faced a $20 million budget with little cash flow alone.

While the board looked for another Jack, the staff did the best they could, adding more vice presidents and staff to carry the load. Although CFO Ted interfaced with the board and became the de facto CEO, he had no real authority to manage operations or staff, so everyone continued to drift along with the board.

At last the board found its perfect CEO—Carl, a charismatic Prince Charming who the board believed would sweep new money into the museum for an ambitious new budget. After all, that's what he did for the science institute. But, as the alumni magazine article revealed, Carl's ability to talk a good game did not really jibe with the facts. The museum "had not finished its strongest year since 1900." In fact, it had been running deficits since Jack left, and eventually Carl's rosy projections of exhibit attendances that did not materialize helped precipitate a crisis.

As it turned out, at his last job Carl led the science institute for only 14 months, hardly enough time to make the impact that he claimed. And the science institute enjoyed an endowment of over $300 million, but BUM's endowment was only around $5 million at the time, not enough to provide a big cash flow or to provide a safety net for deficit budgets. The board obviously didn't explore the true facts about Carl's management experience, nor did it seem to care that Carl openly admitted a lack of financial skill. This was a huge mistake, because all CEOs must have financial skill to manage the business component effectively.

Meanwhile, the board passed over for the job a very strong staff vice-president: fundraiser Sarah. Sarah left and was not replaced for six months. Then Carl hired an acquaintance who commuted back and forth for three months and then resigned. At a critical time when the museum had $18 million in debt, and had traditionally relied on annual campaigns for more than 50 percent of its funding, for four years the board didn't even seem to notice the absence of a major capital campaign.

When hit by a crisis, respond quickly but don't bury your credibility—the museum needs an experienced manager . . .

When the crisis hit, the board chair Peter talked to the newspapers first and the board second. Although it was necessary to counteract bad publicity quickly, he did not have to endorse Carl so strongly before the facts were known, and he certainly should have prepared the board for the bad news no matter how short the time interval.

As a result, the museum's early comments on the reason for the deficits, the continual underestimating of the true impact, and the early sweeping statements of CEO support made the board look silly as more and more information came to light. As a result, it compromised the public's trust and will need to work very hard to regain it.

Lastly, as the crisis broke, and especially when Carl resigned, instead of getting into a public shouting match with county officials, the museum board had a perfect opportunity to bring in a heavyweight interim CEO. The board had the opportunity to both look proactive and to have an ally who could quickly determine the true state of the organization and get it back on track—and allow the board the time to search for the right CEO.

Instead, the board selected a county official, Terry—an insider—who the then board president announced in the press by saying, "At first I was skeptical that Terry could do the job, but he convinced me. His political savvy, fundraising connections, proven leadership, and ability to take the helm on a short notice worked in his favor." This doesn't sound much like a board that realized that fundraising didn't lead to the crises; the lack of a CEO managing the museum business component and the failure of the board to monitor and hold the CEO accountable did.

Salt Mines #2: (Situation)

While we were sleeping . . .

- Right after the May bombshell headline, phone lines are burning. One of the board members, Theresa, is speaking with Peter: "The community is shocked, and we are simply astounded. How did this happen, and why did I have to read about it in the newspaper?" "Calm down," Peter replies, "the papers got hold of this before I had a chance to contact the board. We'll figure all of this out at our meeting tonight."
- Theresa calls several other board members. One muses, "I wonder whether we made a mistake relying on CFO Ted and giving him some of the powers of a CEO." Then he adds, "Well, we did resist when Carl wanted to take those powers away from Ted, but at that point we had to trust Ted. Carl made it plain during his interview that finance wasn't his strong suit . . . it just seemed wise to let Ted continue."
- Three weeks go by. The BUM board votes to cut the budget from $21 million to $14 million after the investment firm that holds the museum loans wants to slash staff from 250 to 115. At the meeting, the president Peter tells the board that the shortages are because of unrealistic budgeting, shortfalls in private fundraising, the sluggish economy, too-rapid growth at the museum, and freeway reconstruction that hampered attendance.

  Carl sums it up by saying, "The museum just grew too fast. We couldn't keep up with the rapid growth in spending and staff as we expanded so dramatically."

  President Peter reads aloud a resolution—"the BUM board has complete confidence in our CEO, Carl, assisting the board to get to the bottom of this"—and asks if the board backs this by consensus. No one votes no. And, of course, every detail of this public meeting was recorded in the paper the next day.
- Carl lays off only 75 staff members, but the curatorial and exhibits staff are cut in half. This cuts almost $3 million per year; other cuts need to be made from areas other than personnel. Bankers still want another $2 million in cuts.
- More and more disclosures hit the papers. The most damaging is the news that CFO Ted started withdrawing endowment funds for operating expenses in the middle of last year. Since then, the fund has gone from $4 million to $400,000. Even before these withdrawals, the fund was considered undersized by national standards; now it stands nearly empty.

  When questioned by a reporter, ex-CFO Ted says, "I have no idea how large the fund is now. My understanding was that, these were our funds and we had the ability to withdraw them. As far as I know, I did nothing wrong because they were used for the museum, not some unauthorized expense." He says that he expected to repay the fund later in the fiscal year, but attendances were down.

- Ex-CFO Ted and ex-fundraising vice president Sarah are talking with the press. Sarah claims that she warned the museum's previous director, Bob, that the museum had been in stagnation for the previous two years and there was a significant risk in standing still. Ted claims that he told the full board after Bob left that they needed to address short-term weaknesses and long-term systemic problems. He also told them last year after the audit that a third straight year had ended with a cash deficit, that the museum had to negotiate the terms of its loans, and that the delay in starting a capital drive had put further strain on funds needed for operations.
- By December, the auditors' report for the previous year is still not finalized. Irregular transactions need to be reclassified; however, the preliminary report states that "the board failed to adequately supervise staff and indirectly fostered a culture that discouraged frank discussions of the risk of aggressive growth."

  In response, the current board president, Larry, writes, "The board trusted management too much, and we accepted optimistic reports. We're truly sorry." Also quoted is a respected sector advisor, who says, "What happened at the museum is understandable. In the real world it's unrealistic to think that volunteer boards can micromanage what goes on. Boards are made up of volunteers who act like volunteers."
- Meanwhile, the county board does its own audit of the museum and releases a scathing report in December. In general, the report cites that the board, in the face of deteriorating deficits, drained its resources and kept its problems secret even as it negotiated a long-term lending agreement with the county.
- BUM leaders release new financial figures for the current fiscal year that are more than 50 percent higher than the figures released in September. Instead of a projected asset loss of $5 million, the loss is expected to be $11 million, leaving the museum with an overall net worth less than $5 million.
- The new museum CEO, Terry, calls the disclosure good because it means that new management is cleansing the books of aggressive accounting methods that masked the real state of the organization.

Salt Mines #2: (Aftermath)

The unwatched pot is sure to boil . . .

- The announcement of runaway deficits prompts county officials to put the new lease/management agreement on hold. There's also a great outcry from the public. One longtime museum lover talks about the fear that staff cuts are gutting everything that makes the museum popular—from the expertise of curators and the teaching impact of museum staff to the talented artists and craftspeople who build the exhibits.

- It also becomes clear as the terrible year drones on that exhibits budgeting and management were severely lacking. One of the disclosures reveals the seeds of the museum's financial problems were sown during Bob's short CEO term almost three years ago. He laid the groundwork for the smashing African exhibit that broke all attendance records last year, but he told the county's auditors that senior managers were divided on how to run this exhibit, which was four times larger than anything they had previously attempted. However, the board backed Bob's plan.

  Although the African exhibit was a creative and public success and the museum gained visibility and admission fees, the exhibit cost more than $5 million with only $2 million coming from donations, and operating costs ran $1 million more than expected. Exacerbating the problem was that this year's budget built in a hefty increase in attendance for the exhibit, but in a small city, attendance peaks in the year an exhibit opens and usually levels off the second and third years, so enrollments ran below expectations, worsening the cash flow problem in the current year also.
- In a letter to the museum board made public shortly before Carl's resignation, the county board executive calls for an immediate business plan to wipe out the $7 million debt by this year's fiscal end of August 31, and says that the county would seek changes in the management structure if the plans were not there. Right after Carl's resignation, the same executive makes a public statement that "this will help restore community trust."

  This angers the museum board, and board president Peter issues a statement in response saying, "The county board letter pushed Carl out, and this has completely stopped the museum's ability to raise funds."
- The county board audit also has another disastrous effect. At year-end, the district attorney announces that his office is opening a criminal investigation into museum practices regarding the manipulation of funds and falsification of information in museum records.

Lesson Primer *Salt Mines* #2: A Sleeping Board a Nightmare Makes

Volunteer board approval is not a pretend game; it carries real consequences. Panic is a heck of a wake-up call . . .

Granted, the museum board got catapulted out of its slumber in a dizzying way—intense media scrutiny and county pressure—but it clearly went into panic mode, reacting in a knee-jerk fashion—immediately announcing the intent to cut the budget by $8 million and to slash staff dramatically—without any idea what such cuts might mean to the museum's long-term mission and programs.

Although such actions looked good to investment firms and in the press, it's the board's job to protect mission, and usually outcomes put into place when the organization is running scared negatively impact future performance. The board announcement set off an internal panic as staff scrambled to keep their jobs. A public outcry ensued from people who understood that cutting curators and exhibit personnel might jeopardize the very things that they loved about the museum—things that made people attend.

The problem is not that expense cutting wasn't part of the immediate solution; it's that it was touted as the only solution to multilayered problems originating from the same source—the failure of the museum board to govern.

Real board policies are understood and followed . . .

Let's look at some of the precipitating events and the part that the museum board played in the "sudden crisis":

- CEO Bob told the auditors that senior managers were divided on how to run the African exhibit—an exhibit four times larger than anything the museum had run to date. But the board backed Bob's plan over staff objections.

  This is a failure of board organizational oversight: The CEO, who had been there less than a year, told the board what it wanted to hear—we can do it!—so the board ignored the warnings of long-term staff who understood the resources needed to actually do it. This doesn't mean that the board should ignore a great opportunity, but it does have a duty to listen to all sides and to hold the CEO accountable for identifying the financial and people resources necessary to make it work.
- The board left CFO Ted totally in charge of finance, providing neither guidance nor oversight. Unless something comes out in later investigations, Ted didn't raid the endowment fund to take his family on a cruise, but genuinely seemed ignorant of the necessity not to commingle reserve and operating funds. Clearly, when desperately seeking funds to pay loans and operating expenses, he saw nothing wrong with using such funds.

  This is a failure of board oversight: Comments by board members such as "our financial reports are so complicated, so how could we know things are bad?" are ludicrous. It's the board's job to make sure it receives clear reports and that it has the financial training to understand them. Furthermore, it is the board's job to create macro-financial policy that protects the organization's assets.

  Having two essential board policies in place—(1) endowment and other reserve funds cannot be used as operating funds and (2) the museum cannot be indebted beyond its ability to repay within 90 days—and monitoring their enforcement would have prevented the raiding of the endowment funds.
- The board knew that the museum ran deficits beginning every fiscal year after Jack's departure. Not only did the board get three years of audit reports that showed cash deficits, but both CFO Ted and fundraising VP Sarah warned the board of short-term weaknesses and long-term revenue/expense problems. The board also knew that the museum relied on an annual campaign from donors for 50 percent of its budget, yet when the operating budget jumped from $10 million to

$20 million, no one realized that annual donations needed to jump $5 million to $10 million to keep pace.

This is a monumental failure of board oversight and performance: The board was a passive bystander, letting CFO Ted do its governance job—managing audits and audit reporting. Contrary to their comments, board members had to know that no annual fundraising campaign was happening and that more cash was being spent than brought in.

Plus, the board let CEO Carl, although he had no financial acumen, discount what Ted said as "exaggerated." The board was clearly relieved when Carl optimistically predicted that proceeds from the African exhibit would make up for everything, even though a simple phone call to most museums would indicate that big exhibits rarely even pay for themselves. So the board and CEO continued to write checks without any thought as to the actual funds in the account.

The list goes on and on. The point is that boards have a real job to do, and when they abdicate that job to CEO and staff, ultimate accountability for the resulting failure falls to governance, not management. The museum's CEOs mismanaged the business component, and the CFO's failure is partly a CEO oversight problem, but in this case, the board hired CEOs without the necessary CEO management skills and knowingly placed a CEO with little financial acumen in charge at a critical time, without performing governance oversight or creating crucial macro-financial policies. The board's job is to see that the system works, not look the other way when it does not.

People in glass houses shouldn't throw stones . . .

Everyone's huffing and puffing to the contrary, the museum's perfect storm started ten years ago as the county announced a wonderful new partnership between the county's public support of the museum combined with a new private, professionally managed nonprofit to take the museum to the next level.

But strong CEO Jack lulled the county officials to sleep just like the museum board. The county had huge challenges with other social services, and the $4 million annual museum contribution was just a small part of its tax, so it gradually reduced its board appointments to 9 out of 20 members, and then as a cost-saving measure stopped its annual audits of the nonprofit.

In reality, the county officials failed the museum board in much the same way as the museum board failed the CEO. They still had nine members on the museum board who at any time could have alerted the county to problems. But instead of presenting a united front, both boards allowed the political battle between the county that holds the purse strings and the museum board that manages the money to erupt into public warfare, further eroding the loss of public confidence and tarnishing the museum's reputation.

Meanwhile, all of the leadership energies that should have been directed toward great new exhibitors, community education, and programs—mission delivery—were tied up in meaningless political squabbling.

Salt Mines #3: (Situation)

Ignoring governance policy leads to bad board conduct...

- Among the continuing disclosures is a revelation that in the January preceding the March headlines, the museum needed $800,000 to make a bond payment. The solution: a bank loan from the president of the bank who is on the BUM board. The executive committee does not disclose the problem to the county board with which it is finalizing the lease agreement, nor to the full board.
- One of the board members, Judy, resigns in June right before the release of the previous year's audit reports. She cites an inherent conflict between her board positions with the county board that provides funding for the museum. She has a parting shot for Carl for whitewashing the facts to the board and the executive committee for not revealing the financial crisis earlier.
- The chair of the audit committee is also one of the bankers who guaranteed the loans, so she steps down; another board member who is president of a bank that is one of the existing creditors also steps down. In addition, the board ends a $100,000 contract with a lobbying firm that employs the daughter of another board member.
- The county audit reveals that the previous fundraising vice president, Sarah, hired a telemarketing firm that her husband ran. The firm raised almost $1 million over the year, but 95 percent of the cost went to expense.

  When questioned about the activity, Sarah says, "This is not a conflict of interest. I told the board president and my development committee about it." She also points to how the endowment fund grew during her term. Although the contract is severed shortly after Sarah leaves, her husband tells the paper that there is no connection between his wife's leaving and his losing the contract.
- Board minutes reveal that preliminary audit statements were handed out at the previous December's board meeting. At the time, the reports show a $2.4 million drop in assets and a $200,000 cash deficit. What the board remembers most is Carl being upbeat and planning for new major exhibits.
- Volunteer president and interim CEO Peter resigns from the board in early July, citing family reasons. The board elects another board member, Larry, to serve in his place as both president and acting CEO. BUM is now facing a reforecast $7 million deficit for its fiscal year ending in August.
- Minutes also reveal that only 6 of the 20 board members were present at the budget presentation made by Carl for the current fiscal year. Such lackadaisical attendance was the norm. The board met every two months, with meetings running around 90 minutes. Attendance ran 50 to 70 percent, and there was no disciplinary action for nonattendance.

- For the past three years, the president, Peter, was only at half the meetings due to a family problem, and he also served on the board of two other large organizations. The board did not have term limits, and many of the board members also served on the boards of other local prestigious institutions.
- Later, some of the members tell the press, "We just didn't see this coming. Our reports were just too complicated and misleading for us to see the financial decline." Yet, BUM's executive committee included a banker, business executives, and a lawyer.

Salt Mines #3: (Aftermath)

A critically wounded museum . . .

- The county, which had been backed into a corner, in June guarantees a bank credit line of $9 million to keep the museum afloat. In return, a new five-member panel of people appointed by the county board president has power over budget and financial management.
- The cuts in staff result in a loss of talent that was uniquely well-versed in the strengths and weaknesses of the museum's artifacts and specimens. The loss of this institutional knowledge is a loss of the city's heritage, which can never be replaced.
- The board's new conflict-of-interest policies correct some of the board's governance policy deficiencies, but the damage to the public's trust and donor base will take a long time to rebuild.
- The political battle between the county and museum board and the focus on micro-financial budget management will hamper the new CEO's ability to manage.

Lesson Primer *Salt Mines* #3: A Board Leads by Example

A nonprofit board that relies on taxpayer dollars must be above reproach.

Boards must avoid the perception of self-dealing . . .

As one consultant publicly said, "We have many of the same people on boards, and they are all interrelated. They are friends. Many don't make meetings or spend time preparing. There's too much overlap of trustees on prominent boards. They can't do a good job on any of these boards."

Not only did some of the board members serve on multiple boards, but the museum board was riddled with potential conflicts of interest. Judy served on the county and museum boards; a banker provided an emergency loan without disclosure; the chair of the audit committee was president of the bank that holds museum loans. These relationships may all have been above reproach, but the public's perception of self-dealing was just as important as actual self-dealing. Essential to nonprofit board service is the duty of loyalty—to selflessly serve for the sole benefit of mission and nonprofit, not self-gain.

Furthermore, clearly at least one staff person didn't understand conflict of interest. Fundraising VP Sarah thought everything was fine as long as she told the president what she was doing. Why should she think any differently in the absence of a clear board conflict-of-interest policy and given the conduct of the board itself?

Board conduct speaks louder than words . . .

The comments of board members—they didn't see this coming—are pretty weak on the surface but make more sense when one realizes that board meetings only occurred every other month, ran no longer than 90 minutes, and were attended by less than 50 percent of the board. It's difficult to see something coming if you are not there to hear about it.

Though an audit committee has an important job to do, it's also pretty obvious that the museum audit committee did little more than listen to the CEO/CFO reports. That brings us to a common theme: volunteers disengage from board committees that become staff committees that just regurgitate reports; volunteers become engaged when they have real work and a real purpose.

Finally, the board president is as important to board performance as the CEO is to staff performance. Board chair Peter attended only half the board meetings, yet the board left him as chair, did nothing as he made statements to the press that reflected badly on the board and museum, and even made him interim CEO. The board is accountable for its own conduct; board policy should be very clear, and poor conduct confronted, especially when that poor conduct comes from the leader.

The Economic Cost of the *Board Fiddles, Rome Burns* Elephant

The cost of the museum board's fiddling while the fate of the entire museum was at risk can only partially be measured in hard dollars. It's clear that millions of dollars are lost, but the erosion of public confidence, the loss of intellectual capital in the form of experienced staff, and the potential loss of the exhibits and history that makes the museum special to the public will only be known as the future unfolds.

As this book goes to press, local corporations, foundations, and other donors have stepped up to contribute $3 million and to fuel what officials hope is a turnaround of the institution's stunning fiscal meltdown. The museum hopes to raise at least $30 million for operations, capital, and replenishing its endowment. Public support is rallying around the museum, but the question is whether the museum is on the right track to justify that support.

Considering how the problem is being summed up does not instill a great deal of confidence:

- The president of a company that advises organizations on how to avoid or work their way out of bankruptcy says, "In a real world, it is unrealistic that boards of nonprofits are going to highly scrutinize and micromanage what is going on. I don't think it is the exception to have a board of volunteers who act like volunteers."

- Large foundation donors state, "We satisfied ourselves that the museum's problems were related to individuals who are no longer there."
- The new board president and CEO's written response to the final audit report was this: "The board relied too heavily on trusted management. This trust dulled the board's critical analysis and lulled it into accepting overly optimistic reports. For this we are truly sorry. The museum had a different understanding of the museum's financial situation than was really happening. The board takes full responsibility for its mistakes and has new fiscal policies in place to promote openness and fiscal responsibility."

Volunteers cannot have it both ways. Volunteer boards cannot be accountable only when things go well, but when things go poorly be excused because they are volunteers. Volunteer boards can govern well, and they must, or the nonprofit is at risk.

The answer is not finance committees or hands-on boards trying to do the CEO's job. The museum's crisis was not precipitated because the board failed to spend hours on the budget or to authorize every expense. Although boards often focus on these tasks instead of sticking to their true responsibilities, it is unreasonable to expect unpaid, part-time volunteers to do what is a full-time job. The museum imploded because the board did not do the basic things for which it is accountable and which volunteers can do:

- Protect mission by creating macro-financial policy that limits system risk
- Develop policies for hiring the right CEO and holding that CEO accountable for performance
- Carry out its business component oversight charge
- Institutionalize policies and practices to monitor its own performance and hold itself accountable for following them

A nonprofit board is ultimately responsible for safeguarding mission and the viability of the organization, and it doesn't matter that they are volunteers. A board that understood its obligations, created board-appropriate strategy and policy, and performed proper oversight would not have allowed BUM to spin out of control.

Summing It Up

In private discussion, many sector insiders abandon their public pretense that volunteer boards can provide consistently good governance. They encourage the CEO to manage the board and governance process behind the scenes. Frankly, this is just plain wrong. It may be more efficient for a talented and strong CEO to do both jobs, but it is not better for nonprofit performance. Both board and CEO have huge responsibilities that are complementary but mutually exclusive; if the CEO does both jobs, there is no oversight and no cross-checks to protect the nonprofit. But most of all, the nonprofit is deprived of the benefits that a strong board can bring. Done right, the board's responsibility for creating and monitoring board policies as well as the oversight duties for mission, CEO, and organization—and fundraising in philanthropic organizations—is an enormous role.

The *Board Fiddles, Rome Burns* elephant cannot flourish when boards understand the importance of policy and strategy throughout the nonprofit. Boards will focus their efforts on governance policy and strategy, and CEOs will focus on operating policy and strategy. The wondrous thing is that when this occurs, not only does everyone in the organization feel empowered and happier—the nonprofit is truly protected, and its performance optimized.

NOTES

1. Glenn H. Tucker, Jean S. Frankel, and Paul D. Meyer, CAE, *The Will to Govern Well: Knowledge, Trust, and Nimbleness* (Foundation of the American Society of Association Executives, 2002).
2. Randy Lidner, "Role Definitions: Leading vs. Managing," *Bostrom Solutions for Association Professionals and Volunteers,* no. 1 (July 29, 2003): 1.
3. Doug Macnamara, "On Creative Abrasion," *Executive Update Online* (April 2004): 8.
4. Peter Drucker, *Managing in the Next Society* (New York: St. Martin's Press, 2002), 47.
5. Griffin B. Bell, Robert B. Fiske, Jr., Robert J. McGuire, G.G. Michelson, and Russell S. Reynolds, Jr., *Report of the Independent Committee to the Board of Directors* (July 2004), 3–4.
6. Julia Moskin, "Culinary Foundation Calls Fiscal Juggling a Possibility," *New York Times,* September 9, 2004.
7. Carol Hymowitz, "Lessons to be Learned on Corporate Values from Year's Blunders," *Wall Street Journal,* sec. 2, December 16, 2003.
8. Harrison Coerver, "Straight Talk on Strategic Planning," *Forum* (October 2003): 14.

CHAPTER 6

The *Smile, Not Skill* Elephant

Well done is better than well said.

—Ben Franklin

Then There Were None: The Disappearing CEO

An Annie E. Casey Foundation research study of executive leadership transitions found that 55 percent of their CEOs are over the age of 50, and 65 percent plan to transition out of their positions by 2009.[1] Another study by CompassPoint anticipates an expected rate of turnover of nonprofit executives during the next five years of 70 to 90 percent.[2]

Horror stories surrounding executive turnover abound from these studies, including one organization that went through seven different executives in a short period of time. Another community development nonprofit lost 25 percent of its funding while flipping three new executives in a 12-month period.

Concurrent with the disappearing CEO are reports within the nonprofit industry that volunteers with little or no leadership experience are increasingly filling board vacancies. As Don Crocker, executive director of the Washington D.C.–based Support Center for Nonprofit Management puts it, "The convergence of increasing executive turnover with inexperienced and unprepared boards poses significant risk for the nonprofit sector."[3]

The trend toward high nonprofit turnover does not stop in the executive suite. A study titled "Help Wanted: Turnover and Vacancy in Nonprofits"[4] reported that 8 percent of paid staff positions are vacant; 30 percent of these positions were vacant for four months or more; and 24 percent of the vacancies are non-CEO management positions.

Given the current need for stronger board and CEO leadership, these trends threaten to exacerbate an already difficult situation. But in adversity there are always seeds of opportunity. Can departing CEO and volunteer leaders be replaced by ones with skills that better align with today's challenges?

In This Chapter

Nonprofits need to reach beyond the "burnout, stress, and low wage" answers that so often dominate turnover discussions. What causes the stress? What makes nonprofits, as Giovinella Gonthier characterizes, "the most uncivil workplace of all"?[5]

The *Mission Impossible, Earth to Board,* and *Board Fiddles, Rome Burns* elephants all act as troublemakers by encouraging the *Smile, Not Skill* elephant's bad behavior. Ironically, the driving force that melds all the elephants into an "uncivil workplace" is something that this book calls the *Code of Nice.* How the *Code of Nice* and the *Smile, Not Skill* elephant work to substitute personality for performance and how that negatively impacts nonprofit performance are the central themes of this chapter. The destructive forces are hard at work in two key relationships: board and CEO; CEO and staff.

A *Live Lesson,* "If the CEO Performs Poorly, Blame the Staff," and a trip to the *Salt Mines* solidify chapter concepts and illustrate the cost of the *Smile, Not Skill* elephant in the nonprofit workplace.

A Brief Introduction: Four Elephants and a Code

The *Smile, Not Skill* elephant does not act in a vacuum—it has a little help from its friends. A short review of their friendly influence and an introduction to the *Code of Nice* is essential in order to understand the *Smile, Not Skill* elephant's harmful behavior.

Mission Impossible Sets the Stage

I'm the Expert is the soul of the *Mission Impossible* elephant. This archetype encourages volunteers to overvalue the benefit component and undervalue the business one. Intentionally or unintentionally, the signal goes out: volunteers work out of dedication and love, so they are valuable and trusted; staff members work for money, so they are not to be trusted. Caring and passion are valued; professional expertise is not.

The problem is magnified in philanthropic nonprofits where volunteers sometimes feel guilty about spending grant or donor monies on "administrative overhead." Couple that with volunteers who believe that staff should not get paid for what volunteers do for free, and the result is a failure to appreciate staff performance and a reticence to invest in nonprofit infrastructure.

Frequently, such attitudes are expressed subtly rather than openly. The following situation shows how this hidden resentment bubbles to the surface:

> A well-known professional staff president, Henry Fogel, was stepping down from his post at the Chicago Symphony Orchestra after 18 years. During these years, the orchestra

gained an international presence for both its music and excellent fiscal model; results of benefit component leadership by maestros such as Georg Solti and business component leadership from Mr. Fogel.

Yet, this is what a music critic, clearly put out by a farewell concert and reception held in Mr. Fogel's honor, writes: "The audience stood and applauded: Champagne was served at intermission. . . . After 18 years of service to the orchestra and cultural community, Fogel certainly deserved a sendoff. . . . But . . . Fogel, lest we forget, is the orchestra's president not its music director."[6]

Enter the *Earth to Board* Elephant

Into the mix, the *Earth to Board* elephant contributes the *Everything Is Wonderful* game. This is the CEO technique of putting a positive spin on organizational activities, thus shielding boards from the true state of CEO and organizational performance—or non-performance.

An interesting study of city managers subtly implies the rewards of playing this game well.[7] In a surprising finding, high leadership effectiveness skills—the ability to take charge and get things done—did not translate to longer CEO tenure. Indeed, the correlation was negative; city managers rating high in leadership effectiveness actually had shorter nonprofit tenures.

Arguably, this may or may not hold true in other types of nonprofits, but the findings do strike a chord with experienced volunteer and staff leaders. They give weight to a well-quoted industry adage—do something and be hated, do nothing and be loved.

Board Fiddles, Rome Burns Gets into the Act

A widespread governance belief is that boards set policy and CEOs implement it. But this kind of thinking encourages boards to lower their expectations of CEO performance.

The *Board Fiddles, Rome Burns* elephant encourages boards to become immersed in business management strategies and to ignore governance policies and strategies—a fertile environment where underperforming CEOs thrive by shifting their accountability onto the board.

The *Code of Nice*

If volunteer attitudes discount the business component, and CEOs shield boards from the true state of organizational or staff performance, how do volunteers measure CEO and staff performance?

The *Code of Nice* steps in to fill the measurement void. Harmony, consensus, and "niceness" are prized above all things, including output. The golden rule is: always be cordial, don't disagree, and never say anything critical in public; of course, anything goes in private. Paid staff is rated by its likeability quotient—a factor known in the media world as the "Q" rating.

Q is simply a volunteer's opinion about how congenial and accommodating the staff member is. In the absence of set goals and success measurements, Q is a tangible standard by which geographically remote volunteers measure staff performance.

Staff members who adhere closely to the *Code of Nice* earn a high Q rating. One tongue-in-cheek staff member describes how to accomplish this feat:

1. Be available, smiling, and cooperative at all times of the day and night.
2. Do special favors for volunteers and their friends.
3. Give all credit for your successful efforts to volunteers or committees.
4. If something goes wrong, staff assumes the blame.
5. Provide volunteer support for things such as finding babysitters.
6. Answer on the spot every call, letter, and e-mail of all members and donors known to vested volunteers.
7. Never say anything critical about a volunteer or a volunteer's performance.
8. Always be positive about staff activities and the CEO.

Of course, boards and other volunteer leaders must also follow the *Code of Nice* in order to gain high Q from peers and staff. The chairman of the board might describe that process in this way:

1. Never say anything critical about the CEO or staff.
2. Don't anger the CEO; back off if your questions are visibly upsetting.
3. Kiss up to the CEO to ensure staff cooperation and a flow of good information.
4. Never criticize a board member's poor performance; work around it.
5. Avoid topics where there may be serious disagreement.
6. Avoid angering any powerful constituent who might bite back after we're out of office.

The *Code of Nice* is pervasive in all areas of the nonprofit industry. The extent of its acceptance is illustrated by a short piece that mourns the death of a longtime CEO in a widely read industry newsletter: "his passing away is noted with the highest compliment that can be paid—he always had a smile on his face." It's difficult to imagine anyone praising a corporate CEO in that manner.

Armed with the knowledge of the *Code of Nice* and the contributions of the elephants fresh in mind, let's return to one of the issues at hand: How do all of these factors converge to impact the board and CEO?

The Board and CEO

Reams and reams of paper are devoted to the relationship and workings of the board and CEO, but without question the most fundamental issue is how boards attract and retain high-performing CEOs. Their success depends on a couple things: (1) hiring the right CEO and (2) adequately supporting and overseeing CEO performance.

Hiring the Right CEO

Time of opportunity or fear . . .

One of the most pivotal times in the life of a nonprofit is when the board faces a vacancy in the CEO office. A pithy saying that characterizes the moment is: Will the board settle for lemons or make lemonade?

Hiring staff is difficult for any organization, but many nonprofit boards find hiring CEOs a particularly angst-ridden experience. Michael Allison, a CompassPoint director who contributed to the study, *Leadership Lost: A Study of Executive Director Tenure and Experience,* finds that:

> Boards of directors dramatically underestimate the risk of bad hires and are "woefully unprepared for the task" of hiring. This is particularly alarming given study findings that indicated an average tenure of three years for 501(c)(3) CEOs.[8]

Allison goes on to note that boards tend to spend as little money as possible on the executive search, viewing the process as an "unwelcome and troubling burden" rather than an opportunity to move the organization in another direction.

It's easy to understand a board's "hurry up and get it over with" attitude considering the situation. Many boards are dependent on the CEO for organizational knowledge and activities: even independent boards rely on CEOs to manage staff and execute administrative functions. They find the prospect of assuming CEO duties on top of board work scary enough, but they must also face the unfun prospect of spending a limited board term hiring and training the new CEO.

Things get particularly contentious if board and CEO roles aren't properly defined or board members have never worked directly with a high-performing CEO. Board members, vested volunteers, and would-be candidates alike come out of the woodwork to offer their ideas on the "ideal CEO." Partisan lobbying and politics accelerate into high gear.

Boards face other potential problems. The departing CEO may be a long-tenured, high-Q executive who earned that rating by keeping a low profile; she or he avoids doing anything significant, and thus is not seen as a target or too powerful. This CEO management model of "smile and do what the board says" will be reflected throughout the staff, so any move to a performance-based CEO also means significant changes throughout the entire organization.

Or, perhaps like the museum board in the Chapter 5 *Live Lesson,* a board is caught in a downward spiral of high CEO and staff turnover. This might be because of a past board failure to correctly align organizational needs with CEO talent. Perhaps a newly hired, high-performing CEO rocked the boat too much, and the board was unwilling or unable to deal with the vested volunteer and staff dissension that followed. Whatever the reason for the turnover—and it could be just plain dumb bad luck—the board is gun-shy and frightened of making another mistake that could send more staff stampeding for the door.

All of these issues illustrate that boards do face real obstacles that make them want to hire a new CEO as soon as possible, but it's essential that they fight this urge and make the time to conduct the hiring process properly.

The First Step: Accurately Defining Mission/Organizational Needs Lemonade is enjoyed by boards that interpret a CEO's departure as a time of opportunity—a period to reflect, assess, and realign mission, CEO, and organization. Mission, culture, and values come from the board: directly through board actions and conduct and indirectly through interaction with the CEO. Failure to practice adequate board leadership in either area reverberates more loudly than any written mission statement and will make the assessment phase particularly difficult.

A good example of how culture emanates from behavior, not words, is found in a study of the National Aeronautics and Space Administration (NASA) after the loss of the space shuttle *Columbia*. An investigative report by Behavioral Science Technology Inc. concluded that NASA's culture did not reflect the values it said it most prized: employees didn't feel comfortable raising safety concerns. Furthermore, in the words of the Columbia Accident Investigation Board, NASA had moved away from a culture of "proving that the shuttle was safe to fly" into a mindset that an individual had to essentially "prove that it wasn't safe to fly."[9]

NASA employees perceived that skills of communication and management were more highly prized than technical skills, that budget constraints affected engineering safety, and that workers should not raise issues. Employees took their cue from the intentional and unintentional behavior of top NASA leadership much more than from their contradictory public rhetoric.

One thing seems very clear: the old NASA board that failed to see the reality of the existing workplace might be hard pressed to accurately define the skill set a new CEO might need. The same holds true for most boards; if they cannot accurately assess culture and organizational needs, they start the CEO hiring process with a very large handicap.

The Second Step: Recognizing the Importance of Management The single biggest mistake that boards tend to make when hiring CEOs is underestimating the need for line management experience. Good people cannot compensate for a bad CEO. After all, the position is the top rung of the nonprofit management ladder; CEOs operate without direct supervision and with only periodic communications from a geographically remote board. In effect, boards throw CEOs into headquarter waters, where they must sink or swim without a life preserver. If CEOs drown, they take their staff down with them.

Isn't it ironic, then, that normally risk-adverse boards are so willing to assume a huge risk by hiring CEOs who lack large-scale management experience? The assumption seems to be that CEOs will get trained on the job. But who does this? Even if board members want the job and have the necessary acumen, they aren't physically present to do the training. And it's equally ludicrous to expect senior staff to train the CEO. That's like asking the interns to train the chief physician!

Specifically, a CEO's track record should clearly demonstrate success in directing and managing staff and organizational resources to achieve stated outcomes. Management theorist and critic Henry Mintzberg sums it up well: "Trying to teach people who have never practiced is worse than a waste of time—it demeans management."[10]

Anti-Performance Hiring Practices But boards engage in other hiring practices that lessen the chances of hiring the right CEO and negatively impact a performance culture. They can be categorized as *Who Me?; Glitz and Glamour; Benefit, Not Business;* and *Fowl Instead of Beef.*

The *Who Me?* Hire One of a board's most far-reaching acts is hiring a CEO. So, what's the first thing that happens when a CEO leaves? The board hires an executive recruiter or appoints a search committee, thereby creating a layer that insulates them from the hiring process. In effect, the board shifts its hiring responsibilities to another party, who does everything but approve the final candidate.

Shouldn't a board seek outside help when faced with such a difficult decision? It's good to employ an objective outside party who can act to provide a fresh look at mission and organization, but the caveat is that boards must own and lead the process, not abdicate their responsibility to someone else.

It's all right to use a recruiter or search committee as a tool in the CEO hiring process, but unless the board is totally engaged each step of the way, the tool leads the process. Too often, boards skip the upfront assessment work, and then hire biased recruiters who do only a cursory, superficial job of analyzing and matching organization and CEO. Sometimes the recruiter is a friend of a board member or represents a company used by the member's employer; frequently they have little or no nonprofit search experience.

Particularly egregious is the practice where the board appoints a search committee, and the search committee hires the recruiter. This really isolates the board from all but the final candidate(s), so the important selection of the next CEO is in the hands of those with vested interests. People who feel strongly about the previous CEO can lobby for membership on the search committee and the chance to pick a particular type of CEO or a friend. Or committee members are distinguished volunteer leaders of the past who may not understand the current state of the nonprofit or its emerging needs.

Also harmful unless handled very carefully is the well-intended but misplaced practice of appointing a staff member to the search committee. In one instance, instead of appointing, the board just asked for a staff volunteer. The result was the presence on the search committee of a first-line staff member who had no idea what the CEO or board did.

None of these actions, in Jim Collins language, puts "the right people on the right bus" or lends positive energy to an intelligent CEO hiring decision. The search committee and executive recruiters won't have to live with the results of their actions, but boards and staff certainly will.

The *Glitz and Glamour* Hire CEO searches, particularly those led by retained executive recruiters, tend to go for the glitter of a big name or impressive credentials over practical experience. Form takes precedence over substance.

Bad recruiters—and there are a lot of bad recruiters—tend to produce lengthy, beautiful CEO position descriptions. The introduction is a feel-good recap of mission and history, sometimes followed by a summary of organizational philosophy and approach. Then comes many pages of responsibilities that derive from interviews with key stakeholders. Boilerplate language of required CEO experience and traits completes the package.

Boards accept such "books" without asking themselves: Is this a job that someone can actually do? Read the responsibilities of a job description plucked from the Web site of a well-known recruiter:

- Work with board to implement all policies and programs
- Work with (15) subcommittees to execute priorities
- Develop and execute fundraising strategy
- Do PR and serve as public spokesperson for the profession
- Identify and cultivate new sources of revenue
- Attend and participate actively in all board and subcommittee meetings
- Manage administration and information systems
- Create weekly e-newsletter to constituents

This particular job description was part of an executive search for an executive director, not a CEO. If these are the expectations for that position, the high survey projections for future CEO burnout and turnover don't seem all that shocking.

Setting aside the fact that it's difficult to believe that one human could actually accomplish all of these tasks well, it's tough to find one resume that lists experience in such diverse areas; so the recruiter focuses on candidates who are well-known in the industry, have recently garnered public accolades or fame, or possess glamour (e.g., Harvard or Yale) credentials.

The board gets carried away by how good such a "catch" looks to stakeholders and the public and forgets all about matching candidate experience with the actual job description. Further encouragement comes from the fact that a "name" hire lowers the risk of blame if the name fails. After all, when things go bad, how can medical association members hold the board responsible if it hires a well-known researcher as CEO? Or if a Washington-based think tank hires a past congressman? Or a large social service agency hires a past presidential candidate?

Glitz and glamour blind boards to a basic fact: In nonprofits that have staff and complex organizations, the number-one job of the CEO is managing staff and organization. Notable and all too frequent is the absence of even the slightest mention of leading and managing staff in CEO ads like our previous example. Degrees, published research papers, or public recognition are not good indicators of success in this area.

This is not to say that glitz and glamour aren't great if the candidate also has a solid track record of successful line and people management. In fact, glitz and glamour combined with appropriate management experience is the very best hire, but there aren't all that many people in this category, and assuming that such a person can be found, the price tag he or she commands may be well beyond most nonprofits' ability to pay.

Last, it may be that glitz and glamour are needed to draw funds or prestige to the nonprofit. That's okay too, but just know that an additional person will need to be actually running the business, and that the nonprofit will need to pay top dollar for two executives. Even for corporations, CEO stardom is waning. Pragmatism and a focus on day-to-day operations are in vogue. In a *Chicago Tribune* article, Ulrike M. Malmendier, an assistant professor of finance at Stanford University notes in a study of CEOs: "The companies of superstar CEOs subsequently underperform."[11]

The *Benefit, Not Business* Hire Boards often feel that the benefit component—the complex, unique make-up of their nonprofit—makes the learning curve overwhelming for an outsider. So their mindset is to limit the search to an inside person or an expert in the benefit field in the mistaken belief that this shortens the learning curve.

Such actions appear logical on the surface, but they fail to consider an important fact: benefit knowledge is not business knowledge. CEOs can gain benefit knowledge through data and volunteer mentoring, while the people management and leadership skills needed to direct the business only comes from years of hands-on experience.

A line manager with a successful track record of leading staff and organization can learn the essentials of the benefit component and become familiar with various stakeholder groups within the first several months. A CEO without top line-management experience will be learning on the job for many years to come at the cost of the people and organization.

Briefly thinking about the way that most boards train CEOs reinforces the point. CEO training programs rely on factual documents and interviews with key stakeholders; they don't teach leadership skills or financial acumen. A CEO with in-depth benefit knowledge but no management experience duplicates the knowledge that board and volunteers already supply, but the board and volunteers do not supply the management knowledge that the CEO lacks.

The *Fowl for Beef* Hire The departing CEO may be a high-Q, low-performing executive who was good at schmoozing, not managing. Because in the absence of objective performance measurements Q equals performance, the board feels that the CEO did a good job. Logically, it wants to search for someone just like the departing CEO. The board may even allow the CEO to name a successor or guide the search process.

This often happens with boards that have no institutionalized methods for monitoring CEO and organizational performance. Few lines of communication are open for honest staff input. Even if a board tries to solicit such feedback once the CEO leaves, it encounters difficulties. Because authentic communication is not the norm, staff members may be hesitant to answer what they interpret as loaded questions.

Sometimes part of the board knows that the departing CEO is board-popular but not staff-popular. In this case, it is especially important to discern why this is the case. Otherwise, the board may hire someone who just perpetuates the problem. And if the board decides that a change is needed at the CEO position and throughout the organization, the board needs to signal those changes and the strategies behind them as much as possible before the actual CEO search. This helps set the stage and preshape staff expectations for the new CEO's arrival.

In certain cases, a board confers the position as a reward to a long-tenured, high-Q senior staffer. This kind of decision is a comfortable fit for a board that wants to avoid the whole search process and continue on as before with a person who mirrors the former CEO and/or the board's personality, interests, and beliefs.

This is not to say that promoting new CEOs from the inside is always wrong. To the contrary, good succession planning that develops internal leaders is one indication of a well-run nonprofit with a forward-thinking board and CEO. But the plain fact is that most nonprofits are not at that point. Boards should cautiously approach appointing internal candidates only after completing the hard work of ensuring that their skill set and talents are the best fit with organizational needs.

Fit should be much, much more than a cozy, comfortable feeling between board and CEO personalities. Fit should refer to the fit between the direction that a nonprofit must go and the best CEO skill set to get there. An added benefit to not settling for just a comfortable fit is, as Robert I. Sutton, who writes in the *Stanford Social Innovation Review,* is quoted in a *Fast Company* article, "Hiring people who make you uncomfortable . . . if you find a candidate who seems talented yet has different beliefs, knowledge and skills than most insiders . . . such people often scout out new trends and direction."[12]

Supporting CEO Performance

Let's assume that a board correctly completes the search process and hires a CEO who matches the organization's needs. After an initial orientation period, the board's next challenge is ongoing CEO support and monitoring.

We already know many of the practices that positively support CEO performance: clear, defined distinctions between governance/management and board/CEO; policy and strategy delegated to the appropriate levels; board policies that spell out good governance practices; measurable board and CEO performance standards; evaluating CEO performance and taking action where warranted.

But even when these practices exist, the board and CEO must work together and consistently apply these practices to daily work life. And there's the rub. How does the board create the culture that best supports CEO efforts, and how does the board encourage the extension of this supportive culture to professional and volunteer staff?

This is a topic that we'll learn more about in Chapter 11—specifically how the *Smile, Not Skill* solutions help boards to encourage a high-performing CEO and staff culture. Now, it's time to return to the other focus of this chapter—the CEO and the staff culture.

The CEO and Staff

A board member tells a volunteer, "We're really lucky. This organization has a great staff that's been here forever." The volunteer walks away feeling blessed that the nonprofit is not beset by the same turnover problems that other nonprofits face. But think about it: Is a staff that's been around forever a blessing—or a curse?

Although boards directly affect staff and members with whom it works closely, most professional and volunteer workers in a reasonably sized nonprofit rarely come into contact with board members or attend board meetings. So most of a nonprofit's culture comes directly from the CEO, not the board. However, a long-tenured CEO creates the same working culture for staff that the board creates for the CEO. If the board doesn't care about management, neither will the CEO. If the board feeds a Q culture, so will the CEO. And, if the board doesn't define what constitutes success, neither will the CEO.

A Q culture is a toxic operating culture that limits individual and organizational innovation, creativity, and outcomes. At first, this hurts only the high-performing staff members; as time goes on and high performers are eliminated, the staff is transformed into a long-tenured Q-thriving group that is harmful to nonprofit productivity.

Signs of such a performance-toxic culture may be open and visible to the board, or it may be hidden behind a *bon homie* façade and lots of maintenance activities disguised as outcomes. We'll discuss the openly toxic culture only briefly. After all, this type of culture is out in the open and visible for all to see. We'll examine in greater detail the more interesting and prevalent kind of performance-toxic culture—the stealth culture that volunteers often mistake for a positive culture.

The Openly Toxic Culture

CEOs lead, direct, and manage staff and organization. Their ethical standards, professionalism, and managerial skills are eventually adopted or rejected throughout the organization; in effect, the CEO *is* the staff culture.

Management studies show that 50 percent of an employee's job satisfaction comes from the relationship with his or her immediate manager. The CEO's relationship with senior staff members greatly impacts their job satisfaction; senior staff members' relationships with their managers greatly impact their job satisfaction; and so on down the line.

This means that a new CEO or a non-Q CEO who cannot manage people or organization sets off a dissonance that boards cannot help but hear. The noise comes from trusted senior staff members first-hand and then from committee members who are close to individual disgruntled staff members.

Unless a nonprofit has a long history of bad CEOs (in which case, staff either clams up or is part of the bad culture), staff as a whole seldom hides CEO problems of this kind from the board. Whether boards chose to ignore or confront the situation is another story, but at least they hear about the problems.

The Stealth Toxic Culture

The stealth toxic culture often goes undetected and is sometimes even confused with a positive working culture. This is the *Code of Nice* or Q culture.

Over time, high-Q, low-outcome CEOs infect the working culture. The Q culture weeds out the fittest and lets the congenial survive. What remains are smiling, volunteer-pleasing staff members who maintain their piece of nonprofit turf well while hindering innovation and change.

So, the nonprofit looks good on the surface; the work gets done, programs are maintained, staff complaints are few, and turnover is low, but underneath it is a different story. The Q staff procrastinates about new ideas and opportunities, using "easy on us" and "volunteer appeal," not "mission need" and "broad constituent appeal," as program selection criteria.

The winner in this game is the staff; they enhance their Q by making the easy seem difficult and by avoiding risky new ventures. The loser is the nonprofit. No one notices as the opportunities to increase mission programs keep slipping by.

Characteristics of the Q Culture

A big question is how do boards recognize that a Q culture exists? After all, a long-tenured CEO and staff might also be a hallmark of a high-performing nonprofit. Fortunately, Q cultures tend to share the following characteristics that performance cultures do not:

- People and process management are limited.
- Innovation and achievement are punished, not rewarded.
- Vested volunteers and long-tenured staff are entrenched.
- Volunteer and staff leaders engage in the *Dance of Deceit*.
- Board term and/or CEO tenure equal reality.

People and Process Management Are Limited High-Q CEOs spend their time currying favor with boards and vested volunteers, not leading and directing staff. Such things as holding useful staff meetings, being available for direct reports, maintaining equitable wage and salary schedules, setting and monitoring annual goals, and developing future staff leaders are always on the back burner.

Senior staff manages the same way. One operational consultant spots this problem by using a simple survey tool in which staff executives anonymously track and allocate their time into various categories. Results often indicate that even managers with many direct reports devote less than 1 percent of their time to management.

Some grantors and nonprofit leaders may think this is great if they view staff as administrative overhead, but they are missing the linkage between good people/process management and high mission performance. The absence of managing means duplicated efforts, inefficient programs, cumbersome operations, unimaginative problem solving, and limited program innovation.

Lack of people and process management lowers the rate of member or donor return. Each dollar buys less service and fewer programs. We can easily see why this is so by looking at the kinds of things missing in a low-management environment:

- **Staff leadership is too busy to meet regularly with direct reports.** People do their own thing without brainstorming and receiving feedback. Problems are solved on the job; crises are precipitated, not avoided. Good ideas fall through the cracks.
- **Interdepartmental meetings do not occur regularly.** One employee does not know what the other is doing. Systems fail and problems occur because what works in one area does not in another. There's little cross-training, so work piles up when someone is absent.
- **Cross-departmental meetings are held only when something's new or there's a crisis.** Meetings are just information dumps rather than a chance to exchange ideas, quickly resolve interdepartmental issues, or accelerate decision making. The same issue gets tackled by multiple departments. Programs are viewed only as they affect a specific area, not the organization.
- **Evaluation of senior staff and department performance is not goal based.** Goals that exist are general in nature and relate to maintaining programs and coordinating volunteer activities. There's no CEO-led planning process that yields volunteer and staff mission goals.
- **Staff is often confused by board actions; the board is confused by staff actions.** The CEO fails to act as the proper conduit between board and staff; board actions conflict with workplace reality. These entities spin their wheels and fill in the blanks by speculating about the actions and motives of the other.
- **Pay levels for CEO and other staff leaders are at market rate; remaining salaries are below market rate.** The CEO subjectively manages salaries without consideration

to any objective wage and salary range. Written staff reviews are not regularly done, and pay raises do not correlate with reviews.

- **Little time is devoted to staff training or grooming future managers.** Bench strength is weak. Services and programs are halted when key managers leave. Lack of outside training limits exposure to the kind of new ideas that can creatively resolve entrenched problems.

The list could go on and on. Boards that adequately perform CEO oversight can spot these problems. The rub is that they can just as easily rationalize and ignore them, because the amazing thing is that projects still get accomplished in cultures that are devoid of good management practices. Capable staff and volunteers will maintain programs by working around bureaucratic nightmares, inefficient procedures, and political craziness.

And that makes it easy for boards to settle for CEO excuses like "we'll do better when it's not so busy" or "senior staff knows what they're doing—they meet when it's necessary." CEOs even receive kudos for eliminating the training budget and keeping salaries low. Expense reduction is always easy, but it takes a lot more vision to understand the value of missed opportunities.

Innovation and Achievement Are Punished, Not Rewarded In Q cultures, CEOs and their staff see their roles only in terms of doing what the volunteer wants rather than challenging volunteer assumptions and leading new efforts. Yet the opposite behavior is what leaders like Ralph Nappi, president of the American Tool Distributors' Association and chair of the Center for Association Leadership, think is necessary for nonprofit survival. In an *Executive Update* article, Mr. Nappi is quoted as saying:

> Association executives now must do more than take orders; they must help craft what those orders will be . . . a leader will find out where the pain points are for members and then develop products and services that address those pain points. The member can tell you about the pain, but if they knew what to do about it, they would have done it.[13]

So what happens when "new-thinking" managers collide with Q-culture staff? Excited by the prospect of uniting professional experience with cause and oblivious to nonprofit behavior, these managers arrive full of energy and new ideas and partner with staff and capable volunteers to confront or work around the entrenched bureaucracies. Things start to happen.

Improvement and the introduction of new programs attract the attention and accolades of volunteers who have long desired such changes. But being out in the open and accountable for the success of the programs also earns new-thinking managers enemies in the vested volunteer and Q staff ranks.

Q managers operate from behind committees and derive power from pleasing vested volunteers. They resent that new-thinking managers do not do this, and they do not want the accountability and extra work that will come if the new management style is adopted. Their complaints add fuel to the rumblings of vested volunteers, who resist what they view as more staff control. And Q-culture CEO allegiance lies with vested volunteers and Q staff. They hear and grant the Q staff's demand for an "equal playing field."

That means the same rights, recognition, salary, and privileges as new-thinking managers without the added responsibilities. Q staff is not asked to shoulder more responsibility or assume the accountability of new programs; new-thinking managers continue to do so but must also coordinate nonmission output committees, support meaningless inside activities, and keep volunteers happy.

Of course, it's much more difficult to succeed at new programs than to maintain existing ones. Inevitably, some new programs fail. Failures count against new-thinking managers, but points are not taken from Q staff for not trying. The situation can be compared to a figure skating competition where skaters get downgraded for falling but gain no extra points for degree of jump difficulty. Before long, skaters stop attempting the more difficult jumps and reduce their performance to safe, lackluster leaps.

And that's exactly what makes Q cultures toxic. The reward for leading and achieving is more work, more enemies, and more chance of failure. By following orders, however, you get the same reward without the extra work and enemies. Which would you chose?

New-thinking managers come to understand these rules and the difficulties that will be encountered with each new change. Either they burn out and leave or—worse yet—they burn out and stay. Neither choice is a very happy ending for the individual or organization.

Vested Volunteers and Staff Are Entrenched One way that staff accumulates Q and job security is by cultivating influential volunteer leaders and turning them into friends. In such a way, staff members create their own little fiefdoms protected by strong member advocates. These fiefdoms do not exist for the good of the nonprofit but for what this small oligarchy defines as good. Consider the lament of the following CEO as recounted on a Web-based list serve:

> My staff director worked closely with a longtime board member who also chaired the development committee. Unfortunately, she spent more time manipulating the board than she did in raising money. When I put the director on notice that her performance should improve, she just stepped up her board communications regarding her value to the organization. Since her performance did not improve, I asked her to leave.
>
> The board member then demanded that the staff director be reinstated and an investigation opened into "CEO improprieties." Luckily, the board chairman was a retired head of personnel who believed in separation of governance and management. He called for a special board session to review the allegations. There, the board member was forced to admit that he had no idea of the development director's real performance or any evidence of CEO malfeasance except for what she told him. He and the rest of the board backed down, and I finally hired a capable new development director.

Staff/volunteer fiefdoms endanger what should be an inherent advantage of the volunteer/staff system: the checks and balances and give and take that make for better decision making. When volunteers and staff members become entrenched over a long period of time, they fail to challenge each other's assumptions and ideas. Such cliques also discourage other volunteers who might contribute new knowledge and better ideas.

Volunteer and Staff Leaders Engage in the Melinda Tuan, in an article for the *Stanford Social Innovation Review,* describes the process by which philanthropies obtain grants as "a dance of deceit."[14] This dance is the process that nonprofits must go through to show low program administration costs in order to attract foundation monies.

Using the term in a slightly different context, volunteers and staff engage in a similar *dance of deceit.* Staff members do the work, but they pretend that the volunteers did. This CEO illustrates the dance as recounts on a newsgroup how he resolved a common board complaint:

> We are a national association, and our board meets monthly via conference call. We have 15 active volunteer committees that also meet monthly. A staff director and a board member are assigned to each committee, and for each call the board member is supposed to report important committee activities.
>
> Needless to say, most of the time the report made to the board was "no report," and committee action items were missed. Then, I started a new procedure where the week before the board meeting, the staff director writes a report for the board member; the board member reads the report on the call, and the board feels informed and happy.

What's really happening here? The staff member is doing the work of the board member, attending the meeting and recording important actions, while the board member is only pretending to do so by reading the staff report. Leaving aside the all-too-obvious observation that a part-time board and staff of seven could not possibly properly liaise on the monthly activities of 15 committees, what possible mission purpose is served by a board member pretending to do the work that someone else did?

The destructive effects of the *dance of deceit* are not difficult to see. The dance reinforces harmful industry stereotypes such as *I'm the Expert.* These archetypes keep nonprofits frozen in the past rather than thriving in the present, because only the benefit component exists, and temporary part-time volunteers can do it all.

Equally important, the *dance of deceit* sows seeds of disrespect and mistrust between the nonprofit's most essential relationship—volunteer and professional staff. The dance acts like a virus running through every nonprofit decision and activity. It's the dance of boards that develop amnesia regarding CEO activities gone awry; it's the dance that Q staff do as they praise committee work in public and laugh at committee ineptness in private; it's the dance of high-Q CEOs who say "yes" at board meetings and undermine board decisions with senior staff and colleagues.

Broadly speaking, the *dance of deceit* keeps high-Q staff employed while forcing would-be high performers to play down their talents. This requirement to avoid confrontation with vested volunteers and lower performance to exist in the *Smile, Not Skill* culture is another big reason why high achievers feel forced to leave the nonprofit industry.

Board Term and/or CEO Tenure Equal Reality Q-driven cultures rarely maintain the good practices that are found in high-performing nonprofits. Things like governance policy manuals, measurable goals for governance and management, written distinctions between governance and management, and assigned accountability for organizational success do not exist.

Neither does objective institutional memory. Q cultures substitute subjective opinion for objective performance measurement; everything is open for interpretation, and anyone can do the interpreting. This fosters a high degree of anxiety and lots of uncertainly, which in turn breeds gossip. Gossip presented as fact passes for organizational communication. Characters can be assassinated by just one bad word broadly circulated in an anecdotal e-mail.

Just as beauty is in the eye of the beholder, so institutional memory is in the eye of the current board and/or CEO. The "facts" of past nonprofit actions are often just the folklore of a long-tenured CEO or vested volunteers. Lacking any institutionalized method of passing along an objective version of history leaves everyone free to reconstruct the folklore to fit their own needs.

A Few Last Words on Stealth Toxic Cultures The presence of any of these signs serves as an early warning system that a toxic culture could develop, and it is wise to heed these early warning signs and nip a toxic culture in the bud before it has the chance to fully form. Once a Q culture is in full bloom, it does not lend itself to quick or easy fixes. Often, the board faces not only the need to replace the CEO but the eventual turnover of many key staff members. Especially painful is confronting entrenched vested volunteers who thrive in toxic cultures.

What's it like when the board hires the wrong CEO, fails to properly oversee that CEO, and friendship is the only way volunteers and staff get anything done? Our *Live Lesson,* "If the CEO Performs Badly, Blame the Staff" and *Salt Mines* exercises will answer this question.

A *Live Lesson*: "If the CEO Fails, Blame the Staff"

Introducing the Principals

For this lesson, our nonprofit is a health care organization that we'll call the National Surgeon's League (NSL). NSL has a reputation for publishing a prestigious research journal and holding a large annual conference with an exhibition hall full of all the latest paraphernalia. The conference traditionally announces the key findings of important research studies done during the year.

In the past, this one conference contributed almost three-quarters of NSL's revenue for the year, but attendance of both regular attendees and vendor partners has dropped precipitously in the past five years. As revenues are continuing to drop, panic is in the air around NSL leaders.

Live Lesson Essentials

- NSL hired a research firm two years ago to do an environmental analysis. The board and multiple planning committees partnered with another consultant, and the result was a 26-page document called the NSL Action Plan.
- The present CEO, Dennis, is a retired surgeon, one of the pioneers in his specialty field. The immediate past president, Gary, who sits on the current board and chaired the board that hired Dennis, brought Dennis in almost two years ago to take charge of staff and execute the Action Plan. In addition, for the first time NSL is facing competitive pressure from another organization that started running a better annual conference. The board wants Dennis to turn around the downward slide and find new sources of revenue.
- Dennis is NSL's third CEO in 18 years. CEO number one was another retired doctor, Monica. Everyone liked her and she held that position for 15 years. However, the next CEO, John, was fired after three years, but not before 75 percent of the staff turned over. Because Monica succeeded and her background was medical, and John did not and his background was managerial, one of the prime search criteria was to find a doctor rather than another association executive.
- Despite Dennis's affability and willingness to concede to the board's wishes, the new president of the board, Erica, is increasingly unhappy with Dennis's performance. Past president Gary does not agree with her assessment; he's been friends with Dennis for years. Erica chairs NSL's five-member executive committee, and Gary is a member of the committee.
- NSL has an operating budget of $4 million. Its staff structure consists of a CEO and 21 full-time staff members, and the volunteer structure includes a fifteen-member board, a five-member executive committee, and ten volunteer committees. Exhibit 6.1 shows the NSL staff organizational chart.

Salt Mines #1: (Situation)

When in doubt, bring in a consultant . . .

- President Erica is talking with one of the executive committee members and says, "I just got another e-mail from the marketing director, who seems to have no idea

EXHIBIT 6.1 THE NSL STAFF ORGANIZATIONAL CHART

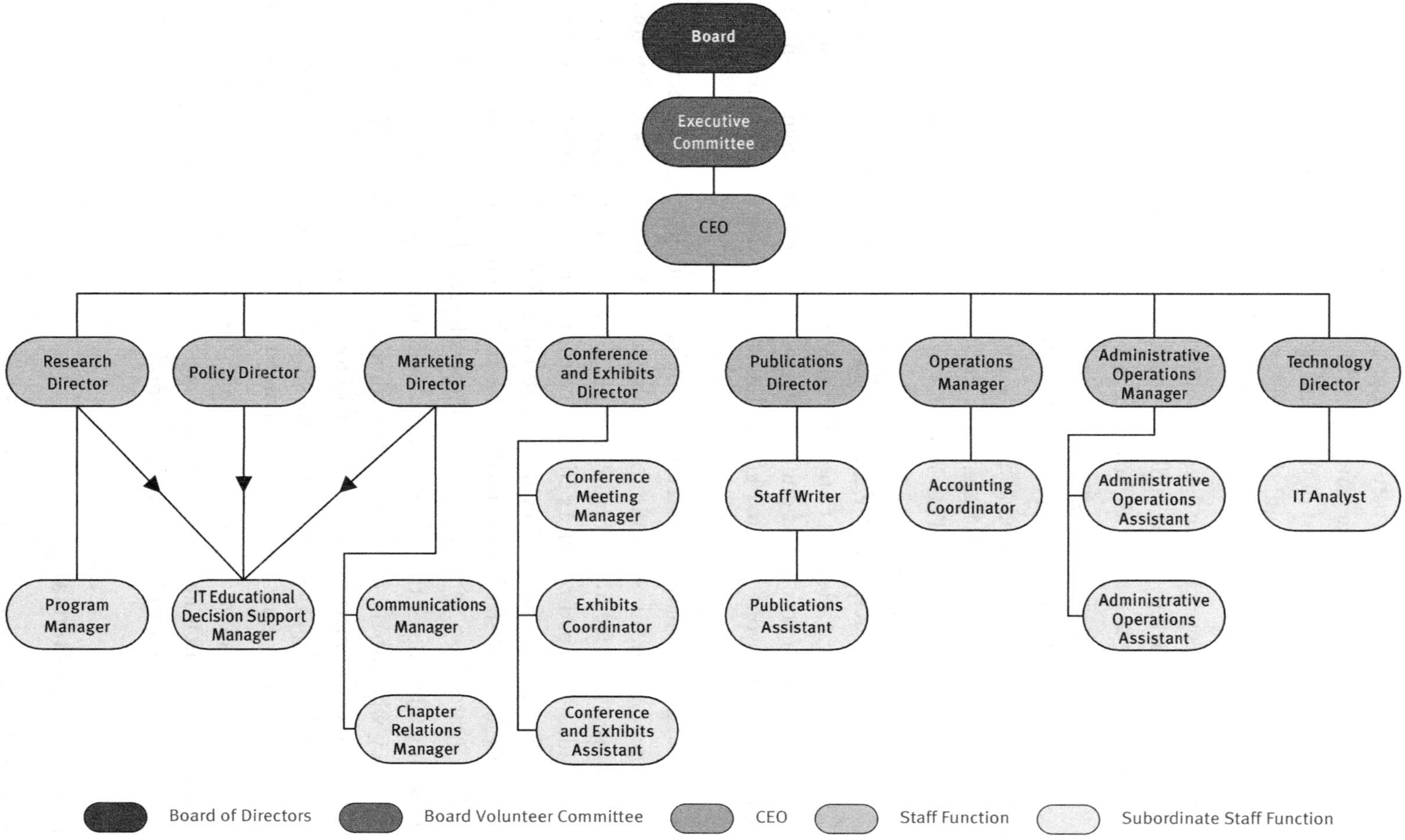

Board

Executive Committee

CEO

Research Director

Policy Director

Marketing Director

Conference and Exhibits Director

Publications Director

Operations Manager

Administrative Operations Manager

Technology Director

Program Manager

IT Educational Decision Support Manager

Communications Manager

Chapter Relations Manager

Conference Meeting Manager

Exhibits Coordinator

Conference and Exhibits Assistant

Staff Writer

Publications Assistant

Accounting Coordinator

Administrative Operations Assistant

Administrative Operations Assistant

IT Analyst

Board of Directors | Board Volunteer Committee | CEO | Staff Function | Subordinate Staff Function what we approved at the board meeting. Our CEO just can't seem to communicate things right." The other member adds, "Well, our past president is against it, but thank goodness the rest of the board agreed to bring in consultants to help us evaluate whether Dennis and the entire staff structure are what we need for the Action Plan."

- Erica is also answering her e-mail—several are from staff directors, all asking for direction on various board endeavors with which they are involved. "Darn," she thinks, "on my last visit I did explain that CEO Dennis is really trying to do a good job, and they should give him more of a chance. Hopefully, this executive coach that we hired can help him communicate more."
- Past president Gary is miffed and talking with a board member. He confides to him, "Dennis is having a rough time. He's a great guy but a couple of staff directors are making his life miserable. They're Erica's friends and talk with her all the time. He doesn't know what to do."

  His colleague responds, "Well, we're just lucky to find him. You know how bad the last CEO was. He didn't know anything about medicine, and no one respected him. At least Dennis speaks our language, and he's certainly giving us more information than anyone ever has before. I'm sure that you've told him not to worry about all this."
- Back at the international office, the consultants set up an initial meeting with staff and send a sign-up schedule for individual interviews with key directors. CEO Dennis, who is feeling increasingly under fire from President Erica, knows that the consultants are part of Erica's efforts to evaluate him, but he thinks that they might actually help his cause. They'll see how much he's trying to do and support his appeal for more staff. He immediately e-mails to the consultants the full 26-page NSL Action Plan and the latest board spreadsheet of tactical activities.
- Meanwhile, one of the staff members sends an e-mail to the incoming president, Nancy, who also sits on the executive committee, complaining, "Dennis just sprang this consultant meeting on us. I'm out of town, another member is on vacation, and we didn't even find out about this until we got back. Then, it was a note in our mailbox saying that some consultants are going to evaluate staff. What is going on?"
- One of the board members sees Nancy at the hospital. Nancy starts talking about some of the staff issues when the board member interrupts with a question, "I didn't realize that's what these consultants are doing. Is there a problem with Dennis's performance?"

Salt Mines #1: (Aftermath)

Figuring out what is happening is a full-time job . . .

- Staff is buzzing. "Who are these consultants and what are they doing here?" The marketing director calls the education director and asks, "Are you going to tell them what's really going on here?" The education director responds, "I'm not sure. CEO Dennis did hire us, and it seems clear that president Erica has it in for him. And both she and incoming president Nancy know how we feel, and nothing happened when we talked with them the last time." The marketing director interjects, "I'm not so sure, maybe that's why the consultant's are here. Let's go to the meeting and see."

- The board is humming. The board at large is trying to figure out what the executive committee is up to. After seeing Nancy, the board member calls another board member and asks, "Did you know what those consultants are really doing? I thought they were just part of the Action Plan initiative, but now I don't know. I bumped into Nancy, and she tried to downplay it, but I think that something is wrong, maybe with Dennis. Do you know anything about this?"
- President Erica sends an e-mail in advance of the consultants' meeting, trying to calm staff fears by stating that the consultants are just part of NSL's ongoing efforts to make sure that staff has the necessary resources and infrastructure to implement the Action Plan.
- The education director meets with the marketing director over lunch saying, "See, this really is the board's attempt to answer our questions. We should tell them that Dennis does nothing and all of it falls on our shoulders. Maybe we'll finally get rid of him and get some real help out here."
- Meanwhile, the longtime operations manager is talking with a friend, "I think the consultants are here to cut staff. I don't think that Dennis likes me very much. I'll talk to a couple of board members to see what they know."

Lesson Primer *Salt Mines* #1: In the Absence of Facts, Everyone Makes Up Their Own

When information does not come from official sources, board and staff friendships are the inside track to what is going on.

In a sense, both President Erica and CEO Dennis are doing the same thing—sharing only partial information, which conveys the impression that ulterior motives are afoot. Human nature being what it is, neither board nor staff will rest until it can get to the bottom of what is really going on—and in the absence of facts, they all make up their own stories.

When uncertainty rules, not much else gets done . . .

When emotions run high, organizational energy gets diverted from mission to fear, anger, and self-survival. Board members try to figure out what the executive committee is doing instead of producing governance outcomes. The operations manager stops any future-oriented projects, thinking future employment is uncertain. Dennis spends his time pandering to board members. Past president Gary spends his time soothing

CEO Dennis's feelings and venting to fellow board members rather than using his informed wisdom to mentor other board members.

Rather than confronting Dennis's poor performance, the executive committee members are arguing among themselves based on their personal feelings about Dennis and each other. Gary refuses to listen to Erica because he thinks she's micromanaging the situation, and he's disgruntled about her changing all the things he did during his term. Erica is doubly angry because she feels Gary is making excuses for what she views as the poor performance of his old pal and colleague Dennis. Incoming president Nancy just wants everyone to get along and things to be settled before she takes office.

The job of a board president is to keep the board on track, not to derail it, and the constant sniping of two of the most influential executive committee members makes meetings contentious. As head of the executive committee, Erica sometimes forgets to tell the board everything that is going on. What a good leader should do at this point is step back, call a timeout, and get everyone focused again on what is important—making sure that mission goals are clear, CEO performance objectives are measurable, and objectively evaluating Dennis's performance.

The job of a CEO is to keep staff on track, prioritizing what is important and focusing all business component resources toward mission delivery. Instead, Dennis creates mayhem by announcing the arrival of the consultants in the most alarming terms and by failing to make sure that all key people were at the kickoff meeting. He fails to see the seriousness of the consultants visit as past president Gary tells him that this is just another instance of Erica's micromanaging.

Salt Mines #2: (Situation)

A rudderless ship drifts . . .

- CEO Dennis tells the consultants, "Every week Erica comes up with more things, and the directors really resist when I tell them that this is what the board wants. You saw my spreadsheet. We have over 25 initiatives underway, and I'm doing all that I can to keep track of everything."
- The monthly executive committee conference call is still going on after an hour and a half. Erica sums up the call, "We need to wrap things up. Dennis's operating report generated a lot of discussion. The main thing is that we get better communications, and the new steering committee will help coordinate information between us, committees, and staff."
- The staff directors continue with their consultant meetings. The technology manager explains, "Dennis invites me sometimes, but I don't go to the monthly meetings. It's mostly about conferences. A board member that I help with his office technology told me something's going on with a Web display at the conference, so I'm going to the next one."

He goes on, "None of the other directors really understand what I do anyway. They just look on my department as a help desk function, but that's not why Dennis hired me. My focus is using technology to create revenue and lower expenses, not to listen to a bunch of complaints about the system. Besides, I told Dennis soon after I was hired that the system was fine, we just needed some upgrades. Now that they're in, people don't use them."

- As the director/consultant interviews continue, what becomes clear is that then-president Gary and CEO Dennis basically created last year's tactics that are part of Action Plan initiatives by themselves, and then just presented the plan to the board for approval. Dennis didn't meet to discuss the plan with staff or solicit any meaningful input from his direct reports. Half the staff directors haven't even seen the results that Dennis includes with his weekly board report. They just do the committee's work and rely on a friend on the executive committee or a committee chair to clue them in as necessary.
- Dennis sends an e-mail to the marketing director, "Where is your weekly report? I need to get my information in to the board, and you're holding me up." He calls out to his assistant, "Tell the conference director to come see me about these registration figures."
- Suzy, the IT decision support manager, is in the conference director's office expressing her frustrations. Suzy works for three directors and is always swamped. She's explaining to the conference manager, "I don't think that the operations department has entered all the registrations yet, but the assistant is out for the day and no one can find anything on the desk. They're really confused over there, and I'm just going to start entering these again myself."

Salt Mines #2: (Aftermath)

And charts its own course . . .

- Incoming president Nancy calls the publications director after the board conference call, because she doesn't understand Dennis's answer about the status of a journal project. The publications director exclaims, "I'm so glad that you called. We've been a little delayed, but those summaries will be out of the next issue of the journal just like the board wants." Nancy pauses for a moment, and then responds, "Well, that's not exactly what we meant. Those summaries are an important part of the journal; we want to explore other suppliers, maybe expand some of the summaries and try a little different format."
- The publications director shoots an e-mail to Dennis letting him know that the board does want the summaries left in the journal, and that it will cost quite a bit at this late date to change the issue, but Nancy told her to do it. Meanwhile, the publications director bumps into the conference director in the lunch room and

says loudly enough to be overheard by the two staff people in the room, "Why do I even bother talking to Dennis? I can't rely on a single thing he says. I can't get to anything on my desk, and now this!"

The conference director looks a little sheepish and says, "Oh, I'm so sorry. I knew that wasn't what the board wanted. Erica mentioned it when we were looking at the conference agenda."

- President Erica asks Dennis why he isn't using the project software that the board authorized to track the progress of items in the Action Plan in order to provide his weekly board report; it would make reviewing everything on the call easier. Dennis responds, "The managers were trained, and they just won't use it, but I'll get on them about it." Erica slams down the phone and e-mails incoming president Nancy. She writes, "I'm so tired of trying to track everything that Dennis does. Every time I think we're making progress, he doesn't follow up."
- Suzy and the conference director manage to find and count the missing enrollments. The conference director enters Dennis's office and shows him the latest conference attendance figures. Dennis says, "Why aren't these figures better? We thought that holding the conference in conjunction with the International Anesthesiologists Society meeting would really bring people in."

  "We did try to tell you that wasn't a good idea. It dilutes the education programs and the conference committee wasn't keen on mingling with the anesthesiologists," the conference director retorts.

  Dennis sighs and says, "Erica wanted this, now look what's happened. The board will blame me." He immediately e-mails Gary to inform him that there may be a problem with the conference numbers, and he wants to discuss it with him before he talks to Erica.
- Suzy resigns a month later. She tells one of the directors, "I really loved my old job as program manager, but it's just too stressful working for so many managers. I don't have any control over how operations does their job, and the technology department doesn't want to explain anything."

  The directors try to talk Suzy out of leaving by offering her another position, but she's already accepted another job. One director moans to the other, "What are we going to do now? We talked Dennis into taking the enrollment work away from the operations manager; he'll just have to figure something else out now."

Lesson Primer *Salt Mines* #2: Many Mini-CEOs Do Not One CEO Make

Another committee and a strong senior staff cannot make up for a weak CEO.

In the absence of top-down priority setting, people set their own priorities. In the absence of a strong CEO leader, the senior staff becomes a collection of mini-CEOs, each directing priorities depending on which board member wants what.

Performance cultures must confront performance problems . . .

The ability to communicate clearly—to understand the reality of what is being said and transmit that reality to someone else—is an essential CEO management skill. Dennis sees his job as just passing board information on to staff verbatim without any sense of strategy or direction. That's bad enough, but he doesn't do a very good job of passing it along verbatim either.

The board must hold the CEO accountable for articulating its mission goals to staff correctly. Although it's clear that he is not and that the majority of the executive committee is frustrated with Dennis's lack of communication skills, they work around rather than confront a serious CEO performance problem. They provide an executive coach to "help Dennis" talk directly with staff and create a "steering committee," to ostensibly help communications.

Dennis echoes the "work-around rather than confront the problem" style of management on staff. Everyone in operations was complaining about the operations manager, so Dennis simply transferred the operations staff to another manager. When the technology manager complained about his title, Dennis made the position a director, without telling anyone why. When the policy manager had problems with the policy assistant, Dennis moved her into the operations department "where she couldn't hurt anything."

The end result is that staff performance weaknesses were not corrected; tasks not performed well just got moved elsewhere. The good performers got punished with more work, and the bad performers got less; the former worked late every night while the latter went home on time. Eventually the good performers like Suzy left, while the poor performers kept the seats warm until an effective CEO was hired.

Process is not outcomes . . .

No one can accomplish 25 initiatives. As an outspoken industry consultant once said, "My cat Buster can design a plan like that, but it's doubtful any of those initiatives will actually be in place in five years." A 26-page Action Plan is doomed from the beginning, but CEO Dennis smiles and says nothing as the board throws in new venture after new venture.

When Dennis joined NSL, the board made it clear that his focus should be stopping the conference hemorrhage and finding alternative revenue sources. So, the board keeps coming up with programs, and Dennis tracks them and reports them as new revenue programs. The staff knows that no real progress is being made on half these programs, but Dennis diligently tracks activities on his spreadsheets, and the board reviews them at each meeting.

The staff directors had no input on the plan initiatives. They let Dennis fill in what he wants because they know half that stuff will fall off the radar screen by the next plan. Dennis stopped having weekly senior staff meetings because it's easier to have the directors e-mail their weekly reports.

What this means is that no one on staff is buying into the goals other than the CEO, and Dennis cannot accomplish these goals directly. One of the reasons to hold meaningful staff meetings is that it is an efficient way to share information, resolve important issues, set priorities, and not have everyone running around trying to solve the same problem. Most of all, these meetings are a place to rally the troops, to keep everyone excited about mission, and to expose problems that may affect the success of ongoing and new programs.

At NSL, directors act in a vacuum, as did the technology director, who upgraded systems without finding out what the users really want. The result is an achievement on the technology director's weekly report, but a system that does little to improve overall office efficiency.

If the CEO doesn't model good management, neither will the staff . . .

Although the first CEO, Monica, was liked by all, she did not manage staff well—most of her directors were Q-managers who worked very well with the volunteer committees that maintained the two major programs, the annual conference, and the research journal. The CEO who followed Monica was terrible, but the board took three years to fire him, and during that time 75 percent of the staff left, including a talented research director who managed the journal and research studies.

Just like the Big USA Museum board, the NSL board saw its CEO problem not as a management one, but as a "get the right technical skills" issue. Unfortunately for NSL, they couldn't have picked a worse strategy. A strong CEO with strong management skills is especially what is needed when the staff organization needs rebuilding.

Dennis did hire some qualified directors; people like the technology director had talent, and in fact most of the directors knew the problems and had the talent to solve them, but they needed a leader to give them direction and a mentor to help them grow and reach their potential. They did not get that, and in turn, they did not provide that environment for their staff; instead, it was every person for him or herself.

Salt Mines #3: (Situation)

If a tree falls in the forest and there's no one there . . .

- The conference director is talking with the consultant and tells her, "One of the things that our surgeon members really want is to be alerted on new techniques immediately. They feel our conference no longer focuses on their higher-level needs, and since our attendances have been down in recent years, some of our best vendors go to a bigger show. We've been talking about this for two years now, but with all the management changes, no one does anything."
- Incoming president Nancy is at dinner with another board member and says, "Part of our membership decline is that our programs are too basic. "Do you remember that committee that I chaired, the one that came up with the idea for a fellowship

program for researchers? Everyone loved the concept, but I have no idea what happened to it. Every time I ask, the research director just tells me that there's no staff for it."

- The staff technology director discovers a great new software package for tracking and distilling the latest surgery techniques. He sends it to the conference director excitedly asking if they can profile this at the upcoming conference. She turns him down.

Salt Mines #3: (Aftermath)

An idea without resources is just a dream . . .

- The research director is having lunch with a colleague and mulling over his previous conversation with the consultants. He complains, "These people really bug me. They asked for ideas on revenue, and I told them—do e-mail alerts on the latest research and offer nonmember pricing for the research journal. Now they want me to talk to Dennis, and you know what he'll do."
- His colleague laughs and responds, "I can't believe you opened your mouth. We're still cleaning up the last new program that Dennis mangled . . . we told him that the fellowship program could not work the way he wanted, but he made us go ahead anyway. Well, the person that I had working on it left, and it's just going to sit there until I have some help."
- Even though the conference director thinks the technology director's new software has merit, she doesn't have time to look at anything new, because she is up to her neck in alligators with the attendance figures down. Plus, as she tells one of her friends, "It must be nice to have lots of time to butt into someone else's area. He should be working on a better enrollment system, not looking at software in his spare time."

Lesson Primer *Salt Mines* #3: The Answer to a Problem Lies Within

Most of the time, the answer to a problem is the question that is never asked.

One of the fallouts from letting staff set their own priorities is that good projects get dropped or simply die when the next activity needs those same resources. Without a high-performing CEO, NSL has no mechanism to consistently ask the right questions or to get staff resources together to share informed wisdom. Activity drowns out any free time for the talent left on staff, and the lack of cooperation and respect between CEO and board makes everything more difficult and even more stressful.

Dennis is focused on process and reports, telling people what to do, and courting influential members. He sits in his office and, even though a director is two doors away, relies on e-mail for his main communication. Staff members likewise stay in their silos, venturing out only when there's a problem. New programs require collaboration and innovation, but the NSL staff is in survival mode. They are keeping their heads down, and the last thing they want to do is risk trying something new.

In the final analysis, it is the responsibility of the CEO to make sure that every director is guided by mission and makes decisions for the benefit of the entire organization, not just the individual or departments. Dennis should generate excitement for mission and mission goals; he should demand action and reward achievement of those goals; and he should motivate the troops when times are tough. Dennis is failing as a leader in all major categories, yet the board fails to recognize and confront his poor performance.

The Economic Cost of the *Smile, Not Skill* Elephant

Let's examine three areas where the cost of our smiling pachyderm is particularly high:

1. Strategic Planning
2. Annual Conference
3. New Programs

Strategic Planning The NSL board spent $75,000 for a research firm to do an environmental analysis. It is important to scan the environment, but if the board was doing its job—not micromanaging staff and connecting with members on an ongoing basis—a majority of this cost might be saved. The board's scanning strategies may rightly include an outside firm, but there were no surprises on this expensive report, just a lot of pages explaining what they already knew from being in the industry.

The board also spent a total of $35,000 to have another consultant work with the board and planning committees to create the final NSL Action Plan. Again, if the board had an ongoing planning process in place, it should be able to define annual mission goals and the CEO should be accountable for working with staff on the initiatives, thus saving most of the consultant's fee.

The current operational audit costs NSL another $25,000, and the executive coach for Dennis is on a retainer of $1,000 per month.

Annual Conference Before the original research director left, this person sounded the alarm for three years that trends were changing and that another competitor would be holding a similar conference in the future. Over the years, each new board talked about this a lot, in particular the need to diversify NSL's offerings so that one program did not contribute so much of the total revenue.

When this research director left, NSL lost the ability to please the market that was its bread and butter—the elite cadre of surgeons who require highly specialized information and education. As NSL dumbed down its conference, the surgeons looked elsewhere for information—and found it from another association. When the surgeons started going to another meeting, vendors who relied on foot traffic started to look at where they were going—and started going too. Within five years, a program that had cleared almost $1 million per year was down to $500,000, and NSL didn't have to lose these funds. The board just needed to select and support the right CEO, and the CEO just needed to lead, but neither did so.

New Programs Failure to deal quickly with a problem CEO caused an erosion of NSL revenue from a major core program, the annual conference. Three additional examples of lost potential revenue are:

- NSL's technology director had a cost-saving idea—convert the education manuals to CD—but he doesn't tell the education manager. This generates yet another lost opportunity cost. Converting education manuals to CD would have saved NSL $20,000 annually.
- Given that some 50,000 surgeons don't belong to NSL but might buy a subscription to e-mail alerts, that's another lost $60,000 of revenue per year (1,000 times $5 per month).
- Incoming president Nancy's fellowship program could have been wildly successful in tuition and increased members.

Summing It Up

This chapter began with the question of whether we can replace a departing CEO and volunteer leaders with people whose skills and experience better align with today's challenges. The answer to this question is "yes," assuming nonprofits hire, support, and properly oversee performance-oriented CEOs and work to prevent Q-cultures from developing.

A quote by Marianne Williamson seems appropriate here: "Your playing small doesn't serve the world. There's nothing enlightened about shrinking so that other people won't feel insecure around you."[15]

A culture that encourages staff members to play down their professional skills in order to be liked is not a culture that encourages performance and innovation. It creates disillusionment and burnout in those who thrill to the challenge of accomplishing something, and it forces the exodus of the people who might successfully build a very different, high-performing nonprofit.

NOTES

1. Paige Hull Teegarden, *Nonprofit Executive Leadership and Transitions Survey* (Maagance Consulting funded by the Annie E. Casey Foundation, 2004), 4.
2. Mike Gallagher, *High Turnover of Executives Hurting Nonprofits* (Council of Michigan Foundations, March 2004), 1.

3. Id.
4. Jeanne Peters, Anushka Fernandopulle, Jan Masaoka, Christina Chan, and Tim Wolfred, *Help Wanted: Turnover and Vacancy in Nonprofits* (CompassPoint, 2002), 2.
5. Noah Isackson, "Giovinella Gonthier: A Civility Engineer," *The Chicago Tribune Magazine* (December 29, 2002): 8.
6. John von Rhein, "CSO Gives Fogel Sendoff with Carter World Premiere," *The Chicago Tribune,* Metro, May 31, 2003.
7. George L. Hanbury, Alka Sapat, and Charles W. Washington, "Know Yourself and Take Charge of Your Own Destiny: The 'Fit' Model of Leadership," *Public Administration Review* 64, no. 5 (September/October 2004): 570.
8. Timothy Wolfred, Mike Allison, and Jan Masaoka, *Leadership Lost: A Study on Executive Director Tenure and Experience* (CompassPoint Nonprofit Services, March 1999).
9. Gwyneth K. Shaw, "NASA Culture Blamed for Shuttle Safety Woes," *The Chicago Tribune,* news 9, April 13, 2004.
10. Henry Mintzberg, "The MBA Menace," *Fast Company* (June 2004): 31.
11. Ulrike M. Malmendier, "For Most CEOs, Stardom Doesn't Equal Success," *Chicago Tribune,* bus. 9, February 14, 2005.
12. Polly LaBarre, "Fresh Start 2002: Weird Ideas that Work," *Fast Company* (January 2002): 54–68.
13. Scott Briscoe, "Leading the Way," *Executive Update,* September 2004.
14. Melinda Tuan, "The Dance of Deceit," *Stanford Social Innovation Review,* Summer 2004.
15. Marianne Williamson, *A Return to Love: Reflections on the Principles of "A Course in Miracles"* (New York, Harper Paperbacks, Reissue edition (April 24, 1996).

CHAPTER 7

The *Read My Lips* Elephant

History will be kind to me because I intend to write it.

—Winston Churchill

Hubris and Nonprofits

Hubris is an interesting word that can easily apply to much of the written and spoken nonprofit language. People engage in hubris as they communicate with excessive pride or arrogance. Nonprofits display the same kind of hubris as they proudly announce organizational activities and new programs that are not supported by marketplace reality.

Nor are nonprofits alone in their tendency toward hubris. Corporations and businesses share this habit. In fact, hubris is so common in business that knowledgeable people tune out the information churned out by public relations machines. But there is a distinct difference between corporate and nonprofit hubris. Corporate hubris does not go unchecked, whereas nonprofit hubris does. Markets punish corporations that can't back up their hype; sales decline, stock prices fall, or companies go bankrupt. Nonprofits, however, are largely immune from such market retributions.

There is nothing wrong with good PR or positioning programs and accomplishments in a positive light, but there is something wrong if this PR lacks any real accomplishment to back it up. Doing is different from rhetoric. At the end of the day, something must exist to show for doing. What lasts is not how something is said, but the reality behind the words and the ability to put ideas into practice.

For nonprofits this presents a dilemma. The sector tends to be populated with right-brained people, idealists with superlative speaking and writing skills who can make even mundane ideas seem lofty and admirable. Grandiose verbiage is easy and addictive; it becomes a way of life when leaders are disconnected from the market reality that might deflate such idealism and rhetoric.

Psychiatrist Gordon Livingston, in his book *Too Soon Old, Too Late Smart,* explains:

> We are not what we think, or what we say, or how we feel. We are what we do. Conversely, in judging other people we need to pay attention not to what they promise but how they behave.[1]

Although Livingston is speaking about individuals, his comment also applies to organizational behavior. Nonprofits are not what their leaders say they are; nonprofits are their mission accomplishments. The *Read My Lips* elephant thrives each time a nonprofit president announces grand plans that are disconnected from the resources needed to deliver those plans. Or when a CEO announces the use of a new technique like the Balanced Scorecard to the board without providing the necessary tools or training for staff to actually use it. As such pronouncements are made, the *Read My Lips* elephant sits next to the affected parties as they share a common thought: "Who the heck is going to do all this?"

In This Chapter

The objective of this chapter is to identify outsized rhetoric and examine why nonprofit leaders so frequently engage in such language. We'll see how the *Read My Lips* elephant influences the actual workplace in the *Live Lesson,* "Great Is Just a State of Mind." And we'll evaluate the quantitative costs of this elephant in terms of organizational performance.

Outsized Rhetoric: Up Close and Personal

Hubris on the Inside

How do we recognize hubris? What signs portend its presence? Outsized rhetoric is so much the norm that it often takes a skeptic who is unafraid of asking pointed questions or a person who is intimately involved in the subject matter to uncover conflicting facts. For example, these situations illustrate the difference between hubris and actual fact:

1. *"The latest glossy annual report (2002) of the American Bible Society proudly lists the famous money manager Sir John Templeton as a senior trustee."*[2]

   Reality: Templeton left the charity's governing board in 1991 and, when queried, knew nothing about the current use of his name.

2. *Upon completion of a refurbished auditorium, the president of the Chicago Symphony states, "to my ears, Orchestra Hall now ranks as one of the finer concert rooms in the world."*[3]

   Reality: Many music critics and dedicated season ticket members consider the auditorium acoustics inferior to the sound enjoyed prior to the "improvements."

In the first example, the American Bible Society (ABS) trades on the name of Mr. Templeton in order to bolster the organization's image. Only an insider or, in this case a reporter, has the knowledge or access to the research necessary to reveal that fact. Interestingly enough, at the time of this news item, ABS was hemorrhaging money and accumulating a history of bad business deals that cost the organization millions of dollars. Employee morale was low, and insiders were leaking a stream of damaging internal documents to the media. But the public pronouncements of the CEO kept indicating that fundraising was strong and morale high.

The Chicago Symphony example illustrates the use of words that indicate a rank order that exists primarily in the subjective mind of the originator rather than an objective outside source. It doesn't take any in-depth knowledge to recognize that words like *premier*, *world-class,* and *foremost authority* might be good indicators of hubris at work. These words should trigger logical questions in the listener's mind (e.g., Does someone really visit and rank all the symphony auditoriums in the world, and if so, what criteria are used?).

Usually such questions voiced aloud elicit answers that go something like this: "We think it is true, so if we say it is true, it must be true." That's the motto of the *Read My Lips* elephant; say something loud enough and often enough, and people will believe it is true.

For example, when BoardSource says it is the premier resource for practical information tools and best practices, training, and leadership development for board members of nonprofit organizations worldwide, we believe it's true. When the ASAE states that it is considered the advocate for the nonprofit sector, we believe that it is.

The reality behind the words "the advocate" and "premier resource" in this example is known to insiders. They might suggest that the ASAE is an advocate for mainly association executives, and BoardSource is a premier resource primarily for philanthropic organizations and foundations.

Use of such outsized rhetoric reaches its zenith at annual meetings and in nonprofit newsletters. Presidents try to impress volunteers with board accomplishments and praise committees for myriad new endeavors while CEOs embellish every staff sneeze with meaning and accomplishment.

Nonprofits even hype accomplishments when it's illogical and slightly silly to do so. A financially challenged professional institute sent a letter to a colleague that shows a unique kind of hubris. It went something like this:

> We've sold our building, are looking for new quarters, and had to reduce expenditures in painful ways in order to survive. We've made significant salary reductions for all staff and will lay off others before the end of the year.
>
> Fortunately, we are able to move forward because the Institute has already experienced new growth—last year we established a new library, began a series of new seminars, and opened a new center. In the coming years, we will provide more programs for

> specific audiences, present courses and workshops in various locations, and participate in more joint programs.
>
> But, despite the drastic cuts and generous loans from several members, unless this appeal is successful, we could end the year with a shortfall; please seriously consider and respond to this request for contributions.

Leaving aside the wisdom of the "we're desperate, please bail us out" style of fund raising, even when a nonprofit is down and out, it cannot resist the temptation to hype programs and services. It seems unlikely that a nonprofit that is selling its building, cutting staff, and reducing expenses in "painful ways" can simultaneously expand programs and services.

Donors withdraw support and members leave a nonprofit when the gap between outsized rhetoric and constituent reality becomes obvious. The situation faced by a member of a large nonprofit illustrates the point. This member needed to correct personal information for the nonprofit's directory.

After sending six e-mails, one fax, and two checks, on the fourth phone call an exasperated employee filling in for the person assigned to make such directory corrections told the member that "personnel cutbacks make things difficult, and the person who does this is on leave, but she'll take care of it when she gets back." Despite the employee's assurances, when the directory came out six months later, the entry was still wrong. While all of this was going on, the member was also receiving from the CEO and president glowing e-mails and publications about all the wonderful new things that nonprofit's pending merger would bring.

Rhetoric may be effective in attracting constituents to a nonprofit, but the reality of the quality of service on "bread and butter" issues is how members judge performance. Although hubris may impress committee members, other nonprofit leaders, or the media, it's irritating and meaningless when constituents cannot experience a reality that backs that excessive confidence.

Hubris on the Outside

Nonprofit advisors sometimes encourage and contribute to the sector's hubris. A classic example is the Drucker Foundation's weekly e-mailed newsletter. One of the Foundation's focuses is innovative nonprofit leadership, and each issue highlights in glowing terms an innovative nonprofit program.

Taken at face value, these programs sound very praiseworthy and successful, and they may very well be so. Yet a phone call to the Drucker Foundation yielded this response to a query regarding the success and sustainability of profiled programs: "Following up is something that we'd like to do, but we just don't have the resources at this time."

The Drucker Foundation rightly deserves kudos for showcasing creative ideas, but whether those programs are successfully put into operation and are sustainable is equally important. Innovation disconnected from the measurement of the marketplace is just another form of hubris. Consider the following story that further illustrates how sector advisors encourage nonprofit hubris. In a widely circulated board newsletter, a board member recounts the following situation:

> Our organization got into trouble when our longtime executive director left. Our reserves quickly went from $700,000 to $75,000. As we were close to broke, the board made the decision not to hire a new ED to save cash and avoid any complication with a possible merger that we were exploring. We agreed that keeping the program staff was the top priority, and though some board members left in disagreement, we assumed the management duties ourselves. Sometimes, we even had to meet weekly.
>
> After several months we realized the merger wasn't going to happen and changed our strategy to finding a new ED and creating an organization that would help him or her succeed. At this point, we let the program staff go and kept only the fundraiser.
>
> What kept us going during these hard times? We really believed in the organization. We had pride in how everybody stepped to the plate. We were successful as we now have a great new executive director and great new board leaders who are taking this nonprofit to new heights.

The newsletter editors praise this board and board member, touting the incident as a reminder that boards are a safety net for nonprofit organizations and that the board stepped up and saved the organization's services for hundreds of young people. However, another interpretation closer to reality might be that the board created the problems that it resolved. Initially, the board failed to monitor the CEO and had no succession plan in place. After the CEO leaves, the board attempts hands-on management part-time, pursuing a bad strategy that costs most of the staff their jobs. But the board believes it did a good job and wins kudos from sector advisors.

This is also an excellent example of the *Nonprofit Trouble Cycle* at work. The board ignores the pending problems, steps into the crisis phase with wrong solutions, and quite probably is committing the same error again as the board rests on its laurels and puts all its faith in a new CEO. Institutional memory records the board as saving the organization rather than almost destroying it, so if the CEO leaves in the same manner as the last one, the trouble cycle just repeats itself.

Global words, unsubstantiated rankings, and unwarranted praise are the droppings that show the *Read My Lips* elephant is lurking. These signs should trigger a skeptic response in constituents, encouraging them to step back and examine if there's any reality behind the words.

Why Are Nonprofits Addicted to Outsized Rhetoric?

Most often, people develop habits and those habits persist because, in some way, the habits are rewarded. And that's the short answer as to why nonprofits are so partial to talk rather than action—it's easier, and it works.

But this short answer belies a much more complicated situation. Hubris works because all nonprofits share a certain kind of leadership and operating culture. That culture tends to encourage and reward rhetoric, while failing to recognize and often punishing doing.

We have discussed many aspects of this culture in previous chapters, but the *Read My Lips* elephant highlights some flaws in this environment. They are:

- Talking is acting.
- The bigger the rhetoric, the better the reward.
- Measurements are missing or faulty.
- Institutional memory is unreliable.

Talking Is Acting

Nonprofits make talking, writing, and analysis their main work. CEOs spend their time preparing and delivering information to boards; boards spend their time talking to constituents about board activities; senior staff members devote large portions of their day to coordinating committees and reporting committee activities to staff and vice versa.

Conversations and the generation of reports are considered output in these nonprofits. Most board and committee meetings involve listening and making decisions that often consist of little more than telling staff to move ahead. The more bells and whistles the report has and the flashier the language of the presentation, the more highly rated is its deliverer and the program.

The better that CEOs can speak and write, the smarter they are perceived to be by their boards and constituents. That's because the quality of their speaking performance can easily be assessed immediately, while the ability to judge whether the CEO actually does what is promised can only be assessed with more difficulty and over time.

If impressive language makes one seem smart, it stands to reason that even more impressive language makes one seem even smarter. Busy volunteers and constituents can't devote the kind of time necessary to determine if impressive words are backed by equally impressive implementations. Neither are they present at the headquarters office to detect any warning that rhetoric does not match delivery. Often, volunteer terms are over before the extent of the negligence becomes clear.

Yet another form of hubris relates to decision making. Boards and CEOs make important decisions, announce them with great fanfare, and congratulate themselves on getting things done. Yet, as they move on to the next agenda item, boards ignore a basic truth: making a decision does not guarantee that things will change, nor that the decision will be carried out.

Nonprofit leadership really believes that "we say" means that "they do." After all, the minutes and memos announcing decisions are immediately distributed; smart people will see the value and intent of the decision and execute it. Although it is understandable that extremely busy leaders might wish this were so, the reality is that only follow-up will determine whether people buy in to the idea and are committed to leadership decisions.

This follow-up is so lacking when the act of making decisions is considered "doing." In reality, decision making, announcing a decision, executing, and evaluating are simply parts of an overall system and process; what's important is the output of these processes —a sustainable mission result.

The Bigger the Rhetoric, the Better the Reward

We already know why CEOs paint everything in the best possible light. Optimistic spin is the accepted language of nonprofits, and CEOs gain Q by exaggerating organizational accomplishments (see discussion of Q culture in Chapter 6). Boards that fail to set up effective CEO monitoring systems are in no position, given the limited and part-time nature of their positions, to determine the validity of CEOs' words.

Plus, many CEOs are expected to be the public face of the nonprofit, to travel continually, be involved in multicommittee activities, as well as give speeches and interviews to media. But they also have a full-time management job. Something has to give, and often the management efforts become shallow. Instead of accomplishing things, CEOs find that they can get away with the appearance of accomplishing, and a meeting where they give a good performance is rewarded much more than a meeting that helps the senior staff.

Outside experts also encourage a different source of misleading rhetoric. One of the best examples is the situation that grant-dependent philanthropic organizations face. These nonprofits depend on foundation and government grants and are under exceptional pressure to overstate program value and understate program cost.

Entities like *Forbes* rate charities by weighing the amount of money a nonprofit spends for charitable purposes against that spent for management, administration, and fundraising. The lower the overhead percentage, the higher the nonprofit rating, and the more individual funders and private contributors are encouraged to give to this organization. As Indiana University author Thomas H. Pollak states:

> Yet many people automatically believe that the lower the costs are, the better nonprofits use donations. This misperception provides significant incentive (for charities) to underreport costs or lump them into program expenses, which people are more willing to fund.[4]

As foundations sometimes fund only program rather than operating expenses, nonprofits are forced to either inflate program expenses or underreport operating costs. This practice has the unfortunate result of making what rating agencies and donors consider a "socially acceptable" level of administrative expense to be an unrealistic figure driven more by underreporting than by what charities need to be effective.

A study conducted by the Center for Philanthropy at Indiana University and the Urban Institute's Center on Nonprofits and Philanthropy found that some 37 percent of nonprofits receiving gifts totaling at least $50,000 listed no fundraising costs.[5] It makes little sense that nonprofits can raise money with no related expenses. Spending money on fundraising and administration is necessary to operate and develop new services.

Nonprofit constituents and the realities of the marketplace strongly encourage nonprofits to ignore this fact, while rewarding with donations and grants the nonprofits that tout important new programs while also touting extremely low administrative costs.

Measurements Are Missing or Faulty

Metrics such as spending ratios are quick, easily understood markers that guide donors to which cause gets their dollars. Fairly or unfairly, nonprofits will continue to be rated in periodicals like *Forbes* and *Money* solely by such finite spending ratios, unless better indicators are developed. But this kind of thinking has significant problems. Nonprofits have a business component, but they are not traditional businesses.

Nonprofits are different from traditional businesses in that they have two equally important components: benefit and business. They must make a profit to continue to exist, but that's not why they exist. Nonprofits exist for their stated mission. Unlike traditional businesses, they perform to a double bottom line. Nonprofits must operate the business effectively (e.g., efficient use of resources and ensuring net revenue), but they must first and foremost manage the benefit or mission in an equally effective manner. Spending ratios measure the efficiency of the business component but indicate little about the effectiveness of the benefit component.

A focus on business measurement without an equal focus on benefit measurement masks the true effectiveness of a nonprofit. It's very possible to operate extremely efficiently on the business side while failing to deliver effective mission outcomes. A sector advisor recounts the following story:

> A nonprofit whose mission is to combat world hunger was offered a $1 million grant. Because there were no administrative expenses associated with the grant, accepting the grant would improve the nonprofit's program spending ratio.
>
> However, the deliverables of the grant just provided window dressing rather than addressing the country's real needs. So the nonprofit turned down the grant and instead designed a campaign to raise the funds that would actually do what the country needed.
>
> The organization's decision resulted in a lower spending ratio, which worsened its ranking in national surveys. But, in reality, the decision reflected a high level of leadership and effective management of the benefit or mission component.

This example paints the dilemma that nonprofits face with only quantitative business measurements. Poor nonprofit leadership would grab the $1-million grant and announce the new program with great fanfare. Lots of activity would follow and, although that activity might not address a real mission need, the accompanying rhetoric would make it seem so. Leadership would get kudos by bagging a great project with little administrative costs. Follow-up to determine the benefit impact or total impact on mission would be unlikely.

That's the danger as increasing media attention focuses on the very public examples of nonprofit inefficiency or malfeasance. Attempts to prevent that malfeasance will center mostly on quantitative measurements of business performance. This myopic focus on only the business component will simply exacerbate the hubris in public announcements of program and performance.

Jeffrey Pfeffer and Robert I. Sutton, in the book *The Knowing-Doing Gap,* explore faulty measurement as one of the reasons why organizations know what they should do but don't do it. They explain that it's not enough to measure something; what you measure must really matter. They cite the following measurement mistakes that organizations are prone to make:[6]

1. *A focus on assessing individual performance.* Factors critical to organizational success are systemic. Organizations focus on assessing individual behavior when organizational success relies on the interdependent relationship of many individuals.

   Nonprofit examples: Staff performance reviews center on department accomplishment when program's success is organization-wide; committee and staff actions are viewed separately.

2. *A focus on end-of-process rather than means to ends.* End-of-process measurements tell how well you have done (past behavior) rather than help in understanding what is going right and what is going wrong (future behavior).

   Nonprofit example: Measuring people on outcomes that are dependent on the contributions of many (e.g., number of new members) without a process measurement of what matters to them and what they can directly affect (e.g., timely processing of applications), thus creating stress and frustration but not a more effective process; board that focuses on budget (past actions) rather than the financial indicators that represent future behavior.

3. *Too many metrics and too complicated a process.* Effective measurements that drive behavior need to be simple enough to focus attention on key elements and fair enough so that people believe they can affect the measures. Instead, organizations focus on complexity and comprehensiveness, things that dilute attention and mix important with trivial, instead of focusing on critical issues and processes.

   Nonprofit example: The tendency to make every line item in a budget important rather than creating two or three key indicators that measure issues critical to business and mission.

4. *Measurement does not reflect the business model.* Measurement lies at the heart of both vision and strategy. In measuring things such as values, measurement will depart

from conventional accounting-based indicators, but companies separate vision and strategy from measurement. Leaders concentrate on important, exciting things like vision and strategy while accounting-type people measure.

Nonprofit example: Vision and strategy belong at the board level; it's up to staff to deliver and measure it.

It's easy to agree with Pfeffer and Sutton—only measure what's important—but actually accomplishing this goal is a much more difficult matter. Boards and CEOs are bound to struggle with defining what really matters, and agreeing on what may sometimes be unconventional measurements is equally difficult. Although each nonprofit has to walk this path alone to find its own unique answers and measurements, the need for a collective effort at tackling this problem is equally important.

Given the growth and strength of the nonprofit sector and the public's desire for quick methods to evaluate nonprofits, the nonprofit sector needs to take the offense on the measurement issue. Otherwise, it risks organizations like McKinsey and Forbes continuing to do the job, which would be a real shame because it's doubtful that such organizations can jettison their profit mindset to define other than business measurements.

We will look at the current state of thought on sector-wide measurements in Chapter 12, as well as examine the results enjoyed by some nonprofits that have succeeded in creating meaningful measurements for their organizations. One thing is certain regarding these efforts: Putting the focus on measuring the outcomes that count is an important step toward elevating acting above talking—and a big step toward eliminating the *Read My Lips* elephant.

Institutional Memory Is Faulty or Nonexistent

Most nonprofits have no institutionalized way to capture organizational knowledge. The most commonly used tool, board minutes, are in this litigious age often reduced to little more than a verbatim recording of approved motions. This creates two problems: (1) there's little downside to embellishing facts verbally, and (2) without a reliable record, opinion has the same weight as fact.

Revising History Throughout Part II, we have confronted situations in which leadership beliefs and proclamations conflict with the reality of what is happening in the *Salt Mines.* Examples abound. The dual volunteer/staff operation structure clouds responsibilities and disguises where decisions are made and work gets done. Boards hear the voice of constituents, but in many cases are hearing the opinions of only vested volunteers. CEOs place a positive spin on organizational activities, while many of those activities never make it to market or quietly go away.

The nonprofit culture of shared accountability coupled with the twin constraints of volunteer leadership—short terms and limited, remote working time—provide the perfect storm for continually revising institutional history. The *Nonprofit Trouble Cycle* exists because of this culture. Given the time lag between cycle phases and the brief nature of volunteer terms, issues created in one cycle rarely attach to the right source in the next. When board or CEO rhetoric does not live up to expectations, that rhetoric can be attributed without much reprisal to a board that is long gone rather than to the rightful (or wrongful) party.

The temptation to increase one's leadership power and stature by using the superlative to embellish endeavors with which one is personally involved and to pass along any problems created to someone else is great indeed. The harm is that this failure to accurately reflect on the good and bad of any endeavor means the organization is condemned to repeat the same problems in the next endeavor.

The advice of a very successful past CEO is illuminating:

> Always use the most optimistic language when announcing new programs. We told the board about a "fabulous" new marketing campaign . . . so the board is telling everyone how fabulous it is. Volunteers will believe what you tell them . . . if you say it's terrific, anyone who's heard otherwise will soon be gone . . . what will stick is "fabulous campaign."

Opinion Is Fact The *Read My Lips* elephant doesn't just appear when hubris or outsized rhetoric are afoot; it is also present when harmful words deliberately distort another's actions or reputation. In a study published in *Psychological Science* magazine, Stephan Lewandowsky writes:

> People build mental models. By the time they receive a retraction, the original misinformation has already become an integral part of that mental model or world view. . . . People continue to rely on misinformation even if they demonstrably remember and understand a subsequent retraction.[7]

Thus the reputation of a senior staff director is inexorably harmed as the CEO unfairly tells all who will listen about the director's usurping of what needs to be under volunteer control. The CEO's words plow fertile ground in the minds of volunteer leaders, who hold the *I'm the Expert* mentality. For these volunteer leaders, no amount of retraction that this is the director's role will erase the negative image created by the CEO's words.

The tendency to hold mental models even when the information is proved false or is retracted provides even more incentive to use words to distort on a grander scale. Paul Volker's second interim report on the United Nation's Oil for Food Program cited adverse management findings of conflict of interest, willful neglect, and incompetence under the current Secretary General, Kofi Annan. Although the finding did not specifically cite Mr. Annan as knowingly guilty of any criminal activity, the report clearly cited conditions that would be grounds for firing for-profit CEOs.

Yet, Mr. Annan issued a statement saying "the inquiry [the report] has cleared me of any wrong-doing."[8] Newspapers quickly rewarded his not-quite-accurate statement with the headlines, "Annan Calls Report Exoneration," and later media stories began with the lead-in, "Kofi exonerated."

It's unrealistic to think that people will not manipulate words and information for their own means, especially in a world where so much information is created and can be distributed in an instant. But, it is not unrealistic to expect volunteer and staff leaders to display the honesty and integrity to engage in that practice as little as possible. It is possible—and given a nonprofit's higher calling—important to create cultures where critical thinking and a reliance on factual information is prized. One useful tool in this endeavor is ways to accurately capture and record the history of major institutional activities. We'll look at how this might be done in Chapter 12.

How all of these concepts play out in real life are illustrated in the *Live Lesson:* "Great Is Just a State of Mind." A few *Salt Mine* exercises enable us to see the *Read My Lips* elephant in action. Finally, we'll see what might have been if this organization had chosen to act rather than to talk.

Live Lesson: "Great Is Just a State of Mind"

Organization and Cast

The subject of our *Live Lesson,* "Great Is Just a State of Mind," is a small foundation, the Healthy Hearts Foundation (HHF). HHF has $3 million in assets and is the education and research arm of a $7 million nonprofit. Its philanthropic cause is women's heart health. The parent nonprofit has chapters in every state and is almost 150 years old; the foundation is 50 years old.

HHF's professional staff includes an executive director named Nanette and four full-time employees. Healthy Heart's board of eight directors is led by the board president, Carrie.

The Rhetoric

HHF's executive director, Nanette, is retiring after a 15-year tenure. While munching on dinner, foundation donors and parent nonprofit members reminisce about foundation activities. HHF's board president, Carrie, mounts the podium and begins her speech:

> For over forty years HHF has been a leader in the fight for the education and prevention of woman's heart disease. We've become well known and respected internationally as an important funding source for women's heart health.
>
> Nanette has spearheaded many of the foundation's past fifteen years' accomplishments. She's helped us:
>
> - Dramatically increase donations each year through successful mail/phone campaigns.

- Effectively partner with the Heartfull Institute and be a contributing member of White House initiatives.
- Successfully educate thousands of women on heart disease.

> Nanette, along with our volunteers, and this board have made our foundation the envy of other like foundations. We thank Nanette for her outstanding service and wish her nothing but the best in the future.

Applause broke out as Carrie finished her speech, and all eyes turned to Nanette. Everyone in the room was sorry to see her go but extremely proud of the foundation's enormous success during her tenure.

And, yes, everyone in the room is feeling just a little anxious. Would it be possible to find another executive director who could fill her shoes?

The Reality

Salt Mines #1: Leader Implies Followers

Reality in the office . . .

The HHF staff is busy sending a government video on heart care to each chapter. As one of the staff members points out:

> "This should help raise awareness of heart issues at our chapters. Can you believe it? Our last survey still shows a large number that are clueless about what the foundation does."

Irritated, the other staff member replies:

> "They don't read our e-mails and newsletters. How many times have we explained things? You'd think that something would click in their minds. We even had the list of heart grant recipients in the last issue."

Reality in the marketplace . . .

If, as Carrie states in her speech, HHF is an internationally respected leader in the fight for prevention and education of women's heart disease, at the very least HHF's chapters should be well aware of that fact.

Carrie's use of the word "international" is also misleading. HHF's parent organization's international presence is limited to only a few Canadian chapters. Setting aside this fact for the moment, it seems fair to assume that a position of true international leadership would not be passive (e.g., the number of education videos distributed or the number of speeches given). An international leader would take a proactive role in educating women throughout the world and participate in major funding for things like cardiac research.

HHF may be an international leader in its board's mind, but contrasted with the above model, HHF's efforts seem limited to their parent chapters, and even that market is not readily following their lead.

Salt Mines #2: Donations, a Shell Game

Rhetoric at the board meeting . . .

Board members are feeling apprehensive about the upcoming executive director search. One board member laments:

> "I just don't know where we're going to find another Nanette. Over the last five years, her mail and phone campaigns increased our donations by over 40 percent."

Another director chimes in:

> "It's just amazing when you think about it; we've granted half a million dollars to Heartfull to combat heart disease. Wow! Well, the board's made it very clear to the recruiter. Any candidates that we interview must be able to continue this kind of fundraising."

Reality in the marketplace . . .

While it's true that HHF granted more than $500,000 to cardiac issues, these funds were granted over a 40-year period. On average, HHF is granting only $12,500 per year, which is a minuscule sum of the total funds granted each year for cardiac care. This makes it very difficult for an objective observer to classify HHF as a major funding source.

Neither did HHF's dramatic increase in donations come from innovative phone and mail campaigns. Rather, donations took a huge jump in the first couple years of Nanette's employment. She was the HHF's first executive director with professional fundraising experience. Nanette quickly displayed her expertise by instituting something that had been previously lacking—structured fundraising campaigns targeted at individual donations. Likewise, she developed a chapter program that required each chapter to make an annual pledge of funds to the foundation.

But contrary to Nanette's board reports and foundation marketing literature, after an initial bump of donations that immediately followed Nanette's new structured funding campaigns, individual donations show no steady upward pattern, and in fact were trending downward when telemarketing expenses were factored in.

Nanette successfully diverted attention from this fact by quietly increasing chapter pledges, which masked the lack of individual donor growth. In effect, she was playing the old shell game—simply taking funds that otherwise would go to the parent shell and moving them under the foundation shell.

Salt Mines #3: The "Me Too" Partner

Reality in the office . . .

Nanette just returned from a visit with their partner, the Heartfull Institute. Turning to her assistant, she complains:

> "It makes me so mad! Once again, Heartfull had an invitational meeting in Washington, and they didn't even let us know until now. We thought government representatives would be at this meeting.

Luckily, I enjoy going to Washington anyway. And, Heartfull's Red Heart campaign really compensates for the hassle and expense of the trip. It's a huge success. Our chapters just love those pins and brochures!"

Her assistant replies:

"The cause-related consultant is still calling. What do I tell him? I know we agreed that his advice is helpful, but he keeps asking if the board has reviewed his latest information and if there's any final decision on the original cause-related campaign proposal. He'd really like to be at the next board meeting. What do you want me to tell him?"

Nanette looks pained and says:

"Darn, I do feel bad about this, but let's continue to stall him. He gives me some good information from time to time. And the board really did like his initial plan, but you know what happened. I brought him in quite a while ago, and while I initially thought this was a good idea, enacting his plan is a huge project that requires a lot of work.

With some of the board members a little hesitant and my retirement so close, it just didn't make sense to start this project and then dump it on a new person. Plus, then the opportunity to partner with Heartfull came along, and we can use their stuff without all the work."

Nanette's assistant felt a little relieved. Although she wasn't looking forward to fending off more of the consultant's calls, she had enough to do without getting all those materials ready for the board again. She replies:

"That's great. With all the new board directors and the success of Heartfull, the board doesn't seem all that interested in reviewing his plan again anyway. They loved your article about our part in the Red Heart campaign in this month's newsletter.

Also, Carrie's looking forward to accompanying you to Washington for the next Heartfull meeting. I can add a bullet about our participation in the next newsletter, if you like. She probably will also want this as part of her board report for HHF's upcoming annual meeting."

Reality in the marketplace . . .

Created just two years ago, the Heartfull Institute, not HHF, is the great success story. Capitalizing on the emerging public interest in women's heart health, Heartfull quickly attracted national attention to its mission of educating women on cardiac care and providing funding and research for the prevention and effective treatment of women's heart disease. Heartfull has recently rolled out its Red Heart campaign, which distributes free educational materials and pins and is greatly contributing to the national awareness of women's cardiac issues.

Heartfull certainly does not consider HHF to be a strong partner; it simply appreciates HHF's efforts as it does others that distribute Heartfull's materials. HHF's $1,000 yearly contribution buys it little in the way of influence on Heartfull's policies and actions. Rather, HHF is a "me too" partner. HHF attends rather than actively participates in Heartfull's public meetings and shakes hands rather than helps Heartfull formulate policy with congressional leaders at Washington gatherings. Heartfull does the work and has the influence; HHF simply tags along for the ride.

The Consequences

Believing Great Is Not Being Great

The Problem The biggest problem when rhetoric does not match reality is that things can't be fixed if no one admits there's a problem. Opportunities are missed when there's no need to search them out. This, in a nutshell, is the consequences of allowing the *Read My Lips* elephant to exist. Greatness isn't achieved when everyone believes they are already there.

Hubris and outsized rhetoric mask the real state of the nonprofit and hinder the kind of critical assessment that distinguishes winning activities from duds. To bring the point home, let's look at what might happen if HHF drops its outsized rhetoric for a moment.

What Might Have Been The board would face the brutal fact that HHF is currently a small player in the field of women's heart health. It would recognize that the increase in donations is limited to the early years of instituting a structured fundraising campaign. The following is a peek at the board meeting that might have been almost eight years ago:

> The board looks over the results of its latest environmental scan. Carrie comments, "This is truly interesting information; there's starting to be universal recognition that men and women suffer heart attacks very differently. Plus, attention is beginning to focus on the fact that heart attacks are a leading source of women's deaths."
>
> Another board member joins in: "About time! At our chapter get-together and when I'm out talking to individual donors, people keep expressing the desire for more cause-related activities . . . maybe some sort of national HHF campaign. They feel that we've added an executive director and staff resources, so now is the opportunity to become a leader on the national level as public attention to women's heart health grows."
>
> Carrie explains, "Well, our chapter pledges are good, but individual donations are leveling off. Telemarketing expense is on the rise, making the latest donation campaign less cost effective. Some sort of annual event that garners public recognition would certainly increase donations across the board."
>
> "I just went to a conference where there was discussion about a new tool called cause-related marketing," Nanette offers. "It's a good way of getting corporate sponsors for national campaigns. Given the changing public environment, this may be a perfect opportunity to do something that all of us would like—increase our impact in cardiac care and deliver more on our mission promises."
>
> Nannette adds, "I'd like to hire the consultant that did the cause-related presentation to assess the current environment, and propose a cause-related campaign for us."

The board enthusiastically approves her request.

You get the picture: This board sees an opportunity to improve HHF's real condition. HHF may currently be a small player with limited funds, but the board sees that environmental conditions—the rising interest in women's cardiac care, combined with added HHF staff and new tools like cause-related marketing—may present an opportunity for HHF to play a much larger role in its mission field. By not being complacent and looking at reality, this could-have-been HHF board is alert to multiple opportunities: (1) the possibility of halting the decline of individual donations, (2) the chance to answer constituent demands for a philanthropy event, and (3) the ability to use changing environmental conditions to grow in influence and deliver on mission.

What Was Turning back to real life, Nanette, to her credit, did educate HHF's board on cause-related marketing, and she produced a consultant who proposes and presents an excellent cause-related marketing plan. But she also is responsible for painting all of HHF's activities in the most outsized rhetoric possible. The board believes that HHF is already doing better than most other foundations, and donations continue to increase. As a consequence, the board had no burning need to become greater; it believed the organization was already great.

Carrie and Nanette were aware that the parent nonprofit's 140 chapters and many of its 100,000 members did want some sort of national event or campaign. But they confused the process of talking about the subject at every board meeting and reviewing the consultant's plan regularly with the act of actually doing something. The board and parent organization went along.

The Cost of Opportunity Lost

The *Read My Lips* elephant substitutes glorious rhetoric for meaningful accomplishment. Nonprofits that believe they are already "best in show" won't recognize or feel the need to seize opportunities knocking at their doors.

HHF has the perfect opportunity to gain national prominence and influence in the field of women's heart health and the chance to better deliver on mission promises, but it talks and doesn't act. The board benchmarks its performance to like foundations that likewise talk a big game and make small impacts in their given philanthropy field. Meanwhile, if one person fails to seize on a market-presented opportunity, another moves in to fill the void. While HHF brags and dithers, others take advantage of the market opportunity, and the Heartfull Institute is born.

Opportunity Lost Quantified

The following is a summary of the events and financial impacts inherent in HHF's failure to seize upon the market opportunity to grow its philanthropy along with the increasing public emphasis on women's cardiac care.

The Opportunity Moves Elsewhere

- Two years ago, founders created the Heartfull Institute. It followed the same logic and actions that were in the cause-related consultant's plan that was presented to the HHF board five years earlier.

The Money Moves Elsewhere

- Heartfull creates its Red Heart campaign and begins with five mega-corporate sponsors donating $25 million. Within five years, its list of corporate sponsors and grantors numbers more than 50.
- Heartfull signs agreements with retailers across the country. Firms like Minute Maid pledge to donate from ten cents up to two dollars for every specially designated product sold in a designated store.

The Leadership Moves Elsewhere

- Through the Heartfull Institute, Heartfull, not HHF, gains national prominence. Red Heart pins and the Red Heart insignia are everywhere. A recent survey shows that in the two years since founding the Heartfull Institute, 60 percent of American women recognize the Red Heart symbol and want to learn more about heart disease; it prompted 45 percent of women to talk with their doctors or get a check-up.
- Washington's prestigious National Institutes of Health (NIH) partners with Heartfull on its latest campaign. HHF is not even listed on Heartfull's Web site as one of 20 contributing Red Heart organizations.
- Heartfull gets the press calls. Heartfull is invited to congressional hearings, and Heartfull is a major advocacy voice on the issue of women's cardiac disease. HHF has no place on the national stage.

It may be widely speculative to put a dollar figure on HHF's opportunity lost, but even modest assumptions would put the loss of sponsorships and other revenue in the neighborhood of millions. However, the true cost is best summarized by an old MasterCard refrain: "There are some things that money can't buy." The total loss of the entire opportunity is priceless.

What is the dollar estimate for the influx of new donors, members, and professional staff that national prominence brings? How do we place a price tag on being able to positively influence the health of women everywhere? Where would all the alleyways and passages that come with being in the middle of cutting-edge heart-health thinking and research lead?

It's not entirely clear whether HHF could have accomplished these things even if it had acted on the consultant's cause-related marketing plan. HHF might be in Heartfull's position now, or it might have failed or even be in a worse position than it is now. But one thing is for certain: HHF has no chance of succeeding if it never even tries.

Summing It Up

Rhetoric is easy, but doing something is hard. The interesting thing about the truth of this statement is that it depends on the audience.

The winners when the *Read My Lips* elephant ploughs through a nonprofit are the current leaders. Their hubris and outsized rhetoric benefit them in the short term at the expense of the long-term health of the nonprofit. HHF's leaders pumped up their attitude and decreased their workload by promoting HHF's greatness. Donors and members are largely unaware of HHF's missed opportunity and are happy with their Red Heart pins and proud to see Carrie represent HHF in Washington.

The loser is the future of HHF and the future of HHF's mission. It is the loss of what might have been versus what is.

NOTES

1. Gordon Livingston, *Too Soon Old, Too Late Smart* (New York: Marlowe and Company, 2004), 7.
2. Tomas Kellner, "American Bible Society Is a Terrific Example of How a Nonprofit Shouldn't Operate," www.forbes.com/forbes/2002/1209/182_print.html (accessed March 17, 2003).
3. Alan Artnet, John von Rhein, and Howard Reich, "How Can Orchestra Hall Reverse a Flawed Redesign?" *Chicago Tribune,* sec. 7, December 1, 2002.
4. Rachel Emma Silverman, "Many Nonprofits Underreport Fund-Raising Costs," *Wall Street Journal,* sec. D, December, 8, 2004.
5. Mark A. Hager, Thomas Pollak, and Patrick H. Rooney, *Nonprofit Overhead Cost Project* (Center on Nonprofits and Philanthropy, Urban Institute Center for Philanthropy, Indiana University, 2004), Brief 1.
6. Jeffery Pfeffer and Robert I. Sutton, *The Knowing-Doing Gap* (Boston: Harvard Business School Publishing, 2000), 138–175.
7. Sharon Begley, "People Believe a 'Fact' That Fits Their View Even if It's Clearly False," *Wall Street Journal,* sec. B, February 4, 2004.
8. Editorial, "Kofi's Accountability," *Wall Street Journal,* sec. A, March 30, 2005.

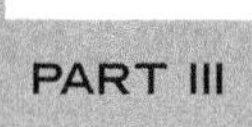

The Elephant Solutions: Good Behavior, Exceptional Results

Make no little plans; they have no magic to stir the blood . . .
make big plans; aim high in hope and work.

—Daniel Burnham

A New Mindset

Nonprofit elephants are redeemable. As real animals, elephants that are ignored and untrained are difficult to control and destroy their surroundings, but with care and education, elephants become tame, dependable, and friendly to humans. So once nonprofits acknowledge the five elephants, they can be trained.

That is the challenge for Part III, "The Elephant Solutions: Good Behavior, Exceptional Results." Each of the five chapters that follow explores one nonprofit elephant in depth, offering "elephant solutions"—ideas and practices that modify harmful elephant behavior and transform unruly guests into well-behaved friends.

A Brief Word on "Best"

Defining great nonprofits is especially risky because uniform, hard data such as ratios of stock returns to market just doesn't exist. Nonprofit "bests" are often defined by consultants who promote their work, questionnaires filled out by presidents or CEOs, or public announcements of innovative programs. Little is done objectively to determine if these programs are produced efficiently or results sustained over the long term.

Thus, Part III does not hold up certain nonprofits as "the best." You will find examples of nonprofits doing the right thing and promising new practices, but these glimpses of doing things right are meant to spark ideas—to show what is, not the best of what can be. When put into practice, the ideas and solutions in *Exposing the Elephants* will help nonprofits realize their own successful, sustained long-term results.

Coaxing Elephants into the Open

Taken together, the five nonprofit elephants reflect the problematic thinking so prevalent in the nonprofit sector today—thinking that keeps nonprofits locked in the past and limits their innovation and achievement. The elephant solutions form the building blocks of a new mindset, one that better positions nonprofits to meet the challenges of the 21st century working environment.

Setting the Stage

It may seem paradoxical, but nonprofits should not even attempt to eliminate the elephants entirely. Even in the best of circumstances, some level of confusion and chaos exists in nonprofits simply because that is the nature of organizations that must blend volunteer and professional resources. Trying to make the elephants disappear entirely would be a frustrating waste of precious resources, because the pesky pachyderms will surely reappear and wreak havoc from time to time.

Rather than seek perfection, it is better to embrace the more pragmatic strategy of accepting the situation for what it is and making it work by institutionalizing the practices that keep their most harmful behaviors at bay. This brings us to a basic question: How will we know good elephant behavior when we see it?

One Behavior, Two Faces

Psychology and experience tell us that the same behavior manifests very differently in individuals depending on environment and upbringing. For example, take the common behavior of parents loving their children. At the positive end of the behavior spectrum, loving parents protect and nurture children who grow into confident, independent, and secure adults; at the negative end, overly possessive parents smother and stifle children who grow into timid, dependent adults. The same behavior—parental love—but the results are very different.

A similar phenomenon applies to our elephants. The goal is to set conditions that favor positive rather than negative elephant behavior and positive rather than negative outcomes. Consider the information in Exhibit III.1, and this idea becomes clearer.

These positive outcomes can be realized if nonprofits embrace their elephants and insist on their good behavior, but, reading between the lines, the challenges are also visible. Once the elephants are coaxed into the open, what strategies and actions actually transform this unruly herd to consistently produce these positive outcomes? And once

EXHIBIT III.1 ELEPHANT BEHAVIOR—POSITIVE OR NEGATIVE OUTCOMES

Elephant	Negative Outcome	Positive Outcome
Mission Impossible	Committees and vested volunteers who consume resources	Mission-oriented groups and volunteers who contribute resources
Earth to Board	Boards that make flawed decisions based on vested input	Boards that make effective decisions based on mission-interested input
Board Fiddles, Rome Burns	Boards engaged in management detail while governance is ignored	Boards that achieve governance outcomes; CEOs who achieve business outcomes
Smile, Not Skill	Congeniality substitutes for performance	Civility expected; performance rewarded
Read My Lips	Leaders who preach bravado unsubstantiated by fact or actual outcomes	Leaders who use rhetoric reflecting real outcomes to promote mission and motivate resources

the transformation takes place, how do such practices become widely accepted and institutionalized?

These topics follow in subsequent chapters, but for now, a quick overview of the five elephant solutions suffices.

The Five Elephant Solutions

Blending scarce volunteer and professional resources to achieve mission results is a messy process; nonprofit elephants are always lurking. The elephant solutions put these beasts on their best behavior and free volunteer and staff leadership to innovate and perform. They are:

1. *Create One Mission Structure* . . . a single volunteer and staff structure

   One structure with clearly articulated volunteer and staff accountabilities equals confident leaders who achieve mission results.

2. *Seek a Shared Reality* . . . relentless governance focus on mission

   A relentless board focus on constituent and mission reality equals a mission-responsive nonprofit.

3. *Develop Policy and Strategy at All Levels* . . . each organizational level is accountable

   Decisions and actions by the right person, in the right place, at the right time yield effective, market-responsive decisions.

4. *Demand Performance* . . . expect civility, reward performance

   A performance culture where high achievers thrive equals innovation and lasting mission results.

5. *Reward Results, Not Rhetoric* . . . eliminate the grandiose language of rhetoric and reward outcomes

Meaningful, clearly articulated goals backed by actual performance equal enthused constituents and lasting mission outcomes.

Summing It Up

The elephant solutions weigh the uniqueness of nonprofits, the constraints on volunteers, and the reality of how work really gets done in a high-performing, dynamic environment. Part III is not about endless lists of "shoulds"—piling more responsibilities on boards that can only devote limited time and attention is not the answer to better governance or CEO management.

The elephant solutions are about appreciating and building equally strong benefit and business components and equally strong volunteer and staff leadership. Think of the situation like the best kind of marriage, a union where strong, equal partners support and encourage the best from each other—a place where good mission leadership and good business leadership grow together.

Nonprofits that institutionalize the elephant solutions will not avoid the occasional bad volunteer president, board member, CEO, or staff director, but they will be able to withstand and move beyond these rough patches and continue to excel.

CHAPTER 8

The *Mission Impossible* Solution: Create One Mission System

The music comes from something that we cannot direct, from a unified whole created among players. . . . When it works, we sit back amazed and grateful.

—Margaret J. Wheatley

Taming the *Mission Impossible* Elephant

Embedded deep in the nonprofit psyche, the *I'm the Expert* archetype drives volunteer behavior and fuels the first and very powerful elephant, *Mission Impossible.* As Chapter 3 illustrates, this elephant is the catalyst for the dual volunteer and staff structures that emit a confusing fog of conflicting roles and power struggles.

This troublesome pachyderm can be tamed. It is possible to change *I'm the Expert* thinking to embrace both benefit and business components. Volunteer and staff leaders can come together to find constructive solutions to the *Mission Impossible* elephant. A single unified volunteer/staff leadership structure can emerge from the fog. Read what one CEO blogger says:

> What I find is that the leadership and the board have in fact been quite hungry for change. They want to set their sights high. They want to stretch, and they want to try major new approaches. I didn't expect this willingness to surface as quickly as it did, and I rejoice.
>
> What I admired most about the board was their commitment and unspoken understanding about how much change they—and this association—would be willing to undertake at one time. Literally, at the end of the day we proposed a fairly significant change in how our annual meetings are programmed. This came after agreeing to shorten the meeting by a full day and eliminating a couple of major events and allowing significant programming by special interest groups against previously protected interests.

Mission-dedicated volunteer and staff leaders know that something is wrong, and they are hungry for answers that address the realities of their workplace. The answer to the *Mission Impossible* elephant is deceptively simple—create a single, unified volunteer and staff structure.

Articulating this concept is one thing, but successfully putting it into practice is quite another, and making it stick beyond one or two volunteer cycles is an even greater challenge!

In This Chapter

Perhaps a little counterintuitive at first, creating a unified structure is a case where the container actually matters more than the contents. The exact flavor of governance, title, or department is less important than that certain concepts drive the design.

All firm foundations start with key planning concepts. This chapter thoroughly examines the keystone concepts that build a unified volunteer and staff structure. We'll see how accountability is embedded at each level and discuss ways to change entrenched *I'm the Expert* beliefs.

Lastly, we'll tackle what Malcolm Gladwell, in his book *The Tipping Point,* calls the "stickiness factor."[1] Once a single organizational system is in place, how do nonprofits make those changes "stick" throughout each new cycle of volunteers?

Elephant Solution One: Create One Mission System

We've already taken a giant first step toward creating one organizational structure. In Chapter 3 we brought the *Mission Impossible* elephant out into the open, revealing its destructive behavior. Volunteer and professional staff energies are consumed by internal politics and infighting rather than producing mission results.

I'm the Expert thinking leads to the conclusion that nonprofits are best protected by volunteers, not staff driving all the real decisions—two competing structures, volunteer and staff, spring into being. The only way to limit the *Mission Impossible* elephant's bad behavior and become a high-mission-performing nonprofit is to merge these two structures into one.

Let's look at a hypothetical example that we'll use throughout this chapter. Assume that there's an organization called the United Medical Association (UMA), and its board wants to make doctors aware of the value of alternative as well as traditional medicine. Exhibit 8.1 illustrates what typically happens when dual structures are in place.

The board assigns the task to its volunteer board committees, but does so through the CEO, Melanie. Melanie delegates the task to two staff directors who are the liaisons for the two board committees. In turn, they contact the board committees and arrange a meeting or time to get together and discuss the issues. Now, let's contrast that with Exhibit 8.2 when one mission structure is in place.

EXHIBIT 8.1 DUAL VOLUNTEER AND STAFF STRUCTURE

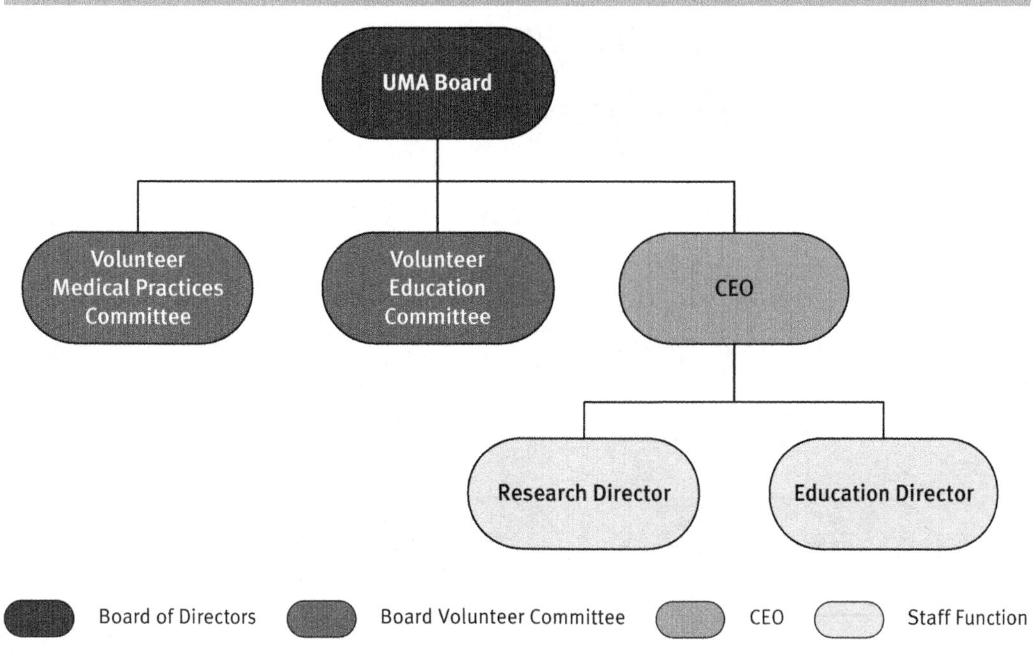

In a one-mission system, boards delegate to CEOs full accountability for a stated board outcome. Under CEO direction, staff directors select and manage the volunteer and expert resources needed to deliver those outcomes.

In the dual system, UMA staff will spend a great deal of time coordinating general board committees that may lack expertise in specific areas like alternative versus traditional medicine practices. Much of the "committee's work" will probably be staff's outcomes under the guise of the committee banner. With one mission structure, staff selects the expert volunteer and other outside resources needed and spends most of its time planning and implementing outcomes. One system supports productivity, and one thwarts it.

Expect the *I'm the Expert* cry, "volunteers not staff should make the decisions" to echo through the volunteer ranks. That makes it very important for advocates to thoroughly understand the concepts that underlie one system and lay a factual groundwork of information to counter arguments and reassure volunteers of the benefits of such a move.

Three important, keystone concepts underlie and support the merger of separate volunteer and staff organizational structures into one. They are:

1. Benefit and business components are equal, complementary parts of one, unified mission system.

EXHIBIT 8.2 ONE MISSION STRUCTURE

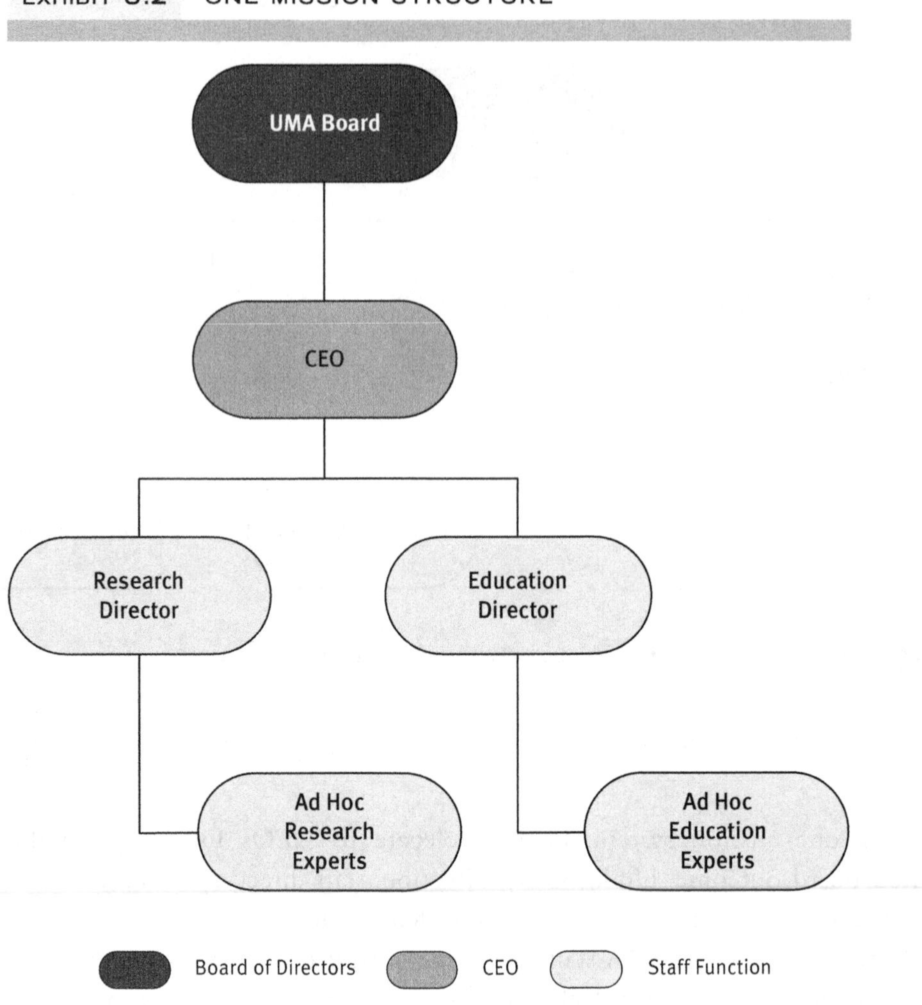

2. Volunteer and staff are equal, complementary parts of a single mission system.
3. Accountability is the key to a high-performing mission system.

Keystone Concept One: Benefit and Business Components Are Equal, Complementary Parts of a Unified Mission System

Benefit and business, volunteer and staff, members or donors—all are interdependent parts of a much bigger whole or a mission system. This shift in perception from piece to whole has the power to revolutionize nonprofit performance.

It's like changing the lens on a camera—altering the lens alters the entire picture. Adjusting the lens of the nonprofit camera to include the panorama of the mission system moves organizational decision making from myopic to global, and short to long term. And that shift greatly increases the chances that decision outcomes will also be positive, lasting mission outcomes.

Mission Systems Thinking Think of the sum total of all nonprofit entities and operations as a mission system. The complicated and exact management principles that underpin the field of systems thinking in general are well beyond the scope of this book, but the basic systems concept can be helpful in expanding *I'm the Expert* thinking into a broader context. Peter Senge, author of *The Fifth Discipline* and a pioneer of systems thinking and learning organizations, describes system thinking as follows:

> Systems thinking is a way of thinking about, and a language for describing and understanding, the forces and interrelationships that shape the behavior of systems. This discipline helps us to see how to change systems more effectively, to act more in tune with the larger processes of the natural and economic world.[2]

Specifically, our mission system consists of these elements: benefit and business components; volunteers and staff; all other constituents and stakeholders; the interrelationship of all the parts; all the decisions, processes, and outcomes therein.

Mission Systems versus Governance Models A mission system is not another new governance model. Nonprofits use governance in a very specific way—to indicate board leadership. But governance in the broader sense of the word and in corporate practice encompasses the entire top leadership of an organization (e.g., board, president, CEO, and other key senior leaders who sit on the board).

Governance in the nonprofit vernacular is just one piece of the mission system—the benefit component for which boards are accountable and the process by which boards do their work. Although some might say this is mincing words, in this case the words really do matter.

Nonprofits spend endless resources searching and implementing new governance systems as the answer to all their problems, but the best of governance models, such as Dr. Carver's Policy Governance Model™,[3] require a level of board education and commitment that is tough to sustain initially and throughout each new board cycle. The more opaque the model—for example, the more unique the language and complexity—the easier it is for vested volunteers to demonize, making it all the harder to adopt and institutionalize the changes.

Exposing the Elephants intends to be as simple, open, and free of new jargon as possible. Although it incorporates the best of governance model thought here, the change from dual operating structures to one mission system is not simply a change of governance models—it is a fundamental shift in perception and values.

Nonprofit leaders don't have to discard their existing governance model but merely adapt it. It's like taking the same ingredients but baking them into a very different pie. While our mission systems chart may look somewhat like a traditional governance model, the concepts and the way the pieces act and interrelate are very different.

Equal Benefit and Business Components Mission systems will achieve maximum performance only when benefit and business components are equal—when boards and CEOs are equally strong. What happens when these relationships are out of whack? When the mission component is strong and the business weak or vice versa? In a nutshell, nonprofits underachieve.

Think of the mission system as a big tennis court with a net dividing benefit and business components. When the benefit component and board are strong, mission outcomes are clear and defined. When the business component and CEO are strong, mission outcomes are delivered. Exhibit 8.3 illustrates such a balanced mission system.

But what happens when the net moves, and the court looks like Exhibit 8.4?

When the benefit component is strong and the business component weak, nonprofits cannot deliver on board mission strategies. Sometimes, this situation even drains resources that other nonprofits might use to serve the same constituents.

Consider the findings of a study of Illinois nonprofits by the Donor's Forum of Chicago.[4] Thirty percent of survey participants had less than $25,000 in revenue, and more than 25 percent of this group had existed for more than 50 years and only 6 percent were new (less than 5 years old). A logical assumption is that organizations with such stagnant growth have a very weak business component

Now, consider what happens when the reverse is true and the court looks like Exhibit 8.5.

When the benefit component is weak and the business component strong, nonprofits lose constituent input and become staff directed. Without a strong volunteer board protecting the benefit component, the staff may deliver profitable, well-executed

EXHIBIT 8.3 EQUAL BENEFIT/BUSINESS COMPONENTS

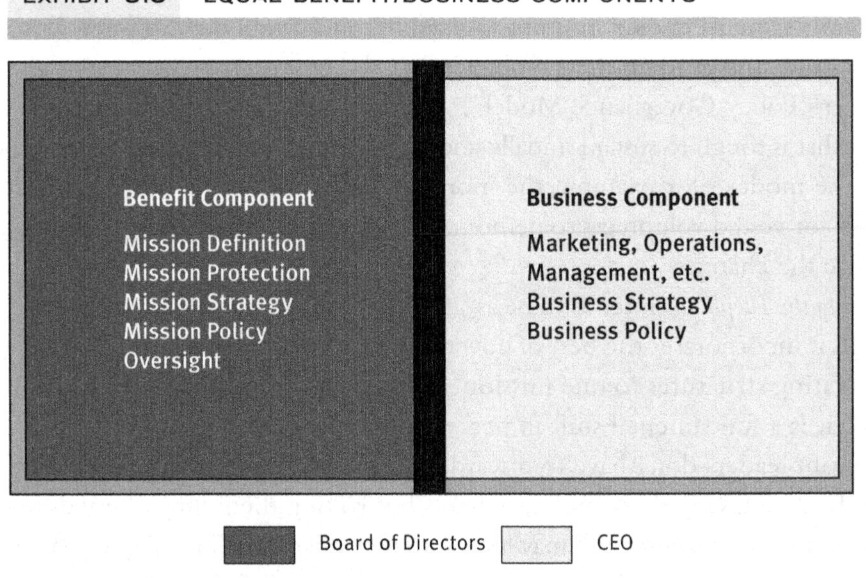

EXHIBIT 8.4 STRONG BENEFIT/WEAK BUSINESS COMPONENTS

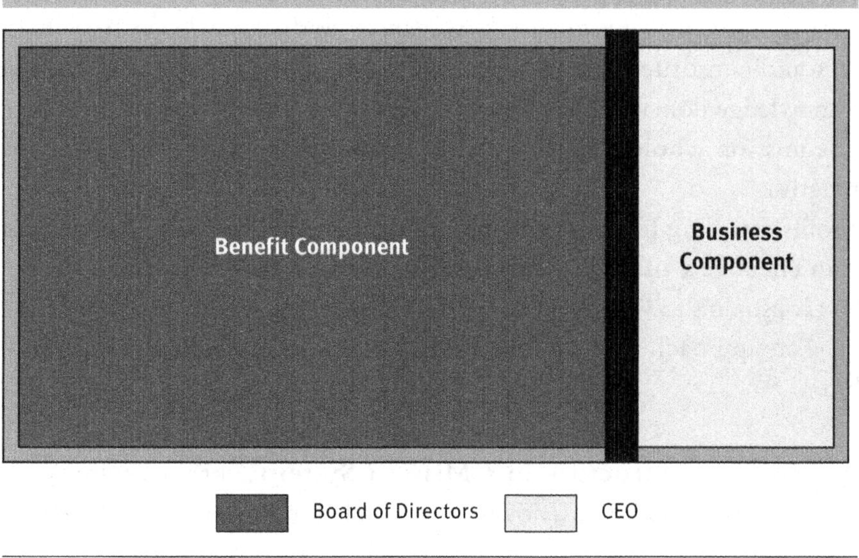

Board of Directors CEO

programs that fail to adequately address the needs of constituents. Or, sometimes a CEO who is unencumbered by active board oversight spins out of control and misuses nonprofit revenues and/or assets.

Say it again, Sam—embracing the equal importance of benefit and business is one key to a high-performing mission system.

EXHIBIT 8.5 STRONG BUSINESS/WEAK BENEFIT COMPONENTS

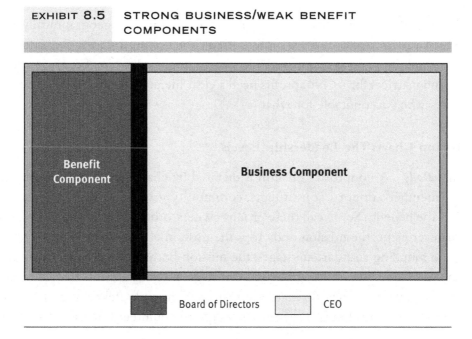

Benefit Component

Business Component

Board of Directors CEO

Keystone Concept Two: Volunteer and Staff Are Equal, Complementary Parts of a Single Mission System

The benefit component—mission and governance—is the knowledge domain of boards, volunteers, and constituents. The business component—management and operations—is the knowledge domain of CEOs and professional staff. Each domain is an essential part of the mission whole; each considers the constraints of its entities but builds on their strengths.

Nonprofits can cling to the outmoded thought that temporary, part-time volunteer leaders can effectively manage a full-time business, or they can acknowledge today's reality. The constraints to volunteer leadership necessitate a different approach in a mature nonprofit—an approach that embraces the equal importance of volunteer and staff leadership.

Volunteer and Staff Structure in a Mission System From a pure systems perspective, organizational charts are not a good vehicle for representing a system. Attempts to portray a dynamic, matrix-type organization on paper almost always descend into a complicated tangle of interlocking circles. That might impress people, but it does little to clarify volunteer and staff reality.

For all the talk about self-directed groups and grassroots decision making, the ability of human beings to make intelligent, responsive, meaningful decisions relies on knowing who is in charge. An extreme example of what happens in the absence of such clarity was seen in the immediate aftermath of Hurricane Katrina in 2005. The lack of clear lines of authority for local, state, and federal officials exacerbated an already catastrophic situation.

The nature of nonprofits, with their ever-changing and geographically remote volunteer leaders, makes it even more difficult for nonprofits to move as far on the systems thinking scale as visionaries like Senge might advocate. So, no interlocking circles and matrices for us. Nonprofits need a clear hierarchal visual representation that illustrates who's accountable for what.

A Mission Chart: The Leadership Levels

Mission Body A nonprofit's mission is dictated by charter and law, but the mission body—members, donors, constituents, community groups—adapts, refines, and/or receives the benefits. Some call these groups owners, others call them stakeholders, but by whatever name, the mission body tops the mission chart.

At the founding and start-up stages, the mission body and volunteer board may be one and the same. But, moving beyond this stage, most nonprofits become too large to directly govern, so they delegate the management and safekeeping of the benefit component and overall mission system oversight to volunteer boards.

Volunteer Boards Like any subordinate, the board answers to the people who bestow its powers—the mission body. To do their job well, boards must be in continual contact with the mission body to determine and articulate that will in decision making and performance. In addition, boards oversee the performance of the entire mission system.

The CEO Boards delegate the management and safekeeping of the business component to CEOs. Although CEOs also operate under the auspices of the mission body, they report directly to boards, not mission bodies. In other words, CEOs take direction from boards, not constituents—an important distinction that will be discussed further in the upcoming section on accountability.

All of these entities constitute the leadership level of the mission system (Exhibit 8.6). The direction of the arrows indicates who delegates (delegator) power to whom (delegate).

Capitalizing on Volunteer and Professional Staff Strengths The leadership of a mission system embraces the strengths of its resources and minimizes its weaknesses. Volunteer boards' duties of benefit and oversight capitalize on volunteer strengths—passion for and experience in benefit or cause—and are not limited by volunteer constraints—temporary time, short terms, and lack of specific business experience.

The business duties of CEOs and professional staff capitalize on staff strengths—permanent, full-time responsibility and experience in nonprofit finance, marketing, operations, education, and general management—and are not limited by staff constraints—

EXHIBIT 8.6 THE LEADERSHIP LEVELS OF A MISSION SYSTEM

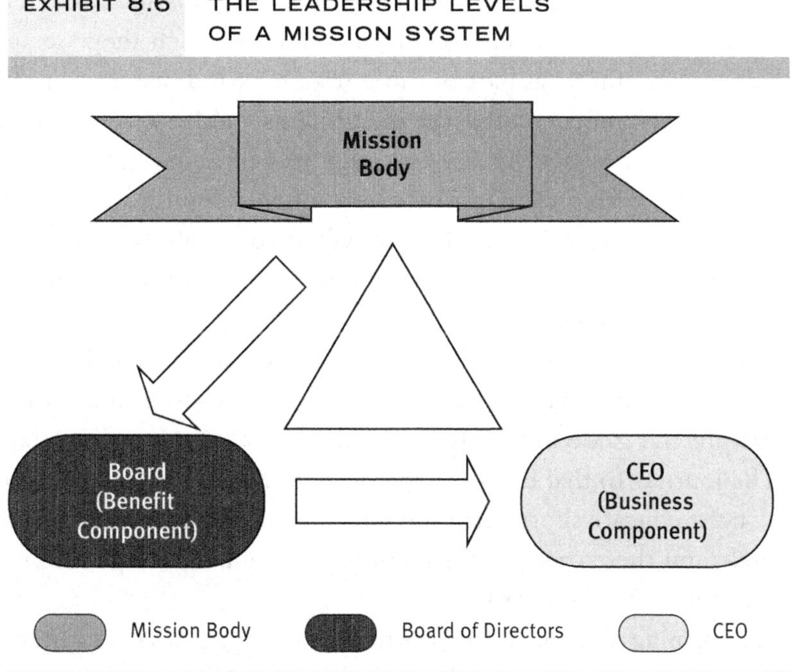

limited expertise and/or day-to-day experience in benefit and lack of direct benefit passion.

A board member may have more management experience than the CEO in certain areas, or a CEO may be a very skilled mission practitioner, but given the limits of their respective volunteer and staff roles, each uses those skills better doing their own jobs rather than the other's.

The Managing and Operating Levels To visualize and chart the managing and operating levels, we must make some reasonable assumptions about the mix of committees and departments that exist in a typical nonprofit. This is merely for illustrative purposes; the actual mix of mission system contents depends on an individual nonprofit's mission and needs.

A further explanation regarding the terms "operations" and "administration" helps clarify their appearance on the chart. *Operations* is generic for work associated with programs and services (i.e., programs specific to that nonprofit such as chapter services, fund development, and community relations). *Administration* is generic for general program support areas such as finance, human resources, and technology.

With this in mind, Exhibit 8.7 illustrates the managing and operating levels.

At this level, the mission chart deviates most from acceptable nonprofit norms. At least conceptually, sector experts and nonprofit leaders agree on the leadership level. Boards report to constituents and CEOs to boards, but no such agreement on the reporting structure of staff and volunteers exists at the managing/operating levels.

Volunteer Groups Board members usually agree that CEOs should determine and manage all resources needed to achieve an outcome for which they are accountable, but add volunteer committees as part of those resources, and that answer changes.

The concept that volunteer committees and groups should report to professional staff is anathema to volunteer leaders. This is especially true in long-entrenched committee structures where committee chair positions are often stepping stones to board and executive committee positions. Few leaders are willing to openly admit that the problem of unclear roles and accountabilities that plague nonprofits lies with the construct and reporting of volunteer groups.

Mission system thinking is pretty simple: the person accountable for an outcome is the person who selects and manages the resources necessary to produce that outcome. This limits the pretend game in which a committee outcome is really a staff outcome in disguise. The journey to that outcome is that staff inherits general resources selected by the board, must educate short-term members during limited meetings on months of staff research, and then arranges for members to rubber-stamp and present these "committee decisions" to the board.

In a high-performing mission system, boards or their delegates select and manage the resources that they need to reach benefit and governance outcomes, and CEOs or their

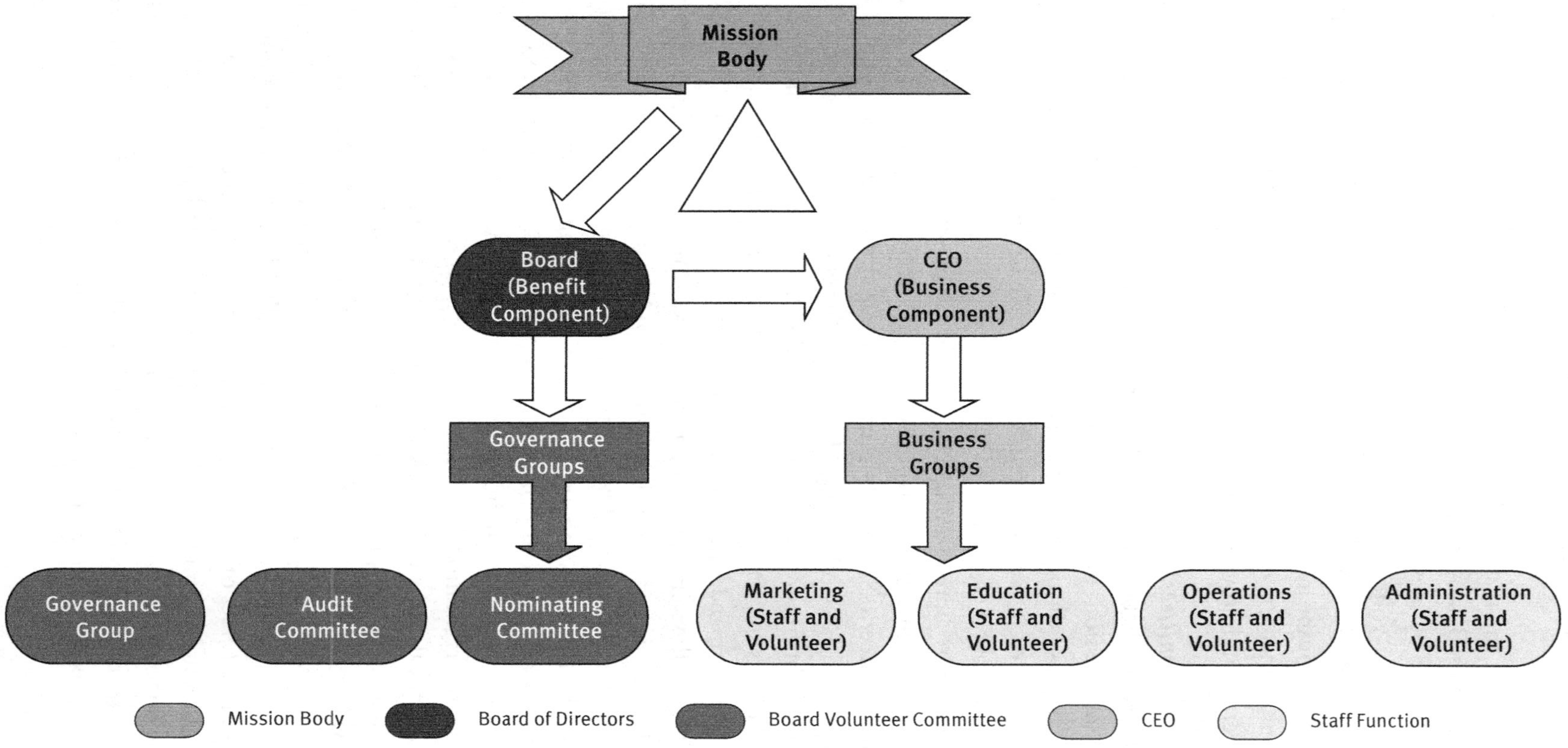

EXHIBIT 8.7 THE MANAGING AND OPERATING LEVELS OF A MISSION SYSTEM

delegates select and manage the resources that they need to reach business and management outcomes. Boards are accountable for benefit or mission outcomes, and CEOs are accountable for business or organizational outcomes.

Because most volunteer resources in a mission system are dedicated to producing business outcomes, most of the volunteer groups will report to the appropriate business manager. The pushback to this kind of thinking will be strong because it flies in the face of entrenched *I'm the Expert* logic. It is an especially hard sell in a nonprofit burdened with several standing versus ad hoc committees.

Standing Committees versus Ad Hoc Groups Under one mission system, standing committees should be limited to those required by law and those representing ongoing, permanent mission need or mission-body sensitivity. They are usually defined in a nonprofit's constitution or bylaws. A good example is the common need for a transparent, open process for nominating people to the board. Another is the need for a credentialing body.

The reasons to limit standing committees are many. First, because they endure over long periods of time, their makeup and purpose often becomes obsolete or unaligned with current needs. Second, because standing committees are defined in nonprofit constitutions/bylaws, changing these committees often results in a knock-down, drag—out fight from committee leaders. Finally, standing committees tend to duplicate staff efforts but report to the board—the *Mission Impossible* elephant at its worst!

Rather than mandating standing committees, nonprofit bylaws should give boards and CEOs the flexibility and power to form committees and volunteer groups as needs dictate. Using our hypothetical nonprofit UMA as an example, the following illustrates the mission benefits of an ad hoc committee versus a standing committee.

The UMA has a standing strategic planning committee. Being asked to serve on this committee is a prestigious prize eagerly sought by past leaders. The UMA decides to address a specific topic: childhood obesity. It's unlikely that the strategic planning committee has the right mix of volunteer resources to specifically address childhood obesity. As is typical, the standing strategic planning committee has ongoing activities on its agenda and cannot quickly address a new issue. It's more than likely that the committee will rely on the CEO Melanie to find and contact the experts—and do the work.

Contrast the standing strategic planning committee with an UMA board-appointed ad hoc group of childhood obesity experts. The board puts the right people on the right bus. Task forces of experts not only get results, but they also engender the enthusiasm and loyalty of constituents who can use special talents to meet a specific goal.

In the one-mission system, any standing committee needed to produce benefit component outcomes is selected and managed by the board, and any committee needed to produce business component outcomes is selected and managed by the CEO.

Keystone Concept Three: Accountability Is the Key to a High-Performing Mission System

A curious tendency of nonprofit leaders is to do everyone else's job but their own. Boards do management, CEOs do governance, and committees often do whatever the strongest member wants. The reason this occurs is in the dual volunteer/staff structure. Everyone is responsible for the same activities, but no one is accountable for the final activity outcome, so parties are free to focus on whatever appeals most to them at the moment.

A high-performing mission system relies on three things:

1. Clear, distinct, and known accountabilities
2. Equally clear, distinct, and known constraints that limit power within those accountabilities
3. Autonomy to operate within these boundaries

Given the myriad responsibilities that lie within global accountabilities, typically each entity should have no more than five such accountabilities. To whittle down to this level, we'll borrow a term that Gladwell uses in his book *Blink*—thin-slicing.[5] Tune out the extraneous process and activities and ask the question: What global outcome do all of the activities produce?

Board Accountability Both board and CEO operate under the umbrella of mission. Both are honor-bound to place the needs of mission first. But these two entities derive their power and accountability from very different sources—the board directly from the mission body and the CEO directly from the board.

In all, boards have three global areas of accountability—benefit, organizational oversight, and financial safekeeping. The mission body directly holds boards accountable for the benefit component. The law holds boards accountable for operating in accordance to its mission and for the purpose for which it gained tax exemption. The mission body and incorporation law hold boards accountable for the integrity of the entire mission system.

Nonprofit boards face some unique challenges in discharging their responsibilities. Unlike for-profit boards that can judge CEO and organizational performance by reviewing profit and stock market indicators, with little need for direct contact with customers, nonprofit boards cannot do the same. Profit is not the sole indicator of good performance, and sometimes, it's just the opposite. A good example of the latter is foundations with large endowment funds that keep using earnings to beget more earnings rather than produce mission outcomes.

Nor can nonprofit boards rely on outside experts or stock market indicators to judge performance. Nonprofit boards define broad mission goals, but CEOs, not boards, implement these goals. The only real way nonprofit boards can judge whether their mission goals are accomplished is to ask their constituents.

Board Accountability: The Benefit Component Boards are accountable for the benefit component—for defining, shaping, and safekeeping mission. Boards translate the will of the mission body into mission strategies. At least annually, boards must define mission goals—what mission outcomes go to which part of the constituency at what cost.

Safekeeping mission not only means setting mission goals, but it also means updating mission by continually scanning the horizon for internal and external trends that might impact mission and mission strategies. Sometimes these two areas—representing constituent will and updating mission—conflict. This is another reason why being a volunteer board member is not for the faint of heart!

To better understand this issue, let's look at another hypothetical example of how the United Medical Association (UMA) board might properly fulfill its mission accountabilities, and then plot what that looks like on our mission system chart.

Assume that the UMA board is watching a patient trend toward alternative rather than traditional medical cures. The board sees this trend continuing and that it might greatly affect its constituency. They also know that a recent constituent survey showed half the members strongly opposed to assimilating alternative medicine ideas into their practices.

Although part of the constituency may object, the UMA board is accountable for safekeeping mission currency, and that means they need to explore any trend that affects their stated mission. They might do so through one of the mission strategies shown in Exhibit 8.8.

In Strategies One and Two, the UMA board retains global accountability for shaping mission but delegates clear responsibility for a specific outcome to either volunteer group, outside vendor, or CEO. Now, contrast that with the strategy shown in Exhibit 8.9—the one favored by most *I'm the Expert* boards in a dual operating structure.

In this third strategy, the board still retains accountability for shaping mission, but it's not clear who is accountable for the outcome. Most likely, the CEO does the same work as she does in the second strategy, but she must work twice as hard to educate and keep a generalist task force involved. If the CEO has no time to coordinate this board group, she simply "pushes the peas around the plate" and lets the task force spin its wheels until the next board comes along.

Despite *I'm the Expert* fears to the contrary, both of the first two strategies can work well. In Strategy One, boards manage the board committee and process; in Strategy Two, boards completely delegate the project to the CEO. If boards really hold CEOs accountable for achieving an outcome, CEOs have no incentive to do other than assemble the best volunteer advisors, subject experts, and staff to achieve that outcome.

EXHIBIT 8.8 UMA MISSION STRATEGY CHOICES

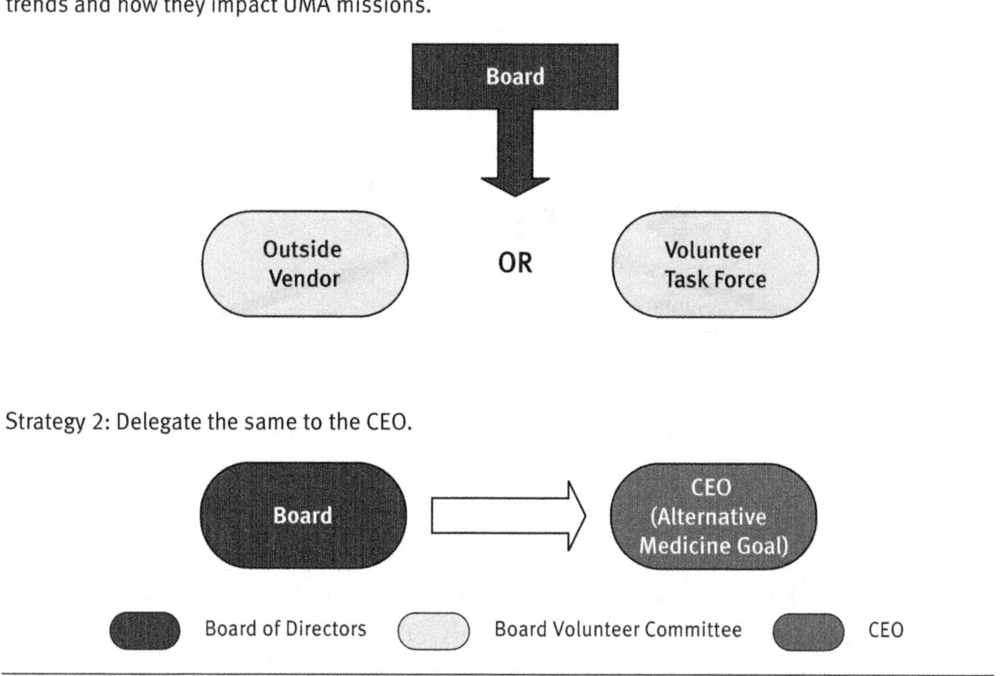

Board Accountability: CEO Leadership and Organizational Effectiveness The board is accountable to the mission body for organizational oversight—in general, for seeing that the nonprofit has the CEO, infrastructure, and resources necessary to achieve mission goals. In a mission system, boards fulfill this accountability by:

1. Hiring the CEO and facilitating CEO success
2. Delegating full business component accountability to the CEO
3. Exercising proper CEO oversight

Chapters 11 and 12 cover these items thoroughly, so we won't spend much time here. However, it is worth repeating an earlier comment—boards do not achieve their mission goals directly. They must rely on CEOs for that. And that means that boards are only high-performing if CEOs are high-performing.

Board Accountability: A Fiscally Healthy, High-Performing Mission System Boards are accountable for fiscal and risk management and for monitoring mission system performance. Both legally and via the expectations of the mission body, boards have fiduciary accountability for ensuring that all parts of the mission system operate ethically and in

EXHIBIT 8.9 DUAL-STRUCTURE STRATEGY

Strategy 3: Select a volunteer task force to summarize alternative medicine trends and propose how those trends impact UMA mission and constituents; direct the CEO to coordinate the process.

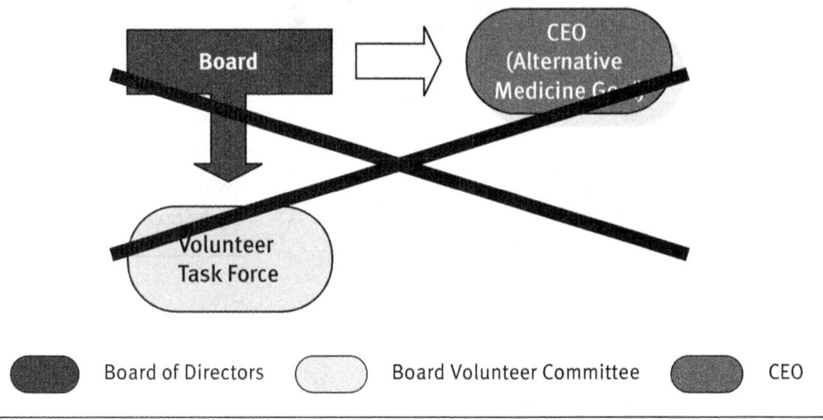

a prudent financial manner. Not only should board policies protect the nonprofit from undue financial risk, but boards must make every effort to make sure that these policies are understood and followed.

Fiduciary accountability is often feared and misunderstood by volunteer boards, so Chapter 11 goes into this topic in depth. Our purpose here is just to recognize that boards are accountable for identifying areas of mission-system-wide risk (e.g., maintaining proper insurance levels, filing income tax returns, maintaining a balanced budget) and creating and monitoring policies that avoid such risk.

Beyond a board's global risk accountability, boards are also accountable for financial and performance oversight. In turn, boards make CEOs accountable for the safety, financial well-being, and performance of the business component, but they must faithfully oversee CEO performance in this area.

The Board Accountability Description The sum of a board's accountabilities equals the *Board Accountability Description*. Ever so much better than a regular job description with its pages of activities, this global document clearly defines the board's accountabilities in terms that constituents can understand. Exhibit 8.10 illustrates a sample Board Accountability Description.

CEO Accountability Boards delegate accountability for a subset of the mission system—the business component—to the CEO. That CEOs report to the board and not the mission body, although somewhat subtle on the surface, has a huge effect on CEO performance.

On the subject of protecting CEOs from constituents, Fareed Zakaria, in *The Future of Freedom,* speaks specifically about the pressure of special-interest groups in modern democracy. Substitute the words "volunteer boards" for "governments," and his ideas resonate in the nonprofit world.

> Governments will have to make hard choices, resist the temptation to pander, and enact policies for the long run. The only possible way this can be achieved in a modern democracy is by insulating some decision-makers from the intense pressures of interest groups, lobbies, and political campaigns—that is to say from the intense pressures of democracy.[6]

The mission body is a form of democracy where the potential for small special-interest groups and vested volunteers hijacking the mission will of the majority is great. By delegating the power to make business decisions to an unelected CEO, the board insulates the CEO from the lobbying of vested interests and a largely uninformed (in regards to the business component) mission body. That leaves CEOs free to make informed business decisions that have long-term consequences based on the greater good of the whole, not the self-interested good of a small oligarchy.

Wise boards expect their CEOs to spend most of their time performing, not politicking. Such boards understand that they, not the CEO, are the elected representatives

EXHIBIT 8.10 BOARD ACCOUNTABILITY DESCRIPTION

Accountability 1: The XYZ board is accountable for the benefit component of the XYZ nonprofit.

Major Responsibilities:

- Connecting with constituents to determine mission, mission needs, and mission satisfaction
- Articulating mission through vision and mission strategies
- Safekeeping mission by shaping it as appropriate to current trends

Accountability 2: The XYZ board is accountable for the global effectiveness of XYZ mission system.

Major Responsibilities:

- Hiring a CEO leader and facilitating conditions conducive to CEO success
- Holding the CEO accountable for the business component
- Holding the CEO accountable for translating mission strategies into business goals and achieving related measurable outcomes
- Monitoring and improving board performance
- Creating and monitoring key indicators of mission system health

Accountability 3: The XYZ board is accountable for maintaining sound fiscal and risk policies.

Major Responsibilities:

- Identifying areas of major financial and ethical risk; setting policies to protect the mission system; ensuring those risks are followed
- Holding the CEO accountable for sound fiscal and ethical practices of the business component

of the mission body, and they are the body directly accountable to the people. They accept managing constituent politics as part of their job without expecting the CEO to run interference.

Contrary to *I'm the Expert* fears, delegating autonomy to the CEO does not mean that CEOs can merrily run away with the ship or guide it far away from mission waters. CEOs are accountable to boards and usually go seriously amuck only when those boards are asleep at the wheel.

One of the clearer definitions of CEO accountabilities is found in Carver's Policy Governance (PG) model. The basic idea is that boards hold CEOs accountable for achieving board-defined outcomes (in PG language, *ends policies*) while avoiding board-set constraints (in PG language, *executive limitations*). Frankly, this is a great model for distinguishing between board and CEO accountabilities, and it works well for boards that are disciplined enough to implement and follow it.

The problem is that this kind of discipline runs counter to the constraints of volunteer leadership. Most volunteer boards either cannot or will not make the time to climb an initially steep learning curve and lack the political skills to institutionalize the model beyond their terms in office. So, in keeping with this book's philosophy of practical ideas that work in the real nonprofit workplace, we'll adapt the best of Dr. Carver's ideas into mission system thinking—with the caveat that our application may or may not be what Carver had in mind at all.

In our mission system, CEOs are accountable for achieving board-defined mission outcomes within the boundaries of board-defined constraints. More specifically, CEOs are accountable for:

1. Achieving board-set mission outcomes
2. Achieving business component outcomes that maximize the effectiveness of all business component resources, practices, programs, and services
3. Operating within the constraints set by federal/state law, nonprofit constitution and/or bylaws, board policies, and commonly understood business practice

CEO Accountability: Achieving Board-Set Mission Outcomes CEOs are accountable for translating board-defined mission outcomes into business component goals—mission programs and services.

Chapter 12 illustrates how this works in detail, but let's create a simple example here. Assume that one of the UMA board strategies is that "physicians will be knowledgeable about alternative medicine cures." The board wants the entire constituency to benefit from this outcome and sets a certain percentage of the next fiscal budget for this endeavor.

Further assume that the CEO Melanie translates this board strategy into business component programs and services and gets board approval that these outcomes achieve the board-defined mission outcome. She then delegates the following program goals to her staff directors:

Staff Practices Director

Goal: Develop an UMA practice statement on alternative medicine and traditional medical practice.

Staff Education Director

Goal: Develop and deliver one continuing education program that teaches how to integrate alternative medicine into traditional practice.

Note that although the CEO retains global accountability for achieving board mission outcomes, she delegates accountability for specific program goals to appropriate staff directors. Just as the CEO and board must agree, the CEO and staff directors must mutually agree upon goals and the measurements that indicate those goals are met. Considering the aforementioned goals, our mission chart might look like Exhibit 8.11.

EXHIBIT 8.11 MISSION CHART

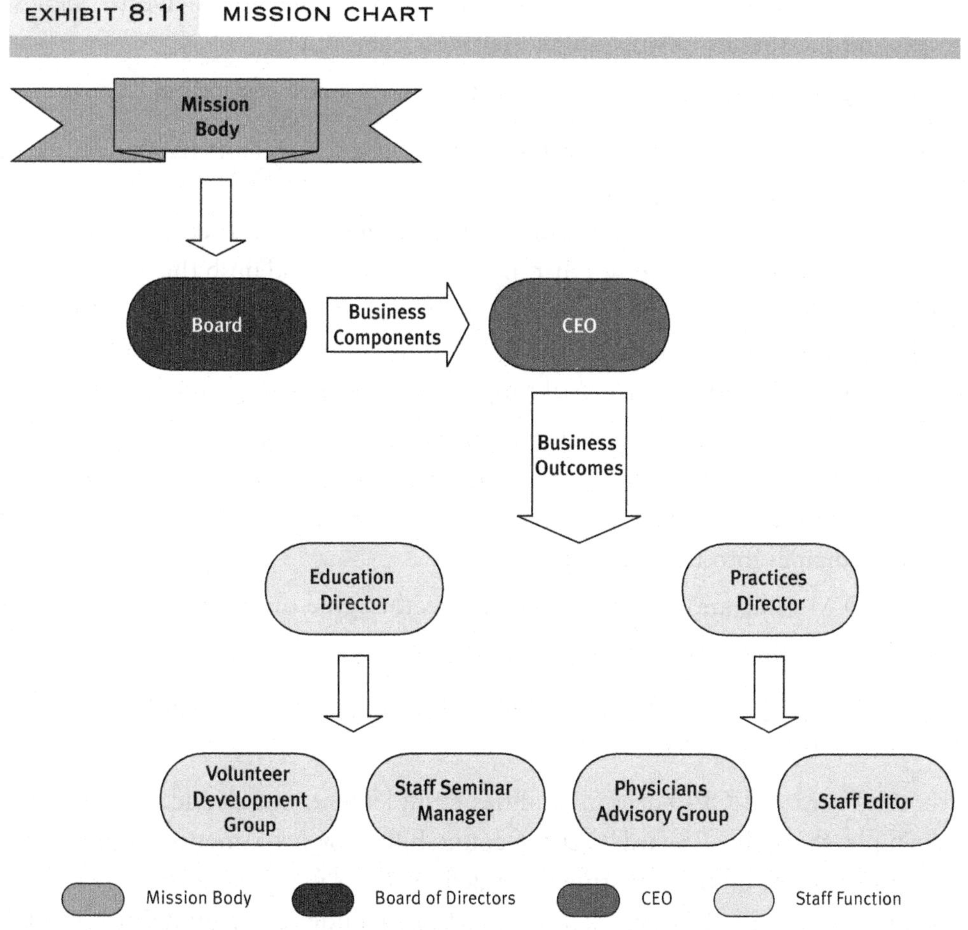

CEO Accountability: Achieving Business Component Outcomes That Maximize the Effectiveness of All Business Component Resources, Practices, Programs, and Services
Globally, CEOs are accountable for continually setting business component goals that improve business component performance. This includes effectively managing the people, infrastructure, and financial resources necessary to support existing programs and services and to deliver new mission goals.

Stop for a minute and think about what this encompasses, and then you'll begin to understand why the CEO position is no place for a beginning manager. Responsibilities within this accountability include:

- Ensuring the financial integrity of the business component: financial planning and budgeting, proper management and safekeeping of all financial assets, effective day-to-day management of revenue and expense, effective management of investments, timely filing of income tax forms, accurate reporting of key financial data, etc.
- Establishing or overseeing all policies and processes related to programs, services, and other business component activities
- Effective leadership of staff and facilitating conditions conducive to their success and the success of mission and business component goals
- Keeping the board informed about significant business component activity

The list could go on and, again, Chapters 11 and 12 fill in that kind of detail, but what's key here are two points.

First, CEOs are accountable not only for maintaining the status quo but also for setting business component outcomes that improve processes and push the envelope. Continually improving practices, programs, and services is much more difficult than simply managing what is there. To illustrate the point using our hypothetical UMA example, a business component performance goal might look like this:

> The UMA has no computerized system for tracking volunteer skills and preferences. This limits the staff's ability to tap into physician volunteers who have specific expertise for volunteer advisory groups (e.g., knowledgeable in the integration of alternative medicines into traditional practice).
>
> The CEO Melanie and the membership director agree on the following goal:
>
> **Membership Director**
>
> *Goal:* Examine methods of collecting and accessing volunteer information, and implement the best system.

Second, board and CEO accountabilities complement, not duplicate, one another. For example, the split of board/CEO accountability for investments might look like this: The board sets global investment guidelines (e.g., percentage of the investment portfolio that is invested in stocks, bonds, and cash); under these guidelines, the CEO directs the day-to-day management processes that maximize portfolio performance.

Boards are accountable for creating broad financial policy and addressing major financial risk; CEOs are accountable for managing the business component financial resources within these board set boundaries. Yet, how many nonprofit boards have investment committees to "manage portfolios." These committees typically meet once or twice a year, trying to duplicate the investment managing job of a full-time CEO and CFO, while neither board or committee address the macro-risk and investment policies for which they are truly accountable and that protect the nonprofit.

CEO Accountability: Operating within the Constraints of Federal/State Law, Nonprofit Constitution/Bylaws, and Board-Set Executive Limits Globally, CEOs are accountable for not violating or allowing practices that violate federal or state law or their nonprofit's constitution and/or bylaws. In addition, they must operate within the boundaries of board policies as set forth in the Board Policy Manual (see Chapter 11). Examples of CEO accountabilities in this area include:

- Meeting all state and federal filing and payment requirements
- Adhering to board-set ethical practices and avoiding conflicts of interest such as personal business relationships with vendors or awarding nonprofit contracts to volunteer friends

The CEO Accountability Description The sum of all a CEO's accountabilities equals a *CEO Accountability Description*. Exhibit 8.12 shows an example.

Board and CEO and the Mission System

How do the three keystone concepts and board/CEO accountabilities interrelate and positively impact the mission system? Returning to our UMA example seems a good way to answer this question. Let's assume that one of the UMA board's mission strategies is this:

Board Mission Strategy: Physicians will be knowledgeable about alternative medicine cures.

The CEO creates and the board agrees to the following business component strategies and goals:

CEO Business Strategy: Develop programs and services to educate physicians on alternative medicine.

Goal: Develop an UMA practice statement on alternative medicine and traditional medical practice.

Goal: Create and deliver one continuing education program that illustrates how to integrate alternative medicine into traditional practice.

This simple example illustrates how board and CEO complement each other and how their respective benefit and business accountabilities mesh. A strong UMA board stays

EXHIBIT 8.12 CEO ACCOUNTABILITY DESCRIPTION

Accountability 1: The XYZ CEO is accountable for achieving XYZ board mission strategies.

Major Responsibilities:

- Translating board mission strategies into business component objectives and goals
- Creating key performance measurements that CEO and board agree prove business component goals are met
- Achieving said business component goals

Accountability 2: The XYZ CEO is accountable for maximizing the effectiveness of all business component resources, practices, programs, and services.

Major Responsibilities:

- Ensuring the financial integrity of the business component: financial planning and budgeting, proper management and safekeeping of all financial assets, effective day-to-day management of revenue and expense, effective management of investments, timely filing of income tax forms, accurate reporting of key financial data, etc.
- Establishing and/or overseeing all policies and processes related to programs, services, and other business component activities
- Effective leadership of staff and facilitating conditions conducive to their success and the success of mission and business component goals
- Keeping the board informed about significant business component activity
- Keeping the staff informed about significant benefit component activity

Accountability 3: The XYZ CEO is accountable for operating within the constraints of federal/state law, nonprofit constitution/bylaws, and board-set executive limits.

Major Responsibilities:

- Meeting all state and federal law: includes filing and payment requirements
- Adhering to board policies as set forth in the Board Policy Manual; includes avoiding conflict of interest such as personal business relationships with vendors or awarding nonprofit contracts to volunteer friends

---

alert to trends and creates mission strategies to keep mission relevant. If mission goes astray (e.g., the alternative medicine trend is ignored), that's the board's fault, and it is accountable to the mission body. Over time, constituents punish such poor performance by electing new volunteer leaders.

A strong CEO takes the board's mission strategy and translates it into appropriate mission programs, but if those programs aren't on target (e.g., education programs don't create alternative medicine training), that's the CEO's fault, and she is accountable to the UMA board. The board will factor the failure to properly deliver business component goals into the CEO's performance review.

The beauty of a mission system with global accountabilities is that when the board and CEO do their jobs, the mission system is positively affected. When one or both do not, they are held accountable, the problem is identified, and the likelihood of it being repeated is lessened.

Embracing the keystone concepts makes it relatively simple to accept the structure, relationships, and interactions of a single mission system. But gaining this insight and implementing the policies and practices that support the one-mission system is a much more complicated task—one that requires a radically different mindset than that found in most nonprofits today.

Making the Changes Stick

Peter Senge provides an interesting insight into why so many nonprofit change initiatives are not sustained:

> Some people think that the "structure" of the organization is the organizational chart. Others think that "structure" means the design of organizational work flow and processes. But in systems thinking the "structure" is the pattern of interrelationships among key components of the system.
>
> Beware the easiest, fastest solution. People prefer to intervene in a system at the level of rules, physical structure, work processes, material and information flows, reward systems, and control mechanisms—where the elements are more visible and it requires less skill to work with them. But as you move to the more intangible elements, such as people's deep-seated attitudes and beliefs, your leverage for effective change increases. You come closer to looking at the underlying reasons why the rules, physical structure, and work processes take their current form.[7]

Simply implementing a new structure, be it governance or management, will not in itself have a long-term, positive effect on the mission system. Thinking systemically requires rejecting surface solutions and standing up to the political pressure to find an easy solution. If the behavior of vested volunteers is the real problem, then circumventing that behavior with a new governance structure is not going to fix the problem. If the real problem is the failure of the CEO to supply the board with key financial data, implementing the Balanced Scorecard is not going to improve CEO performance.

Change needs to start in the minds and hearts of a few brave nonprofit leaders and then slowly expand and become part of the fabric and culture of the nonprofit. This will not happen quickly, or without a continuing effort toward change. Nonprofits face a steep uphill climb, and a little help from your friends is just what the next section provides.

Cultivating a Different Mindset

An analogy applies here: Plants don't grow because a gardener stands over them yelling "grow." Rather, seeds germinate because they are planted in fertile soil in a favorable climate. The same concept applies to changing the behavior of the *Mission Impossible* elephant and *I'm the Expert* attitudes. Nonprofits can use the following five tools to meet this challenge:

1. Reframe the argument
2. Address *I'm the Expert* fears openly

3. Prepare for vested arguments
4. Target key decision makers early
5. Practice, practice, practice

Reframe the Argument Too many times, potential changes at the leadership level are preceded by a grand announcement that goes something like this: "We're appointing a task force that will propose changes to make our governance structure stronger and better." Once such a pronouncement is made, two things happen simultaneously. Old-timers grumble "not again," and vested volunteers meet in covert groups to plan their attack.

Why not try a different approach? Don't position the pending changes as a new governance structure; in fact, don't make any grand announcement at all. As Nike says, Just Do It! Discuss the changes in the context of an ongoing process of improving board and staff processes and adapting to environmental changes (e.g., the need for capacity building or increased competition for funds, programs, services, or volunteer time).

After all, boards and CEOs do share accountability for improving governance and business processes, respectively. Position the move from a dual operating structure to one mission system as just one goal in a continuous process of improving leadership effectiveness. The following is a simple plan that illustrates just such a strategy:

Step 1: Board and CEO review the current volunteer structure and create a plan and timeline for reviewing the activities of each committee.

Step 2: The board selects a respected, independent party that works with each committee chair and staff liaison to assess the actions and outcomes of each committee. The independent party may be an outside consultant or inside "sage," but it's essential that volunteer and staff leaders respect the impartiality of whoever is selected.

Step 3: The independent party reviews the minutes and works with participants to evaluate the committee's effectiveness (e.g., does it duplicate another entity? engage mostly in activity or outcomes? could outcomes be better produced elsewhere?). Sample activities/questions might include:

1. List the lasting outcomes from the past five year's committee minutes.
2. Are those outcomes benefit or business work? Accountable to board or CEO?
3. Figure the percentage of committee time spent on activities versus outcomes.
4. Who really produced the outcomes (e.g., did the research, wrote the information, etc.)?
5. Were the outcomes implemented? What positive mission system change occurred? Was it measurable?

6. Who is accountable for ongoing outcome success? How is it measured?
7. Who performs oversight and how?

The point is that boards and CEOs don't need to rile everyone up by tackling the whole process at once, but can systematically target areas one at a time and gradually transform the whole structure.

Openly Address *I'm the Expert* Fears Subliminal fears must be exposed to the light of day and addressed in an open and factual manner. Most nonprofit leaders harbor some *I'm the Expert* prejudices, and just telling them that they are wrong won't make them change. In fact, quite the opposite, because most of the time it just makes those attitudes more entrenched.

Instead, create safe opportunities for volunteers to vocalize their fears, and then use logic and example to frame the fear and show that an alternative outcome is at variance with what they fear most. We can see how this technique works by looking at some of the most common *I'm the Expert* fears.

Fear of CEO Power If key volunteer leaders view the board as weak—if their friends are not on the board or proposed changes veer from the course set during their board terms, this may very well be the case—they fear that a strong CEO will overpower the board, and staff, not volunteers, will control the nonprofit.

This is where boards need political savvy and connectedness with key volunteers and constituents. This creates informal opportunities to illustrate through example how the board/CEO relationship really works, how boards exercise accountability, and how board policies and practices effectively balance CEO power. These kinds of informal conversations show a strong board that cares about the opinions of its constituents and that engenders the trust of constituents. Such reassurance can only come from the board, because CEO efforts in this vein will be seen as partisan and self-serving.

What kind of dialogue should occur? Certainly, boards should develop talking points that are a primer of the keystone concepts. Plenty of pithy examples that illustrate these concepts in situations unique to their nonprofit will drive home the benefits of thinking and acting as a one-mission system. Most important, boards need to highlight the transparent safeguards embedded in board policy that protect the nonprofit from abuses of power at all levels.

Fear of Limited Volunteer Involvement Longtime volunteers who love volunteer action fear that a strong board and CEO in a structure with few standing committees will severely limit volunteer opportunities. That fear escalates exponentially when staff selects and manages volunteer resources. But, in fact, just the opposite is true. Fear that people can't volunteer runs counter to the fact that more people volunteer when their time commitment is respected through real work and achievement of real goals. A strong staff component can both engage new volunteers and develop a new membership base.

Consider the response of Nataki Foodall, staff manager for young professionals for the National Urban Leagues of New York, as she tackled a common association complaint—the graying of the member base and the lack of engaged young professional members:

> In two years we've grown from four Young Professional (YP) affiliate chapters to 40, and our budget has grown from $57,000 to $1.2 million thanks to the growth. The formula for our successes is remembering the "3Ts" of young professionals—**time, tempo, and transition.**
>
> **Time:** YPs are in a career-building stage and many work 50 to 60 hours per week. We need to work on their clock and fit opportunities into the time they have available.
>
> **Tempo:** YPs have good ideas and want to do them immediately. To meet that need, we created a special account of money they can access in a week. The account is funded by personal and chapter gifts. It provides seed money, and the YPs love the ability to run with their ideas. We've taken some of these successful ideas and implemented them nationwide.
>
> **Transition:** This is the greatest challenge—YPs live in a constant transition with career, life, and relationships. We work to find ways to keep them engaged throughout the life changes. Eventually they get used to the new job, new spouse, or new baby and come back to us as they can.
>
> One thing that helped fuel our growth was redefining what it means to be involved as a YP. We teach our YPs there are three ways to be active: They can be a doer, a donor, or a door opener. This mind shift has created a lot of new opportunities for us.[8]

Use Existing Trends to Mitigate Fears Another approach is to introduce outside studies that support the need for change. Such studies reassure volunteers that their nonprofit is forward thinking and ahead of the curve. For example, the following excerpt from an *Association Management* article dovetails nicely into support of the keystone concepts:

> **Volunteers want short assignments:** Reluctance to commit to a long-term volunteer assignment is so prevalent that it's moving from a trend to an established fact. Members are stressed and time-starved. Yet we have earned the reputation of rewarding good volunteer work with more volunteer work, meaning we often burn out our best people.
>
> - Supports the argument for eliminating standing committees and involving volunteers in specific, time-limited projects and task forces.
>
> **Volunteers prefer multitasking opportunities:** Volunteering is a leisure time activity in which members participate after filling the priority demands of job and family. They will do all sorts of tasks if they enjoy what they are doing and the people they are doing it with.
>
> - Supports the argument that more volunteers are out there—a strong staff can use creative methods like encouraging families to volunteer together, recruiting groups of friends to volunteer together and enjoy each other's company while helping the less fortunate or advancing your profession.

The article also illustrates how to add an element of fun to such surveys. It contains the following true-or-false quiz that reveals interesting statistics about the changing attitudes about volunteer work:

1. *Volunteerism continues to decline because of today's hectic lifestyle.*
   False. In the most recent numbers from the Bureau of Labor Statistics, 63.8 million people did volunteer work in 2003, up from the 59.8 million in 2002.
2. *Women are more likely than men to serve as volunteers.*
   True. Women volunteer at a higher rate than men, a relationship that holds true across age groups, education levels, and other major characteristics. For 2003, 32.2 percent of women did volunteer work, compared to 25.1 percent of men.
3. *Because they have more time on their hands, retirees are the most likely group to volunteer.*
   False. The Labor Department finds that the age group most likely to volunteer is 35- to 44-year-olds, at 34.7 percent.
4. *The estimated hourly value of volunteer time is less than the minimum wage.*
   False. The Independent Sector estimates that the estimated hourly value of volunteer time in 2003 was $17.19 per hour.
5. *You can double the number of your volunteers by simply asking people to participate.*
   True. The Independent Sector calls it "the power of the ask," citing statistics that reveal that the percentage of people who volunteer when asked is 71 percent, compared to the 29 percent who volunteer on their own.[9]

Fear That Staff Will Not Seek the Informed Wisdom of Volunteers When followed to their logical conclusions, some fears simply don't make sense, and this is one of them. If you know that you'll truly be held accountable for an outcome, what do you do? Hang out with your buddies and party or seek the resources you need to achieve a successful outcome? An experienced staff director who is accountable for a walk-a-thon and whose performance is measured by donations and volunteer/participant feedback has a huge incentive to find and select appropriate volunteer and staff resources.

Other than logic, tangible things like an active online volunteer database reassure constituents that volunteer opportunities exist. The best systems allow constituents to update their volunteer interests and skills online, and again volunteers trust what they can see and control. Part of the CEO's job is to make sure that staff directors tap into the base and continually engage qualified, new volunteers.

Furthermore, if key volunteers have specific mission-related concerns regarding the members of a specific committee or group, boards can address those concerns through board policies that define selection criteria (e.g., term limits or requiring a certain number of new members per term). Note, the words "mission-related"—that is the only time that boards should consider this option.

Be Ready for Vested Arguments Although most constituents and volunteers have an open mind and will listen to logic and facts, a small percentage of vested volunteers will not. Once this group emerges, boards should not waste their time trying to convince the "unconvinceable"—jump over their heads and work on those who still have open minds.

No matter how gradually boards and CEOs try to change to one mission system, vested volunteers will emerge and lobby against the changes with their "members want" arguments. In particular, they will take advantage of the confusion that surrounds any change by twisting small bits of information out of context and using inflammatory conclusions to rally the masses.

In this vein, it's illuminating to understand what Alexander Hamilton and James Madison did when facing a contentious debate over our national constitution: they used the Federalist papers to rationally spell out their arguments and inform and persuade a largely uninformed populace. Boards need to find their talented Madisons and Hamiltons and publicly lay out the concepts, logic, and benefits of proposed changes ahead of the predictable partisan demagoguery of vested volunteers.

Target Key Decision Makers Early Another idea that Gladwell introduces in *The Tipping Point* is the concept of *connectors*—a small amount of people who link to everyone else in a few small steps.[10] These connectors know everyone and can rapidly spread the word throughout an entire population. Most of the rest of us link to the world through those special people.

As an ongoing practice, boards and CEOs should identify and communicate with nonprofit connectors at all levels of the organization. Such people not only influence the opinion of others, but they also give boards a quick pulse check of constituent opinion. In the face of global change such as the shift to one mission system, it is essential that boards know these people and work to gain their understanding, approval, and advocacy of proposed changes. However, it's possible and even probable that some of these connectors are the vested volunteers of the previous section. If so, boards must know what they are up against and commit the additional resources that will be necessary to counteract a strong vested influence.

Practice, Practice, Practice It may seem obvious—boards must embrace and model the keystone concepts—but sometimes the obvious is the easiest thing to overlook.

Someone once said that a new behavior becomes a new habit only after being repeated at least 15 times. The keystone concepts are a new way of thinking and acting. Appreciating the equal importance of volunteer and staff leadership, acknowledging their boundaries, and making mission-wide decisions doesn't just happen; it requires conscious thought and practice at every meeting and in every action.

Everybody uses the same global words and then just goes back to business as usual. To prevent this, evaluative time should be an essential part of every board agenda, an idea that we will explore more in later chapters. One good habit is to devote the last hour of each board meeting to an objective wrap-up and review of board performance. Although board presidents are accountable for effective board performance, they may want to appoint an independent ombudsman or governance group that is not part of the meeting for this task.

Boards need time alone, without the CEO, for these discussions. It's just easier to keep face when answering questions such as:

- Did we follow the policies outlined in the Board Policy Manual?
- Did discussions center on board accountability?
- Are motions activity or outcomes?
- Did our decisions consider all parts of the mission system?
- Are all directives to the CEO clear?
- How do motions positively impact the mission system?

Whatever method boards choose, it's important that they don't assume that others will embrace the keystone concepts unless these concepts are integral to board behavior. Needless to say, it takes a great deal of work and a lot of perseverance to change attitudes and culture. This leads us to the final section in this chapter: What comes after concepts are accepted and the *Mission Impossible* elephant is behaving?

Institutionalizing the One-Mission System

Once the dual system is gone and the mission system is in place, nonprofits must keep the changes in place and the mission system thriving beyond just one or two board cycles. The key is a three-pronged attack in the following areas: nonprofit bylaws, board policies, and board recruitment.

Constitution and Bylaws Things stated in nonprofit constitution and bylaws are instantly institutionalized, because these documents are legally enforceable and difficult to change. So, adding the keystone concepts and global leadership accountabilities to nonprofit bylaws in effect institutionalizes the framework of the mission system.

The basic strategy is simple: bylaws should contain important, global guidelines; the Board Policy Manual should detail more specific guidelines. Institutionalize the keystone concepts and global leadership accountabilities in nonprofit bylaws; institutionalize the responsibilities, limits, and process in the Board Policy Manual. The bylaws cement the broad mission system framework while delegating wide latitude for boards to align board policies and governance process as circumstances and environment dictate.

Advisory groups like the ASAE and BoardSource all provide model templates for drafting a nonprofit constitution, and attorneys specializing in nonprofit law are more than ready to help in this endeavor. Other than some tweaks added by differing incorporation law in various states, however, the basic format is pretty simple. The following illustrates the most common format, and the bold type indicates where one-mission system language might be inserted.

Article I:
Nonprofit name and location

Article II:
Mission as shown on IRS application and articles of incorporation

Articles III-X:
Separate articles that define such things as: makeup of members or constituent bodies; organizational entities like chapters; dues structures; etc.

Articles X-X:
Separate articles pertaining to state incorporation laws such as: time and place of meeting; voting requirements; officers, etc.

Articles X-X:
Separate articles detailing the authority and duties of the board of members, board president, CEO, and standing committees

(Add one-mission concepts and leadership accountabilities here; ideally, there should be no standing committees, but rather delegate global authority to the board and CEO to form volunteer groups as needed.)

Articles X-X:

Separate articles containing various housekeeping details such as what happens if the nonprofit dissolves or the procedures by which to amend the constitution

Boards may run into a real problem when they try to execute this simple concept. As noted previously, established nonprofits may be saddled with years of bylaws detail and a number of standing committees. Boards in such a nonprofit will need to employ every tactic mentioned in the earlier sections to get the votes to change the bylaws.

In some cases, existing bylaws are not specific. Boards need to assess whether the timing is right to add such language or whether that action would trigger a firestorm of resistance. Where the voting body is large, boards may need to educate parties that have no institutional knowledge or experience and meet only once a year on the rationale behind the necessary amendments.

It's certainly better to institutionalize the mission system in the bylaws, but if that is politically difficult, boards may chose to define mission system changes in the Board Policy Manual and wait to change the bylaws once the benefits of a mission system become clear.

Board Policies Chapter 11 discusses at length the kind of detail that the Board Policy Manual should contain. Just know that this is a very different animal than the traditional operating manual disguised as a board manual, nor is it a well-written tome that gathers dust on the shelf. The Board Policy Manual is a true governing document, and it's the best place to institutionalize the detail of the mission system's structure, relationships, limits, and process.

Board Recruitment and Orientation Once the mission system is institutionalized in bylaws and board policies, each new board member must commit to the form and substance of these laws and policies. Existing boards must make sure that both board recruitment and board orientation ensure this commitment upfront.

Board Recruitment Whatever form board recruitment takes (e.g., nominating committee, private board selection, public election), the process must ensure that candidates are knowledgeable about existing bylaws and board policy and that they understand that serving on the board requires embracing these concepts and policies.

That doesn't mean that candidates cannot propose changes and improvements to board policies once elected, because they can and they should. It does mean that candidates accept the totality of mission system and the fact that board service means maintaining and improving the existing system, not totally blowing it up and starting over again each new term.

Board Orientation All new board members should start their term with a complete orientation led by current and past volunteer leaders. This is not a short orientation on general duties of board members with a "meet the staff" handshake. This is a working session where the board chairperson and key leaders thoroughly discuss the keystone concepts, the Board Policy Manual, the board strategies currently underway, and the workings and process of meetings.

As we shall soon see, these last two strategies—institutionalizing changes through board policies and board recruitment/orientation—are not only the key to institutionalizing the good behavior of the *Mission Impossible* elephant but institutionalizing the positive behavior of all the elephants that follow.

Summing It Up

Making the leap from separate volunteer and staff structures to a one-mission system requires equal measures of leadership, patience, and perseverance. The reward for all this work is a high-performing organization that maximizes mission outcomes. Not a bad trade-off!

Notes

1. Malcolm Gladwell, *The Tipping Point* (New York: Bay Back Books/Little, Brown and Company, 2000, 2002), 89.
2. Peter Senge, Art Kleiner, Charlotte Roberts, Richard B. Ross, and Bryan J. Smith, *The Fifth Discipline Fieldbook* (New York: Doubleday, 1994), 6.
3. John Carver, *Boards That Make a Difference* (San Francisco: Jossey-Bass, 1997).
4. Kirsten A. Grønbjerg, Curtis Child, *Illinois Nonprofits: A Profile of Charities and Advocacy Organizations* (Chicago, IL: Donors Forum of Chicago, December 2003).
5. Malcolm Gladwell, *Blink: The Power of Thinking without Thinking* (New York: Little, Brown and Company, 2005), 18.
6. Fareed Zakaria, *The Future of Freedom* (New York: W. W. Norton, 2003), 242.
7. See note 2, 90–93.
8. Conversation, "The Voice of Young Professionals," *Executive IdeaLinks* (August 2005).
9. Susan J. Ellis, "Tracking Volunteer Trends," *Association Management* (January 2005): 72.
10. See note 1.

CHAPTER 9

The *Earth to Board* Solution: A Shared Reality

Leadership should be born out of the understanding of the needs of those who would be affected by it.

—Marian Anderson

TAMING THE *EARTH TO BOARD* ELEPHANT

On a recent survey of nonprofits, more than half of respondents reported membership levels flat or declining over the past three years. Nonprofit leaders share a common concern: current and prospective members, constituents, and donors are drifting away. A causative factor in this migration may well be a failure to understand stakeholder needs, identify trends affecting those needs, and adapt programs and services accordingly.

This is the *Earth to Board* elephant's territory. The pachyderm runs rampant through nonprofits that cannot distinguish the reality of the mission body from the noise of its parts. And it's most at home in nonprofits whose boards lack a strategic and systemic method of directly connecting with the mission body.

In This Chapter

The *Earth to Board* elephant calms down as nonprofits apply the second elephant solution—seeking a shared reality. Boards must relentlessly pursue mission feedback both within and outside the nonprofit, honing skills that assess the true state of the organization and aligning their decisions with that reality. Doing all this well requires a level of board discipline and leadership that truly separates the exceptional boards from the ordinary ones.

Elephant Solution Two: Seek a Shared Reality

We know from Chapter 4 that if boards are to understand constituent reality, they must distinguish the voices of the mission parts—volunteers, vested volunteers, and CEO—from the whole of the mission body. Somehow, boards must hear the voice of an amorphous whole.

Strategically Connecting with the Mission Body

The much-touted and well-applauded concept—connect with the mission body—in reality leaves boards just scratching their heads. What the heck does this really mean? How do they do it? Some board members think they already do, others think it's silly, still others believe the real work is budgets, and most simply have no idea where to start.

Boards often believe that their credibility with communities and consultants rests with their ability to speak with authority (e.g., to cite various experts, recount operational detail, or make data-driven decisions), but credibility and its relative respect are earned when boards demonstrate a deep, caring understanding of the constituents they serve.

The wonderful thing is that these conversations engage and ignite the benefit fires of board members, not the discussions of finance and operations that normally fill board agendas. Such conversations allow volunteer leaders' signature strength—a passion for benefit—to shine as they discuss benefit concerns and challenges.

It's one of those lovely win-win situations. Boards gain confidence as they play to their strengths by understanding and connecting with the mission body. The mission body gains confidence as they feel leaders are really listening and understanding their situation. As boards and constituents authentically engage in open-ended conversation, the true reality of constituent values emerges, giving boards the opportunity to convert their values into mission goals.

Knowing what constituents want makes boards much less vulnerable to the *vr-room* effect—the amplified voices of a few vested volunteers. As a consequence, boards are more apt to make decisions grounded in constituent reality that positively affect the mission system.

Once boards realize the value of dialogue and move beyond the admittedly uncomfortable initial conversations, they begin to see exciting opportunities. The four main venues where boards can directly connect with the mission body are:

1. Regular board business
2. Communities
3. Online surveys, blogs, and Podcasts
4. New models

Regular Board Business Multitasking can be good. Not only is it possible for boards to execute their connecting accountability in conjunction with the regular course of work, but sometimes it's downright advisable. Take the example of Indianapolis-based Noble of Indiana, a nonprofit that provides therapeutic treatment and vocational/life-skills training to children and adults with disabilities. This is what they did when facing cuts in governmental grants and a million-dollar shortfall:

> The Noble board adopted the Raising More Money funding model—a technique that focuses on building an emotional tie between donor and organization. The goal is to allow people to see the organization in action, share its vision, demonstrate its needs, and then engage potential supporters in a meaningful way.
>
> In the first year, the nonprofit held 20 "Noble Mornings" at its facility for potential donors—one-hour orientations over coffee and muffins that told the Noble story. Attendees felt connected with mission and vision, and the result was new donors and donations that surpassed expectations.[1]

In this case, Noble was connecting with an important segment of its mission body—potential donors. The Noble Mornings served two purposes. First, the Noble board executed a task often dreaded by board members—fundraising—not uncomfortably by asking people to write a check, but by allowing passionate board volunteers to do what they do best—inviting people to get to know the organization and making them aware of nonprofit mission and financial need. At the same time, the Noble board was connecting with constituents and building the kind of loyalty that provides a ready pipeline for donations and stakeholder input.

Another idea for making outreach a part of regular board business is to include an outreach event at each board meeting. Almost all boards hold regular meetings, attend regional and annual meetings, and have board retreats. Schedule an outreach event at each of these meetings. For example, one nonprofit created a series of outreach programs it called "the coffee connections." Setting aside an extra afternoon at each regularly scheduled board meeting, the board invites randomly selected mission body members for coffee and conversation.

Ask yourself, how flattered would you be if the board of your nonprofit invited you to coffee simply to ask your opinion and get your feedback? These connections don't have to be grand, expensive events. In an increasingly artificial world, people are more touched by authentic gestures. A board that humbly and sincerely asks for the opinion of its constituents is a much greater reward than champagne and caviar.

But that doesn't mean such events are just social chit-chat or the meet-and-greet cocktail parties that occur at every nonprofit convention or gala. No, connection events are very different. They are strategically planned to solicit the constituent feedback needed for sound mission decisions.

A connection event is an intense conversation between boards and constituents to mutually explore critical mission issues—a new mission goal, an anticipated environmental pressure, or a new global challenge. Any topic is fair game with one caveat: topics must fall within the board's, not the CEO's, accountability scope.

Planning an ongoing series of strategic conversations with the mission body takes time but is not difficult. Exhibit 9.1 shows the kind of pre-event framework that boards might use to implement connection events.

Whatever the topic or format, the outcome of a connection event should always be a shared understanding of issues, a mutual appreciation of each other's viewpoint, and new ideas for addressing the issue at hand. And it almost goes without saying: don't even try to hold such a session without a true willingness to listen to participants and genuinely consider their feedback when making decisions related to session topics.

Communities In the previous examples, boards control the participant population and event topics. Communities, however, present a different challenge. A community is a group of people who form a connection over time through interacting regularly around shared experiences. Other than possibly having control over the categories, boards do not control who participates.

The term *community* is rapidly becoming an overused buzzword—cited by some as a new way that nonprofits can become more relevant and by others as something nonprofits already do well. This is one of those wonderful times when both views are right; nonprofits really are communities, and leaders just need to understand how to capitalize on the richness of opportunity that their already-thriving constituent communities bring.

Communities present the opportunity for dialogue, but many nonprofits only monologue with their communities, thereby missing the opportunity for a rich two-way relationship. Instead of just thinking of communities as opportunities to sell services and talk to constituents, nonprofit leaders should view them as places to gauge mission relevance.

Sometimes national headquarters of nonprofits try to limit direct board participation in these groups. That's because board members tend to send staff scurrying in response to each individual comment that they interpret as community feedback. So national offices

EXHIBIT 9.1 A CONNECTION EVENT PLAN

Event Task	Example
1. Identify no more than two or three issues	Reasons for the falloff of younger members
2. Identify invitees	Members under 40 belonging to the nonprofit for three or more years
3. Define session outcomes	Top five reasons why invitees joined; top three things valued and top three irritants
4. Create a list of strategic questions; identify and coach session leaders/recorders	What is your favorite program and why? What would you like to see less of?
5. Invite attendees and hold sessions	Write and mail/e-mail invitations
6. Summarize the findings	Use an online database easily accessible to current and new boards
7. Follow up with attendees; be prepared to act and communicate actions to session participants	Send thank-you communications; share session outcome and ongoing communications on actions and progress

generally put controls on the activities of such communities, which greatly reduces the chances of true board/community dialogue.

Although limiting or moderating communities and newsgroups does have some advantages—arguably to increase the value of the dialogue—nonprofits escape liability for what is said by groups when they make it known that the groups are unmonitored. In return, they are rewarded (and sometimes dismayed) by hearing the unvarnished views of mission body individuals.

Communities at their best are self-organizing and self-sustaining, and organizations that do not try to control the dialogue and simply provide the technology and minimal service support (advertising the meetings or answering questions) can gain great insights into the real world of that community.

One example is what came to be known as *Fast Company*'s Company of Friends. *Fast Company* magazine had cells of readers that wanted to meet with other readers. The magazine supported self-forming local cells by publicizing meetings and offering magazine resources, while volunteer coordinators handled local efforts and communicated with *Fast Company* headquarters. Because this network had few controls and truly reflected local opinions, it became a rich two-way dialogue between headquarters and subscribers.

An example of this in the nonprofit world is the Institute of Electrical and Electronics Engineers (IEEE). It supports more than 100 online communities, each offering members things like the latest sector news, reference materials, bibliographies of journal papers and conference proceedings, white papers, and open discussion groups. Think of the value such information is to users and the instant source of feedback it supplies to nonprofit leaders.

You might say, well that's fine for technical groups like the IEEE, but it won't work for small community-based groups. How could we support it? The better question might be: How can you afford not to when all it takes is a Web site and one nonprofit leader who is willing to marshal the resources to get started? Done right, communities do most of the work themselves.

Online Surveys, Blogs, and Podcasts Most nonprofits use technology in some form as a facilitator of online communities, newsgroups (a specialized type of community), information, and surveys. Targeted surveys, particularly online surveys designed for rapid dissemination and response, are an important tool for soliciting constituent feedback. Today it's easier than ever to construct and administer such small-scale surveys online by using services such as Zoomerang (www.zoomerang.com), which provides easy-to-use templates and tabulates data in several formats.

One caveat, however, is that online surveys are a passive rather than a direct form of communication. Surveys are open to having their results misconstrued if questions are misleading or the specific mix of respondents is misunderstood. In addition, sometimes survey questions fail to address the real issues, and the survey provider appears out of touch or to be simply garnering support for a decision that has already been made.

A good example of this is the member who could not get a directory listing corrected. In the heat of battle, the member received an online survey to rate new services under consideration, but offering no chance to rate the "bread and butter" membership services that were broken and personally mattered the most to this member.

Some organizations, however, are beginning to adapt the online survey concept in innovative ways that do encourage two-way conversation. A colleague who donates to Heifer International received an e-mail from that organization asking her to join a special group of contributors and friends as a HeiferVoices Advisory Panel member. Up to once a month, she would be invited to participate in online focus groups and surveys and contribute to the decisions that would help Heifer reach its goal to lift 23 million people to self-reliance by the year 2010.

Other emerging tools like blogs and podcasts are especially popular now, and sector publications are full of good advice on where to find vendors and how to use these tools. Blogs can be a way of initiating or sustaining community interaction and thus can be a legitimate source of constituent opinion, but too often, blogs are simply glorified one-way newsletters. Perfectly good blogs like the California Manufacturers and Technology Association (www.cmta.net/weblog_daily.php) and *Buzzboard* from the National School Boards Association (www.nsba.org/boardbuzz) just coordinate and gather news links for members. No doubt these blogs are of value to members, but they are of little use to a board seeking to gain a broader opinion of its mission body.

Podcasts are "audio-blogs" where content is in audio files rather than text. In effect, organizations can create their own radio show with a few simple pieces of software and hardware. A good tutorial on the process can be found at PodCastTools.com. Like blogs, podcasts are a great way to broadcast a message, but care must be taken to authentically solicit listener feedback if they are to be used as a board connection tool. It seems appropriate to close this section with the reminder that just because something's on a Web site (or in a book or magazine for that matter) doesn't mean that it isn't just so much blather. Blogs at this stage are places for strong individuals to sound off on positions that may or may not have mainstream traction. Nonprofit leaders have to stifle the urge to react and give individual comment too much weight. One emerging trend is the appearance of consolidators of blog information—sites that visit several blogs on given topics. Such a consolidator might help transform this technology into a useful connection tool in the future.

New Models Some nonprofits are experimenting with new feedback models that help leaders gain a deeper understanding of constituent reality. Take the example of the Financial Planning Association (FPA), which is transforming itself into a culture defined by conversation. Its goal is to include every stakeholder in conversations around topics that matter most to the nonprofit—a worthy achievement indeed.

A detailed look at FPA's journey toward its goal is detailed in a thought-provoking article in the *Journal of Association Leadership* issue titled "The Café Model: Engaging Associations in Meaningful Conversations." The basic gist is this:

> The goal of the FPA is leaders (volunteer and staff) engaging in authentic conversations with members about critical topics. The tool is the "café" local groups that are conversations between four to five people.
>
> The FPA started with town hall meetings—a mostly one-way dialogue vehicle—then drove the meetings out to the chapter level. These morphed into knowledge cafés based on the World Café model (the World Café, www.theworldcafe.com). Cafés start with a full group meeting and then break into groups of four to five participants with a Café-trained facilitator.
>
> FPA's theme for the first year's 15 Cafés was: What one question—if addressed—would change the financial planning profession? The Cafés were billed as input to the board on the future of the profession, a very compelling theme.[2]

Three types of cafés emerged during the FPA meetings: member, event-driven, and purpose-driven. The curious thing is that no matter what the kick-off question or type of café, the FPA found that the conversation always seemed to center on the public's understanding of the value of financial planning leadership—exactly the conversation that the FPA needs to have in order to probe the relevance of its mission system.

Understanding the Real State of the Organization

Boards insulate themselves from organizational reality by creating organizational vibes that opinions are not welcome and that they wish to receive information mostly from the CEO. Two practices that promote these situations are (1) encouraging a Q culture (see Chapter 6) and (2) playing the CEO's *Everything Is Wonderful* game (see Chapter 4). Boards can limit such activities by developing a collective nose that sniffs out the real state of CEO and organizational performance.

How do boards cultivate such a nose? By understanding and implementing three important concepts:

1. Don't manage staff; do communicate with staff.
2. Avoid a forced positive environment; celebrate both success and failure.
3. Encourage performance, not bravado.

Don't Manage Staff; Do Communicate with Staff We know that boards are accountable for the benefit component and CEOs for the business component, but this does not mean that all communications between staff and board should come from the CEO.

In an attempt to avoid meddling, boards allow themselves to be boxed into funneling all communications through the CEO. This may stop board meddling—more likely it changes into covert meddling—but it prevents boards from seeing the organization from other than the CEO's vantage point. This makes it extremely difficult for boards to fulfill a major accountability—independently monitoring CEO and organizational performance.

How can you get around this problem? Understand and drive home the distinction between communicating versus directing and information versus action. Boards should communicate regularly with staff, but they should not direct staff. CEOs should communicate with people who report to senior staff but should request action only through senior staff.

Another way of saying this is that nonprofit leaders must learn the art of communicating without usurping another's authority.

Clear Roles and Accountabilities Engender Open Communications No matter how refined the interpersonal skills of any individual leader, the ability to communicate, not direct, to gain information and not imply action only resides comfortably in a trusting culture. And an important element of a trusting culture is a shared understanding and acceptance of clear, distinct roles and accountabilities.

Volunteer board presidents and CEOs who trust each other to act within their distinct areas of accountability are not likely to view private CEO/board member conversations as violating the "only speak to the board as a whole" rule or board/staff conversations as breaking the "only speak with the CEO" rule.

When all mission system participants know and respect each other's areas of authority, it opens the way for an open culture in which communication among all levels of the mission system is the norm. Conversation is prized as a way of exchanging informed wisdom, not as a way of circumventing the person in command.

The Art of Communicating without Usurping Authority When lines of authority are clear, nonprofit leaders still must cultivate the art of staying in touch without usurping authority. Although our discussion here centers on boards, the concepts apply equally to CEOs, who should be well versed in this essential management skill.

Each conversation between board and CEO or board and staff is an opportunity to build trust or create mistrust, to gain ideas or stifle innovation, to understand reality or spread misconceptions—in total, to enrich or weaken the relationship. Boards that approach CEO and staff conversations with a genuine interest to listen and learn not only gain useful information but also earn the respect of people who feel that their opinions are valued.

Boards that direct staff to perform outcomes independent of CEO direction not only undermine the CEO's authority, but they also undermine their own. They sow mistrust among employees and lose the opportunity for new ideas and candid feedback on the true state of the organization.

Consider the following examples that illustrate the subtle but very real difference between communicating and directing.

Example One:

Directing: The board agrees on key operating indicators and receives regular monitoring reports. A board member says to the controller, "I'd like these figures in a different format. Please send them to me."

Communicating: The board member says to the controller, "I appreciate your work on these reports. They're very helpful. What do you think about changing the format a little like this? Can you think of other information that might be helpful or changes that you'd like to make it even more understandable?

Example Two:

Directing: A board member tells the education director, "We need a seminar on XYZ."

Communicating: The board member to the education director: "I was talking with a member of our chapter. They're expressing a need for a seminar on XYZ. What do you think?

The directing scenarios have a common link: they do not encourage two-way exchanges of information. Instead, the board member usurps the CEO's authority for providing board monitoring reports and the education director's authority for determining education programs and then directs that party to act. Staff will always interpret a board member's "need" as "do."

The communicating scenarios encourage an exchange of informed wisdoms that should lead to a better shared understanding of the situation. Let's be a fly on the staff and board room wall and identify the wake that follows in the aftermath of the first directing example.

Example One:

Directing: The board agrees on key operating indicators and receives regular monitoring reports. A board member says to the controller, "I'd like to see these figures in a different format. Please send them to me."

Aftermath ***(assumes a good controller/CEO relationship):***

Controller to CEO: "He wants these figures in a different format. What do you want me to do?"

The CEO wonders what the board is up to behind his back and thinks, maybe this guy is a problem. What ensues is a tap dance between participants as the CEO talks with the board member and then the controller. The controller is nervous that he's in the middle of the board member and the CEO.

Now let's look at the wake left by the communication example.

Example One:

Communicating: The board member says to the controller, "I appreciate your work on these reports. They're very helpful. What do you think about changing the format a little like this? Can you think of other information that might be helpful or changes that you'd like to make it even more understandable?"

Aftermath ***(assumes a good controller/CEO relationship):***

Controller to board member: "That's an interesting idea. That might also help us with another problem. We'll bat it around a little here."

The CEO and controller work on this a little using the board member as a sounding board for their ideas. The CEO and board member present possible changes at the next board meeting, and other suggestions are made. This leads to a modified report that is more useful to all participants.

In this example, the controller looks at things from the board member's vantage point and gets a new idea from the conversation. In the previous example, the education director thinks "yes, that new seminar might be a good addition" and brings it to the education committee to evaluate in the context of planned offerings.

Communicating yields positive results even if the suggestions are not implemented. For instance, say the board member is simply uninformed and the proposed report or seminar already exists. Then, the controller helps the unaware board member to read the existing report. Or, in the case of the education director, the seminar already exists, but this raises the possibility that the current offering's title and marketing might be unclear.

How do boards increase the chances of receiving the positive results that flow from communicating and avoiding the negative consequences of directing? First, create board awareness of communicating versus directing. Use examples like the previous ones drawn from specific nonprofit experiences. Second, avoid using words or phrases that imply action or stop conversation and raise defenses such as:

- Action verbs that directly or indirectly imply action: *need, do, want, give, provide*
- Using the "you" word: *you should do this, you didn't call*

The beauty of bumping into people and the art of impromptu conversations is that you never know what tidbit will come out. Effective communication means that both parties walk away from the conversation with a better understanding of each other's reality and the possibility that the conversation has sparked in the other the beginning of a great new idea.

The Dark Side of Communication No matter how trusting the culture or how skilled the nonprofit leader, these conversations carry inherent risks. Part of the responsibility of participants in an open culture is not to use conversations to place the other person in jeopardy. To avoid this, boards must sidestep two very common roadblocks to successful communications outcomes: (1) "so and so" said this and (2) failure to keep things in perspective.

Avoiding "So and So" Said This Let's consider the communicating versus directing scenarios in the previous sections and assume in the first example that the board member goes back to the CEO and says something like this: "I talked to the controller, and he told me that we're not looking at the XYZ figure. Why aren't you doing this?"

The CEO instantly feels attacked and is angry at the board member for invading his turf as well as suspicious of the controller's motives, who did not come to him first. Now, consider a different approach. The board member goes to the CEO and says: "We've been reviewing the monitoring report, and I did some brainstorming with your controller. What do you think about adding the XYZ figure to the report?" The CEO is free to share in the discussion without feeling defensive.

As these examples show, it is possible to get the communicating thing right: the board member does not direct the controller in the initial conversation but then he blows it with a threatening follow-up CEO conversation. This damages the relationship between CEO, board member, and controller, and a nonproductive political battle may commence. But when the board member simply uses the information gleaned in conversation—avoiding "the controller said"—to share ideas with the CEO, the relationship between all parties stays positive.

Keeping Things in Perspective Let's consider the second example in communicating and assume this: the education director unloads on the board member, telling him how much pressure the CEO is creating to bring in more attendance and how volunteers just aren't doing their jobs. What should the board member do in this case?

Keep the conversation in perspective. Has the education department been under pressure, and the director is just blowing off steam during a bad day? Don't assume; do ask questions and seek information that brings the conversation into context. How is the CEO bringing pressure to bear? Have there been conversations with the CEO about the concerns? Where are the volunteers falling short of expectations?

Rather than charge into action or ignore such complaints as negative, this board member has a real opportunity to let the staff director vent and, depending on the situation, just listen or be able to provide counsel that helps the director remedy the situation. Learning to deal effectively with such problems encourages individual growth and builds strong staff leadership.

The education director may not just be having a bad day, however. Other directors may have the same concerns, or the education director may already have tried to remedy the situation with the CEO. Keeping things in perspective means staying alert to small signs that may indicate much deeper problems but not taking action until a trend is confirmed.

Avoid a Forced Positive Environment; Celebrate Both Success and Failure When a staff director expresses a serious concern to a board member, any action that a board member takes often adversely boomerangs back to that director. The board member does not reside in the day-to-day staff workplace, and board members' actions usually tread on the CEO's business component turf. Board members cannot control either the interpretation or the effect of their actions in the workplace, but the CEO does, and that's usually not good news for the staff director.

Thus, a false-positive culture develops, previously burned staff members quickly learn to say nothing when board members are present, and conversations are only occasions for self-congratulation and reassuring each other that "everything is wonderful." Nothing burns out people more than dealing with the same problem over and over again because it's forbidden to admit the problem exists in the first place—our elephants in the flesh!

This is tricky territory. No one enjoys hearing negative comments or wants to encourage a whiny problem-oriented culture. The answer lies in not painting problems and failure with a globally negative brush and staying alert to warning signs.

Consider Failure and Success in the Same Light False-positive cultures cannot take hold when leaders see failure and success as equal parts of doing. In a culture of risk and innovation, some things work and some things do not. Exceptional organizations realize that overcoming problems and learning by failures is how they improve.

Discussing problems is an important part of getting the pieces right and adjusting to changes over time. When nonprofit leaders give equal respect to failure and success, as well as problem and solution, there is no need to avoid reality or falsely hype the latest program.

Let's be very clear here: we're not encouraging discussion of the day-to-day gripes about inconsequential things that inhabit every workplace, but advocating open discussion of serious problems that impede mission productivity (e.g., a dramatic falloff of volunteers or a systemic failure to conduct performance reviews).

Pay Attention to the Blinking Red Lights False-positive cultures will not take hold if nonprofit leaders are alert to the early warning signs that indicate such a culture may be developing, including the following:

- CEOs who say yes to every board request
- Senior staff members who sit silently at board meetings
- Capable staff directors who are in the office at all hours of the day and night
- Board members who rarely disagree
- Claims that every program is going well
- Lots of activity but few mission results

Encourage Performance, Not Bravado A performance culture means that goals and measurable outcomes are defined and widely communicated. In such a culture, talking cannot substitute for achieving goals, and bravado cannot mask the truth of monitoring reports and key indicators.

It takes a lot of work to identify goals, create goal measurements, define key indicators, and design monitoring reports. That's why these subjects are discussed in detail in the next two chapters. But completing such efforts allows boards to objectively assess the true state of the mission system directly.

Grounding Board Decisions in Mission Reality

Board actions tend to veer away from mission reality when board behavior or board politics get in the way of intelligent decision making. If board decisions are to align effectively with mission system reality, they cannot be unduly influenced by one strong individual or the consensus process.

Confronting the Dysfunctional Board Member Let's create an example nonprofit, the Institute for International Health (IIH), and listen in on a hypothetical board meeting. The background for this situation is that the IIH board decides to distribute a vaccine to countries that are beset by the bird flu epidemic. That decision was made only after seeking extensive stakeholder and constituent feedback, which is overwhelmingly in favor of the benefit of the vaccine over the risk of negative donor or constituent reaction.

In the process, many board members had to resolve conflicted feelings, but only members A and B voted "no" on the final motion.

Board meeting:

Member A: I'm hearing lots of complaints. This kind of negative reaction is really bad. We could lose major donors.

Chairperson: We knew this might happen. This program would especially step on the toes of some drug companies that are major IIH donors. But we have PR ready to answer these concerns, and I would encourage each of you to talk with individuals and groups to help increase their understanding of this program.

Member B: But I talked with Robert, who's one of our largest donors. His company will not continue donating to IIH if we go ahead with this program. He knows a lot of people, and he may convince them to do the same. The board had trouble with this decision in the first place. Maybe we better revisit it now before real damage is done.

What the chairperson does next will either keep the board aligned with the reality of mission body feedback or realign the board with the reality of a few strong board opinions. Here's what happens in both cases:

Keeping the board aligned with mission body reality:

Chairperson: I appreciate your comments. We knew the risk, which is why we did such extensive stakeholder surveys to be sure this direction is what our constituents want. We've implemented our PR plan for dealing with complaints and adverse publicity and have measurements to track our progress carefully along the way. The project has just begun, and we need time to let our strategies work. It's just way too early to draw any conclusions yet.

Member A: (Breaking in) We know people are unhappy. If we wait, our reputation will be ruined; donors will be gone. We need to revisit this decision right now.

Chairperson: Let's get a sense of how everyone feels. Is anyone else getting negative feedback?

An open discussion ensues and reveals that complaints are originating from two major drug company donors. The chairperson takes an informal vote to determine if the board wants to discuss the program more.

Chairperson: The board's agreed (with members A and B opposed) that negative feedback is pretty much anticipated, and there's no need to reopen discussion on this decision. We'll continue to closely assess program progress. If we start to experience a larger than expected donor drop-off or we have critical new information that means we're not meeting goals, then we'll rethink our strategies.

Keeping the board aligned with a few strong board opinions:

Member B: Let me go back to why we should never have made this decision in the first place.

She follows with a recitation of all the objections from previous board discussions.

Another Member: You do have a point. These are concerns that many of us shared. It is possible we made the wrong decision. Robert is very powerful, and I don't like to see our donors upset.

Chairperson: I want everyone to be comfortable with our decision, so let's talk about this some more.

An open discussion ensues, covering the same pre-motion ground. After two hours, the board agrees to take another look at all the previous research and discuss it further at the next board meeting. Meanwhile, they direct the CEO to tell staff to halt implementation until the board looks at things again.

This example shows that dysfunctional doesn't necessarily mean out of control or acting irrationally. Board members A and B are passionate about the IIH and feel that the board is not acting in the best interest of the organization. But their vested personal interest—member A's spouse works for a drug company and member B is close friends with A—dysfunctionally colors their ability to represent the public good. No amount of discussion will convince member A to change.

Member A will waste board time going over the same ground if the chairperson allows it, and may even change the view of a board that lets emotion sway fact. That's because boards that are willing to tackle tough issues and seize new opportunities can never be 100 percent sure they are right and often defer to the member who does seem sure. That's another reason why it is so important for boards to systematically connect with constituents. It grounds them in reality when trouble hits and the inevitable second-guessing of a few board members starts.

Consensus Process Should Not Trump Consensus Decision The act of achieving consensus cannot become more important than the decision itself. In other words, effective board decisions must result in positive action in the benefit component or mission system, and that can only happen when the outcome of consensus decisions resolves the original issue. This may seem to be an obvious point, but this is another concept that is simple to understand in the abstract but often breaks down in practice.

Let's go back to our IIH example and consider the scenario where the IIH board allows a few strong opinions to control the agenda. Let's also assume that the board members go home and review the previous information, and as the board reconvenes, members become frustrated as members A and B keep going over the same arguments. It's getting time for the meeting to end and—voilà!—someone comes up with a compromise.

> *Consensus Member:* We can't seem to agree on a course of action. Members A and B have really good points—the loss of Robert's donations may be just the tip of the iceberg. So, let's delay implementation of this program for six months and put together a task force that can resolve some of Robert's concerns and then move ahead with the program.
>
> *Chairperson:* Do we have a consensus on this plan of action?
>
> All members indicate their approval. Everyone breathes a sigh of relief and goes home.

What just happened here? Most members did not want to step on the toes of members A and B—after all, they are so confident of their stance, and who can be sure what the right thing is? The board just wants to resolve this tough subject and walk away friends. But the original issue was providing quick aid for a rapidly spreading epidemic, and a six-month delay means a lifetime to those who are infected. The outcome of the IIH meeting was board consensus, not resolving the mission problem at hand.

Bad consensus decision making plagues average boards. To protect themselves from elevating consensus over mission system outcome, boards must make critical questions part of the consensus decision process. No matter how eager the board is to move on or how lengthy the meeting, never vote on a consensus decision unless the board addresses a paramount question: Given the original issue, does our action deliver the desired outcome? Exhibit 9.2 shows what IIH's questions might be.

EXHIBIT 9.2 CONSENSUS DECISION CHECK

Original Issue: Decrease the spread of bird flu epidemic among Asian populations at risk.

Mission system outcomes:

1. Address most critical concern: distribute vaccine; lower prevaccine rate of infection by 30%
2. Identify and prioritize other critical concerns of rapid spread of disease in Asia

Consensus Decision: Delay the program for six months; appoint a task force to address drug company concerns.

Consensus decision outcomes:

1. Keep drug company donors happy

Does the consensus decision resolve the issue?

Consensus outcomes versus mission outcomes:

1. Delaying the program fails to address the most critical need for vaccine.
2. Mission recipients are Asian partners and their citizens, not drug companies.

Aligning consensus decisions with mission reality takes just a flip chart and the willingness to brutally assess whether the consensus decision addresses the original mission outcomes. The board president or chairperson is the first line of defense in making sure this gets done, because keeping the board on track is part of the job of overseeing board performance. But CEOs also have a vested interest in good board decisions and a responsibility to share informed wisdom—if the board chairperson does not do the job, the CEO should step in before the final vote is taken and guide the board appropriately.

Making the Changes Stick

Cultivating a Different Mindset

Changes to attitudes and beliefs must precede a shift to nonprofits seeking a shared reality. How nonprofit boards ready themselves and their organizations to make this quantum shift lie in an organizational willingness to value the following four activities:

1. Searching for causative data
2. Asking the right questions
3. Engaging in real conversations
4. Sharing wisdom

Searching for Causative Data Nonprofit leaders who wait for reality to rise above the din may wait a very long time. The board and CEO of any complex nonprofit are beset by a loud clamor of voices at any given moment; it takes little effort to respond to the loudest voice but a great deal of effort to extract the essential from the surrounding noise. Leaders must learn to think logically and to probe gently for the causative data that usually lurks beneath the surface of any situation.

Think Logically Obviously, if they think about it, boards have no difficulty distinguishing volunteer from nonvolunteer. Likewise, they should have no problem distinguishing their respective input, but the problem is that they don't think about it.

Boards meet and greet at each annual conference and talk to committee and chapter members all the time, but they don't stop to think that these volunteer conversations may—or may not—accurately reflect the viewpoint of the larger mission body. Feedback is important, but it is even more important to think and understand who is giving the feedback and the point of view from which that feedback comes.

Probe Gently In the heat of battle, consider a timeout to think and probe for the reality of the situation. This is an especially good technique to employ during major decisions on contentious topics. For example, after conducting systematic research and receiving constituent input, a board defines a new mission goal: "improve our national image." The CEO delivers a new logo and campaign, but just prior to rollout, a groundswell of "this isn't what members want" complaints start coming in. What does the board do?

They should resist the first instinct to panic and start questioning their decision. Call a timeout and probe for the reality of the situation. Assuming this board is close to constituents, they should have the contacts and confidence to ask the kinds of questions that lead to a response appropriate to the reality of the situation. Questions might include:

1. Is the groundswell really a large number of constituents? Is it many different constituents or mostly originating from one angry person or group of people that is influencing the uninformed?
2. Does the negative feedback reflect mission concerns (e.g., the new logo doesn't reflect the mission)? Or does it reflect self-interest (e.g., we created the old logo and don't want it to change)?
3. What is the percentage of negative comments to positive? Is this the *vr-room* effect of a few strong voices that negate the more silent approval voice of the majority?

Asking the Right Questions Sprinkled throughout this chapter is the value of asking questions. Staff members wait and hope that boards will ask the right questions. The board adds a new PR committee and the CEO agrees; the staff waits for a single board member to ask what are the financial or people resources needed to support such a committee. The CEO makes a global statement that contradicts what was previously said, and the staff waits for a board member to ask why the difference.

Asking the right questions in these situations yields not only rich feedback to the issue at hand but also important clues about the state of management and organization. If the CEO agrees to the new committee but when questioned cannot pinpoint resources, then that says something about CEO performance.

The sister to the art of communication is the art of investigative inquiry—stay curious and ask pertinent questions—and the reward is staff respect and a better understanding of the situation.

Engaging in Real Conversations and Sharing Wisdom Most nonprofits are populated with volunteer and staff leaders who understand the real issues and are willing to share that knowledge. They possess the talent and capability to resolve problems and seize opportunity, if they are given the chance.

A major part of a leader's job is not to do the work but to create the conditions that allow others to do the job. Survey after survey shows that above money and position, people want respect, to be heard, and to feel they make a difference. Nonprofit leaders must ask themselves: What is the most important thing we should be talking about? Then they should create the opportunities for the right people to talk.

Because leaders tend to turn to the same key people for ideas and problem solvers, the assumption is that others don't have ideas or the talent to make the same contributions. This issue is not discussed openly, but leader behavior readily reflects this belief in the workplace. Each time boards or CEOs make decisions that affect mission system entities without giving those entities the opportunity to share their wisdom and engage in real conversation, the message goes out: We don't value your opinion or think you have anything to contribute.

One way to not change this mindset is to call sporadic meetings and ask "what do you think?" A good example that illustrates why this doesn't work is the situation faced by a colleague as he became CEO of a nonprofit that had a large, experienced staff. Used to managing people, he called a staff meeting expecting an open give-and-take conversation among managers. Instead, his "what do you think?" question met with complete silence. Why? Because candid staff comments in the past either yielded nothing or a negative payback, so no one trusted management and was willing to share opinions on important things.

Boards should give real conversations with staff and volunteers in the field the same priority as connecting with the mission body. There are so many ways to do this well, but here are just a few ideas.

Ongoing Brainstorming or Think Sessions Normalize the use of think sessions as a way to explore new issues or resolve problems. Delegate the responsibility for the sessions downward, and develop a model by which anyone at any level may facilitate such a session. The caveat is that the topic of the session should fall within the accountability of that level. For example, a simple model for a CEO-level brainstorming session might look like this:

Session Leader: Define issue; define outcome; map the mission entities affected; select participants

Issue: How to share information among various volunteer and staff groups

Outcome: A user-friendly, systemic way to input and access information among groups; session outcomes include a wish list of user needs that define system requirements

Mission Entities: Map experience requirement, and then have CEO and members work with volunteer and staff groups to select appropriate participants

This looks remarkably like the board model for planning mission body connecting events, and the same concepts do apply. The trick is to make these sessions the norm rather than a one-shot affair. Also important is the necessity to define the kind of experience necessary to participate and to make those requirements known. Treating participant selection objectively treats people as adults. They can assess if they possess the skills to contribute to this particular group rather than feel that such sessions are just a perk for the manager's favorite people.

Innovative Group Meetings Ralph Nappi, president of the American Machine Tool Distributors Association (AMTDA), has a unique way of adding value to attending AMTDA's annual meetings. His organization helps its members take information gleaned at annual meetings and apply it directly to their workplace. AMTDA created Leadership Forums—groups of eight or nine people that meet three times a year to share how they are implementing what they learned. It facilitates the meetings, develops agendas, and monitors progress between meetings.[3]

What a great idea! Not only do the forums allow annual meeting participants the chance to share their ideas with other nonprofits, but they also provide a critical indicator to assess the value of AMTDA's annual meeting education.

Another example is that of Denise Casalino, manager of Chicago's Wacker Drive reconstruction project, which ran for two years and threatened large-scale disruption of Chicago businesses:

> Casalino met constantly with the appropriate mission system entities to lessen the stress and financial fallout caused by the massive project. She listened at these meetings, stitching together a makeshift hotel driveway and taxicab stand to provide important accesses to high-rises when stranded by closures.
>
> She did things like teaching a Wacker reroute to police officers and motorists after terra cotta falling from a high-rise closed an alternate route and temporarily changing the Chicago skyline for a frantic bride who complained that a bridge closure ruined pictures that were six months in the planning.[4]

The Wacker rehabilitation was an unprecedented success because stakeholders were given the opportunity to share their concerns with someone who really listened, and those real conversations were backed up by real actions that averted many potential crises.

Institutionalizing a Shared Reality

A visionary board and CEO embrace a new mindset and a commitment to seek a shared reality with the mission body and all its parts. They begin to see success in their outreach efforts—organization-wide, people are beginning to talk about what is really important.

How do these leaders keep the momentum going and prevent the next board or the next from reverting back to the same-old, same-old routine? A Board Policy Manual (see Chapter 10) is certainly one key. Others include ongoing training and scenario playing.

Board Policies and Orientation Once boards define a systematic way of connecting with the mission body, that process should be institutionalized under the board accountability section in a Board Policy Manual. It might look something like this:

> **Board Accountability One: The XYZ board is accountable for the benefit component of the XYZ nonprofit.**
>
> *Major Responsibilities:* Connecting with constituents to determine mission will, mission needs, and mission satisfaction
>
> *Annual Mission Goal:* A series of stakeholder outreach meetings will be part of the yearly (name) mission plan and yearly board agenda.

This is an example of a broad strategy that leaves boards free to fill in the details (e.g., type, place, topic of meetings in the tactical part of the annual mission plan). Boards might choose to be much more specific depending on the political situation. In the same way, boards might commit to seeking causative data under the appropriate board accountability, and that might look like this:

> **Accountability Two: The XYZ board is accountable for the overall effectiveness of XYZ mission system.**
>
> *Major Responsibilities:* The XYZ board will systemically seek factual, explanatory, and causative data and the input of all affected mission body entities prior to making major decisions, assessing in advance the outcome of such decisions on the appropriate mission system parts.

Note that the board makes this statement in the context of its own performance within the sphere of its decision-making authority—benefit and mission system. Because the CEO, not the board, is directly accountable for the business component, the board includes the same statement as part of the detailed CEO responsibilities (e.g., in CEO Accountability Two, the XYZ CEO is accountable for maximizing the effectiveness of all business component resources, practices, programs, and services).

Annual Board Agenda One of the features of *Policy Governance* that even non-Carver-loving boards can readily embrace is the concept of an annual board agenda (see Chapter 10 for Dr. Carver's Policy Governance Model). The process goes like this: first boards create a "permanent" calendar that includes all relatively stable board events and deadlines (e.g., strategic planning, CEO performance review, and budget). This yearly framework should not change much and is inherited by each successive board. Then, all the sitting board needs to do is fill in specific dates and activities related to that year's specific goals.

In other words, each new board inherits the permanent calendar as a starting point and then constructs specific agendas based on that year's board plan. This amazingly simple idea almost instantly improves board performance, which the next chapter illustrates in more detail.

The permanent annual calendar is a wonderful tool for institutionalizing ongoing outreach events and organizational activities. It serves as an oversight instrument in and of itself, making it impossible for boards to overlook important recurring events.

Training and Ongoing Scenario Playing Because board orientation and training are critical to institutionalizing new practices and policies, board orientations should thoroughly cover the linkage between connecting with stakeholders and effective governance. Sessions should provide a grounding in the importance of organization-wide communications and the differences between communicating and directing. These topics should also be part of staff orientations.

Orientation is a good first step, but much more is needed than a one-time orientation if the thinking and practices needed to perpetuate a shared reality are to be institutionalized.

Communicating Doesn't Come Naturally A wonderful adage is "the illusion of communications is that it is achieved." Everyone thinks they communicate, but the problem is that communication recipients may not be hearing what the senders intend.

This is one of those areas where business advisors all agree—real communications and interpersonal skills are sadly lacking at most companies—but this is also an area that business leaders just pretend to address. The good news is that the global need for improving interpersonal skills is generating some useful books and information on what to do, so hopefully, more and more leaders will pay attention.

Nonprofits can be truly revolutionary by providing special ongoing communications training internally. What might this training look like? It could take a very simple form. *Fierce Conversations* by Susan Scott is a wonderful book that contains many thought-provoking ideas and a finite framework for approaching important conversations.[5] Nonprofits that really wish to improve communication might make an annual commitment of $3,000 to $5,000 and hire a qualified consultant to facilitate a communications session with board and senior staff. If funds allow, expand the training organization-wide. The return on investment in the form of problem solving, new ideas, and programs will be exponential.

If funds do not allow for a consultant, perhaps the board and CEO can agree to appoint a particularly talented volunteer or staff manager to create an annual training session based on Scott's or similar books.

Scenario Playing Because boards often have trouble communicating without directing CEOs and staff, they tend to underestimate the impact of their statements on staff morale. Therefore, communication training should always include scenario playing in the initial training and in follow-up sessions.

Obviously, this takes work on the part of nonprofit leaders to capture real situations as they occur and turn them into usable cases. But the best way to recognize unhelpful behavior and learn new ways to communicate is to see how each issue plays out in real situations that mean something to the participants.

Summing It Up

Nonprofits face the big challenge of attracting and keeping new members and retaining and soliciting new donors. Perhaps they should heed the findings of a decades-old report that resonates even more strongly now. The report, *Meaningful Chaos,* published by the nonpartisan Harwood Institute for Public Innovation, examined how people form relationships with public concerns. The report found that people form attachments when they feel three standards of authenticity are met:

1. Discussions reflect a base of reality—the context of their lives, what is at issue for them and society, their daily language.
2. Information sources reflect an understanding of their experiences and value.
3. People want the story straight—they want to "be squared" with.[6]

Seeking a shared reality not only encourages effective organizational decisions, but strategically connecting with constituents and stakeholders and authentically seeking their feedback engenders a loyalty that no amount of money can buy.

NOTES

1. Carole Schweitzer, "Creative Thinkers Tackle Tough Issues," *Associations Now* (Washington, DC: ASAE and the Center for Association Leadership, October 2005): 89; reprinted with permission.
2. Kim Porto and Janet McCallen, "The Café Model: Engaging Associations in Meaningful Conversations," *Journal of Association Leadership* (Fall 2004): 21.

3. "AMTDA Leadership Forum," www.amtda.org/education/leadership_forum.htm (accessed April 16, 2006).
4. Jon Hilkevitch, "Wacker Meets Clock; Here's a Big Reason," *Chicago Tribune,* sec. 1, November 26, 2002.
5. Susan Scott, *Fierce Conversations* (New York: Berkley Publishing Group, 2004).
6. Richard Harwood, *Meaningful Chaos: How People Form Relationships with Public Concern* (Bethesda, MD: Harwood Institute for Public Innovation, 1993).

CHAPTER 10

The *Board Fiddles, Rome Burns* Solution: Develop Policy and Strategy at Every Level

Never tell people how to do things. Tell them what to do and they will surprise you with their ingenuity.

—George S. Patton

TAMING THE *BOARD FIDDLES, ROME BURNS* ELEPHANT

The concept that boards make policies and staff implements them does not work in the reality of today's dynamic workplace. Pretending that this concept does work gives rise to the *Board Fiddles, Rome Burns* elephant. The ability to respond quickly and effectively is sacrificed for the illusion of limiting risk and protecting nonprofit assets.

The third elephant solution—develop policy and strategy at every level—requires a very different mindset. Boards do not own the policy and strategy domain. Instead, part of that domain belongs where the action occurs—at each level. The people who are most knowledgeable about the activity and accountable for the outcomes are the right people to create the policies and strategies that govern those outcomes.

With the parameters of responsibility for strategy and policy established and documented in the Board Policy Manual, each level can be held accountable for its area of influence. The *Board Fiddles, Rome Burns* elephant is under control, and the organization is protected and thrives.

In This Chapter

We'll explore how policy and strategy look at each mission system level and how to delegate strategy and policy powers safely. Applying these concepts to the real nonprofit workplace is exciting, especially in two areas that boards tend to rubberstamp a CEO decisions the most: strategic planning and budgeting.

Step by step, a workable planning model will emerge—each level contributes to an effective, ongoing strategic planning process that promotes exceptional year-round mission system performance.

Elephant Solution Three: Develop Policy and Strategy at All Levels

Delegating Policy and Strategy Authority

Delegating power-making authority without careful consideration to appropriate power and controls is foolhardy at best. Granting power always involves risk; the chances that subordinates will do things exactly as bosses like are minimal. This risk, plus the inevitable mistakes that occur along the way, is why managers are reluctant to delegate. It just seems easier and safer to do it themselves.

The problem is that doing it yourself in nonprofits of any size or complexity is rapidly becoming impossible. The humbling reality is that although subordinates do things differently, they often do things better. When held accountable for outcomes and delegated the appropriate authority and resources to achieve those outcomes, engaged people find creative solutions to problems and create and sustain innovative new programs.

Each level leader makes hundreds of decisions a week and is technically forming new policy and strategy all the time. What top leaders really want are managers who have a sense of policy rather than just a literal understanding; thus, given new circumstances, they will properly develop level-appropriate new policies and strategies.

The organizational reward for the risks of delegation is motivated managers, quicker, better decisions, improved productivity, and more ideas and innovation. The trick to reaping these rewards and avoiding the disasters that uncontrolled delegation can bring is following some basic guidelines:

1. Delegate appropriate power
2. Set controls and perform oversight
3. Make sharing informed wisdom the norm

Delegate Appropriate Power Each mission level should have powers appropriate to fulfill their accountability for achieving expected outcomes. A quick rule of thumb that helps sort out the accountable party and appropriate power is Chapter 5's three "W" questions: Consider the activity or outcome and ask: (1) Where does the activity occur? (2) What is the span of control? and (3) What is the time horizon?

If the policy activity is part of the mission component or the entire mission system and activities are mostly future oriented, the board owns it; if the policy activity is part of the business component and occurs mostly in the next one to five years, the CEO owns it; if the activity is directly part of a department or area and activities take place mostly in the current year, the board committee or managers who report to the CEO own it. Exhibit 10.1 provides a quick visual guide for these concepts.

Control and Oversight The ability to create policy and strategy is the power to take action and influence organizational outcomes. Delegating authority is not abdicating responsibility—it requires tight controls. If the board, CEO, or manager delegates policy power without defining limits or accepting accountability for oversight, the integrity of the mission system rests with individuals—and bad things can result.

Over the long term, delegated power leads to effective organizational decisions only if systemic controls are in place that protect against risky decisions or individual malfeasance. Effective delegation relies on multiple levels of controls: existing policy, limits to power, and oversight.

Existing Policy The first level of control is that delegated power is immediately subordinate to the policies and strategies of the levels above. For example, the CEO may delegate the power to create ad placement policy to the marketing director, but that director can only create ad policy that follows CEO and board policies. If the board's policy dictates that the full nonprofit name must be used, and the CEO's policy dictates that the official logo must be on all advertising, then the marketing director cannot use a nonprofit nickname without a logo in an advertisement.

EXHIBIT 10.1 DELEGATION AT A GLANCE

Accountable Level	Span of Control	Time Horizon
Board	**Global:** • Benefit component • Oversight of mission system • Oversight of business component Example: ethics policies govern the entire mission system	**Future:** • Policies into perpetuity • Strategies and planning for future Ethics policies govern future actions
CEO	**Global:** • Business component Example: program policies	• Majority of activities for **1- to 3-year horizon** Program activities in current year
CEO or Board Direct Reports	**Limited:** • Department or area Example: policies for holding seminars	• Majority of time **day to day and current year** Activity for seminars daily and throughout current year

Limits to Power When delegating power, delegators must also define the scope of that power. This can be accomplished in one of two ways: defining what can be done or defining what cannot be done. An analogy is the difference between European and English law: European law says that nothing is permitted unless legally sanctioned; English law says that everything is permissible unless legally prohibited.

Specifying all the conditions under which the given power may be exercised is a heavy burden to the delegator. It's impossible to conceive of every situation that may arise for events that occur daily. Delegating solely in this way seems to undermine the most desired outcomes of delegation—quick response and more effective decision making.

The second way of delegating—whatever is not forbidden is allowable—seems a much better practice in today's dynamic, competitive environment. Identify high-risk areas, limit power in those areas, and make sure those policies are followed. A good example of this style is when boards give CEOs the broad power to make business component policy and strategy, but they do not want the CEO or anyone else breaking the law. So, the board creates a policy that limits the CEO's power—all officers, volunteers, and staff will operate within applicable state and federal laws. The CEO retains broad business component policy powers, but the board limits this power to lawful activities.

Oversight and Accountability The delegator must exercise proper oversight: ensuring that the delegatee is operating within the given span of control; creating new policies as necessary; and monitoring organizational activities to make sure defined goals are achieved. Most important, leaders must hold themselves and their direct reports accountable when power is abused, bad policy is made, or the desired outcomes are not achieved.

Let's say that the marketing director in our previous example really goofs. The director follows board and CEO marketing policies but places an ad in a totally unsuitable publication that negatively impacts the nonprofit's image. It's up to the CEO to decide if this is a reasonable mistake that any person in the position might make. If so, the CEO limits the position's power by defining a new CEO policy that governs which publications are desirable. But, if not—and in this case it seems reasonable to assume that a marketing director who is accountable for positively promoting the nonprofit's image should know what publications do that—it's an individual performance problem that the CEO must confront.

The board makes the same kind of decision: Did the CEO fail to put in place policies that protect the nonprofit's image, or is the problem the result of one individual's bad performance? This kind of assessment is an essential ingredient of delegated power. When something goes awry, often it's not the policy that's the problem, rather it's the performance problem of an individual manager who did not follow the policy or use good judgment in applying it. Nonprofit leaders often avoid confronting such individual performance problems and prefer to just create a new policy, thus confusing everyone who already understands and applies the original policy correctly.

Shared Wisdom as Norm Policies and strategies exist not to punish, but to clarify the rules of the game and illuminate the values and goals of the nonprofit. Knowing, accepting, and living by these rules promotes trust among parties and gives all mission system entities the confidence to make decisions and take action without undue fear of punishment.

Such trust frees all levels to communicate and share wisdom without fear. The troubles and risks of delegated power are only worth the effort if that power leads to better decisions, improved processes, and sustainable programs, and that only happens when communications are transparent and wisdom is widely shared. In the absence of this norm, department managers build silos of power, creating policies and strategies that work only for that department and not the mission system as a whole.

Policy and Strategy at the Board Level

We just examined how to delegate power and previously discussed in Chapter 5 which policies and strategies belong at the board, CEO, and division levels. Now we will see how each level uses those powers to contribute to exceptional mission performance. The best way to do that is to watch them in action. Meet a hypothetical association, the Universal Dentist Society (UDS):

- The UDS has implemented Elephant Solutions One and Two: One Mission System and A Shared Reality.
- Exhibit 10.2 shows the UDS calendar of major events.

As the calendar implies, everyone at UDS has a very full plate, starting with the board.

Board Mission Statement Policy Mission policy and strategy is where effective boards spend a majority of time, and the most fundamental and potent of the weapons in the board's mission policy arsenal is the mission statement.

Clear Mission Statement Policy Prior to this current year, the UDS board reviewed and changed its mission statement policy. It wanted a less wordy statement, something that painted a vivid picture at a glance and screamed to all mission system stakeholders: This is why UDS exists! Here's what the UDS board did:

- Through connection events and stakeholder input, reviewed current mission policy with questions like: Is the current mission statement clear and succinct? Is it internalized and driving behavior through the nonprofit? Does it reflect current conditions? Will it remain applicable given coming trends?
- Gathered information and compared other mission statements; for example, the board looked at these statements:
    1. The American Cancer Society's Web site international mission statement is: "capacity building in developing cancer societies and in collaboration with

EXHIBIT 10.2 UDS CALENDAR OF MAJOR EVENTS

Month	Event
January	• New fiscal year budget and plan • New board term • Board meeting—late January
February	
March	• Board meeting—late March
April	
May	
June	• Board meeting—mid-June • Annual board planning session
July	
August	• Annual CEO planning session
September	
October	
November	• Board meeting—early November
December	• Board term ends 12/31 • Fiscal year ends

other cancer-related organizations through the world in carrying out shared strategic directions."[1]

2. The Institute of Electrical and Electronics Engineer's mission statement is: "The IEEE promotes the engineering process of creating, developing, integrating, sharing, and applying knowledge about electro and information technologies and sciences for the benefit of humanity and profession."[2]
3. The Greater Chicago Food Depository's Web site mission statement is: "providing food for the hungry (while striving to end hunger in our community)."[3]
4. A board member's son works for a manufacturing company that makes parts for heart valves. Their mission is: "we save lives."

- After reviewing the group's recommendations, the UDS board streamlined its mission statement to **"protecting the public's oral health."**
- The UDS board developed a 30-second "elevator speech" to introduce the new mission statement at connection events and to other stakeholders. The CEO did the same throughout the business component.

UDS wants a mission statement that captures why UDS exists but is short enough to fit on a T-shirt and memorable enough to stay in the minds and hearts of everyone. Although the board reviewed all the excellent information available on creating vision and mission statements, it did not lose focus—a good mission statement inspires the troops. The Greater Chicago Food Depository staff can directly connect their efforts with doing good—food packed with their hands feeds hungry people; IEEE staff may not find it so easy to connect how a seminar on an esoteric topic benefits humanity.

Applying Mission Statement Policy Once a mission statement is short and memorable, boards use that statement as the driver for creating annual mission goals. The UDS board creates these goals at its board planning meeting:

- The UDS board holds an annual board planning session each June (Exhibit 10.2). Although this session is the official kick-off of the next fiscal year planning cycle, it is simply one point in a strategic process that continues throughout the calendar year.
- At the board planning session, the board reviews the mission and trend data that it continually collects from ongoing connecting events and board-identified sources. Although the mission statement rarely changes, such discussions always yield a more complete collective understanding of mission and a renewed commitment by board and staff.
- As one of the major planning session outcomes, the UDS board approves three broad mission goals for the next fiscal year:

  Mission Statement: Protecting the Public's Oral Health

  1. Advance professional education
     - Provide programs that educate dentists in specialty areas
  2. Advocate for Oral Health Profession
     - Increase governmental influence
  3. Advance public awareness and education
     - Expand public awareness of UDS professional standards

Avoiding "Mission Creep" Keeping mission relevant also means avoiding "mission creep" —the gradual expansion of programs and services into areas that are not directly related to mission. A good example of what this term means comes from city government, the New Orleans Levee District, whose mission is to protect New Orleans from flooding.

> The New Orleans Levee District board gradually bought or seized acres of land for flood-control but became more interested in using the land for places of amusement and recreation. It built two marinas, subdivided tracts for development that became the priciest real estate in town, constructing parks, walking paths, and fountains up and down the levees, sometimes with taxes generated for flood control.
>
> In more recent years, the board hatched and then abandoned a company—Floodcom—to string fiber-optic cable through the levees and signed a lease with the floating Belle of Orleans casino to help boost business at its lakefront marina.

The levee board justified its actions in a 1995 brochure: "We protect against hurricanes, floods and boredom."[4]

The levee board allowed mission system activities to stray well beyond the bounds of the mission charge; recreation marinas and parks are not the reason that the levee districts exist, but updating the levees to prevent floods is. The UDS board protects itself against such mission creep by holding the CEO accountable for annually reviewing existing programs against mission relevance.

The UDS CEO uses a very simple method of evaluating programs. Exhibit 10.3 shows the form that UDS uses to compare the results of each program to mission outcomes. The findings, along with program recommendations, are sent to board members prior to the June planning session. The Board and CEO discuss the report and any recommendations at that meeting, including recommendations to discontinue any programs that either serve only a few vested interests or seriously stray from mission.

Policies for Mission Currency Board strategy also includes scanning the horizon for the trends, challenges, threats, and opportunities that may affect mission in the future. Although some boards may delegate this responsibility to CEOs under the guise of "please provide us with the information," boards are accountable for these strategies, not CEOs.

In the Internet age, boards can do this work directly or manage it via a board task force quite easily. The UDS board has an ongoing process for determining which trends are important. The board does the following:

1. Oversees a year-round process for collecting trend information—connecting events, brainstorming sessions, surveys, board speakers, etc.
2. Reviews new information at each board meeting, but formally summarizes new information at the June board planning session; uses that data to build mission goals for the next fiscal year.
3. Uses important questions to evaluate which trends affect mission goals:
    - Does the trend affect UDS purpose and mission? Will UDS miss future opportunities if it doesn't act?
    - Does UDS have the willingness and ability to act? Is it able to invest time, learning, and effort?
    - Does the trend speak to UDS's deepest convictions and vision?

EXHIBIT 10.3 UDS PROGRAM EVALUATION FORM

Inputs	Activities	Outputs	Outcomes
What resources are needed to run the program?	What does the program do?	What happens as a result of the program?	What mission outcome is achieved?

Trend information emerges over time. The June board planning meeting relies on the scanning data gathered over the previous year, and the board uses that data to build mission goals, but an experienced UDS board also identifies any new issues and trends that should be explored in the next fiscal year. This means when the new board takes office on January 1, it hits the ground running, immediately discussing and planning tactics at its first meeting rather than deciding what it should do.

This eliminates what is a major danger in nonprofits—a tendency not to capture the work and informed wisdom of previous boards. Too often, each new board spends the year trying to determine what is important, or a new president or board member comes into the office with a personal agenda that may be quite different from the projects already underway. This tendency to reinvent the wheel is what keeps boards on the lowest levels of the learning curve.

Summarizing Board Mission Policies and Strategies Let's step back a moment and see how the UDS focus on macro-mission policy and strategy promotes a strategic and ongoing UDS planning system:

- Experienced board leaders kick off the June planning session. The mission statement, ongoing connection event feedback, and research findings frame the discussions—topics that encourage meaningful conversations that engage leaders on real issues.
- The session is a time for reflection when many different viewpoints can come together—where little bits of information spark new ideas and where disparate pieces of information start melding into a meaningful whole.
- Although this is a board planning session, the board borrows the informed wisdom of CEO and staff leaders in creating mission goals that consider the collective impact on the mission system. Contrast that with the normal board planning process—a new board succumbs to what one strong board member or CEO dictates as goals or has a consultant come in and lead the discussion to yield yet another vision/goal/strategy plan.
- Everyone leaves the June meeting full of energy and with a renewed sense of mission and organization. The CEO leaves with a set of board marching orders that provide the framework for the CEO/staff planning sessions that follow.

Overseeing Mission System and Business Component Performance Boards focus their mission system oversight policy and strategy efforts on three main categories:

1. Oversight of CEO
2. Oversight of the business component
3. Oversight of the board

Oversight of CEO Arguably the clearest of board accountabilities, boards must ensure that the nonprofit has the right leadership. For most nonprofits of any size, this means hiring the right CEO and providing effective CEO counseling and monitoring.

Policies That Define CEO Scope Boards delegate business component management to the CEO, but they must do so in a way that protects the mission system. They do this by identifying and addressing critical areas where CEO actions could endanger the health of the nonprofit as a whole.

In other words, it is a bad risk to waste board time creating lots of little rules that allow large wrongs. UDS doesn't attempt to curtail CEO activities at the lowest levels (e.g., limiting spending authority to very small amounts); instead, it creates policies that protect the system from abuses of CEO power (e.g., operating and reserve funds cannot be commingled). Although identifying such critical operating areas is specific to each nonprofit, in general, such UDS macro-policies cover:

- Fair treatment of members, donors, volunteers, and employees
- Financial policies related to budget, financial transactions, and accounting practices
- Financial policies related to asset protection
- CEO conduct related to transparent communications and support to the board

Policies That Define CEO Performance Boards hold CEOs accountable for business component performance, so they must measure that performance objectively. Frankly, they will spend an incredible amount of time in this area if they attempt to define activity-level goals and measurements, because it's impossible for volunteers to do this in any meaningful way. Doing so requires a level of knowledge that cannot be known from an occasional, remote vantage point.

So the UDS board focuses on benefit strategies—it defines mission goals at the June board planning session and then expects the CEO to focus on benefit strategies—translating mission goals into objectives and identifying success measurements at the August CEO planning sessions. The board and CEO discuss, modify, and agree on the final product at their November meeting. These are the outputs from that November meeting:

Mission Statement One (board policy): Advance professional education

Mission Goal One (board policy): Provide programs that educate dentists in specialty areas

Strategy One (CEO strategy): Create a portfolio of programs for each major specialty

1. Evaluate existing programs in specialty categories (Identify success measurements and time parameter)
2. Develop one new program for each (Identify success measurements and time parameter)

Mission Statement Two (board policy): Advocate for oral health profession

Mission Goal Two (board policy): Increase governmental influence

Strategy One (CEO strategy): Evaluate opening a Washington office

1. Review pro-forma for Washington offices (Identify success measurements and time parameter)
2. Identify key governmental policy over the past five years—assess effectiveness of lobbying from the national office compared with potential effectiveness from a Washington office (Identify success measurements and time parameter)

Mission Statement Three (board policy): Advance public awareness and education

Mission Goal Three (board policy): Expand public awareness of UDS professional standards

Strategy One (CEO strategy): Use regional TV to promote UDS dentists

1. Develop a series of TV ads to promote public awareness (Identify success measurements and time parameter)

Reviewing CEO Performance The board and CEO agree on each major CEO strategy and how to measure strategy success. During the year, boards and CEO track key indicators to monitor progress toward mission goals.

The UDS board sits down with the CEO in November for the CEO annual performance review, but there are no surprises. This review is just the end point in a process whereby the board and CEO mutually discuss organizational performance and mission goals progress to date throughout the year. The annual CEO performance review is an opportunity to step back and candidly reflect on the year in total, reward the CEO accordingly, and plan for training and support for the upcoming year.

Oversight of the Business Component Obviously, hiring the right CEO, creating an environment conducive for CEO success, and monitoring CEO performance is one kind of organizational oversight, but boards also need to monitor organizational performance directly without getting mired in the details, or the *Board Fiddles, Rome Burns* elephant will take over.

With the CEO, the UDS board identifies the activities that are central to the success of mission and organization, and the board holds the CEO accountable for defining measurements to monitor their performance. Initially, this is difficult work, and the need to consistently tweak and add new knowledge to improve measurements and indicators makes it even more difficult, but the process is worth it. Monitoring a good set of indicators gives the UDS board a way to oversee operations effectively without fruitlessly spending all their time trying to understand and control every activity. Chapter 12 addresses such indicators and measurements in detail.

Overseeing organizational performance also means the UDS board understands the infrastructure and resources necessary to achieve mission outcomes and expects and supports CEO efforts to supply them. It rejects a literal interpretation of sector advice that says that boards determine the organizational resources necessary because it knows that board members are not in the best position to select new computer systems and dictate the hiring of staff directors.

Most of all, the UDS board knows that programs need resources, and it never supports new goals without first understanding their impact throughout the system. The board expects and holds the CEO accountable for accurately defining business component impact and identifying resources.

Overseeing Financial Performance Financial performance oversight challenges boards more than any other area. The temptation to stray from overseeing financial performance into financial management is almost overwhelming. Inevitably, boards will cross this line occasionally, but not to worry. Revisiting the distinction between macro-financial policy, which is the work of boards, and managing within financial policy, which is the work of CEOs, brings things back into focus.

Macro-Financial Policy Macro-financial policies are board directives that protect the financial integrity of the global mission system. In general, these policies define conduct and limits to power for all mission system entities. Roughly, they fall into two main categories:

1. Ethics and conflict of interest policies
2. Investment and financial policies

Ethics and Conflict of Interest Policies Ideally, boards tackle these policies as a whole. They create a statement of values that defines the principles it upholds, a code of ethics that articulates the ethical principles that all must follow, and a conflict of interest policy that prohibits individuals from using assets or funds for personal gain.

Articulating a statement of values and a code of ethics can take quite a bit of time. These are overarching documents, and boards are right to involve member groups and take the time to get it right. In the meantime, boards should have at least a simple conflict of interest policy in place. All nonprofit leaders—boards members, committee members, CEO, and staff—complete an annual conflict of interest form that does the following:

- Defines conflict of interest and to whom it applies
- Requires regular disclosure of information that relates to conflict of interest
- Specifies procedures for handling potential or actual conflicts of interest when they occur

The UDS board implemented a complete set of ethics and conflict of interest policies. This is the process it followed:

1. Develop a statement of values—the values unique to mission that should guide the conduct of mission entities and all activities in the mission system.
2. From the statement of values, develop a code of ethics that shows how these values are practiced.
3. Ensure that the code of ethics covers areas such as global employment practices (equal opportunity, harassment, etc.); issues of privacy (records, disclosure); issues of communication (advertising, access to information); vendor relationships (negotiating contract); and conflicts of interest (outside employment, disclosure of financial interests, family members).
4. Add the statements and code to the Board Policy Manual; create a process for review and adherence to code.

Increasing public scrutiny, particularly in philanthropies whose main source of funding is government grants and public donations, means that nonprofit boards must aggressively avoid even the perception of corruption. It's important to stay ahead of the curve and make sure that good ethics policies are firmly in place and strictly followed.

Consider the example of the National Institutes of Health (NIH), which implemented tough new standards to prevent staff scientists from moonlighting for pharmaceutical and biotechnology companies. As NIH board member Elias Zerhouni says, "We believe that we need to hold the NIH and ourselves as scientists at NIH to a higher standard, because we do have national, public-health responsibilities."[5]

Nonprofit boards like UDS can tap into many resources to help craft good policy in this area. Looking at value and ethics statements on the Web sites of existing organizations provides many good ideas; the ASAE has sample statements and helpful resources on its Web site; the Independent Sector has a compendium of resources, including a checklist for developing a code of ethics; and the Ethics Resource Center offers an ethics toolkit on its Web site, www.ethics.org.

Investment and Financial Policies Instead of spending all of their time expecting the CEO to inform members about every detail of budget and program planning—the business activities of the CEO—boards like UDS's provide direction to CEOs by creating macro-financial policies that limit risk in areas critical to the mission system.

Let's examine what macro-financial policy looks like and see what boards should and should not be doing.

Investments:

Boards should: Create an investment asset allocation policy (e.g., 60 percent equities, 30 percent bonds, and 20 percent cash).

Boards should not: Dictate a particular investment firm or buy a certain stock.

Boards should: Review monthly investment statements and evaluate portfolio versus market performance.

Boards should not: Approve each stock trade.

Finances:

Boards should: Develop overall budget policies (e.g., expenses should not exceed revenues in each fiscal year).

Boards should not: Demand that CEOs get board approval each time an individual line item varies from the budget.

Boards should: Determine the annual target percentage of net revenue that goes into reserves.

Boards should not: Demand that CEOs reforecast the budget for monthly fluctuations.

The 13-member UDS board does not have an investment or finance committee. It believes that every board member has a fiduciary responsibility to oversee finance and understand financial reports. Members receive initial training on all UDS finances and financial reporting at board orientation, and individuals can request additional training as needed.

The UDS board holds its CEO accountable for day-to-day financial and investment management, but it is careful to define and limit that power in the Board Policy Manual (e.g., the CEO can make purchases but must attain comparative prices for anything over $100,000). The board also expects the CEO to provide clear monthly reports, reviews those reports, and closely follows monthly investment statements.

The UDS board has an audit committee and considers this committee an essential part of its oversight policies. The committee chair is a board member who is an expert in finance, and the other two committee members are appointees skilled in finance. The chair guides the committee in performing the following functions:

- Selecting, retaining, and terminating outside auditors
- Reviewing UDS's significant accounting and reporting principles
- Examining audit results and investigating to make sure that exceptions are resolved
- Communicating with the CEO before, during, and after the audit
- Approving and presenting the audit report to the board

The audit committee works for the board, not the CEO, and the CEO is not a committee member. The board does not expect the CEO to coordinate committee activities, but it does encourage open communications between the audit committee and CEO on all matters. The committee is a watchdog for the board, tracking any audit report exceptions or shortcomings, making sure that they are resolved, and bringing any continuing issues—the same exceptions on more than one audit report—to the incoming board's attention.

Boards can turn to the American Institute of Certified Public Accountants (AICPA) for help. The AICPA created the Audit Committee Effectiveness Center in response to concerns for increased governance. The AICPA offers a Nonprofit Audit Committee toolkit on its Web site (www.aicpa.org). This comprehensive kit is an A-to-Z guide for creating and sustaining an effective audit committee.

Budgets and Budget Reports The budget itself is not macro-financial policy. It is a management tool that forecasts future financial performance and reflects how well actual performance matches budget predictions. In other words, budgets are planning tools; budget reports reflect the reality of what happened.

Thus, the activity of creating budgets and the daily tracking of revenue and expenses reflected in monthly reporting are an essential part of CEO management, but not the work of boards. Boards that focus on budgets spend the better part of their meetings discussing past activities, which are under CEO not board control, rather than addressing future areas that are under board control—creating and monitoring risk policies, performing oversight, and holding CEOs accountable for financial performance.

The unfortunate reality is that CEOs and staff catch on quickly when boards micromanage budgets. They realize that a shortfall of actual-to-budget prompts board censure, so they project forecasts and future budgets that are ultraconservative. What often results is an unexpected surplus at the end of the year that should have been used to produce more mission outcomes throughout the year.

The UDS board considers both positive and negative variances of actual-to-budget as just part of management's response to real and unforeseen events rather than CEO ineptitude. It focuses board activities on macro-policy that links mission to financial performance and oversees financial performance as a whole. Specifically, the board does the following:

1. Begins the annual planning process by setting overall guidelines for the budget (e.g., a net surplus for the year or a certain percentage of net revenue must go to permanent reserves) at the June board planning meeting
2. Links mission goals to budget by determining the allocation of dollars to budget categories (e.g., what percentage of total budget should be devoted to the mission goal of "more dentist education"?)
3. Ensures that effective monthly and yearly budget and financial reporting are in place (e.g., monthly budget reports clearly indicate: budget; actual; percentage variance of actual to budget; forecast if different from budget; trend analysis such as previous year's budget and actual; aggregate categories)
4. Ensures that all board members are oriented to budget and finance and that they read and understand the financial reports (e.g., reviewing the monthly reports for

major category variances and making sure that the CEO supplies information regarding these variances with monthly reports)

Oversight of the Board The mission body delegates power to boards, so, theoretically, the mission body should oversee board performance. However, in practice, such a diverse body cannot do this except by voting board members in and out of office. Therefore, boards need to institutionalize policies and practices that monitor their own performance.

The UDS board articulates such policies in its Board Policy Manual. Here are the general categories that govern UDS board performance:

- Board accountability description
- Issues governing conduct (e.g., orienting new members, ongoing board development, monitoring board performance)
- Board recruitment and election
- Annual board calendar and yearly board agenda
- Authority and duties of the president or chairperson
- Board Code of Conduct
- Board committee philosophy and principles

Board Recruitment and Election Boards often give short shrift to their accountability for perpetuating an effective volunteer board. Their responsibility goes well beyond simply having policies that define an open and transparent nomination and election process. Boards need to actively identify, mentor, and recruit board candidates whose skills align with current and emerging mission needs.

Assuming boards are scanning the future and keeping their mission current, new mission needs may necessitate new board member skills. If more fundraising is a goal, it may be necessary to recruit members who can make large donations and access large donors. If a national image is needed to reach large donors, recruiting a famous personality who can open doors (e.g., Audrey Hepburn and UNICEF) makes sense. The UDS board may want to recruit a Washington insider to help achieve one of its mission goals: increase governmental influence.

It's important that candidate requirements clearly define these expectations upfront. One philanthropic nonprofit requires a commitment of $10,000 per year from each board member (either through outside donations or a personal check), and requires that board candidates and members sign a document that outlines this and other board responsibilities. The chairperson holds board members accountable by reading the names of those who have not reached their goal at each board meeting.

Boards need to think of recruiting as a process, avoiding the common election scenario where, close to deadline, boards suddenly realize that there are no good board candidates. A frantic last-minute search for people does not generate an outstanding board. Boards need an effective, ongoing set of strategies throughout their term to identify and recruit the right candidates. Ideas for doing so are plentiful: (1) make recruitment a part of regularly scheduled connection events; (2) invite a few attendees to meet with the board over lunch, discuss requirements, and then ask for the name of one person they think might be a good candidate; (3) place a newspaper ad that reads "Help Wanted: Volunteer Board Member" and (4) strategically target member groups that may have members with the requisite skills.

Many nonprofits use some kind of nominating committee to assist in this process. Bylaws and board policies assign a variety of functions to these groups, including recruiting candidates, creating the candidate slate, holding the elections, and evaluating board performance. That approach is fine as long as boards are prepared to nominate people to this committee who understand candidate requirements, board policies, and good board performance. It's useless to have volunteers with no exposure or knowledge of board service serve on a committee that selects board candidates.

What boards must not do is abdicate to the nominating committee their accountability for identifying and recruiting the right board members and perpetuating an effective board.

Board Assessment High-performing boards are self-aware; they follow policies and are committed to improving board conduct and performance. Self-improvement is accepted by every member, and each board meeting is another opportunity to further performance. Improving performance is not a stop-and-start process or a push to create a new governance structure after each *Nonprofit Trouble Cycle,* but an institutionalized habit embedded in every meeting and action.

UDS builds an evaluation period into the end of each meeting agenda, making it known that members cannot schedule flights and leave before candidly evaluating member conduct and whether meeting outcomes are achieved. It also annually sets aside a time, November, for a formal board self-evaluation. It uses the results to provide ideas and recommendations for policy change at the January meeting.

Many different thoughts exist on how to do board assessment, but boards like UDS can make one of three choices: (1) self-assessment, (2) outside help, or (3) volunteer groups. Boards that go the self-assessment route will find an abundance of guides that provide a ready-made framework to follow. At the time of this book's publication, the following tools are available: McKinsey & Company has a wonderful, free self-assessment tool; nonprofit association Web sites like ASAE and Boardsource have a wealth of free information; and Carter McNamara's site (www.managementhelp.org) offers self-evaluation and other free board tools.

Some well-functioning boards may want to do the whole process themselves, but others may feel it is better to use an outside facilitator. Such facilitators are trained in doing such evaluations and should be able to present uncomfortable truths in an acceptable way to sensitive board members. No matter how skilled the board members, they may still want an objective eye—an outside person or perhaps a widely respected and trusted volunteer—who sits in on board meetings and provides new and interesting insights.

Governance Committees One of the current trends to improve governance is expanding the nominations committee into a "governance" committee. In addition to creating a slate of board candidates, the committee assesses board performance by observing and seeking feedback from board and management, most of the time via questionnaire.

This is another one of those good concepts that is just not practical or sustainable given the nonprofit culture. Deciding to go this route is fraught with danger, and boards should approach with extreme caution. Assessing board performance is difficult unless committee members have the knowledge and expertise to recognize good board performance, and in any case, questionnaires are personal reflections, and the reality of judging performance is being able to directly see it, which means attending board meetings and additional meeting expense.

Most problematic, boards may find themselves in the same position as staff when coordinating committees, because more time is needed to inform and train people than is realized in positive gain. Even when nominating members are knowledgeable of good board performance, they need another set of skills to administer a questionnaire and share the results with understandably defensive board members. Done poorly, the result is hurt and angry board members, which does little to improve the board's overall performance.

Policy and Strategy at the CEO Level

If boards are busy creating policies and strategies to perform their benefit component and mission system oversight accountabilities, what's left for CEOs to do? Plenty! CEOs are accountable for the policies and strategies that achieve mission goals and maximize business component performance.

Achieving Mission Goals Once boards define mission goals, CEOs develop the program objectives that achieve those goals. Let's return to our UDS example and see what strategies the CEO creates for the board's first mission goal: "Provide programs that educate dentists in specialty areas."

- At the June board planning meeting, board and CEO discuss the intent and resources needed to achieve the stated board goal.
- At the August CEO planning sessions, the CEO discusses this goal with staff; in the following months, senior staff works with their staff and volunteer groups to agree upon strategies in their areas. The end of that process yields this:

  (CEO Accountable) Mission Objective 1.1: Create a portfolio of seminars for each major specialty. (Target: total of three seminars in each category by 12/31)

(CEO Accountable) Mission Objective 1.2: Create a series of brochures that highlight each specialty. (Target: brochure template by 12/31)

Except for finance, the toughest area for boards to fully delegate accountability and avoid meddling is program work. Generally, at least one member of the board has volunteer experience in any given program area and tries to get the board to micromanage those programs. However, program policies and strategies—creating, developing, implementing, sustaining, and tracking programs and services—are business component pieces and thus belong to the CEO.

The people who are accountable for the outcomes are in the best position to understand the resources needed and how those resources must interlink to produce and maintain programs. Boards should properly oversee CEO performance but delegate the policy and strategy approval necessary to lead these areas directly to CEOs. Boards should not delegate these powers to committees, which expect to be informed of every program activity but not be present or accountable for any program outcome.

Maximizing Business Component Performance CEOs are also fully accountable for ensuring that the engine that delivers mission goals is up-to-date and operating as effectively as humanly possible. For example, when the UDS office needed remodeling, the board had no idea what the staff needed to be most productive, so it held the CEO accountable for approving and directing the entire process. When it became obvious that a new computer system was needed, the UDS board expected the CEO to find and approve the vendor and direct the entire process.

Policy and Strategy at the Division, Committee, and Lower Levels

The board and CEO delegate the policy and strategy power to committee and division level that is appropriate for the accountabilities assigned to that area. The board delegates accountability for the audit process to the audit committee, and the CEO delegates accountability for achieving a given objective to the department director.

We can see how this process works by observing the actions of the UDS senior staff following the August CEO Planning Session. This is what the education director does:

- The CEO delegates accountability for defining and achieving the tactics needed to achieve *Mission Objective 1.1:* Create a portfolio of seminars for each major specialty. (Target: total of three seminars in each category by 12/31)
- The education director meets with her staff and volunteer advisory groups and determines the following:

  (Education Director Accountable) Initiative 1.1: Determine specialty categories.

  (Education Director Accountable) Tactic 1.1: Create volunteer advisory group. *(Volunteer Group Accountable) Tactic 1.1a:* Develop specialty groupings; evaluate current seminars and sort into identified groups.

Division managers continue delegating policy and strategy downward, giving authority for a limited scope of department activities to their subordinates. For example, the UDS education director delegates the seminar evaluation process to the education program assistant, who is accountable for developing the policies and strategies necessary to evaluate the quality of each seminar held.

It is worth noting here that there is a difference between being accountable for something and actually doing the work. The *I'm the Expert* part of a volunteer looks at Initiative 1.1 and says, "The education director can't define our specialties." The volunteer is right, but that's not what the education director is doing. No one expects corporate managers that are accountable for creating products to actually make those products themselves; rather, they find the expert help that can do so. Delegating accountability to the education director provides the strongest of incentives for that person to find the best resources to get the job done—and, that's the volunteers.

Delegating authority down to the lowest levels has another benefit; each level has an incentive for seeing that the other level does its job. The board looks bad if new specialty programs are not developed; the CEO looks bad if the education director fails to properly identify areas and the seminars are not successful; and the volunteer group looks bad if topics are not what peers want. And no one likes to look bad!

Making the Changes Stick

Holding every level accountable for creating and implementing the policies and strategies appropriate for the level is an essential step in the journey toward exceptional nonprofit performance. But taking this step requires releasing old thinking patterns, creating some new habits, and using some new tools.

Cultivating a Different Mindset

The archetype embedded in the nonprofit psyche is that boards are the policy-making body—period. Luckily, one good way to break this mindset is to visually show volunteers a better system—how much more productive boards are when they are not immersed in the policy work that belongs to the CEO and how much better protected the organization is when they actually do board work. One important tool that can help do this is the Annual Calendar.

Use the Annual Calendar to Inform and Educate

It's What You Get, Not What You Give Up Boards that delegate policy and strategy to the appropriate levels ensure a stronger, more mission-focused nonprofit, not a staff-dominated one. This means more, not less, of everything stakeholders like: programs developed faster, more opportunity for volunteers to participate in small impromptu volunteer advisor groups, and more organizational self-confidence to try new things and improve on existing programs.

One reason that volunteer leaders so often cling to the concept of boards approving everything is that they cannot imagine what boards would do otherwise. And that's where creating an annual board calendar that shows the differences between board macro-policy and CEO management policy can help volunteers understand the real work of boards.

Using the UDS basic calendar (Exhibit 10.2), let's fill in some UDS major annual activities. Exhibit 10.4 shows the results.

EXHIBIT 10.4 UDS ANNUAL CALENDAR OF MAJOR EVENTS

Month	Board	CEO

January	• Orientation for new board member
	• Board Meeting. Agenda items include:
	  ○ Finalize board meeting dates; decide connection events schedule
	  ○ Action plan for research and data gathering for issues identified at past June planning session—results due for current year June session
	  ○ Discuss any surprises from year-end reports
	  ○ Evaluate progress on mission goals and objectives
	  ○ Evaluate board performance
		• New annual plan and budget in place
		• Attend board meeting; report on mission goal progress and issues from year-end

February	• March meeting prework ○ Send prework reports	• Send unaudited year-end financial reports to the board
March	Audit committee meeting: • Meet with outside audit firm as preliminary to March/April audit • Board meeting • Connection event	• Coordinate on-site auditors • Attend board meeting—report on mission goal progress
April	• Nominating committee meeting • June session prework ○ Send prework reports	• Start annual program evaluation
May	• Board receives preliminary audit findings—discusses findings during board conference call with audit chair, CEO, and CFO • June session prework ○ Send prework reports	• Evaluation report out to board

(continues)

EXHIBIT 10.4 UDS ANNUAL CALENDAR (CONTINUED)

Month	Board	CEO
June	• Board elections • Annual board planning sessions. Agenda items include: ◦ Develop mission strategies and plan ◦ Set CEO planning and budget oversight guidelines ◦ Create annual board calendar (includes connecting event and board meeting schedules) ◦ Review existing board policies ◦ Review programs for mission "creep" ◦ Identify mission trends for coming year ◦ Audit committee, auditors meet with board to discuss audit report	• Attend board planning session—report on mission goal progress and financial performance to date • Support information or recommendation on the Program Evaluation Report
July		
August		• Annual CEO Planning Session ◦ Review board mission plan ◦ Develop business strategies and plan ◦ Draft supporting budget
September	• Board and CEO discuss mission strategies and proposed programs—budget problems are reviewed as necessary	• CEO/staff meetings on plan objectives and tactics • Staff/volunteer meetings on plan objectives and tactics
October	• Board approves CEO strategies and programs	• CEO presents strategies and programs to board
November	• Board meeting. Agenda includes: ◦ Finalize annual plan and budget ◦ Create preliminary January agenda and prework ◦ CEO performance evaluation	• CEO presents final strategic plan and budget • CEO presents recap of year's performance to objectives
December	• Board term ends 12/31 • Fiscal year ends • Board chair. January prework ◦ Send prework reports • Board term ends	• Fiscal year ends

Drive Home the Concept That Accountability Is Strength, Not Risk When reasonable volunteers think about the situation, most would agree that knowledgeable people in the thick of the action who are held responsible for the outcomes of those actions are much more likely to create effective policies and approve decisions than those who are not there. They just need to be educated that volunteer boards best retain control of these activities through oversight, not by approving activities of which they have little knowledge.

Boards that delegate power actually gain power in the form of board time to concentrate on what really matters—macro-policy. Once volunteers better understand all that entails, they begin to accept its benefits. A good analogy to use is that shareholders own companies but hand over their management to experienced people who have the time and energy to do it. They retain ultimate control, but realize that they cannot run the company themselves. They delegate that task to management professionals because they know that professionals, not amateurs, will maximize their return.

The same holds true for nonprofits: volunteer leaders have neither the time nor the direct management experience over the long term to run the nonprofit well, and that's why they hire professionals. By giving up some control, boards can devote their time to mission and constituents.

Yearly Board Agendas Keep Board Focus Complementing the annual board calendar is laying out a whole year of board agendas in advance. Publishing these agendas not only helps educate other volunteers to the board's real work, but it also allows them to provide input on important topics in a timely fashion.

To develop the agendas, the board takes the known calendar events, the planning issues that come out of the July board planning meeting, and re-occurring agenda issues and creates a preliminary agenda for each board meeting occurring in the fiscal year.

Doing so alerts board members to upcoming agenda items, so they can determine in advance what information and resources are needed to tackle the issue. The chairperson can assign premeeting work (prework) that board members can complete between meetings. Constructing agendas in advance not only encourages board members to come prepared and meetings to be more productive, it also keeps members engaged and focused throughout the year.

Institutionalizing Policies and Strategy Powers

The Board Policy Manual The Board Policy Manual is the best vehicle for institutionalizing mission and oversight policy and strategy. The Manual serves as a guidebook that defines good governance practice, a vehicle for continuity of leadership from one board to the next, and a training instrument for new board directors. It's also a notice tool for prospective board nominees—here's what we expect, so don't apply unless you are able and willing to follow these rules and do this work.

In addition, the Manual is the framework by which the board monitors everyone's performance, including its own. The CEO can help the board in its efforts, but the board, not the CEO, is accountable for creating, maintaining, and practicing good governance as set forth in this manual.

EXHIBIT 10.5 BOARD POLICY MANUAL—SAMPLE CONTENTS

CEO Policies
- CEO accountability description
- Limits to CEO authority
- Macro-board policies for:
  - Finance
  - Investment
  - Budget and planning
  - Staff and management
  - Board support

Board Policies
- Board accountability description
- Limits to board authority
- Board/CEO conduct
- Evaluation of CEO performance
- Annual agenda planning
- Board performance:
  - Code of meeting conduct
  - Role of president
  - Treatment of board committees
  - Commitment to board orientation and training
- Recruiting and electing board members

Mission System Policies
- Volunteer/staff mission structure
- Mission statement
- Statement of values
- Code of ethics
- Conflict of interest
- Annual mission goals
- Annual CEO objectives

One of the best examples of the kinds of board macro-policies that should be in the Board Policy Manual is contained in the Carver book, *Reinventing Your Board.*[6] The book's appendices illustrate a sample board manual with a generic set of policies that all boards, not just those aspiring to the Carver governance model, can adapt to their own organizations.

Exhibit 10.5 shows the general areas that Carver's and most Board Policy Manuals should cover.

Summing It Up

McKinsey & Company created quite a splash in a 2003 *Harvard Business Review* article when it stated that the nonprofit sector could capture an extra $100 billion per year in increased social benefit by making changes in the way it operates.

The changes that McKinsey cites—changing fundraising, distributing funds more quickly, streamlining and restructuring the way services are provided, and reducing administrative costs—are challenges to improve business component performance. Boards cannot do this directly, but they can delegate accountability for doing it to someone who can—the CEO—and monitor performance to make sure the right results are achieved.

When boards do this, they free their time for the exciting, real job of governance, a job that with the right knowledge and the right tools, volunteer boards can and will do well.

NOTES

1. American Cancer Society, www.cancer.org/docroot/AA/content/AA_1_1_ACS_Mission_Statement.asp (accessed December 19, 2005).

2. Institute of Electrical and Electronics Engineers, www.ieee.org/web/about us/visionmission.html (accessed December 19, 2005).
3. The Greater Chicago Food Depository, www.chicagosfoodbank.org/aboutus/mission.html (accessed June 21, 2005).
4. Ann Carrns, "Long Before Flood, New Orleans System Was Prime for Leaks," *Wall Street Journal,* sec. A.1, November 25, 2005.
5. Davis Willman, "Ethics Rules Tightened for Researchers at NIH," *Chicago Tribune,* News, p. 13, February 2, 2005.
6. John Carver and Miriam Mayhew Carver, *Reinventing Your Board* (San Francisco: Jossey-Bass, 1997), 189–207.

CHAPTER 11

The *Smile, Not Skill* Solution: Demand Performance

If you refuse to accept anything but the best, you very often get it.

—Somerset Maugham

TAMING THE *SMILE, NOT SKILL* ELEPHANT

Nonprofits face an amazing opportunity over the next decade. With CEO turnover rates projected at almost 70 percent in the next four years, boards have a unique chance to anticipate present and future mission system needs and hire CEOs whose experience and skills closely align with those needs.

This opportunity coincides with another trend—experienced corporate managers who are retiring from companies but seeking new careers in the nonprofit world. These managers want to put the expertise and skills built over many years of for-profit practice into helping others. Nonprofits face a dilemma: they may attract this potential management force, but once on board, can they retain it?

Effective managers thrive on challenge and achievement, but the *Smile, Not Skill* elephant drives a work culture based on congeniality. Nonprofits can successfully resolve this conundrum by taming the *Smile, Not Skill* elephant—retraining the lumbering pachyderm to value professional achievement over congeniality.

In This Chapter

Performance cultures begin with boards. If boards hire skilled CEOs and reward CEO performance, then CEOs will hire skilled professional staff and reward achievement; if boards continually seek to improve their own performance and hold CEOs accountable, then CEOs will convey those same values with staff.

The key to the Elephant Solution Four is "Demand Performance." The *Smile, Not Skill* elephant behaves when boards and CEOs work in tandem to build a high-performing mission system where congeniality is expected but achievement is rewarded.

ELEPHANT SOLUTION FOUR: DEMAND PERFORMANCE

Boards and Performance

Boards play an essential part in perpetuating performance cultures. First, they create the infrastructure that makes such a culture possible, and then they interact with a limited number of individuals—CEOs and other volunteer leaders—whose actions build and sustain the culture. Boards that are serious about a high-performing mission system should take these steps:

1. Identify, create, and institutionalize the policies and practices that yield a high-performing mission system—the five elephant solutions.
2. Hire the right CEO and hold the CEO accountable for performance.
3. Set the conditions that are most conducive for CEO and mission success.

This section focuses on these board actions, specifically the practices that promote the successful hiring and retention of high-performing CEOs. To illustrate best practices, we have created a model nonprofit, a hypothetical philanthropic organization that we will call Education Stops Poverty (ESP). Essential information that you need to know is:

- The ESP board is over the first huge hurdle—it has implemented Elephant Solutions One, Two, and Three.
- ESP's mission is: "defeat poverty through education."
- The ESP board has 9 members, and the number of professional staff is 15.
- ESP has chapters in 20 states.

Board Must Hire High-Performing CEOs

The biggest challenge for boards that want a high-performing mission system is to identify a high-performing CEO who aligns with their mission needs. Chapter 6 illustrated what boards should not do—bad hiring practices—and now let's find out what they should do—how to improve the odds of hiring the right CEO.

The Assessing Phase When boards rush into the hiring process, they act like the harried homeowner who slaps paint onto a wall that's not properly prepared; they will just need to repaint at a later date. Failure to take the time to accurately assess CEO needs upfront leads to a death spiral of frequent CEO turnover, and few things sap the energy of the entire mission system more quickly.

Face the brutal facts upfront—realistically assess where the organization is and where it needs to be—the current state of the organization against future mission needs. Admittedly, this is more easily said than done, because boards and senior staff find these kinds of candid discussions particularly difficult.

The answer is prepare upfront and have a genuine desire to hear the answers. Although the particular details of a CEO's departure make each situation a little different, here are the general practices that our example nonprofit, Education Stops Poverty (ESP), follows when it needs to hire a CEO:

- **Create a plan.**

  The ESP board:

  1. (Board with CEO) Meets with the outgoing CEO to review and discuss issues like the mission achievements of the last few years, the current year's plan and progress to date, and any data available from the board's ongoing trend analysis and connection events.

     The CEO provides a written report of work in progress with a summary of each staff director's ongoing major initiatives.

     Outcome: A summary identifying the current state of the organization, any gaps between current and future needs, as well as gaps between board support received and board support needed.

  2. (Board alone) Develops a hiring strategy and plan. Here the board looks at the state of the board to assess readiness to hire and hiring strategies. Discussion questions might include: (1) Are there gaps between board and CEO view of the organization? (2) What's the frequency of CEO turnover? And what does that tell us? (3) What additional CEO skills are needed? (4) Do board and CEO viewpoint align?

     Outcome: A candid board discussion and collective agreement on the state of the organization, future needs, and the CEO skills and experience necessary. A written report that includes the summary report of the state of the organization and the hiring strategy plan (e.g., board alone, executive search group, volunteer selection committee, retreat facilitators).

- **Hold a board/senior staff retreat.**

  The ESP board knows that not only is the CEO's departure stressful for the board, but it is also a difficult and uncertain time for the staff. That's why as soon as the CEO announces the resignation, the ESP board needs to:

  1. Speak with staff, explaining the general approach to the hiring process, disclosing the date of the Board/CEO meeting, answering questions, and agreeing on the date and agenda for a board/senior staff retreat.

     Outcome: Staff fears are mitigated by providing information and a set time to share their ideas and suggestions.

2. Collect data. The board also alerts staff to reports or information needed for the retreat. Depending on the gaps identified in the hiring strategy report and the specific hiring process, the board collects any surveys or information documented in that report.

   Outcome: Gain factual information to disseminate prior to the retreat.

3. Holds a board/senior staff retreat. The key to doing this successfully is pre-work: setting the stage for a genuine two-way discussion, sharing in advance the outcomes from the board/CEO meeting, and having all the data out prior to the meeting. ESP finds it helpful to have staff suggest names of any trusted volunteer leaders who might serve as facilitator, and then mutually agree upon this person to lead the discussions.

   Outcome: Compare board, CEO, and staff viewpoints; encourage a good working relationship between board and key senior staff during a CEO absence, gain more insight into staff CEO needs, and adjust the state of the organization document as needed.

- **Summarize findings in CEO Hiring Blueprint.**

  1. Create the Blueprint. This is the top-level information in the ESP CEO Hiring Blueprint:

     Current State of ESP

     – Trend list of past five years' mission outcomes
     – Progress to date on current-year mission goals
     – Summary of major department initiatives underway
     – Summary of any major initiative needing CEO approval and action in the immediate future

     Future State of ESP

     – Projection of major mission outcomes for the immediate and long-term future
     – Current/future organizational and CEO performance gaps identified
     – Needed CEO experience and skills defined

     Ideal CEO Experience and Skills

     – Summary of major qualifications

     Hiring Process

     – Define inside or outside resources
     – Time table
     – CEO interview process

     CEO Orientation and Material

     – Orientation manual and orientation process identified and ready

This is ESP's hiring process, but ESP already has the elephant solutions in place. Many nonprofits may still have those pesky elephants hanging around, and even worse, they may already have an entrenched Q-culture.

The bad news is that nonprofits cannot leap from a Q-staff to a high-performing staff in a single bound; the good news is that boards that are genuinely interested in improving performance can get there in steps, and relatively quickly if they hire the right CEO. Although it will take longer to get all key people in place, a high-performing CEO can instill a performance attitude and culture almost immediately; meanwhile, the board can be implementing the elephant solutions. The key is finding that CEO leader, and realizing that nonprofits already ruled by the smiley elephant can rarely do this alone.

Go It Alone or Bring in Help How do boards know if they are facing the brutal facts of the present and accurately assessing future needs? It's reasonable to assume that boards that practice good governance "know what they know"; boards know if mission system thinking, processes, and ongoing practices like connecting events and environmental scanning are in place. If so, these boards usually have a realistic read on the actual state and future needs of the nonprofit. Upon the CEO's departure, they follow ESP's process and move relatively easily to the next step of hiring the CEO.

A board that is not governing well faces a much tougher challenge. One of two situations probably exists. The board "knows that it doesn't know" and will seek help, or the board "doesn't know that it doesn't know"—it thinks everything is fine and won't ask for help. To be blunt, unless boards have devoted a great deal of meeting energy to the kinds of things contained in elephant solution practices, they should assume that they fall into the latter category. Assume that they cannot assess the situation objectively, and choose the safe course—seek outside help.

A consultant or skilled interim CEO comes into an organization not only with the experience to do the analysis but without the baggage of being perceived as biased toward any specific position or stakeholder group. Such a person can provide the clear, crisp, fresh perspective that comes from being on the outside looking in, and can offer frank observations and candid comments without the fear of stepping on volunteer or staff toes. But there are several strong caveats here:

1. Don't hire a board member's friend unless that friend truly has the credentials and references to support the skill to objectively facilitate what will be difficult and sometimes confrontational meetings.
2. Consultants or interim CEOs are only as good as the board that hires and manages them. The board, not the outside source, must own and lead this process. Board members should still follow ESP's good hiring practices, but the first step—create a plan—will take much longer. The board president, in particular, plays a key role in stewarding this process and creating an environment that encourages real dialogue.

3. Boards should not waste money to hire a consultant and go through the process unless the whole board agrees and is serious about achieving a realistic read on the current state of the organization, future needs, the work necessary to get there, and the desire to hire the right CEO.

A Word on Hiring Interim CEOs An interim director can help boards assess the current state of the organization, provide an objective audit of staff and operation, and keep the forward momentum of current projects and goals. There's also a growing recognition in the nonprofit sector that interim CEOs can help an organization change direction and set the stage for the permanent CEO's success.

The ugly little wrinkle to an otherwise emerging good practice is the tendency for boards to name an inside board member or senior staff member to the interim post rather than an outside person. A quick Google Web search yields the following: "The Charles Darwin Foundation names their director of administration as interim executive director"[1] or "Michigan Tech Fund names the Fund's chief financial officer as interim executive director."[2]

Although these may be good choices, naming inside parties is frequently about the board's comfort with this person rather than an attempt to seek help in assessing things objectively. Plus, even if insiders try to be objective, they still must deal with stakeholder perceptions of bias. Insiders may find it very difficult to overcome this bias and to risk objective evaluation, particularly if the board does not want to face hard realities.

Appointing insiders as interim CEOs also reflects a board attitude that senior staff does the real work anyway. Why spend the money and go to the trouble of hiring an outsider who needs to be trained, when it's much easier to have a long-tenured, high-Q senior staff person hold down the fort? Or even worse, the board can't decide on one staff director and appoints co-interim directors. Every decision requires a meeting, and an already apprehensive staff now has two temporary bosses to deal with.

An inside—or for that matter, an outside—interim CEO who lacks the skills or authority to manage increases staff uncertainty and lends nothing toward helping the board understand the real state of the organization or its CEO needs. And what does the board do if an insider throws his or her hat into the CEO ring and loses? At a minimum, they will find it difficult to switch back from manager to peer.

Naming a board member is especially problematic. Volunteer leaders who are not in the office on a day-to-day basis woefully underestimate the influence and output of an effective, strong CEO. Everything visible to the board looks placid and regal when, in effect, all the action is below the water line.

Governing can be done well on a part-time basis, but directing the business cannot. Board members who would be appalled at placing amateurs in charge of their own businesses think nothing of putting themselves in charge of managing the nonprofit. This is just another form of devaluing CEO management—to say nothing of the difficulties that board interim CEOs face in switching back from management to governance.

Summing up the Assessing Phase Boards that institutionalize good governance practice will be more than capable of navigating the assessment phase alone; boards that have not put good governance in place need outside help. That help might come in the form of a trusted consultant or it might come in the form of an interim CEO. Whatever the choice, a CEO vacancy provides a small window of opportunity for objective outside assessment and finding a CEO who aligns with those defined organizational needs, so boards should not throw that opportunity away.

Hiring a CEO Moving beyond the assessment phase and into the actual hiring phase, the individual needs of a nonprofit will dictate the list of specific CEO experience and skills the candidate needs. However, if boards are to successfully build high-performing cultures and attract high-performing CEOs, it's imperative that:

1. New CEOs should be experienced line managers.
2. CEO title, job description, and salary do matter and must align.

Universal #1: CEOs Should Be Experienced Line Managers

Choosing the right CEO is the greatest gift that boards can bestow on staff and organization. So do them a favor: hire an experienced line manager. Boards greatly improve their odds of doing so if they seek CEOs who demonstrate a successful track record of directing and managing a multidisciplinary staff and organization to achieve stated outcomes.

Put succinctly, if CEOs do not practice good management, neither will their staff. Boards cannot settle for just the appearance of management experience on a CEO resume. They must dig in and make every effort to find out if the applicant really is an experienced leader. As psychiatrist Gordon Livingston states in his thought-provoking book, *Too Soon Old, Too Late Smart,* "We are not what we think, or what we say, or how we feel. *We are what we do.* Conversely, in judging other people we need to pay attention not to what they promise but to how they behave."[3]

The ESP board uses two good tools for sniffing out whether CEO candidates are just talking a good game or if their words are backed by real achievement: situational interviewing and a strategic approach to candidate references. Let's take a quick look at each practice.

Situational Interviewing

- Define two or three management challenges that actually occurred at ESP, and ask the candidate how to resolve the situations.
- Pick one or two achievements from the candidate's resume and ask the candidate to explain in detail the approach, actions, problems, and people/resource issues involved.

- Ask candidates to describe their management style—a recent senior staff performance review, the successful resolution of a difficult performance problem, a meeting with a successful outcome, or the handling of a difficult board problem.

Strategic Approach to References

- Ask for a reference from each organization: (1) from an immediate supervisor or a board member and (2) from a subordinate.
- Agree on the top one or two management skills needed, and then create management situations that call for those skills. Describe these situations and ask the reference what the candidate would do.

Universal #2: CEO Title, Job Description, and Salary Do Matter and Must Align

The second universal of CEO hiring follows closely on the heels of the first: Title, job description, and salary do matter. They reflect the importance boards place on staff leadership—title, job, and salary should align with the accountability that boards delegate to CEOs.

The indiscriminate use of title in the absence of any correlation with salary and/or accountability contributes to the public's cynicism regarding nonprofit management. When titles like CEO, executive director, president, and administrative director are used in a homogenized way, the effect is to downgrade the chief staff officer position in general. This lends to the perception that a corporate CEO's responsibilities far exceed those of a nonprofit CEO.

Align Title with Description The following words on a CEO position description —supervise the office staff and implement board decisions—do not align with the title of CEO. An agency description asking for "a principle executive officer to discharge all duties of that office" and "direct strategies and staff in all fundraising, financial, promotional, and organizational activities" does.

The first description actually advertises for a CEO at a $120,000 salary, and the second for an administrative/executive director at a salary of $40,000. The problem is that a CEO may be attracted to what is basically an administrative position with a title of CEO and high salary, but that person will not be a fit for the work culture. In the second case, boards will not be able to hire a high-performing CEO, yet they clearly want someone who can do that caliber of work in the position.

An interesting sidebar to this discussion is the role that gender plays in the misalignment of nonprofit titles and salaries. Exhibit 11.1 highlights the findings of interesting studies on the subject.[4, 5]

Align CEO Pay with Market Rate A common reason that boards publicly cite for paying CEOs less than market rate is "lack of funds." Although this appears to be true on

EXHIBIT 11.1 GENDER, TITLE, AND SALARY

Trends in CEO Title and Salary

Statistics show interesting trends with regards to the experience, titles, and salaries of men and women CEOs. The study *"Daring to Lead: Nonprofit Executive Directors and Their Work Experience"* found the following:

- Women substantially outnumber men in nonprofit executive director positions; in most regions they make up 60 percent of the population.
- Only 36 percent of executives were promoted from within their own organizations; nearly two-thirds were in the position for the first time.
- Women executives are paid less than their male counterparts for the same jobs. The differential is especially acute among large agencies.
- Men disproportionately lead large agencies; although men make up 38 percent of the (executive director) population, they run 55 percent for the agencies with annual budgets of $5 million or more.

The population for this study is mostly 501(c)(3) organizations, but a quick, nonscientific review of gender/titles and size of organizations in association directories like the ASAE's seems to show the same pattern—larger associations are headed by males; those titles tend to be CEO or president.

These statistics may reflect some public attitudes that help keep both title and salary for smaller nonprofits and female-headed nonprofits below market. They are:

1. Public archetypes about gender
2. Traditional female behavior and attitude

One of the archetypes strongly held by the public is that men are tougher than women. This attitude is often present among board members. Boards may see male CEO candidates as better able to make the tough decisions necessary in a larger nonprofit. Higher pay and title accrue to these tougher jobs, but traditional attitudes and behaviors of women may also play a role. In the past, volunteer ranks and leadership were filled with women who did not work outside of the home. Some found self-esteem and fulfillment from unpaid nonprofit leadership jobs in much the same way as women do now in paid corporate jobs. Others were temperamentally predisposed to give unstintingly of themselves for a good cause. Both groups held the traditional female values of giving and supporting causes, and many were willing to work behind the scenes while others got the credit.

Some of this generation of women graduated to the CEO and other staff management spots as times changed, and nonprofits grew. But these women do not associate themselves with the trappings and power of CEO positions and so are much more uncomfortable asking for such than their male counterparts. Plus, some remember the days when they did the same work and did not get paid, so they have conflicted feelings about salary in general.

Although it might be argued that women managers are better suited than men to the collaborative, team-oriented leadership culture found in nonprofits, an equally good case might also be made that current senior women managers are more comfortable sharing rather than shouldering full accountability and power. This gives boards, particularly philanthropic boards, leeway to avoid paying competitive rates if a ready supply of these women will tolerate lower than market titles and salaries. Such public archetypes about gender coupled with nonassertive female behavior combines to keep salaries and titles lower than they should be in some nonprofits. As the CompassPoint study also recommends,

> Women executives would be wise to take notice of their pay relative to male peers. . . . organizations need to value positions appropriately for the qualities of leadership the organization demands. When executives purposely suppress their salaries, they make a demeaning statement about their own talents and their organization, and set boards up for a rude awakening when they leave.

the surface, more often it is a short-sighted excuse or a fear rather than reality if boards delegate full business component accountability to the CEO, and let the CEO handle the rest.

An experienced, talented CEO who enjoys the full confidence of a board that is willing to delegate the appropriate powers can eventually raise the funds or find the revenue sources necessary to support growth and operations, and that includes the necessary expense of competitive staff salaries. The story that a program officer from a local foundation tells is illuminating.

A small arts group had come to the foundation asking for a grant to run a capital campaign. The organization operated on a shoestring budget, and the founder and executive director kept his own salary very low as a way to help the organization make ends meet. The program officer did an assessment of the organization and determined that there was no way the organization could run a successful capital campaign with existing staff. However, it was impossible to find a talented fundraiser to work with the organization since the executive director's salary was so low, and the other salaries went down from there.

Rather than walking away, the program officer explained the situation to the executive director, asked that the executive director double that salary (with a grant from this foundation), and then hire an experienced development director to run the capital campaign. The results were phenomenal. They hired a new staff person to lead the capital campaign, and the organization took off. It developed a strong donor base, reserves, decently paid staff, and sustainable arts programs for the community.

Creating the Conditions for CEO and Mission System Success

Certain board practices support high-performing CEOs. These are the same practices that CEOs need to lead the business component, and that board, staff, and volunteers must practice to sustain a high-performing mission system. Because boards set the tone, we tackle the issues here mostly from the perspective of board to CEO, but just keep in mind that they hold equally true for each entity and every level.

Was the CEO Dead When You Hired Him or Did You Kill Him? Many of the board practices that positively support CEO performance are familiar by now: creating one mission structure, seeking a shared reality, and delegating policy and strategy to the appropriate levels. But, even when these practices are finally in place, each existing board and incoming board must work to consistently apply the practices to daily work life.

Upon reflection, few people would argue against boards promoting the culture that best supports CEO success; the challenge is specifically how to do that. Let's look at six specific practices that our ESP board takes on and that all boards can employ:

1. Governance is important; do it.
2. Institutionalize objective trust; eliminate Q trust.

3. Feed CEO performance; starve CEO politics.
4. Provide extra support during times of change.
5. Confront the devil you know.
6. Don't blur the line between professional staff and volunteers.

Governance Is Important; Do It Such a simple statement and yet so powerful: governance is an important job, and doing that job is the best support boards can give CEOs. This means that the president, not the CEO, creates the meeting agenda; important issues get discussed at the board table, not at break; the board, not staff, develops and orients new board members; committees aren't created without reason or resources; the board reaches out to constituents and cultivates major donors.

To use a trite but apt phrase: boards must walk the talk. Boards cannot expect others to do their jobs if they ignore their own. ESP models a learning culture for staff by doing its job and by setting aside time at every board meeting to monitor and improve board performance with questions like:

- Does the president chair the meeting effectively? Why or why not?
- Do agenda items relate to governance? Why?
- Do all board members contribute or does one member dominate?
- Is feedback from key stakeholders sought and considered?
- Does the board scan the horizon and take action regarding trends and environmental issues?

Doing this doesn't have to be drudgery. Using board policies, create a checklist for good board conduct; assign someone at each meeting to check off the list and report in the last hour. Make it okay to goof up by awarding funny gifts for bad behavior. The idea is that everyone makes mistakes; doing it wrong is how everyone learns to do it right the next time. If the board is having problems in one area, assign a member or ask the CEO to construct a short case study from events specific to the nonprofit, then work through it as a group at the next meeting.

Nonprofits do not get into trouble because they don't understand the concepts of governance; they get into trouble because they don't know how to apply or don't practice those concepts in the workplace. Failures of firms like WorldCom and Enron, or the scandals of The United Way and Red Cross don't happen because their very accomplished boards don't know how to govern, it's because they *did not* govern.

Institutionalize Objective-Based Trust; Eliminate Q-Based Trust *Trust* is a lovely word and a lovely concept. The problem is that trust too often is subjective, based on likeability rather than performance. If the CEO talks a good game and board members like the person, they trust the CEO. This kind of trust gets boards and organizations into big trouble.

ESP understands that the proper board and CEO relationship is not a friendship; its board president and CEO are not best buddies. Nice board members find it hard enough to harshly criticize the CEO when warranted, but it's virtually impossible to hold the CEO's feet to the fire when the board and CEO are friends.

Rather than trust CEOs as friends, the ESP board builds a culture of objective trust. Objective trust derives from a secure environment where the rules of the game are open and transparent, and measurements of performance are defined and followed. The ESP CEO trusts the board because the CEO is secure in the knowledge that, if board-defined goals and measurements are met, performance will be positively judged. And the ESP board trusts its CEO because the board understands how to objectively evaluate CEO performance.

Conversely, when personality or Q-based trust takes over, and boards like CEOs, they trust them to do the right thing. CEOs must schmooze board members, because they know a member liking them leads to a good review. Performance-oriented CEOs do not thrive in such a culture because what constitutes good versus poor performance is undefined, and they cannot accurately predict how boards will judge their performance.

With Q-based trust, CEOs cannot operate freely; they must pander to each board member's subjective opinion as to what constitutes CEO performance. This situation encourages CEOs to avoid confrontation and assume as little risk as possible. This translates into avoiding any and all new opportunities that might alienate any part of the board or related vested constituents.

In contrast, in a secure, objective trust-based culture, CEOs are free to stretch the boundaries, innovate, and seize new opportunities, because they are secure in the knowledge that they will be judged on the basis of known, objective measurements, not personality.

Feed CEO Performance; Starve CEO Politics The majority of a CEO's time should be spent performing, not politicking. In general, one mark of a productive, healthy culture is that both board and staff leaders spend no more than 20 percent of their time dealing with board and volunteer politics. Doing otherwise is wasting donor and member dollars on internal issues, and certainly "we support politics" is not a very good mission statement. However, in the absence of clear outcomes and success measurements, the *Code of Nice* encourages precisely the kind of subjective, Q-based culture that violates the first principle of Management 101—take the subjectivity out; being friends makes it very hard to analyze performance objectively.

Q-based CEOs spend most of their time managing board and volunteer politics, not managing staff and organization. They stay in power by becoming friends with board members and retaining a personal relationship with influential leaders. The well-publicized squabble of Disney shareholders, board, and management provides a unique, public look inside such kinds of board rooms. CEO Eisner's standard operating procedure was to lavish attention on individual board members, soliciting the views of key directors, inviting them to lunch, and plotting with individual board members.

The Disney high offices are an example of a culture rife with the politics that come from private conversations where performance is judged in secret and characters are assassinated without a person's knowledge. Gossip becomes the main form of communication, and organizational energy is directed toward figuring the real meaning behind official leadership communication and action.

The ESP board insulates its CEO from the lobby of vested volunteers and partisan donors, ensuring that CEO decisions are made for the good of the whole, not the benefit of the few. It deals with vested volunteers directly, rather than expecting its CEO to continually spend time justifying the staff's right to act. As long as its CEO is acting within board policy, the ESP board confronts such vested volunteer activity with as little involvement from the CEO as possible.

If boards accept an overly political culture, then CEOs and staff will spend the better part of their valuable time soothing ruffled vested volunteer feathers and dealing with the political shenanigans rampant in such environments. It is inevitable, even in performance-based cultures, that CEOs and staff will sometimes form friendships with volunteer leaders and vice versa, and CEOs will and should cultivate good board relations. The point is that friend relationships are minimal and should not hijack the authority of those officially accountable or usurp the approved route for decision making.

Provide Extra Support during Times of Change Change and discord go hand in hand; at least initially, some member or constituent segment or staff member will be upset by the changes. Even the best change strategies won't always work in the first iteration; in fact, some will fail outright, which gives everyone something to complain about.

In times of major change, how a board tolerates discord, how it counsels vested volunteers and other stakeholders, and how it counsels and monitors CEO performance will largely determine the success or failure of the change effort. Here are some practices the ESP board follows when the organization is undergoing major change:

- ESP understands that major change to governance and management instantly creates a politically charged culture. The board strategically prepares in advance for the inevitable discord that accompanies change and provides special CEO support and oversight during such times.
- The board supports and rewards intelligent CEO failures as well as outright successes. It understands that all untried programs need tweaking that, in turn, converts failure into success the next time. It does not allow such setbacks to tar the CEO and derail the change process.
- The ESP board does not hire a CEO and say "make it happen," and then later add "but don't make anyone unhappy." When ESP first made the leap to a performance culture, it hired a new CEO to strengthen staff leadership. The board supported the CEO as new employees were recruited with a different mix of skills. It understood that some long-term, high-Q staff members who previously hid behind

committees might not relish coming out into the open and shouldering more accountability. It resisted the temptation, when confronted with vested people who were upset by needed change, to privately question if the CEO was doing the right thing because people are upset, and helped smooth over their complaints to influential volunteer friends.

Confront the Devil You Know Too often, boards may like CEOs, but realize their limitations. They don't have the heart to get rid of the person, but neither are they successful at improving CEO performance. However, because they are comfortable with the CEO, they find it easier to live with the situation, and let a good senior staff make up for what the CEO lacks.

Or, boards feel stuck with mediocre or bad CEOs because they fear that they can't find anyone better. Whatever the reason, boards that tolerate rather than confront poor performance cannot build a high-performing mission system. Instead, such tolerance creates a sick culture where boards move around the CEO and senior staff productivity suffers. How this happens is aptly recounted by a colleague:

> My president is a great guy, but he has the habit of calling my staff directors and asking about their departments and how things are going overall. He sometimes asks that they make changes to existing formats; at the last staff meeting one of the directors asked if she reports to me or the president.

The ESP board does not allow its actions to undercut the CEO's authority with staff in this way, nor does it blur board and CEO roles. The board does not want staff directors chasing their tails as they duplicate information and action, or putting them in a situation where they must make the uncomfortable choice of not acting on the president's request—or acting on it and alienating the CEO.

The ESP board understands that when board members are in continual touch with and giving directions to non-CEO staff members, it's either a sign of bad governance practices or poor CEO performance. Either way, they confront the problem directly and act quickly to resolve it. The board knows that failure to address poor performance—the CEOs or the board's—creates a culture where low performance becomes the norm, which is anathema to high achievers and one reason for their departure from the nonprofit sector.

Don't Blur the Line between Professional Staff and Volunteers Eavesdrop on any gathering of CEOs and staff leaders and you're likely to hear at least one conversation that sounds like this: "I love my job, but it's difficult to wear so many hats and continually juggle more balls in the air." Although on the surface this may not seem much different than the complaints of corporate managers in an increasingly 24/7 world, one thing differentiates nonprofit talk. These activities are not a means to an outcome; they are the outcome.

A high-Q, board-pleasing CEO rarely says no to any board request; boards and volunteer committees come to expect this can-do spirit and expect all staff to act on every volunteer idea. Philanthropic nonprofits naturally want to do more to address the very real needs that surround them. Often, this means the CEO and senior staff work weekends and evenings to accommodate the ever-increasing board and committee activities and a myriad of new programs.

Thus the line between professional paid staff and volunteer staff becomes blurred. Because volunteers are donating evening and weekend time without being paid, they expect staff to do the same. Staff's apparent willingness to do so swells the volunteer heart as they publicly voice their pride of "our hardworking staff." It's a sign of how much staff cares. What it really signifies is a culture that is poised to lose its best performers.

An example of the harm that comes from this kind of thinking is found in the actions of a board president of a health care nonprofit:

> The board had scheduled an all-weekend board meeting, which, as customary, would be attended only by the CEO. The Friday of the meeting, the president came to headquarters and fired the CEO; that afternoon the president asked that all senior staff attend the Friday evening through Sunday afternoon board meeting. Three of the senior staff had prior weekend commitments and could not attend all three days.
>
> At the board meeting the following week, the board president complained that "senior staff was unwilling to devote their time to the organization." As another board member put it, "we may need a clean-up of senior staff, not just the CEO."
>
> The message perceived by key senior staff members who had long worked day and night to cover for a poorly performing CEO was this: "The board does not respect your time and doesn't care how many hours you spend here; if you care, you'll volunteer your free time just like us."

Volunteerism is a service performed by people of their own free will, not something they are forced to do. The ESP board has a much different attitude toward its CEO and professional staff than the board in the example just discussed. Admirably, ESP board members and other volunteers donate many hours to the nonprofit, but they do so of their own free will, because they derive personal satisfaction from volunteer work. If their own employers expected them to routinely spend evenings and weekends working for the company on an unpaid basis, they'd think, "Are you crazy?" and eventually leave that employer.

The ESP board thinks this same logic applies to its professional staff. Although nonprofit senior managers accept that their jobs sometimes require copious hours outside of the office—it comes with the territory—the ESP board respects their time and does not schedule more board, committee, and task force activities over weekends, nor does it commit to projects without any thought to resources. It does not expect professional staff to volunteer their off-hours to make all of this happen.

This new mindset also extends to respecting the time of volunteers. The ESP board realizes that lots of meaningless internal activities, politics, and rambling meetings are precisely what many volunteers are trying to escape in their nine-to-five jobs. Productive people do not want to waste scarce off-time doing activities that are frustrating and without purpose, and ESP volunteer and staff leaders do their best to avoid such kinds of activities and politics.

Set High Standards, and They Will Come An old saying is, "set high expectations and people work up to them; set low expectations and people work down to them." When the *Code of Nice* dominates organizational culture, the focus is on supporting and pleasing volunteers, not using professional skills to achieve mission outcomes. An interesting observation on this topic comes from an item in the *Board Café*,[6] a newsletter of CompassPoint:

> The governance role is an outsider's role, holding the organization, and specifically the executive staff, to high standards of performance. While most managers work hard to do a good job, it is not in the manager's personal interest to make her own job harder.

While one could argue that high-performing CEOs welcome a challenge and do not simply seek to make their jobs easier, it is true that board oversight demands that boards assume the opposite. However, boards sometimes need to look at CEO leadership differently; sometimes good performance leadership flies in the face of conventional wisdom. Marshall Goldsmith, a preeminent executive coach, puts it this way:

> If you read the literature, you'll see that much of it exaggerates—if not glamorizes—the leader's contribution. The implication is that everything grows out of the leader . . . take the leader out of the equation and people will behave like lost children.
>
> This is hokum. As the ancient proverb says, "The best leader, people do not notice. When the best leader's work is done, the people say "we did it ourselves."[7]

The ESP board recognizes that good CEO leadership is subtle and often silent. It's recognized by the people who are directly affected, but it may not be readily apparent to board members. Although it expects the majority of CEO time to be spent on management, the ESP board knows that some of the positive indicators of CEO leadership are impossible to gauge from a distance. It gauges the evidence of good CEO leadership by talking with key staff members and observing whether the CEO exhibits good leadership practices, such as:

- Setting conditions whereby others can and want to be successful
- Acting as the catalyst that sparks synergies among direct reports
- Helping staff appreciate and use each other's talents
- Resolving interdepartmental roadblocks
- Monitoring individual and organizational performance
- Chairing stimulating meetings
- Encouraging innovative new ideas and programs

When boards do not allow time for CEO leadership and management, and expect a high level of CEO performance, overall organizational performance suffers. Potential staff leaders have no day-to-day role model, and they are not challenged to ever-higher performance and do not challenge their subordinates. Archetype research done by sector leaders and the American Society for Quality after the September 11 attacks provide important insights into the importance of setting the bar high:

> Americans thrive when failure strikes, but first organizations must set into motion the climate that unleashes a person's willingness to help weather uncertain times. We prefer big challenges that seem insurmountable, but need information about what is going on and what needs to be done. Don't tell us how to get the job done; set us loose to try new ideas and beat the odds.[8]

CEOs and Performance

We've just covered how boards support a performance culture. Now, it's time to see CEOs in action. In a sense, if boards do their job, CEOs just carry on. With effective board policies and elephant solutions as a sound infrastructure, CEOs cultivate the same practices as boards in order to support performance.

But that's where the similarity ends; there's a huge difference between board oversight and CEO management. Temporary, part-time boards do not live in the daily workplace that they oversee, nor do they need to deliver hands-on manager-to-manager support like CEOs.

CEOs must breathe the same air as the staff they manage—a staff that has far less management experience and needs direction and mentoring for professional and personal growth. Because the only way to achieve mission goals is through staff, CEOs have no higher calling than motivating this workforce and challenging them to realize their personal best.

***PER* for Performance** For the purposes of the sections that follow, we explore three crucial elements that go beyond the board practices just discussed. They can be summarized by the word *PER*—CEOs must embrace all three elements if they are to build and sustain a culture that inspires a high-performing staff. They are:

1. Managing people is a **P**riority.
2. Sharing wisdom is **E**ssential.
3. Achieving results is **R**ewarded.

It's one thing to recognize *PER* practices and quite another to distinguish a *PER* from a Q-driven workplace. Although anyone can step inside a nonprofit office and immediately feel a buzz or lack of buzz of energy, it's not so easy to see if that hum is the sound of producing outcomes or just doing everything. However, the picture becomes much clearer if we spend some time with the CEO, because the practices of this top person will pretty much tell the tale.

Toward that purpose, we'll follow in the footsteps of two very different CEOs: (1) Michael, a Q-culture CEO who left our example nonprofit (ESP) more than 10 years ago, and (2) Aidan, his successor, who embraces *PER*. Observing Michael and Aidan in action gives us a clear picture of what distinguishes *PER* workplaces and how such workplaces foster a motivated and performance-oriented staff.

Make People Management a Priority

> The ESP director of marketing, Mark, is sitting in CEO Michael's office as he comes in. Michael's running about 15 minutes late for their meeting—Mark's annual performance review. Michael sits down at his desk and says, "Sorry, Mark. It's just crazy today, but I don't want to postpone this again." As he says that, the phone rings, he answers it, and, in an aside, says to Mark, "It's the president; this will just take a minute."
>
> The call lasts ten minutes. As Michael turns back to Mark, he hands him a one-page review form with a number of checked-off boxes and tells him, "You know I like you, and it's been a pretty good year. You're doing fine. Just take a look at this later, sign it, and let me know if there's anything you'd like to discuss."

An old saying—people will forget what you say, but they never forget how you made them feel—applies here. Michael sends mixed messages to Mark: He says, "I like you," but his actions say, "You are personally not worth my undivided attention, and your professional performance and growth is not really important to me."

Assuming Mark is a good performer, he leaves feeling diminished as a person and angry that his performance goes unnoticed, but the damage goes beyond a demoralized employee. CEO Michael lost the opportunity to generate excitement about mission and organization and to tap into an employee's vision and unspoken ideas. Contrast this with the way Aidan handles the same situation:

> Aidan is reviewing his notes as, right on time, the director of fundraising, Tom, is at the door. He motions for Tom to sit at the conference table, closes the door, and joins Tom at the table. "Tom, we discuss your performance frequently, so there are no surprises here. It's just good to take a moment each year to step back and discuss the year's accomplishments, your career, and where you and the organization can go in the coming year."
>
> Aidan and Tom spend the next hour reviewing the past year's fundraising performance—winners and losers—and the fundraising objectives that they'd already agreed upon for the upcoming year. Aidan clasps Tom's hand and, as he is leaving, says, "Just think, if the donations from your annual telethon again exceed estimates, we may be able to expand our scholarship program internationally earlier than expected, maybe next year."
>
> As Tom leaves, Aidan picks up his messages, one of which is a call from the president, which he returns shortly.

Tom leaves the office feeling personally valued and professionally excited at the chance to better last year's performance.

Since management is his priority, Aidan views performance reviews as a time to connect, evaluate, and create a shared vision for the future; Michael, like many CEOs, views annual reviews as a chore. Such attitudes are a self-fulfilling prophecy: Aidan's time ultimately results in Tom delivering more mission outcomes; Michael's time results in a higher volunteer Q-rating, but the loss of ideas and a potential loss of a valued manager in the future.

Value Staff

What employees say they want is remarkably consistent. Survey after survey shows that the top two things they want from managers are (1) to feel their opinions are valued and (2) to be treated fairly. The conundrum is that the *PER* practices that would fulfill these desires take a back seat to the much flashier illusion of leadership in the form of charismatic CEOs with grand visions.

This kind of CEO and all CEOs say that they value people, but staff people are a jaded bunch that discount much of what leaders say and pay much more attention to what they do. It's the chance encounters that either motivate an employee to come to work or to be just a warm body plodding through the day. It's managers doing the small things that are really big things in people's work lives: a CEO who enters an elevator and says hi and calls you by name, a manager who takes an interest in an employee's career path and training, supervisors saying thank you and praising a special effort. The e-mail that one of CEO Michael's former managers anonymously circulated in the office shows the work attitude that develops when such things are absent:

My Top Ten Management Tips for Michael

1. Never give me work in the morning; always wait until 4 P.M.
2. If it's a "rush" thing, run in and interrupt me every 10 minutes to see how it's going.
3. If my arms are full of papers or books, don't open the door for me.
4. If you give me more than one job, don't tell me the priority.
5. If I do a job that pleases you, keep it a secret.
6. If you don't like my work, tell everyone.
7. Be nice only when the job I'm doing benefits you personally.
8. Wait until a project is almost done to provide important input.
9. Tell me all the little problems you have with your boss.
10. Always leave without telling me where you are going.

Respecting Staff Time Valuing staff opinion is more than listening—it is actively allowing the staff person the time necessary to foster individual thinking and creativity.

Q-based cultures that are riddled with volunteer activities are the antithesis of this. As professor and director of the Quality of Life Research Center, Mihaly Csikszentmihalyi says in his book, *Creativity,* "Keeping constantly busy is commendable. . . . But constant busyness is not a good prescription for creativity."[9]

Csikszentmihalyi found that creativity comes from exposure to a wide variety of ideas alternating with slack periods where those ideas reassemble in new ways. Much of current thinking mimics Csikszentmihalyi's early writings. *Time* magazine recently explored the latest research on staying mentally sharp and found that contrary to popular belief, being busy every minute—multitasking—takes a heavy toll on the quality of output; more work may get done but the work is of lower quality. One study found that once workers were interrupted, it took them 25 minutes to return to the original task.[10]

Coalescing all of these ideas into action, farsighted CEOs create "thinking time" and encourage staff people to gain a wide variety of experiences outside of the office in order to gain fresh perspectives on new ways of working and new services and programs. Here are a few ways that CEO Aidan carves out white space for his staff:

- Hanging a "do not disturb" sign on cubicles when employees need uninterrupted time
- Setting aside private spaces where employees can work in quiet and without distractions
- Not assuming that productive staff is loafing when they chat in the kitchen or brainstorm ideas at impromptu times
- Encouraging staff to group e-mails and phone calls and return them at certain times of the day
- Promoting good e-mail etiquette; avoiding "reply all" types of e-mails that eat up time and have multiple people solving the same problem
- Stopping by cubes and pausing in hallways to talk with people and ask their opinions
- Realizing that people balance office hours with learning hours, family hours, community hours, and everything else that constitutes their lives; not calling vacationing managers on the cell phone, or expecting a grieving worker to be in the office the afternoon after the funeral of a loved one
- Defining work parameters and letting staff people find workable solutions that build more flexibility into their work lives

Treating Staff Fairly Staff people want a level playing field when it comes to structure—to know that the same rules are in place for everyone and transparent for anyone to understand. This means:

- Wage and salary guidelines are in place and shared with employees.
- Salaries are ideally at market or at least at market to other area nonprofits.

- Fair employment practices exist and are in writing.
- New employees are oriented to department and mission.
- Vacation and benefits policies exist and apply to everyone.
- Formal performance reviews and salary increases occur at least annually.
- Everyone has access to learning and training.

But CEOs like Aidan know that the perception of fairness relies on much, much more than such finite rules. People want to feel that CEOs are objective and that they have a chance for promotion as openings occur. Managers need to sit down with the people they manage, learn what drives them, and help them map career paths. They need to groom people for promotion, identify necessary training, and, when possible, promote from within.

CEOs do not treat staff fairly when they enforce a set of rigid personnel rules because it's easier to punish everyone than to address individual circumstances or individual personnel problems. In fact, nothing demotivates people like the equal treatment of unequals. Aidan cannot hire an incompetent manager, and then treat that manager the same as the productive managers. When performance problems are left unaddressed, high performers must assume an ever-increasing workload, which eventually affects their attitude and productivity.

Share Wisdom

In a Q-culture, power derives from close personal relationships with powerful volunteer leaders, but in a performance culture power derives from achieving results. Achieving outcomes depends on how well CEOs clearly articulate goals and direct the process; it depends on communication and the sharing of informed wisdom. While it's true that CEOs garner few outward kudos for making staff feel valued, they gain outright scorn for misusing one of the most potent tools for sharing wisdom—the staff meeting.

The Power of Meetings Let's observe Michael and Aidan as they conduct their 9 A.M. weekly senior staff meetings. Both share the same general agenda items, but here's Michael in action:

> Michael chats and waits as the senior staff trickle into the meeting room. As the last director, Bill, strides into the room 20 minutes late, Michael starts the meeting. Michael speaks: "I'd like to discuss the open house on Tuesday," and spends the next 15 minutes going over details, which results in another 15 minutes of discussion from participants.
>
> Then, Michael tackles the other three items on his agenda: the decrease in membership numbers, the pending budget review, and the coming board meeting agenda, which takes another hour. Total meeting time is almost two hours.

Aidan handles the same meeting very differently:

> Aidan starts the meeting at 9 A.M., acknowledging Bill as he enters but not stopping the meeting in progress. Aidan opens with, "let's do our roundtable." Each of his five directors spends five to ten minutes reviewing the top three priorities in their areas. This takes 30 minutes.
>
> Aidan, meanwhile, is listening and deciding which of these items needs further discussion. He says, "Our membership numbers aren't on target, and that revenue is critical to other new programs this year." He asks the membership director to assemble needed information and to schedule a meeting specifically to identify problems and brainstorm solutions. This takes five minutes.
>
> In five minutes, all agree on criteria and a date for the budget review. Several problems related to department issues are openly discussed and resolved to everyone's satisfaction. This takes 20 minutes. Total meeting time is a little over an hour.

One Meeting Does Not Fit All Patrick Lencioni, in his book, *Death by Meeting,* has an intriguing idea: meetings have such a bad reputation because the people attending them are bored to death. Lencioni believes:

- **Meetings have no drama.** They should be dynamic—people interacting on important things essential to their work lives. Instead, most meetings are information dumps, and meeting leaders seek to avoid conflict among participants.
- **Meetings lack contextual structure.** Because everyone hates meetings, leaders try to minimize meeting time by surfacing everything at one weekly meeting. Unfortunately, everyone who attends wants something different, so everyone walks away dissatisfied.[11]

Aidan follows some of the best pieces of Lencioni's advice. He creates drama in meetings by painting a picture of how activities relate to mission and encourages differing opinions among his managers. He uses various kinds of meetings and makes sure that participants understand the purpose and come prepared for each of the following:

- **The Five-Minute Daily Meeting.** Lencioni recommends starting the day with a daily five-minute check-in meeting where managers share that day's activities and schedules. Aidan uses a more practical solution—an online center where managers quickly post and access the same information first thing each morning.
- **The Weekly Senior Staff Meeting.** Aidan's weekly staff meeting is tactical in nature—meant to review essential activities and metrics and surface interdepartmental obstacles and issues. Aidan asks the kind of questions that solicit the concerns of each director and that if left unresolved might undermine suggested solutions. When someone raises a concern, it's treated with respect and examination—"tell me more"—not the frustrated response—"that's your problem, just resolve it."

- **Monthly Strategic Meetings.** Rather than getting bogged down in lengthy discussions, Aidan defers strategic problems that surface in weekly meetings to a monthly meeting where one or two critical issues can be explored in depth. This allows directors time to discuss these issues with their staff in advance and come to the meeting prepared to address cross-departmental concerns and make critical decisions.
- **Periodic Strategy Meetings.** Aidan also holds periodic strategy meetings (at least quarterly) to review strategy and key issues with all staff.

Lencioni and Aidan illustrate a whole new mindset about meetings—not as drudgery where meeting leaders dump information, but as dynamic two-way communication where each participant comes prepared to communicate and address critical concerns. When CEOs like Aidan lead meetings such as these, people are energized and sharing wisdom is fun.

One nonprofit, the American Industrial Hygiene Association (AIHA), even went one step farther—they made their actual meeting space fun and creative. Staff painted the room a wonderful color and added funky pillows and knickknacks. Dubbed the "polka-dot room," because some items have polka dots, users reported thinking more freely and creatively in a space designed to inspire them.[12]

The Importance of Think Sessions Another important way to value and capture employee opinions and ideas is something that we call a "think session." It's a fun way to break the office routine and to coalesce all those disparate pieces of information that staff gains through outside education and non-organizational-related activities. Some ideas for these sessions are:

- Each manager or staff person takes a turn and brings to the table a topic that the person finds intriguing (e.g., a book, a news program, a current event), but the person is responsible for summarizing the information and facilitating the conversation.
- At the beginning of each weekly staff meeting, have one director give a five-minute recap of something new that they read and that caught their eye.
- Bring in a Myers-Briggs expert and have a fun session analyzing management styles or a sector leader to discuss a topic of general interest to participants.

CEOs can expand the idea of *think sessions* well beyond just staff. Bring groups of community leaders or constituents together to brainstorm critical issues. Send someone to a retreat, where exposure to very different people can stimulate ideas. The idea is to make sharing wisdom part of the culture—to give people the confidence to debate ideas and use those ideas to further both their own learning and new mission output.

Reward the Right Things

Csikszentmihalyi, in his seminal book, *Flow, The Psychology of Optimal Experience,* discusses the conditions that promote "flow"—a euphoric state from which people derive optimum satisfaction.[13] In less academic language, these conditions are:

1. Concrete goals and manageable rules are in place.
2. Skills are in sync with the desired action and goals.
3. Regular, clear feedback on progress and the opportunity to continually improve exist.
4. Distractions are screened out and concentration is possible.

Translating this back into our topic, because flow conditions foster high individual productivity, it seems reasonable to assume that CEOs should create the same conditions to foster a high-performing culture. We already know that CEOs must:

1. Define clear policies (manageable rules) and articulate goals (mission objectives)
2. Ensure that staff experience and training is commensurate with achieving goals
3. Create workplace conditions where staff can focus on the tasks at hand

But, there's one flow condition we have not discussed fully—the need to provide feedback and the opportunity to improve.

Reward Output, Not Activity In order for CEOs to provide clear feedback on goal progress, they must focus individual and organizational energy on that goal and reward progress toward that goal. Staff people then use that feedback to correct and improve the skills and processes that are directed toward reaching that goal. To better illustrate the point, let's return to CEO Aidan as he meets with a senior manager, Teri:

> Aidan inquires, "How are we coming along on expanding the reach of our research journal beyond our membership?"
>
> Teri explains, "We're working on it . . . The new members of the editorial board wanted to survey readers and find out if we need to develop two new research journals. It's taking a lot of my time right now."
>
> "I recall discussing that at length at last year's planning meeting . . . We don't have the resources to develop more journals, nor is that something that our survey of current readers wanted," responds Aidan.
>
> "Yes, I agree, but we know that nonmembers are really interested in our existing journal and have good ideas for how to market to them. I'll wrap up this survey and get the editorial board back in focus," says Teri.

What Aidan does is gently remind his manager of the goal's objectives, and that she is letting the editorial board sidetrack her. He provides her with the opportunity to correct the situation, and this helps her hone her skills in dealing with volunteer groups that may stray outside of a stated mission objective.

Keeping the focus on output and rewarding the eventual output achievements allow people to show off their skills and be excited for their successes. Successful programs or a time-saving new process make everyone happy, and that makes the workplace even more productive.

Reward Success and Failure A huge part of optimizing performance and an integral part of improving is the ability to learn from mistakes and do it better the next time. Sustaining a performance culture requires not only focusing on output, but also treating successful output and unsuccessful output as equal parts of the normal course of business.

Let's say that Teri later returns to Aidan's office with a copy of the editorial board's survey in hand. Even though the survey represents a failure to stay on track, Teri's not afraid to look at the results and see if they might lead to something equally as useful. More specifically, sometimes going down the wrong path leads to insights that would never come to light by following a linear journey down the right path.

The confidence to make decisions and risk new ventures comes from knowing that if you are making rational decisions and taking reasonable actions, you will not be vilified when those efforts go unavoidably wrong. Pushing the envelope, challenging people, or whatever you want to call it, all come from creating an environment where it's okay to fail, and that takes CEOs who openly admit and learn from their mistakes and encourage everyone to do the same. CEOs may find it difficult to hold their tongues when managers make a whopping big error, but the benefits that are realized by simply saying, "Let's give credit for taking a chance, and what are we going to do the next time, or what new direction does this open up?" are well worth the effort.

Reward Good Management Within the depths of a nonprofit's professional and volunteer staff are the answers to every business component question; it just needs good management practice within a sustained performance culture to bring those ideas out. CEOs like Aidan know this and mentor and provide outside training to help managers hone their management skills.

Aidan rewards good management by recognizing the people who do it; he expects managers to develop other managers from within and compliments them on those efforts. He praises the manager who turns in all performance reviews on time, and views good management results as an achievement in much the same way as any successful program or service.

CEOs also reward good management by being an advocate for its practice to boards and volunteers. They help volunteer leaders understand that the time taken to manage people is far overshadowed by the mission outcomes those people produce, and they help volunteers understand that staff people are not overhead but the crucial link to mission delivery. It's Aidan taking the time to explain to his president why he's returning his call a little later, recounting Tom's excitement and what that excitement might mean to long-term mission outcomes.

Making the Changes Stick

The benefits of a performance culture have to be sticky enough to resonate with nonprofit leaders, and performance practices must be embedded deeply enough in the mission system to survive over the long term. But boards cannot directly impact employees beyond the CEO and senior management team, nor in many nonprofits can CEOs touch every volunteer and professional staff person.

What they can do is alter their view of what being a volunteer or staff leader means. Performance cultures depend on leaders who see their role as identifying the barriers to staff self-motivation and productivity, doing everything within their power to remove those barriers, and acting as a catalyst to inspire the ideas and the efforts of all. This switch in mindset is part of an overall shift in thinking that needs to take place.

Cultivating a Different Mindset

Preventing the lumbering *Smile, Not Skill* elephant from squashing performance requires a sustained campaign to change hearts and minds that stretches well beyond a single board term or even one CEO's tenure. It requires educating volunteers and staff people to work together bound by shared success, not by forming friendly cliques and lots of committee activities.

A change of mindset is needed to reorient volunteer expectations regarding staff, reorient staff expectations regarding volunteers, and educate all on performance roles.

Reorient Volunteer Expectations Regarding Staff Volunteers become used to a personalized, concierge-level of service from Q-culture staff because that's what their volunteer experiences tell them to expect. When they stop seeing staff as simply coordinating committees, begin to understand the cost of using staff resources in that manner, and experience working with staff as professionals who produce desired outcomes, they begin to look at staff resources in a different way.

The joy of successful programs and services, the thrill of doing things more efficiently, the satisfaction of reaching more of a community's needs—these are the fun things that replace meetings that beget more meetings and committees that produce activity.

Reorient Staff Expectations Regarding Volunteers Behind closed doors, many staff people view volunteers as a burden that must be endured because that's what their past experiences tell them. They are afraid to seek volunteer help and input because they view these resources as just making their job harder.

Once the elephant solutions are in place and staff sees a board and CEO that sustain and promote a performance culture, they begin to appreciate and are no longer afraid to draw upon the rich benefit knowledge that is so available throughout the constituency.

Systemically Educate Volunteers, Staff, and Constituents on Performance Roles Educate everyone on the difference between congeniality as a given and congeniality that either substitutes for or gets in the way of achieving mission results. Create nonprofit-specific examples of what happens when:

- Nice board members fail to discuss the real issues.
- CEOs tell boards what they want to hear at the cost of staff productivity.
- Senior staff is coordinating committee activities instead of doing mission objectives.
- The time it takes to bring a new committee up to speed versus the mission benefit achieved.

Institutionalizing a Performance Culture

Beyond the tools of previous chapters—board and staff orientation, the Board Policy Manual, and training—the key to institutionalizing a performance culture is capturing the informed wisdom gained by trial and error and making it transparent and easily accessible to all. If you don't understand where you have been and where you are, it's difficult to do it better the next time.

A high-performing culture continually builds its knowledge base, doing more of what it does well, and avoiding the same mistakes in future performance. The lessons-learned approach helps nonprofits in this endeavor.

The Lessons Learned Approach Boards, CEOs, senior staff and volunteer leaders need a lessons-learned session at appropriate times before, during, and after any major project or program. For example, boards would tap into the lessons-learned information prior to nominating a new audit committee and borrow on that informed wisdom when making their selections. They share any key experiences by adding to that knowledge base for the next board to tap into. Board chairs do the same within the powers delegated by the boards.

CEOs and senior managers also tap into the same lessons-learned system, referring to the system before instituting new programs and processes and recording their specific lessons learned as they go along. Ideally, organizations could have a specific software program dedicated to this process, but even small nonprofits can instill this mentality and create a paper file that is openly accessible to all.

Let's look at the very simple way that the ESP board and CEO Aidan do this:

- ESP volunteer and staff leaders and managers are accountable for holding a lessons-learned session after program launches, major committee or process improvements, change initiatives, or anything else that leaders deem necessary.
- Volunteer and staff leaders use the simple form shown in Exhibit 11.2.

EXHIBIT 11.2 LESSONS-LEARNED TEMPLATE

LESSONS-LEARNED SUMMARY

Outcome: ______________________________

Prepared by: ______________________________

Date (MM/DD/YYYY): ______________________________

The purpose of this report is to record and transfer the collective wisdom gained from this experience so that the entire organization may benefit. Lessons-Learned helps us to:

- Repeat desirable outcomes
- Avoid undesirable outcomes

A. Identify what went well and why.
B. Identify what could have been done better and how.
C. Did anything go differently than expected?
D. What serious issues were encountered during the activity and how were they dealt with?
E. What improvements would you recommend for similar activity in the future?
F. What were the most valuable lessons learned?

Summing It Up

There are two styles of management: (1) where the leader has all the ideas and expects people to just execute them, or (2) where the leader sets the conditions and is the catalyst for people who have the ideas and can execute them. In the distant past, nonprofits could afford style one, because they could keep pace with all the ideas coming from volunteer leaders or the CEO. In today's more complex world and in a knowledge-based performance culture, management style two is not only more appropriate, it's essential.

The key to high-performing workforces lies deep inside the hearts and minds of staff and volunteers; it is up to boards and CEOs to provide the effective leadership that can unlock this potential avalanche of programs and services.

Notes

1. "Charles Darwin Foundation Announces Interim Executive Director," *Galapagos Conservation Trust: Newsroom* (February 5, 2004), www.gct.org/feb04_3.html (accessed November 2, 2004).
2. "Fund Names Gail Mroz Interim Executive Director," *Michigan Tech Fund* (April 21, 2004), www.mtf.mtu.edu/features/new_position.php (accessed November 2, 2004).
3. Gordon Livingston, *Too Soon Old, Too Late Smart* (New York: Marlowe and Company, 2004).
4. CompassPoint Nonprofit Services, *Daring to Lead: Nonprofit Executive Directors and Their Work Experience,* August 2001, 3.
5. Id., 34.
6. Jan Masoaka and Mike Allison, "Why Boards Don't Govern," *The Board Café* (October 2004), 3.
7. Marshall Goldsmith, "It's Not About the Coach," *Fast Company* (October 2004), 120.
8. Linda Schwartz, "Putting Research to Work: Americans Actually Excel in Chaos and Crisis," *Center for Association Resources,* www.association-resources.com/carpages/puttingresearch.pdf (accessed October 25, 2004).
9. Mihaly Csikszentmihalyi, *Creativity, Flow and the Psychology of Discovery and Invention* (New York: HarperCollins, 1996), 353.
10. Claudia Wallis, "How to Tune Up Your Brain," *Time* (January 16, 2006), 73–76.
11. Patrick Lencioni, *Death by Meeting* (San Francisco: Jossey-Bass, 2004), 223–248.
12. "A Room of Their Own," *Associations Now* (February 2006), 13.
13. Mihaly Csikszentmihalyi, *Flow, the Psychology of Optimal Experience* (New York: Harper & Row, 1990).

CHAPTER 12

The *Read My Lips* Solution: Reward Results, Not Rhetoric

Not everything that matters can be counted, and not everything that can be counted matters.

—Albert Einstein

Taming the *Read My Lips* Elephant

The way companies build brands and acquire loyal followers is by delivering products that delight and please consumers. Great marketing may initially attract consumers, but only an equally great product keeps them coming back.

Nonprofits that engage in rhetoric that is not backed by results may impress uninformed constituents, but they will not fool the people these results are supposed to impact. In an ever-increasing competitive and information-rich environment, members, donors, communities, and other stakeholders expect results and are increasingly vocal when their expectations are unrealized.

Survival and taming the *Read My Lips* elephant necessitates that nonprofits not only talk about great new programs, but also implement and sustain those programs. Leaders must back outsized rhetoric with outsized mission results.

In This Chapter

A difference exists between what nonprofit leaders say and what nonprofits deliver. Elephant Solution Five—Reward Results, Not Rhetoric—works to eliminate that difference and get "leader talk" and "nonprofit do" on the same page.

This chapter contains ideas and practices that help nonprofits deliver what they promise. Implementing the first four elephant solutions is part of the answer, but taming the

Read My Lips elephant requires special tools beyond what we have already discussed. Measuring mission performance is a large part of the solution, but without finite market metrics, such as stock price, and with the added wrinkle of benefit and business components, accurately measuring nonprofit success is tricky.

Tricky, but not impossible—rewarding results, not rhetoric is a journey. Consistently moving forward one step at a time eventually leads to arriving at the ultimate destination—sustainable mission programs.

Elephant Solution Five: Reward Results, Not Rhetoric

Eliminating the Difference between Talk and Output

CNN broadcaster Judy Woodruff, in an interview discussing media coverage trends of associations, advises nonprofits "to be as straight as possible . . . tell it like it is." Furthermore, she explains, "The press has never been—and is even less today—interested in meetings, conferences, and things like that. What we look for are clear explanations of how your policy affects real people."[1]

Ms. Woodruff's comments are a reflection of constituent attitudes at large—tell us about things that directly impact our lives or beliefs and deliver results that we can touch and feel. This is the challenge that nonprofits must meet today if they are to stay relevant to the constituents they serve.

Making the switch from the hyperbole that announces fabulous-sounding activities to announcements that reflect the kind of positive mission benefit that constituents can feel requires taking five different steps:

1. Implement the first four elephant solutions.
2. Determine what constitutes results.
3. Differentiate between meaningless activity and productive process.
4. Measure both benefit and business results.
5. Reward results, not rhetoric in disguise.

Step One: Tamed Elephants Provide the Necessary Infrastructure Taming the first four elephants is an essential step in making the shift from rhetoric to results. A brief look at each elephant quickly reiterates why:

Mission Impossible—One mission structure assigns accountability, and accountability leads to mission results.

Earth to Board—Boards that connect with the reality of constituents accurately define mission needs and goals.

Board Fiddles, Rome Burns—Boards focus on mission policies, CEOs on business policies; the mission system is protected and productive.

Smile, Not Skill—A high level of leadership performance delivers sustainable results.

Without implementation of the infrastructure of the elephant solutions, nonprofits will find it difficult to take the next steps.

Step Two: Determining What Constitutes Results At an annual meeting, a volunteer president triumphantly presents the report of the strategic planning committee, and a CEO proudly recounts attendance at a Washington meeting. Both people tout these events as accomplishments—results—yet both events are activities—just inputs—not results.

Jim Collins, in his monograph, *Good to Great and the Social Sectors,* defines this problem as a "confusion of inputs and outputs."[2] He cites the New York City Police Department (NYPD) as an example that illustrates this difference. The department initially measured input—items like arrests made and reports taken—but the police commissioner correctly interpreted that people really wanted less crime and shifted the spotlight to the ultimate goal of reducing crime.

Let's look at how this shift away from inputs or activity toward output or mission results changes actions and rhetoric, in this specific case within the police department. The police commissioner (our volunteer board) defines the output or mission goal—reduce crime—and then creates a success measurement of "a double-digit annual reduction in felony crimes." Police Captains (our CEOs) must create department objectives and strategies that achieve this output—reduce crime in their precinct. They can't hide behind rhetoric saying "we're great because we made 30 percent more arrests last year." Everyone sees this as just one indicator of a successful activity that says little about the desired results—a lowering of the overall crime rate.

The shift away from rhetoric toward results gets made because a police commissioner or mission-oriented board ask themselves the questions—why do we exist, and who do we exist for?—and use the answers to identify the ultimate mission outcomes. Once mission success is defined, the entire mission system adjusts the lens through which it views performance. All actions and activities must move the mission system toward that mission goal. In Collins' example, police captains were held accountable for reducing the crime rate, and a failure to reduce crime in their precincts is why "75 percent of commanders eventually found themselves ejected from their positions."[3]

Like the police commissioner, boards must connect with constituents and stakeholders and identify the ultimate mission goals. If boards do this correctly, CEOs and the rest of the mission system have the prism through which they can separate talking and activity from doing and results.

Inflating Mission Results Is Misidentifying Mission Results There's a delicate balance between setting the mission bar high enough—mission should inspire and challenge—and setting the mission artificially high. Inflating mission goals beyond what can be accomplished or using rhetoric that inflates expectations beyond what can realistically be delivered leads to accomplishing less not more.

In our example, the police commissioner set the bar high—a double-digit decline in felony rates—and that challenged the police system to a high level of performance in order to meet that goal. But if New York's mayor announces in a grandiose speech that the goal is to end crime in New York or leads people to believe the reduction in crime rate will be immediate, people's expectations are set too high.

Now, even if the police department achieves a double-digit reduction in crime rate per year, New York residents will be disappointed and morale in the department will decline because no amount of effort will meet expectations. Overreaching and over-promising undermines the efforts of those expected to deliver these promises and disappoints those who receive the benefit—the perfect environment for failure to sustain the effort.

Step Three: Differentiating between Meaningless Activity and Productive Process The ability to distinguish activity from result and shifting the focus to measuring results doesn't mean that all activities are nonproductive or that they shouldn't be measured. Just the opposite: reaching the ultimate mission goal is not an all-or-nothing marker of success, but the result of many activities successfully completed along the way. The question that boards and CEOs should ask themselves about all nonprofit activities is whether such activities are part of a meaningful process on the way toward a goal.

If, for example, boards use a committee of expert people to assess competitive issues, the meetings and reports of this group are activities, but they are meaningful activities. The committee provides recommendations as part of the productive process that the board uses to keep mission current. However, if boards appoint volunteer generalists to a planning committee and the committee just listens to information while the "committee recommendations" are actually the CEO's decisions, then some of the CEO's activities are part of a meaningful board process, but the committee meetings are meaningless activity.

Meaningful process activities are important milestones by which we can track progress toward mission goals; meaningless activities simply drain the life out of everyone in the mission system.

Step Four: Measuring Both Benefit and Business Results Measuring performance is a subject of huge interest and controversy within both the public and private sectors. The attempt to evaluate and rate philanthropies and foundations is at an all-time high as scores of nonprofit groups, like the Wise Giving Alliance and rating agencies like Forbes, attempt to create a universal set of standards and metrics by which donors can evaluate such nonprofits. At the opposite end of the spectrum are the nonprofit insiders that insist all nonprofits are unique and that something as amorphous as mission cannot be effectively measured.

A plethora of information exists on the best methods to actually evaluate and measure performance. Although much of this information is excellent and conceptually useful, few nonprofit leaders have the time to read it. Some of the information focuses on elaborate processes of measurement that are difficult to support, given the volunteer/staff leadership dynamic. Even if the concepts are excellent, they may not be useful anyway, because it's not the conceptual process of measurement that is difficult. It's actually doing it—and doing it consistently.

Measuring in General Globally, the measurement process is deceptively simple, although each new measurement system will label and group the steps differently, most systems provide the following advice:

1. Decide what is meaningful.
2. Measure what is meaningful.
3. Track progress.
4. Recognize and reward success.
5. Capture knowledge and improve performance.

Because it's sometimes difficult to distinguish activity from meaningful process and to define ultimate mission success, nonprofits can become so tangled in inputs and outputs that they try to measure everything. Then, nascent attempts to measure performance quickly fall by the wayside. What follows are practical ideas for approaching measurement that can be phased in slowly and adapted easily to the uniqueness of specific nonprofits.

Measuring What's Meaningful What's meaningful for a corporation or company is profit; what's meaningful for a nonprofit is delivery of mission. An excess of revenue over expense is relatively easy to determine in finite metrics, but defining mission outcomes in such terms is not. Collins has good advice for boards at this stage: "hold yourself accountable for progress in outputs, *even if those outputs defy measurement*."[4]

In other words, don't get hung up on precise measurements, because measuring business component success often lends itself to numbers, whereas measuring benefit component success does not. Take heart in the knowledge that there's no one "right" set of measurements. Just take the plunge and start aiming for a balanced set of measures that considers both benefit and business components.

In the mid-1990s, Drs. Robert Kaplan (Harvard Business School) and David Norton introduced a strategic approach to management and measurement that they called the "Balanced Scorecard."[5] While adapting this system in total from the private to the nonprofit sector is time consuming, challenging, and may well prove to be beyond the reach of most nonprofits, the authors' basic concept of balanced measurements—measuring performance from different perspectives—is excellent and adapts well to the nonprofit challenge of measuring both benefit and business components.

A term the government uses for a balanced set of performance measures is a "family of measures." Nonprofits can adapt this concept and approach measuring performance by creating a family of three measures:

1. *Mission measures*: Defines mission goal success and progress toward that success (board mission and mission goals)
2. *Activity measures*: Defines objective and strategy success and progress (CEO objectives and strategies)
3. *Tactics measures*: Defines key indicators that track business component processes critical to mission system health (operating initiatives and tactics)

The Family of Measures: Mission Measures Nonprofits can use several methods of measuring mission outcomes depending on the organization and available resources. First, if a nonprofit's mission is narrowly defined (e.g., the mission of America's Second Harvest is to "feed the hungry"), mission success can be defined quantitatively. America's Second Harvest just counts the amount of food collected and distributed. Second, if a nonprofit has the resources, it can invest in ongoing research that determines whether its activities achieve the results promised. For example, a sorority whose mission is to train women as leaders can commission studies that track the careers of alumni over a period of time.

But most nonprofits do not define their missions narrowly. Rather, missions are usually glaringly global, nor do many cash-strapped nonprofits have the resources for ongoing studies on mission outcomes. That's where the third method comes in: nonprofits can develop micro-level goals that, if achieved, imply success on the grander scale of mission. To see how this works, let's return to our example nonprofit from Chapter 11, Education Stops Poverty (ESP), and see how it measures mission success:

- ESP's mission statement is "defeat poverty through education." This mission is broad and not so easy to quantify; poverty is a multifaceted problem, and measuring the direct effect of education in this mix is complicated.
- ESP scanning studies reflect that students who drop out of high school are most likely to earn salaries below the poverty levels. The ESP board feels that it's a reasonable assumption that increasing the number of poverty-level students who graduate from high school increases the likelihood that students can earn a living above the poverty level.
- The ESP board measures mission success by the number of schools offering ESP programs, and comparing their graduation rates with schools not offering ESP programs.

The ESP board makes a reasonable assumption: if it meets its goal of increasing the high school graduation rate, it's successfully achieving its mission to defeat poverty. This sets the bar for every ESP program and service: all must be geared to increasing the rate of graduation for poverty-level students.

The Family of Measures: Activity Measures Activity measures track the business component programs that deliver mission outcomes. These are all existing and new programs and services that comprise current-year objectives and strategies.

For example, two of ESP's existing programs are Get-Ahead, an after-school tutoring program, and Child-Watch, a free day care service. The Get-Ahead program measures the number of students enrolled and whether they maintain a C grade point average or above; the Child-Watch program measures the rate of graduation for unwed student mothers. Both are quantitative measurements of business component output that track ESP's progress toward reaching its ultimate mission goal—defeating poverty through education.

The Family of Measures: Tactics Measures Tactics measurements are mostly quantitative metrics or key indicators that track business component processes critical to mission system health. For example, some of ESP's key indicators are:

- Amount and growth of grant dollars
- Amount and growth of fundraising dollars
- Attendance at fundraisers
- Staffing level and turnover
- Staff training and internal process indicators

Exhibit 12.1 shows how the family of measures fit together and how they tie back to the strategic planning process of the nonprofit.

The Right Measurements Bring Focus and Accountability It takes time and thought to develop a family of measures, and trial and error to hone these measurements to a number that truly reflect a nonprofit's most critical issues. The ideal starting point is the most difficult—defining how to measure mission success. But, once that's done, all levels can contribute to the process.

Take the real-life example of the nonprofit Room to Read, the brainchild of former Microsoft employee John Wood. The nonprofit mixes financial and nonfinancial measurements to appeal to the emotions and minds of donors and workers alike. At a Northwestern University lecture in 2005, Wood succinctly defined the success of his mission statement (world change starts with educated children) as "helping 10 million children in the developing world gain the lifelong gift of reading." Room to Read offers just a few programs, but all of these programs clearly link to mission. Read the following and see what a powerful marketing tool measuring outcomes can be:

> Since our inception as a nonprofit entity in 2000, we have impacted the lives of over 755,000 children by:
>
> - Constructing 197 schools
> - Establishing over 2,565 libraries
> - Publishing 77 new local language children's titles representing over 600,000 books

EXHIBIT 12.1 ESP FAMILY OF MEASURES

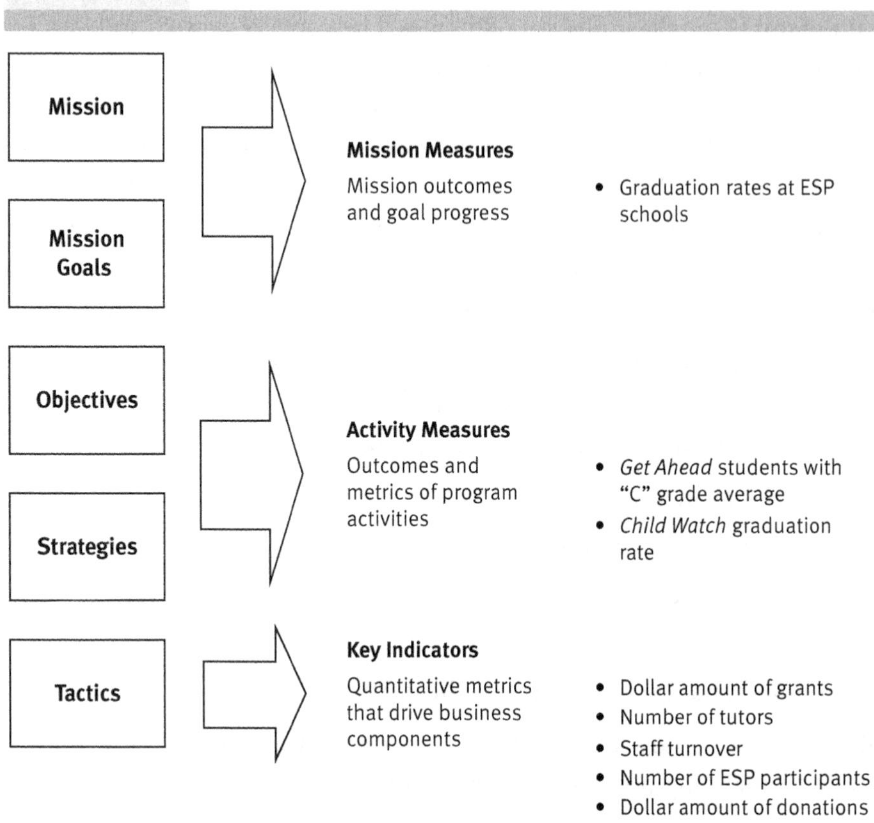

- Donating over 1.1 million English language children's books
- Establishing 60 computer labs and 25 language labs
- Funding over 1,757 long-term scholarships for girls[6]

Donors access the Web site www.roomtoread.org and can see that an $8,000 donation builds a new school, and then click on photos that show the building process and the smiling faces of the school children who benefit. Are Room to Read's measurements perfect? Probably not, but the nonprofit consistently and relentlessly tracks both mission outcomes and process measurements and uses those outcomes to inspire and motivate.

When Wood and other Room to Read leaders talk, it's not empty rhetoric—what they deliver is equally impressive. Admittedly, it is much easier for start-up organizations like Room to Read to do things right from the beginning than for behemoth, long established mission systems like the American Medical Association or The United Way to create and implement a meaningful family of measures. But, even large organizations can use a tortoise approach to measurement, eschewing the temptation to revamp with a splashy, complicated measuring process in favor of gradually and carefully defining a family of measures.

As long as nonprofits implement the four elephant solutions and boards identify the ultimate mission goals, CEOs can work with department directors to define measurement programs and metrics for key indicators. Once departments understand the ultimate mission goals, they are well equipped to identify and measure the department activities and programs that are meaningful toward reaching that goal.

Step Five: Avoiding Rewards to Results That Are Just Rhetoric in Disguise Once established, a family of measures must be linked to accountability and performance appraisal. Boards can judge CEO performance and objectively reward CEOs for achieving mission and activity outcomes. Professional staff members are evaluated and rewarded on the basis of achieving activity outcomes and some tactic outcomes. Public praise regarding performance becomes linked with actually achieving the desired outcome.

Less obvious is the need to link the public awards of the nonprofits to mission. One of the ways that many nonprofits gain favorable press is by announcing prestigious scholarships, research grants, or other awards. Approaching epidemic proportions is the outsized rhetoric surrounding the ever-increasing number of sector think tank and university "best nonprofit" awards. Although the intent of such recognition and awards seems sometimes more about increasing the stature of the awarders rather than benefiting the awardees, most are well-intentioned efforts to further mission cause. The apparent lack of forethought that goes into the awards, however, often makes a mockery of mission. Consider the following newspaper editorial:

> In Philadelphia this coming Sunday, the American Public Health Association (APHA) plans to hand out its "oldest and most prestigious award," the Sedgwick Memorial Medal, to one (name of doctor) . . . we can't help but point out that this doctor deserves much more public health attention as one of nine physicians who are at the center of a growing scandal over silicosis and asbestos diagnoses.
>
> APHA's executive director . . . told us that the group's award committee was aware of the Texas litigation, but did not feel it warranted changing its decision. "We think his work in public health is extraordinary, and this is for a lifetime of work."
>
> The organization's Web site says it is "devoted to improving the public's health." It could start by reserving its award for doctors who actually do so.[7]

Furthermore, sector "best of nonprofit" awards, like the American Society of Association Executives' (ASAE's) "Associations Advance America Awards," rely on responses from nonprofit leaders who complete a form that touts their own program successes. Awarders have no real vetting process to investigate the efficiency or sustainability of programs. The "best practices" on one nonprofit leadership Web site describes innovative ideas and best practices, but most of the stories are submitted by consultants showcasing work done with that "best practice" client.

For rhetoric to match actions, awards should align with mission, and awardees should be vetted by a process that tests the actions behind the words. On a different side of the same coin, when voluntary standards are in place, if nonprofits say they follow these standards, they need to be sure they actually do. In today's era of investigative reporting, charities are especially hard hit when they do not live up to their word, and their problems reflect badly on the whole sector. Consider the effect on organizations that offered child-sponsorship programs when a series of critical articles concluded that "in many cases, one-on-one child sponsorship was just a marketing tool and that the money didn't get to the child who was supposed to benefit."[8]

Part of taming the *Results, Not Rhetoric* elephant happens when nonprofits take the lead in backing up surveys and awards with substance, and in setting meaningful standards before rating agencies and regulators do it for them. As this book is being written, there are some positive signs that this change is happening to some degree. The Panel on the Nonprofit Sector helped shape a softer version of the nonprofit reforms passed in 2005, and the many efforts underway from places like the American Institute of Philanthropy, Maryland's *Standard of Excellence* codes of conduct, and so on are attempting to voluntarily provide standards that attempt to address issues relating to benefit and business component measurements.

Making the Changes Stick

Cultivating a Different Mindset

Substitute "How Can We Measure It" for "What We Do Can't Be Measured" All nonprofits are unique in what they do and whom they serve, but that should not be an excuse for avoiding the difficult work of evaluating benefit and business performance. Once leaders begin to realize that it's not all about numbers but really about evaluating the vitality and success of mission, the mental roadblock against measuring performance begins to yield.

One key to making this happen is ensuring that everyone knows that defining success or outcomes is always possible. Sometimes, that means numbers, sometimes achieving mini-goals that reasonably imply mission success. In the rare circumstances when evaluation is just too time consuming, it means the faith to know that a link to mission is there.

The concept of a family of measures that can be assembled over time helps nonprofit leaders develop the confidence to get started on the path of developing a consistent set of measurements that accurately reflect mission progress, program success, and financial health.

Shift the Dialogue Away from Tactic to Mission Measures Tactic measures, mainly key indicators of activities that relate to the resources that drive nonprofit efforts, consume a great deal of CEO management time, but they shouldn't be a major part of board time. Otherwise, it reinforces the misdirected ideas of some rating agencies that the efficiency of nonprofits is solely measured by business component expense ratios. Unfortunately, this is precisely where the uniqueness of each nonprofit's mission can dictate wildly differing administrative and resources needs.

In general, people don't ask what the management overhead is for Lexus or General Motors, because it's not why they buy these cars. They buy for the prestige and safety of the car and on the basis of previous driving experiences. Donors and members don't give dollars or join organizations because they know their expense ratios; they donate because they believe in a cause or have needs that the nonprofit can fill. It's not that such ratios don't matter; it's that ratios need to be set in context. Nonprofit leaders as a whole need to dialogue with raters on this topic and bring some much-needed sanity to the mistaken idea that delivering mission should cost nothing.

Boards that fit a family of measures on a sheet or two of paper create an oversight tool that allows them to monitor operations efficiently and spend the majority of time on mission work. Kaplan and Norton create a very useful image of how this works—balanced measures are like the indicators on the dashboard of a car. There are many gauges on that dashboard—our mission, activity, and tactic measurements—but drivers only quickly check things like fuel and water levels and any indicator lights that are flashing yellow or red. They spend the majority of their time driving the car safely to its destination. The destination for nonprofits is mission—that's where boards drive the car and that's where constituents live.

Make "Giving Them What They Want" More Important Than "Telling Them What You Do" Just like Room to Read, nonprofits must clearly show that they deliver the promised mission benefits. The action of a nonprofit that provides funds for small charities illustrates this point:

> After Hurricane Katrina, a foundation was interested in a charity that was collecting cell phones for victims of the hurricane. The foundation exchanged seven e-mails and five phone calls to try and get answers about the group's funding and other issues to no avail.
>
> As the head of the foundation relates, "If you are doing what you say you are doing, then it should be a prominent part of your organization. You need to show you are putting phones in people's hands."[9]

The charity did not receive the funds. Showing that you deliver—actually seeing the schools and children on the Room to Read Web site—is worth thousands of speeches that simply say those schools and children exist.

Think of Measurement as a Steady Stream of Singles, Rather Than Hitting the Ball out of the Park Because of their unique need to blend volunteer and professional talents, in the nonprofit sector, consistency constitutes achievement. The overwhelming urge of every new board or CEO is to prove their worth by implementing the latest measuring system or the newest program requiring a sweeping change in direction.

One way to view this problem on a massive scale is to look at what happens to government programs. The National Partnership for Reinventing Government was created in the late 1990s to dramatically reform the way government works. The list of ambitious achievements included some 1,200 specific changes to make government better. It's difficult to tell how many of the grandiose announcements of accomplishments listed on their Web site are backed by real sustainable results, but one thing is evident—the Web site is archived, and all the outsized announcements and promises ended the minute the next administration took office.[10]

Fortunately, most nonprofits don't face the kind of enormous problems that governments face, but that makes the same kind of behavior—abruptly ending innovative programs as new nonprofit leaders come into office—all the more unacceptable in other than the government sector. Rather than making a grandiose announcement that their organization is switching to the latest and greatest new measuring process, nonprofit leaders would be wise to quietly begin creating and using a simple and consistent family of measures that can be sustained beyond one board.

Realizing the High Stakes of "Business as Usual" The danger of more government regulation to cure what is a small but very visible number of true nonprofit scandals is very real. The fact that most of the attention is currently focused on public charities shouldn't be viewed with relief by membership and other nonprofits. The public doesn't make distinctions between kinds of nonprofits, and attitudes and regulations targeted at one group will also dramatically affect all nonprofits. Consider the comments of Brookings Institution Fellow, Paul Light:

> . . . the number of Americans who said they had a lot of confidence in charitable institutions held steady until the winter of 2002, when it began to fall. By August, the number of Americans who said they had no confidence in charitable organizations had doubled to 16 percent, while the number saying they had a lot of confidence had fallen from 25 percent to 19 percent.[11]

Regulation is rarely the answer to performance problems. Many times the "cure" is worse than the "disease," because outsiders fail to understand and address root causes. The five big nonprofit elephants discussed in Part II will not be regulated away; only nonprofit leaders can free the sector from these beasts within that are at the heart of the headline scandals.

If leaders do not address the real problems quickly and if they cannot effectively promote an authentically stronger image to the public at large, the current rumblings of the media and regulatory bodies could result in something that seemed unimaginable before—onerous government regulation and the ultimate loss of tax-exempt status for many types of nonprofits.

Institutionalizing Results, Not Rhetoric

Institutionalizing a culture where actual results are more important than inflated talk is, in part, accomplished by use of all the tools studied so far in the "Making It Stick" sections of Part III. However, two of these tools are especially important: (1) sustaining an effective strategic planning process and (2) maintaining knowledge systems.

Sustaining a strategic planning process supported by an effective system of measurements shifts the focus from talk to performance. When board, CEO, staff, and volunteer are accountable for clear, mission meaningful goals and performance is measured and rewarded by how well those goals are achieved, mission resources rely on results not talk.

Knowledge systems, places where important nonprofit activities and results can be permanently retained, are also an important part of keeping rhetoric real.

Mission goals, objectives, strategies, and tactics should link to a financial knowledge system where program activities are tagged and transactions tracked and aggregated into meaningful financial reports. The outcomes of board connection events, important governmental meetings, think sessions, lessons-learned, and the like should also be systematically recorded and transparent to all.

Such systems can be simple—manual or PC-based for small nonprofits, more complicated software-driven systems for larger ones—whatever the form, they are key to realistically assessing organizational activities and outcomes over a continuum of time, learning from past successes and mistakes to do it better the next time, and passing institutional knowledge on from one board and CEO to the next.

Summing It Up

A quote in the feedback section of *Fast Company* magazine seems an apt summary for this chapter:

> Through 25 years of consulting, I've watched a parade of new management techniques . . . all leading American industry to salvation. I propose a panacea: I'll go from company to company, cut out the fads that produce "meetings and paperwork," and bring companies back to well-thought-out plans, good measurements, and simple and effective controls—ideas that might actually cure everything.[12]

Redirecting energies toward doing the fundamentals well—delivering mission and measuring performance—moves nonprofit leaders away from the splashy announcements of unsustainable programs to the equally impressive announcements of how real people benefit from real mission programs. Seen in a certain light, that is a big cure for what's afflicting nonprofits today.

Notes

1. Kristin Clarke, "A Chat with CNN's Judy Woodruff," *Associations Now,* November 2005, 14.

2. Jim Collins, *Good to Great and the Social Sectors* (Jim Collins, 2006), 4.
3. Id.
4. Id., 5.
5. Robert S. Kaplan and David P. Norton, *The Balanced Scorecard: Translating Strategy into Action* (Boston: Harvard Business School Press, 1996).
6. "Learn About Us," www.roomtoread.org/about.html (accessed February 11, 2006).
7. Editorial, "Doctor of the Year," *Wall Street Journal,* sec. A16, December 8, 2005.
8. Michael M. Phillips, "Big Charities Pursue Certification to Quell Fears of Funding Abuse," *Wall Street Journal,* sec. A, March 9, 2005.
9. Elizabeth Bernstein, "Doing Well at Doing Good," *Wall Street Journal,* sec. R4, November 28, 2005.
10. *National Partnership for Reinventing Government,* http://govinfo.library.unt.edu/npr/index.htm (accessed February 11, 2006).
11. Paul C. Light, "The Content of Their Character: The State of the Nonprofit Workforce," *The Nonprofit Quarterly,* vol. 9, no. 3 (Fall 2002).
12. James Coulter, "Feedback, Gladwell Tidings," *Fast Company,* 92 (March 2005).

Exceptional Nonprofits

There is one thing stronger than all the world, and that is an idea whose time has come.

—Victor Hugo

Transforming Unruly Pachyderms into Well-Behaved Guests

The Pretense-Reality Gap

There's a way an institution appears to get things done—then, there's the way things actually get done. The larger the gap between the two, the more organizational energy is drained by the dissonance. The presence of the nonprofit elephants widens this gap into a gaping chasm, but taming the elephants shrinks the gap and frees an enormous amount of energy for mission work.

Defining the Gap Numerous studies such as McKinsey and Company's "The Nonprofit Sector's $100 Billion Opportunity" attempt to define, estimate, or measure different aspects of the pretense-reality gap. The reaction to the McKinsey study, in particular, reveals the difficulties inherent in such studies.

In 2003, former New Jersey senator Bill Bradley, then advisor to McKinsey's Institute on the Nonprofit Sector, and Paul Jansen and Less Silverman, both McKinsey directors, published an article in the *Harvard Business Review* suggesting that the nonprofit sector could capture an extra $100 billion a year by making changes to the way it operates.[1] Nonprofit leaders immediately attacked the number, shredding the methodology that led to the study's conclusions.

Nonprofit elephants certainly fueled this attack—the volunteer *I'm the Expert* thinking that "McKinsey is a business and doesn't understand volunteer and benefit work" and the staff *Smile, Not Skill* thinking that "McKinsey is right, but those volunteers are preventing us from doing our jobs." Nonprofit leaders also rightly feared the public's reaction; inadvertently, the McKinsey report added to the steady stream of negative nonprofit publicity after the Red Cross September 11th scandals.

Unfortunately, the cumulative effect is that the term "waste" stuck in people's minds. A 2005 survey by Paul Light indicates the growing problem. Two-thirds of the public believe that nonprofits waste money, almost one-half believe that nonprofit executives are paid too much, and only 13 percent feel nonprofits spend money wisely.[2]

What's frightening is, although the public is right that nonprofits should operate more efficiently, it is way off track as to why it does not. It's not because nonprofit managers are incompetent or nonprofits waste money on high executive salaries and administrative costs. Waste occurs because of a sector mindset that causes volunteer and staff talent to be used for everything other than its real expertise. Boards have skills and a real job to do, and CEOs have skills and a real job to do, but too often both are stuck doing something else. Therein lies the pretense-reality gap.

Measuring the Gap If a business places into management a group of people with no experience who can work when they want and who cannot be criticized because they are good people working for free, would anyone be able to run such a business well? No, yet current nonprofit dogma encourages nonprofit boards and CEOs to pretend that it can. This pretense not only consumes their time, but forces volunteer and staff people to find innovative work-arounds to get the job done.

Like McKinsey, this book could make some logical assumptions to come up with a quantitative cost that represents the energy devoured by the pretense-reality gap. Or, we can just add up the losses described in Part II's *Live Lessons* that run into millions for only a handful of organizations. However, instead, let's just choose to accept what we know logically to be true: The number is huge. Now the focus can be on solutions to the problems before that number becomes much worse.

Closing the Gap The presence of unruly nonprofit elephants does two things: (1) prevents boards from being strong and doing important work and (2) prevents CEOs from being strong and doing important work. Taming these elephants frees boards and CEOs to openly use their strengths, and the pretense-reality gap begins to decrease. Exhibit C.1 summarizes how elephant problems are transformed into elephant solutions.

On a chart, the elephant solutions look linear and clean, but in reality, they are a quantum leap away from the mindset of most nonprofit leaders today. Fully embracing the constraints to volunteer leadership, the existence of both benefit and business, and the equal importance of volunteer and professional staff will take a great deal of dialogue and a great deal of action. Current talented nonprofit leaders must swim upstream, acting as change agents and tilting a system that encourages maintaining the status quo into a new direction that favors innovation and increased mission achievement.

EXHIBIT C.1 THE FIVE ELEPHANT PROBLEMS AND THE FIVE ELEPHANT SOLUTIONS

Elephant Problem	Elephant Solution
***Mission Impossible* Elephant** • Thrives on the confusion that surrounds the failure to recognize constraints to volunteer leadership and the equal importance of benefit and business Result: less mission achievement as duplicative volunteer/staff roles and responsibilities direct energies to politics and power struggles	***Mission Impossible* Solution** • Create one mission system Benefit: greater mission achievement as confident benefit and business component leaders focus their complimentary strengths on mission outcomes
***Earth to Board* Elephant** • Thrives as boards fail to distinguish the voice of constituents from that of volunteers and staff Result: boards that do not properly interpret and satisfy mission needs	***Earth to Board* Solution** • Seek a shared reality Benefit: mission success as boards systematically connect with constituents and accurately anticipate their needs
***Board Fiddles, Rome Burns* Elephant** • Thrives when all policy and strategy—benefit and business component—is centralized at the board level Result: unnecessary risk to the mission system as boards rubberstamp CEO and committee decisions and fail to address governance issues	***Board Fiddles, Rome Burns* Solution** • Develop policy and strategy at governance and business component levels Benefit: mission system protection through effective board governance and greater mission outcomes through effective CEO management
***Smile, Not Skill* Elephant** • Thrives in a Q-culture where congeniality is rewarded over performance Results: a failure to seize mission opportunities, a lower level of performance, and the loss of high-performing staff and volunteers	***Smile, Not Skill* Solution** • Demand performance Benefit: a high-performing organization where high achievers thrive and achieve lasting mission results
***Read My Lips* Elephant** • Thrives when grandiose rhetoric masks the real state of programs and activities Results: a failure to deliver mission outcomes and disillusioned constituents and public	***Read My Lips* Solution** • Reward results, not rhetoric Benefit: Sustained mission outcomes and satisfied mission recipients

This burden falls heavily on the shoulders of already stressed volunteer boards and CEOs. They must do all this in the messy real world of dysfunctional mission systems and a crushing workload. They cannot do it alone. The nonprofit sector needs to stand together—charitable, foundations, professional, and trade organizations alike—to help current leaders tackle the real problems. Not only does this take a united front, but it needs leaders that can educate the public, framing public discussions away from cutting "administrative" costs and in simple, nonhubris language, describing the contributions that nonprofits currently make and how much more will be realized as nonprofits thrive in the future.

Exceptional Nonprofits Meet Future Challenges

If nonprofit elephants are tamed, what opportunities might be realized with all the newly found energies of volunteers and staff? To answer the question, let's take a quick look at some important trends affecting the nonprofit sector, and how exceptional nonprofits might meet the inherent challenges.

Predicting trends is a popular sport and information abounds. Every nonprofit advisory group issues its list, and nonprofit experts fill books on the subject. All cite changes such as the shift from industry to information, globalization, changes in demographics, and the splintering of interests within societies. We narrow our focus here to three trends that promise abundant nonprofit opportunities: (1) the localization of the global, (2) the emergence of second careers and a changing volunteer workforce, and (3) the need for social connection.

The Localization of the Global

Appearing on a news show and discussing an update to his popular book, *The World Is Flat, New York Times* Pulitzer Prize–winner Thomas Friedman discussed what he sees as "the mother of all inflection points," the convergence of several events that make it possible to stay small but go global:

- The personal computer that allows us to be not only the author of digital content but to send it around
- The Internet that gives us the ability to send our content to everyone for free
- The presence of workflow software that allows us to work on each other's content together

Friedman makes a convincing case that the convergence of these three things flattens the world for corporations. In effect, a small local business can compete for business on a global scale; the little guy with a computer in India can compete for the same tax preparation work that used to go only to large New York accounting firms. And as more people start to take advantage of this convergence, more opportunities emerge for new businesses and new innovations.[3]

Implications for Nonprofits Firms are emerging that provide office software on the Web—that means for a nominal monthly fee, a small office gets extensive and updated software without the expense of buying software, hiring someone to run a network, or having the knowledge and funds to keep software up to date. Every day new firms will emerge at the intersection of this convergence, and in turn, provide ever more services that can be leveraged by resource-starved nonprofits.

The flip side is that anyone who wants to start a new nonprofit can do so with few resources by leveraging such technology to produce a very large impact. Their ability to stay local but go global presents a competitive challenge to nonprofits stuck in the old mindset. It won't be enough to grind out the same general meetings and education for increasingly segmented constituents.

This fundamentally changing society opens up new exciting areas for nonprofits. So far most of the true innovation is coming from social entrepreneurs and start-up nonprofits that see a specific need and use emerging knowledge to fill it. Exceptional nonprofits can use their newfound energies to seize these exciting new opportunities. The chance to leverage staff and information; segment markets, audiences, and services; collaborate and serve constituents in ever-increasing ways is simply limitless.

The Emergence of Second Careers and a Changing Volunteer Workforce

The face of retirement is changing, and for the first time people are facing the challenge of what to do with the second half of their lives. Two trends are starting to emerge: starting a second and different career or staying in the same job and creating a parallel career in a different field. Concurrent with these trends is a changing attitude in the young—an increasing interest in volunteer service.

The Emergence of Second Careers The people who want second careers often have risen to the middle-management ranks in business and after 20 years or more are facing companies that are shrinking their workforces or jobs that no longer present a challenge. Others are approaching retirement age and want to use their considerable talents to continue working at a less hectic pace. Still others are disenchanted with the corporate world and are looking for something that has more meaning.

All of these trends supply a large number of skilled professional managers who are interested in integrating life values and work, and who want something different. This presents several challenges for nonprofits: retaining the talent that might be subject to the same yearnings and attracting the best of the job switchers.

The emerging workforce of experienced professionals age 50 and older in particular holds great potential for nonprofits in terms of new leaders and the chance to use this new workforce to supply new services. In a survey of 1,000 adults ages 50 to 70, nearly three in five adults in their fifties said that they want to use the next stage of their lives to improve the quality of life in their communities. A good example of this trend is a retired doctor who recruited 55 retired doctors and opened a clinic for people who could not afford medical care. He estimates that "two thirds of the country's 160,000 retired doctors would come out of retirement to work free of charge . . . and could provide much, if not most, of the care for the uninsured in America if they were properly organized."[4]

The Emergence of Parallel Careers Another breed of second careers is the rise of social entrepreneurs. These people are usually very successful in their primary career (e.g., CEOs like Bill Gates, doctors, lawyers, professors) and love their work but want a different challenge. So, they continue to work in their field but start another activity part-time, usually a nonprofit.

A Changing Volunteer Workforce and Business Attitude The culture of volunteering is growing among younger people. According to a national study conducted annually by UCLA's Higher Education Research Institute, volunteerism among the young has risen dramatically in the last decade. In 1989, 66 percent of university freshman reported doing volunteer work in their last year of high school, and that number jumped to 83 percent in 2003.[5]

Nonprofit-related content is exploding at business schools, with the focus on entrepreneurial solutions of social problems. MBA graduates are bringing a new sense of corporate social responsibility that echoes the dialogue of "doing better" taking place at businesses today. Firms like Leo Burnett are trying to combine social consciousness with good business practice. Burnett, trying to showcase its ad capabilities while contributing to what it considers to be its civic responsibilities, launched a marketing campaign to provide marketing services for an unknown nonprofit seeking to become "as familiar as Habitat for Humanity."[6]

On June 1, 2004, Revenue Ruling 2004-51 provided a ruling by which tax-exempt organizations may safely enter into joint ventures with for-profits without fear of losing their exemptions or being subject to unrelated business income tax (UBIT).[7] This opens the possibility of nonprofits having access to capital markets while businesses assuage a social consciousness.

Implications for Nonprofits Will the corporate professionals who are turning to the nonprofit sector for inspiration and challenge find it? They will at exceptional nonprofits with their performance cultures that are open to the risk of new opportunities and the thrill of achievement. So will youthful volunteers who need to see a direct link between their volunteer efforts and mission achievement.

The new opportunities that are opening up for collaboration between nonprofits and private business are equally exciting, but only exceptional nonprofits will have the leadership that can benefit from corporate partnerships without losing mission focus.

Knowledge is no longer controlled in ivory towers; the potential is that passionate amateurs, professionals, and volunteers can collaborate and use distributed know-how to solve complex problems—and exceptional nonprofits can be their partners.

The Need for Social Connection

In his book *Bowling Alone,* author Robert D. Putnam discusses a decline in Americans' "social capital"—their connection with others.[8] He cites the decline in people's desire for group activities (e.g., more people are bowling, but fewer people are joining leagues; memberships in Massachusetts PTAs are decreasing; social connections like dinner parties and get-togethers are on the decline). He feels that these connections are an important way that people work together, and that we need to invent new ways of connecting.

Implications for Nonprofits Busy people are missing the sense of social connection in their lives. They are looking for new commonalities, but also for ways to gain more free time, for help in isolating knowledge in volumes of information, and for quality in what they receive and clarity in what they read.

In ways that are unimaginable now, exceptional nonprofits will find new modes of communicating and leveraging the convergence of technologies and their own collaboration tools to support innovative new communities of learning and sharing wisdom. They will be first in line to discover new ways of creating value for these communities and supporting their growth.

Exceptional Nonprofits and the Future

Too often, nonprofits look on the outside for answers—the latest process or consultant—to meet their challenges when the power to make them better lies within. Instead of clearly defining their mission and limiting the elephants so that volunteers and staff can excel, nonprofit leaders engage in an endless dance of inside struggles of "who does what and how" that drains the energies of all.

A pithy old saying seems germane here—if you want a butterfly, don't put lipstick on a caterpillar and declare it a success. Instead of creating butterflies, large established nonprofits' leaders expend their energies on rhetoric that masks caterpillars in disguise—or worse yet, caterpillars that don't exist. Rank-and-file volunteer and staff members are great at maintaining caterpillars—existing programs—and they can be equally great at innovating butterflies if leadership brings out that talent.

But, there's a reason that AT&T did not introduce the cell phone and that overnight package service wasn't introduced by the U.S. Post Office. These cultures did not support the innovative people that had those innovative ideas and, right now, neither do nonprofits. The solutions to improved performance, sustained mission programs, and innovative new services and programs may lie inside, but it requires real nonprofit leadership to tap into this rich wealth of knowledge and challenge people for answers.

Nonprofit employees and volunteers come to work energized and ready to accomplish something worthwhile, but they are too busy fighting elephants to put these energies to full use. What should nonprofits' leaders do? The answer to an old children's joke—how do you eat an elephant?—provides the clue: One bite at a time. There's no quick fix or magical solution by which the elephants yield their power all at once, but by consistently taking the small practical steps described in this book and confronting each elephant in turn, boards and CEOs can banish the thinking that limits performance and transform their organizations into exceptional mission systems.

The elephant solutions are ideas whose time has come. In an era of unparalleled nonprofit growth and increasing economic importance, we need these truly exceptional nonprofits to emerge. They are the nonprofits that have the potential to create a different workplace, a place where workers have a meaningful and balanced life and yet achieve mission goals that positively benefit society.

We need this world where nonprofits reach their full potential and create unlimited butterflies, and the time to do it is NOW.

NOTES

1. Bill Bradley, Paul Jansen, and Les Silverman, "The Nonprofit Sector's $100 Billion Opportunity," *Harvard Business Review* 81, no.5, May 2003.
2. Paul C. Light, "Rebuilding Confidence in Charitable Organizations," *Public Service Brief, New York University Robert F. Wagner School of Public Service,* no.1, October 2005.
3. *Foreign Exchange with Fareed Zakaria,* interview with Thomas Friedman, January 7, 2006.
4. Kelly Greene, "Tapping Talent, Experience of those Age 60-Plus," *Wall Street Journal,* sec. B12, November 29, 2005.
5. Joann Klimkiewicz, "Kids These Days are More Volunteer Conscious," *Chicago Tribune,* sec. 5, October 27, 2005.
6. Brian Steinberg, "Leo Burnett Pursues Nonprofit Work," *Wall Street Journal,* sec. B5, November 25, 2005.
7. George T. Dillon and Matthew M. Wilkins, "True Sustainability: A New Model to Aid Nonprofits in Developing Self-Sustaining Revenue," *GuideStar* (May 2005), www.guidestar.org/news/features/sustainability.jsp (accessed May 6, 2005).
8. Robert D. Putnam, *Bowling Alone: The Collapse and Revival of American Community* (New York: Simon and Schuster, 2000).

Index

C

I

J

K

L

M

Q

R

S

CPSIA information can be obtained
at www.ICGtesting.com
Printed in the USA
LVOW03s0249180216
475595LV00004B/7/P